Praise for *A New History of the Peloponnesian War*

'An insightful, highly readable history of the first all-out war in western history. Tritle knows Greek history and he knows what war does to soldiers and civilians alike.'

Tom Palaima, University of Texas at Austin

'Not another paraphrase of Thucydides, Tritle's sensitive new history of the great war between Athens and Sparta marshals the literary and material evidence to explore the human and societal experience, showing once again that military history extends far beyond the battlefield.'

Waldemar Heckel, University of Calgary

'Swift narrative, mastery of modern scholarship, and unusual integration of classical literature. Like his great source Thucydides, the author was a soldier, and the terrible brutality of war is immanent.'

Mortimer Chambers, UCLA

'By helping us understand broadly and deeply the human and social dimension of this war, Tritle's book brilliantly justifies its ambitious title of a "new history" of an often-treated old war.'

Kurt A. Raaflaub, Brown University

D1563643

A NEW HISTORY OF THE PELOPONNESIAN WAR

LAWRENCE A. TRITLE

⊛ WILEY-BLACKWELL

A John Wiley & Sons, Ltd., Publication

This edition first published 2010
© 2010 Lawrence A. Tritle

Blackwell Publishing was acquired by John Wiley & Sons in February 2007. Blackwell's publishing program has been merged with Wiley's global Scientific, Technical, and Medical business to form Wiley-Blackwell.

Registered Office
John Wiley & Sons Ltd, The Atrium, Southern Gate, Chichester, West Sussex, PO19 8SQ, United Kingdom

Editorial Offices
350 Main Street, Malden, MA 02148-5020, USA
9600 Garsington Road, Oxford, OX4 2DQ, UK
The Atrium, Southern Gate, Chichester, West Sussex, PO19 8SQ, UK

For details of our global editorial offices, for customer services, and for information about how to apply for permission to reuse the copyright material in this book please see our website at www.wiley.com/wiley-blackwell.

The right of Lawrence A. Tritle to be identified as the author of this work has been asserted in accordance with the Copyright, Designs and Patents Act 1988.

Wiley also publishes its books in a variety of electronic formats. Some content that appears in print may not be available in electronic books.

Designations used by companies to distinguish their products are often claimed as trademarks. All brand names and product names used in this book are trade names, service marks, trademarks or registered trademarks of their respective owners. The publisher is not associated with any product or vendor mentioned in this book. This publication is designed to provide accurate and authoritative information in regard to the subject matter covered. It is sold on the understanding that the publisher is not engaged in rendering professional services. If professional advice or other expert assistance is required, the services of a competent professional should be sought.

Library of Congress Cataloging-in-Publication Data

Tritle, Lawrence A., 1946-
   A new history of the Peloponnesian War / Lawrence A. Tritle.
       p.   cm.
   Includes bibliographical references and index.
   ISBN 978-1-4051-2250-4 (hardcover : alk. paper) – ISBN 978-1-4051-2251-1 (pbk. : alk. paper)   1. Greece–History–Peloponnesian War, 431-404 B.C.   2. Greece–History–Peloponnesian War, 431-404 B.C.–Influence.   3. Greece–History–Peloponnesian War, 431-404 B.C.–Historiography.   4. Athens (Greece)–Intellectual life.   I. Title.
   DF229.T74 2010
   938'.05–dc22

                                                                                    2009020186

A catalogue record for this book is available from the British Library.

Set in 10.5/13 pt Minion by SNP Best-set Typesetter Ltd., Hong Kong

I   2010

For

my Mom, Dorothy B. Tritle

and

Najwa *habibti*

and

those who have seen the elephant

and brought it home

CONTENTS

ILLUSTRATIONS

MAPS

ABBREVIATIONS

Titles of periodical literature are generally abbreviated in accordance with those listed in *L' Année philologique*. Names of ancient authors and titles of works are mostly abbreviated as listed in the *Oxford Classical Dictionary* (see below) or LSJ = H.G. Liddell and R. Scott, *A Greek-English Lexicon*, 9th ed., rev. by H.S. Jones and R. McKenzie (Oxford, 1940).

The following should also be noted:

APF	J.K. Davies, *Athenian Propertied Families*. Oxford, 1971.
ATL	B.D. Meritt, H.T. Wade-Gery, and M.F. McGregor, eds. *The Athenian Tribute Lists*, 4 vols. Cambridge and Princeton for American School of Classical Studies, Athens, 1939–53.
Beloch	K.J. Beloch, *Griechische Geschichte*. 2nd ed. 4 vols. Strassburg, Berlin, Leipzig, 1912–27.
CAH	*Cambridge Ancient History*, ed. by J.B. Bury *et al.*, 1st ed., 12 vols. Cambridge, 1923–39; with a new edition (e.g., second and third), 1970–2001.
FGrHist	*Die Fragmente der griechischen Historiker*. F. Jacoby, ed. Vol. 1–2, Berlin, 1923–26. Vol. 3, Leiden, 1940–58.
Fornara	C.W. Fornara, ed. and trans., *Translated Documents of Greece and Rome*. Vol. 1. *Archaic Times to the End of the Peloponnesian War*. 2nd ed. Cambridge, 1983.

Gomme	A.W. Gomme. *A Historical Commentary on Thucydides.* Vols. 1–3. Oxford, 1945–56.
Gomme-Andrewes-Dover	A.W. Gomme, A. Andrewes, and K.J. Dover. *A Historical Commentary on Thucydides.* Vols. 4–5. Oxford, 1970–81.
Hornblower	S. Hornblower. *A Commentary on Thucydides.* 3 vols. Oxford, 1991–2008.
IG	*Inscriptiones Graecae.* Berlin, 1873–.
ML	R. Meiggs and D.M. Lewis, eds., *Greek Historical Inscriptions to the End of the Fifth Century B.C.* Rev. ed. Oxford, 1988.
PA	J. Kirchner, *Prosopographia Attica.* 2 vols. Berlin, 1901.
P-B	P. Poralla, *A Prosopography of Lacedaemonians from the Earliest Times to the Death of Alexander the Great.* 2nd ed., by A.S. Bradford. Chicago, 1985.
RE	*Realencyclopädie der klassischen Altertumswissenschaft.* Ed. by Pauly-Wissowa-Kroll. Stuttgart, 1894–1980.
*OCD*³	*Oxford Classical Dictionary.* S. Hornblower and A. Spawforth, eds. 3rd ed., rev. Oxford, 2003.
Pritchett	W.K. Pritchett. *The Greek State at War.* 5 vols. Berkeley and Los Angeles, 1971–91.

CHRONOLOGY

Please note: all three-digit dates are BC/BCE; fifth century and fourth century, when referred to as such, should be understood as BC/BCE. 'Common era' dates, when used, will be identified as AD/CE; nineteenth and twentieth (centuries) and all four-digit dates should be taken as modern.

	Political-Military Events	Social-Cultural Events
490–78	Era of the Persian Wars: Athens burned by invading Persians	
490	Battle of Marathon: Athens defeats invading Persian army	
480	Battles of Thermopylae/ Artemisium and Salamis	
479	Battles of Plataea/Mycale: Persian defeat complete	
478/7	Establishment of Delian League under Athenian leadership	
472		Aeschylus, *Persians*[1]
c.469/8–6	Battle of Eurymedon	
468		Sophocles premiers
466/5	Revolt and suppression of Naxos by Athens	
464 (?)	Earthquake in Sparta	

[1] Readers should note that few dates for the performance of Attic drama are secure. Their discussion below is placed where it seems most likely. This applies as well to the dates assigned to works of art.

	Political-Military Events	Social-Cultural Events
458		Aeschylus, *Oresteia*
455		Euripides premiers
451/0	Five Years Truce (Athens and Sparta's Peloponnesian League) Pericles' law restricting Athenian citizenship	
450–30		Era of sculptor Phidias
449 (?)	Peace of Callias, end of war with Persia	
447–32		Building of Parthenon, Athens
446/5	Revolt and reconquest of Euboea by Athens Thirty Years Peace ending 'First' Peloponnesian War	
c.441–39	Revolt and suppression of Samos by Athens	
438		Euripides, *Alcestis* Sophocles, *Antigone* (?)
437		Building of the Propylaea, Athens (to c. 432)
435	Outbreak of hostilities between Corcyra and Corinth	
433/2 (?)	Megarian Decree enacted by Athens Dispute between Corcyra and Corinth, now joined by Athens, leads to battle of Sybota Two Congresses at Sparta: Sparta and its allies vote that Athens had broken the Thirty Years Peace Spartan embassies to Athens (at least four) seeking negotiations (into 431)	

	Political-Military Events	Social-Cultural Events
431, spring	Theban attack on Plataea leads to full-scale mobilization of armies and outbreak of Peloponnesian War's first phase, the Archidamian War Final Spartan embassy (Melesippus) to Athens First of annual Peloponnesian invasions of Attica begins	Euripides, *Medea*
430–28	Plague in Athens; death of Pericles	
428		Euripides, *Hippolytus* Euripides, *Andromache* (?) Sophocles, *Oedipus Tyrannus* (?)
427	Civil War in Corcyra Revolt of Mytilene on Lesbos Rise to prominence of Athenian politician Cleon	Gorgias arrives in Athens
426	Campaigns of Demosthenes in western Greece	Aristophanes, *Babylonians*
425	Athenian victory at Sphacteria/ Pylos	Aristophanes, *Acharnians*
424	Failure of the Athenian general Thucydides in northern Greece; in exile as historian of the War Battle of Delium Congress of Gela, Athenians leave Sicily	Aristophanes, *Knights*
423	One-year truce between Athens and Sparta	Aristophanes, *Clouds*
422/1	Deaths of the generals Brasidas (Sparta) and Cleon (Athens) at Amphipolis Peace of Nicias ends the Archidamian War Fifty-year alliance between Athens and Sparta	Euripides, *Suppliant Women* (?) Aristophanes, *Peace*

	Political-Military Events	Social-Cultural Events
420		Polyclitus'*Hera* at Argos
420–415		Gorgias, *Encomium of Helen*
420–410		Temple of Athena Nike balustrade Temple of Apollo *Epikourios*, Bassai
420–410		Era of artists Zeuxis and Parrhasius
419	Athenian alliance with Argos and allies	
418	Battle of Mantinea	
416/15	Athenian attack and destruction of Melos	Euripides, *Heracles* (?) Euripides, *Trojan Women* Mutilation of the *Hermai*, Athens Profanation of the Mysteries, Athens
415/14	Athenian Expedition sails for Sicily Alcibiades recalled from Sicily to stand trial in Athens – his flight to Sparta	Aristophanes, *Birds*
413	Defeat of Athenian forces in Sicily Sparta declares war on Athens; Agis occupies Decelea in Attica	
412	Revolt of Chios and other Athenian allies Athenians open the 'iron fund', a cash reserve on the acropolis New phase of the Peloponnesian War, the Ionian War, begins Persian intervention in the Greek war begins	Euripides, *Helen* and *Andromeda*

	Political-Military Events	Social-Cultural Events
411/10	Alcibiades arrives in Ionia/the eastern Aegean, he begins intriguing with Persians, later Athenians Athenian naval victory at Cynossema; recovery of Cyzicus follows Oligarchic coup of the '400' overthrows the Athenian democracy followed by a 'mini-terror'	Aristophanes, *Lysistrata* and *Thesmophoriazusae*
410	Counter-revolution in Athens overthrows the '400' – democracy restored	
409–8		Completion of Erechtheum Sophocles, *Philoctetes* Euripides, *Orestes*
408	Capture of Byzantium	
407	Alcibiades returns in triumph to Athens, soon after elected general Arrival of the Persian prince Cyrus in Sardis	
406	Athenian defeat at Notium – Alcibiades falls from power, returns into exile Athenian victory over the Spartan fleet at Arginusae Athens rejects Spartan peace overtures Athenians condemn and execute the generals in command at Arginusae	Deaths of Euripides (Macedon) and Sophocles (Athens)

	Political-Military Events	Social-Cultural Events
405/4	Spartan commander Lysander assumes de facto command of Spartan Aegean forces	Aristophanes, *Frogs*
	Spartan destruction of the Athenian fleet at Aegospotami	
	Athens, besieged by land and sea, surrenders	
	Athens becomes member of Sparta's Peloponnesian League (?)	
404/3	The Thirty Tyrants rule Athens, democracy overthrown, civil war follows; democracy restored following Spartan intervention	
401/0	Expedition of Cyrus, followed by his death at Cunaxa; Greek mercenaries fight their way to Hellespont	Sophocles, *Oedipus at Colonus* staged
399		Trial and death of Socrates

ACKNOWLEDGMENTS

Like the course of the Peloponnesian War, writing this book took a few unscheduled detours on the road of life, but those delays have in some instances proved helpful in writing what follows. Some arguments advanced here were previewed in my textbook account, *The Peloponnesian War* (Westport: Greenwood Press, 2004) and are now recounted in elaborated form. Anonymous readers of that book offered some useful criticisms which have been taken to heart. Without the contributions of my forerunners, especially Victor Davis Hanson, B.W. Henderson, Donald Kagan, and J.F. Lazenby, and especially Thucydides, this book would be very different indeed. Their military-political discussions allowed me to broaden the discourse and call attention to the impact of the war, particularly its violence and the toll it took on culture and society. I hope this and the attention to the literature and art will explain if not justify my title of a 'new history' of a very old topic.

Much of what follows reflects my teaching and thoughts broadly on war and violence since 1996 when I began to think about what war was really about rather than how wars started and the directions they took, subjects long familiar to historians. I have to admit that the stimulus to this was reading Jonathan Shay's *Achilles in Vietnam* (1994) which not only suggested this line of investigation, but also revealed much to me about my own experiences in Vietnam as a young infantry officer. During these years conversations with Waldemar Heckel, John Lee, John Ma, Tom Palaima, Kurt Raaflaub, Jonathan Shay, and Hans van Wees have been helpful, though none should be thought responsible for what follows. But I do thank them for their friendship and encouragement as well as their own very important contributions. My research assistant Gordon Stuart read various drafts and his comments helped ensure that the text was accessible to students and those unfamiliar with ancient Greek history and the

Peloponnesian War. The technical expertise of Henry Au proved no less valuable in preparing the manuscript. Many other thanks are also due, first to Blackwell's Al Bertrand, who took on this project and held up through its delays and those of its companion, *Alexander the Great: A New History* (with W. Heckel, 2009) – thanks Al!. Thanks and gratitude also go to the staffs of Art Resource, New York (especially Humberto DeLuigi), the American School of Classical Studies, Athens (and Ms. Jan Jordan), the J. Paul Getty Museum, Malibu, and John Ma of Corpus Christi College, Oxford, for their assistance in gathering the images illustrating this book. Finally, a College Fellowship from Bellarmine College, Loyola Marymount University, enabled me to complete this book during the fall 2009 semester.

The spelling and presentation of Greek names and technical terms is a thorny issue over which scholars continue to wrangle much to the confusion of non-specialists. James Whitley's advice seems eminently sensible, and I too have tried to be consistent in my inconsistency, preferring the familiar anglicized forms for well-known personal names (so Thucydides and not Thoukydides) and places (so Syracuse and not Syrakousai) so that those readers unfamiliar with things Greek might investigate more easily on their own. On the other hand, I have transliterated technical terms (e.g., *strategos*, general) and some place names (e.g., Kerameikos, the 'national' cemetery in Athens) not so much for effect as for some sort of authenticity.

Larry Tritle
Los Angeles, May 2009

PREFACE

From 431 to 404 a war raged across the Greek world from Sicily to the eastern Aegean, today's modern Turkey, now known as the Peloponnesian War. Such violence was not an unusual feature of Greek life, as Homer's great poems tell and as the philosopher Heraclitus soon after proclaimed (c. 500) – 'war is the father of all things'.[1] But when this war broke out it seemed to at least one Greek, an Athenian aristocrat named Thucydides, that it would be different, that it would be, as one modern scholar has suggested, 'a war like no other'.[2] Thucydides' account of this war is at once analytic and philosophical, poignant and emotional. His treatment of how two powerful states and their allies became locked in conflict has provided generations of historians and political scientists with an introduction to the subject of war and peace, war and violence, in general the ways of great powers.[3]

Yet much of the modern treatment of the Peloponnesian War continues to examine the war much as Thucydides did – as a military and political conflict that unsuspecting readers might think took place in a social and cultural vacuum. This may be seen in two recent histories of the war, those of N. Bagnall and G. Hutchinson, which focus on military events and, for the most part, retell Thucydides' story but without probing his text critically or paying attention to the traumas and anxieties people were then facing.[4] Such military oriented accounts as these, I would argue, give a false impression of life at the time. This may be seen in the experience of modern American society during the Vietnam and Iraq Wars. Here in the 1960s and the first years of the twenty-first century, fighting and dying were accompanied by the making of movies, the writing of novels and poetry, the contributions of artists: in short the intellectual and cultural life of society continued unabated.

Such was life in Athens and the rest of Greece too. In 427, the same year that witnessed the surrender of Plataea and the revolt of Mytilene, Gorgias of Leontini arrived in Athens and took the city by storm. Not by force of arms, but by his public lectures in which he dazzled the Athenians with rhetorical displays not seen before.[5] In a lecture tour that took him across Greece, Gorgias spoke in praise of Helen, absolving her of responsibility for launching a thousand ships in the greatest war of them all. In the middle of his speech, he alluded to what must have been a common sight on the streets and public places of Greece: men left emotionally spent by the horrors of war, unable to work or do much else.[6]

Such 'psych' cases, as they might be referred to today, explain too Euripides' horrific drama of the greatest of heroes, Heracles, who returns from 'war' only to kill his wife and children, the same kind of story that made the headlines of many American newspapers in 2003 with the Fort Bragg murders.[7] In my view, too little attention has been paid to the contemporaneity of wartime Athenian drama, especially tragedy, in which authors cloaked their ideas and responses to the times in the language and imagery of myth.[8] The *Antigone* of Sophocles, for example, is hardly different from the 'non-fiction novels' of Truman Capote and Norman Mailer, which blur the line between fiction and reality.[9] Michael Vickers has a point in noting that 'the audience (of a Greek drama) did not go to the theatre to learn yet more of the history of the House of Laius, any more than we read *Animal Farm* to learn about the everyday lives of countryfolk'.[10]

Other authors in other times have aimed to do likewise. In Elizabethan England, Shakespeare used the 'tragedy' of Julius Caesar to reflect on monarchy and royal succession at a time when to do so openly might lead to censorship or worse (as happened perhaps to Christopher Marlowe). The so-called 'war plays' of Euripides and Sophocles then may be interpreted profitably in this light, as recent readings and performances of these authors have shown in the empathetic responses of Iraq War veterans and West Point cadets alike.[11]

It also seems to me that in writing about war in the early twenty-first century it is crucial to pay attention to the impact of war's violence on society and culture. In reading the accounts of the Peloponnesian War by Donald Kagan, J.F. Lazenby, and Victor Hanson, the inattention to this reality is striking. But then none of them has heard a shot fired in anger or worried about going into battle. I have. Additionally, I have known soldiers like the Spartan officer, later mercenary commander, Clearchus, who was a war-lover, who got stoked on the prospects of fighting. Such experience enables me to appreciate the stories of such men, and those who told them, and so many others that lay hidden in the seemingly classic – or perfect – tradition.[12]

Over the last thirty years, researchers in psychology and biology have explored the impact of violence and what it does to the human body and psyche – how violence not only changes character but also the brain, and how this affects not only individuals but societies at large.[13] Cases of hysterical blindness in Herodotus and in other ancient sources find counterparts in not just the two World Wars, but in a group of Cambodian women living today in Long Beach, California.[14] That soldiers and civilians in ancient Greece would have suffered such a seemingly modern reaction to war's violence will strike some as an idiosyncratic modern interpretation. Yet this is what is revealed upon critical examination. True, historians usually shy away from use of psychology and related disciplines, sometimes simply dismissing the former derisively as 'psychohistory'. But the admonition of American historian William Langer, who urged historians not to fear psychology as some sort of a bogyman remains a persuasive criticism of this view.[15]

Every thinking person, not only the historian, needs to understand the corrosive affect of violence and its impact on human society. As Simone Weil reflected and wrote in 1940s wartime France, 'violence overwhelms those it touches' and makes the possibility of death a constant force in the thought and lives of those who experience it.[16] Such an understanding shaped Thucydides' account of the Peloponnesian War. In his analysis of the civil strife, what the Greeks called *stasis*, that ripped through the Greek city of Corcyra and so many other communities including his own, Thucydides remarked that war is a 'violent teacher' – that its violence brings people down to the level of their circumstances (Thuc. 3.82.3).[17] Euripides and Sophocles understood this reality as well, and studying their dramas brings to life the conditions and plights of Greeks at war.

The inattention to the full range of the Greek experience with war and violence is complicated further by the knowledge of the authors, from Thucydides to his modern day counterparts. That is, they know what the course of the war will be, how it will turn out. Much has been written, for example, of the foreshadowing of Thucydides, who wrote his history of the war knowing how it ended. There are many such examples of this, but a notable one occurs in his fifth book (5.26) where Thucydides introduces the war for a second time. Here he discusses the Peace of Nicias (421), which seemed to end the war after ten years but did not, only taking it in new directions, both in terms of geography (the Athenian expedition to Sicily) and increased levels of violence (the destruction of Melos).

Such foreknowledge, moreover, creates interpretative problems both for Thucydides and the historians who followed him. For Thucydides it leads him to attribute ideas and arguments to the speakers in his history that may not have been there, and to later historians to accept these. An example of this may be seen in Lazenby's account of the war and his observation that from the beginning of the conflict the Spartans and the Corinthians knew that in going to war with Athens they must incite Athens' allies to rebel and build a navy with Greek and barbarian help.[18] Indeed this is what happened at the war's end. But how the Spartans and Corinthians could have imagined this in the debates at the beginning of the war is far from clear.

A better way to approach a modern understanding of the Peloponnesian War is to follow the events chronologically, not knowing any better than the Greeks did at the time of what was likely to happen, from one day, one month, one year to the next. David Lewis once remarked that 'as wars go on, they are more and more likely to form their own pattern and less likely to throw light on their causes'.[19] Not only this, but in cases of protracted periods of war, like the Peloponnesian War but also the Hundred Years and Thirty Years Wars, those fighting at the end will not have the same understanding of events that started the conflict as those at its inception.

No less deceiving is another historiographic commonplace, the idea that wars 'end' in a nice and tidy fashion, until the next one anyway. In the case of Athens in 404, there was no peace, just war of another kind – an uncivil civil war – that took more lives before it too 'ended'. This study, then, does not conclude with the peace – such as it was – that descended on Greece in 404. Rather it closes with some of the consequences of a long and brutal conflict: not just an Athenian civil war, but the sensational trial and execution of Socrates; and war's human toll of another kind, the hungry mercenary soldier. This approach may seem 'historicist' but it is not. It is rather a critical one that seeks to understand the conflict on its own terms, from the inside so to speak, as R.G. Collingwood suggested in his *Idea of History*. Above I noted Heraclitus' pronouncement on war as 'the father of all things'. The reality of this can be seen in the surviving sources of the Peloponnesian War – in the literature both comedy and tragedy, and the history of Thucydides. It can also be seen in the art and in the responses of people to what they witnessed. A modern spin on Heraclitus may be found in the words of Vietnam veteran and novelist Tim O'Brien:

War is hell, but that's not the half of it,
because war is also mystery and terror and
adventure and courage and discovery and
holiness and pity and despair and longing and
love. War is nasty; war is fun. War is
thrilling; war is drudgery. War makes you a
man; war makes you dead.

and some of that too will appear in the pages to follow.[20]

Notes

1 F B10 (*Vorsokr.* 22); Fränkel 1973: 376 notes that Heraclitus turned upside
down a most cherished Greek conviction, i.e., that law is the father of all.

2 Hanson 2005.

3 This begins with Thomas Hobbes' landmark translation of Thucydides. Even
today political scientists define Thucydides' analysis of the nature and conduct
of politics and power as Realism. See e.g., Lebow 2003: 65.

4 Both Bagnall 2004: 196 and Hutchinson 2006: 113–15, e.g., note that two
Spartan officers were condemned for cowardice for refusing to follow orders
given them at the battle of Mantinea. Neither notes that one was the brother
of a Spartan king, then at odds with others in Sparta, a sure explanation for the
condemnations. For further discussion see pp. 124–5.

5 Guthrie 1971: 270.

6 See pp. 74–5, 158–60.

7 See pp. 127–8.

8 The debate began with Wilamowitz's attack on Nietzsche and his 1872 *Birth of
Tragedy*, 'Future Philology' (1872/3). For a thoughtful overview of this occasionally impassioned dialogue see Griffin 1999: 73–94 and Goldhill 1997: 324–
47 (still valuable is Ehrenberg 1954: 2–3); for other views see Meier 1993: 5,
Tritle 2000, Vickers 2008, P. Easterling, 'tragedy, Greek', *OCD*[3] 1541, and
Pelling 1997: 213–24. The comedy of Aristophanes and its contemporary flavor
have long been recognized by readers and scholars. Discussions are numerous,
but see MacDowell 1995, Dover 1972, Ehrenberg 1962, and Sidwell 2009; also
Appendix A.

9 Eksteins 1989: 4.

10 Vickers 2008: 16.

11 On modern readings and presentations of Athenian tragedy and the reactions
of audiences of veterans and cadets, see stories in the *Los Angeles Times*, August
15, 2008 (p. B3) and the *New York Times*, September 19, 2008 (p. A18).

12 See pp. 90, 193–5, 235–6 and Tritle 2004.

13 The literature here is extensive, but Herman 1992, Scarry 1985, and Shay 1994, 2004, as well as Sapolsky 1994, 1997, offer valuable discussions of the psychological and biological consequences of stress and violence.

14 Hdt. 6.117.2–3, with LiDonnici 1995: 109 (hysterical blindness in ancient Greece); Shephard 2000 (trauma in World Wars); Tritle 2000: 8, n.16 (Cambodian women).

15 See Langer 1963 and Tritle 2002 for further discussion.

16 Weil 2003: 57–8.

17 Hanson 2005: 86 obscures the passage, translating it as 'a tough schoolmaster'.

18 Lazenby 2004: 253.

19 Lewis 1997: 19.

20 Collingwood 1946; O'Brien 1990: 80.

Prelude

A BAND OF BROTHERS

Plataea, August 1, 479 – the Spartan Arimnestus was the greatest of many heroes on this day. That evening many Greeks must have dropped by his tent to shake his hand and praise his glory.[1] In the fury of battle, he had killed Mardonius – cousin of the Persian Great King Xerxes and commander of his army – with a rock, crushing his skull (Plut. *Arist.* 19.1).[2] His deed energized his fellow Spartans and they fell upon Mardonius' elite troops, slaughtering them and with that Persian resistance collapsed. The Persians fled to their fortified camp, but it afforded them little refuge. Joining forces, Athenians, Spartans, and other Greeks stormed the camp, killing, destroying, and looting as they worked their way through it. Few Persians would have survived.

After the battle discussion among the Greeks focused on the prize of valor – whose would it be? Athenians and Spartans, leaders of the vast coalition formed to oppose the Persians, in typical agonistic fashion wanted the prize for themselves and challenged its award to another. The wrangling was heated, threatening to make futile the sacrifices of so many – Leonidas and the 300 at Thermopylae, the Athenian abandonment of their city to the Persians, and so much more. But now new heroes intervened. Aristides of Athens calmed the passions of his countrymen, and then Cleocritus of Corinth proposed that the prize should go to another – not his own city, the third greatest of Greece, but tiny Plataea which had sacrificed its lands to the greater glory of all. The compromise was appealing. Persian spoils were given over to the Plataeans to rebuild their sanctuaries and provide honors to the fallen Greek heroes.[3] Over time the individual cities dedicated monuments to the honored dead and their glories and sacrifices at Plataea. Tourists then, like the Greek writers Pausanias and Plutarch hundreds of years later, would have seen a landscape not very different from Gettysburg or Waterloo today.[4]

The Persian Wars had united the Greeks, or at least most of them. Led by Athens and Sparta they created a Hellenic League to discuss how they would respond to the Persian demands and, in spite of their competitiveness and pride – individual and civic – they had devised a formula of command for their land and naval forces. But unity was short-lived. After Plataea, and a crushing naval defeat inflicted on the Persians at Mycale supposedly the same day, Pausanias, the victor of Plataea, led the Greeks in clearing the northern Aegean of remaining Persian bases.[5] But, Pausanias' overbearing manner soon alienated the other Greeks, and the Spartans called him home and surrendered to the Athenians leadership of the ongoing war against Persia.

Other signs of disunity and jealousy appeared in the following decades. Aristides worked and died making the new Athenian-led alliance – the Delian League – viable, promoting its virtues around the Greek world (Plut. *Arist.* 24–26). His rival at home, Themistocles, the man who had done more than any other to make the Hellenic League work, found many enemies who combined to ostracize him and drive him to the court of the Persian king. Here he was welcomed, given sanctuary and a home. A similar fate befell Pausanias, condemned to death and finding it in Sparta's temple of Athena, walled in and left to starve (Thuc. 1.126–139). A disastrous earthquake in Sparta c. 464 spawned revolt and bitter fighting in which Mardonius' killer Arimnestus died a hero's death fighting the Messenians.[6]

By 450 Greek 'unity' was a fading memory and in its place two rival and armed camps, one led by Athens, the other Sparta, had risen. The sons and grandsons of those brothers-in-arms who had fought the Persians now found themselves in conflict with each other. In Athens, Pericles, whose father Xanthippus had defeated the Persians at Mycale, now emerged as the dominant figure in the Athenian democracy. This he did after pushing aside his rival Cimon, whose father Miltiades had led the Athenians in victory at Marathon in 490, and then Cimon's kinsman, Thucydides, son of Melesias. At Sparta Pericles' royal guest-friend, Archidamus II, whose grandfather Leotychidas had commanded Greek forces against the Persians, faced a new generation of Spartans possessing little memory of Greek unity, seeing in Athens only a threat. This included his own son Agis, who succeeded him and suffered the humiliation of the cuckold as Pericles' ward Alcibiades seduced his wife Timaea. And at Plataea, Spartan interests were represented by Lacon, 'Spartan', the son of Aeimnestus, who had stood at the side of the Spartan Callicrates, mortally wounded at the beginning of the great battle of 479. As he lay dying Callicrates only complained that he had not struck a blow for the cause, but that was enough for Aeimnestus to name his son for him.[7] In 427 Lacon would attempt to dissuade the Spartans from destroying his city. He failed (Thuc. 3.52.5). Another player in these events was the Athenian Thucydides, son of Olorus, a kinsman of Pericles' rivals Cimon and Thucydides. In exile from Athens after a battlefield failure, Thucydides would record the actions of his generation.

In spring 431, Pericles' friend Archidamus would lead an army of Spartans and Peloponnesian allies into Attica where it burned and ravaged the countryside, attempting to goad the Athenians into battle. This the Athenians refused, but soon taking advantage of their naval power struck the Spartans and their allies in vulnerable and lightly defended quarters. These initial campaigns followed three years of contested negotiations over a series of disputes involving Athens, Corinth, and Sparta and began the great Peloponnesian War of 431–404. In the end Sparta would prevail, but only by accepting Persian aid and surrendering to the Persians the Greeks of Asia, liberated by the Athenians a generation before. The struggles of these men contrast sharply with the achievements of their fathers and grandfathers who had fought and beaten the Persians, and who had united Greece in the process.

Notes

1 Plut. *Arist.* 19.8, dates the battle to third Boedromion of the Athenian calendar. The Julian date is uncertain, but should fall between mid-July and August 1. For Arimnestus, see Hdt. 9.64, Plut. *Arist.* 19.1, with Hornblower 1: 443–4; cf. Flower & Marincola 2002: 220, and n. 4 below.

2 A detail not usually noted but making clear the fierceness of hoplite battle . For further discussion of the violence of battle in ancient Greece see pp. 99–104 (Delium) and pp. 123–6 (Mantinea).

3 Plut. *Arist.* 20.1–3, with Flower & Marincola 2002: 33–4.

4 Paus. 9.4, with Habicht 1985: 75.

5 Such timing is doubtful; see Hdt. 9.100–1, with Flower & Marincola 2002: 276–9.

6 Hdt. 9.64.2, sometime c. 464–457/6 (on the Messenian Revolt see pp. 10–11).

7 Hdt. 9.72.2, with Hornblower 1: 443–4.

1

'FROM THIS THE CORINTHIANS DEVELOPED THEIR BITTER HATRED FOR THE ATHENIANS'

In 480/79 Athens and Sparta had led the Hellenic League to victory, defending Greece against the massive invasion of the Persian Great King Xerxes. Led by the Athenians at Salamis, the Spartans at Plataea, the Greeks had crushed the invading Persians. Not content with a simple defense, the Greeks then pursued the Persians into Ionia, perhaps hoping even now of liberating the Greeks of Asia from Persian domination.

The Persian defeat led to sharply divergent paths for the two states that had shared the burdens of command. Sparta, always eager to avoid obligations far from home, was traditionally not inclined to hunt down a defeated enemy (Thuc. 5.73.4). Early on Pausanias had led the Greeks against the Persians, but his leadership was too Spartan for the Greeks and they complained. The Persian style of dress and manner that he also adopted proved no less offensive. In the end the Spartans yielded to the many complaints and recalled him home, c. 478.[1]

Put on trial but acquitted, Pausanias continued his highhanded ways in the years that followed, immodestly claiming that the victory over the Persians was his doing alone. More serious, he perhaps began to intrigue with Sparta's serf-slaves, the helots.[2] He may have schemed some sort of revolution in which he promised them freedom and rights as citizens if they would back him.[3] Incriminating dealings with the Persians soon after surfaced and the ruling board of ephors issued orders for his arrest. Pausanias fled as a suppliant to the temple of Athena on the Spartan acropolis where he sought sanctuary. Walled up in the temple on the ephors' orders, he was pulled out barely alive. His death (c. 470) outside avoided pollution of the sacred precinct and effectively ended Spartan activities abroad for some time (Thuc. 1.132.5-134).[4]

Athens after the Persians

Pausanias' misadventures and Spartan reluctance to become involved in overseas military operations handed to the Athenians leadership of the Greeks in the fight against the Persians. Spartan leadership, seen by many Greeks as corrupt and arrogant, gave way to the Athenians, who, on account of their democracy, may have been perceived as more open and friendly. Shortly after Pausanias' recall home, the Athenians took the initiative and established a new military alliance, the Delian League, to continue the war against the Persians (478/7). Established on Delos, Apollo's sacred island, the Athenians organized the Greeks for what some imagined would be a permanent war. Rich and populous communities, especially those on the prosperous islands of Chios, Lesbos, and Samos, provided ships and crews in the military expeditions that the Athenians led and became more powerful themselves. Communities too small or disinclined to serve in person were assessed financial contributions. The Persian War veteran and hero Aristides established these initially, his nickname 'the Just' persuading the Greeks that their monies would be handled judiciously.[5] Later known as *phoros*, or tribute, these monies were paid into a war treasury kept at Delos and were administered by a board of Athenian officials called the *hellenotamiai*, or 'treasurers of the Greeks'.[6] The first assessment totaled some 460 talents, a vast sum. The Athenians regulated the tribute and kept lists (which were published) of the assessments and how these changed in the years that followed.[7] So armed and funded, the Athenians acquired incredible military power enabling them to lead expeditions throughout the Aegean and eastern Mediterranean world.[8]

Just as the Spartans faced the challenges posed by a successful wartime leader, so too did the Athenians. In the first years after the Persian defeat, Themistocles, the architect of victory at Salamis, dominated the city and engineered its recovery. He foiled a Spartan attempt to dissuade the Athenians from rebuilding their city walls, which would have left the city vulnerable to future attack. But the fickleness of the Athenian democracy, the jealousies a successful figure like Themistocles faced from enemies eager to see him fall, led to his political eclipse. In about 474/3 the Athenians ostracized him and the vote may have been rigged.[9] In 1937 a hoard of ostraca, or voting tokens, was found in an old well on the acropolis of Athens. Of some 191 pieces, all but one bore his name. Upon study only fourteen different hands could be read, evidence that a group of his enemies had surely gathered, written out the ostraca and then handed them out on voting day.[10] There is no way of knowing if these ostraca date from 474/3 or not, but they clearly indicate that Themistocles had enemies and that they were organized. Bound by the law, Themistocles left Athens and for a time resided in nearby Euboea. But then he too was caught up in the Pausanias scandal and fled to Asia where the new Great King, Artaxerxes I, son of his late rival Xerxes, gave him shelter. His former enemies welcomed him warmly and years later Themistocles died an honored exile.[11]

Themistocles, however, had his defenders in Athens and not long after his ostracism, one of them, the Marathon veteran and playwright Aeschylus, reminded the Athenians of Themistocles' service to the state. His drama *Persians*, staged in 472/1, not only commemorated the victory over the enemy, but indirectly praised the now dishonored Themistocles. Interesting too is the identity of the *choregos*, the individual responsible for providing the chorus with costumes and training. Pericles, son of Xanthippus and a wartime ally of Themistocles and scion of Athens' grandest family, made his public debut as Aeschylus' benefactor, subtly showing too where his political sympathies lay.[12]

By 467/6, some members of the Delian League began tiring of wartime life as the Persian threat receded: there seemed little reason for a military alliance, forged in the euphoria of victory, to continue. Such was the case with Naxos, an island state, which now withdrew from the alliance. The Athenians, however, did not see things this way. When making their agreement, members of the new league had ceremoniously dumped into the sea lumps of iron and pledged that until the iron floated, they would remain loyal to their oaths of membership. The Athenians saw the Naxians as oath-breakers and so responded with great force. Attacked and subdued by veteran Athenian forces, the Naxians were compelled to dismantle their city-wall and pay penalties as they were forced back into the League.[13] The allies, quickly becoming subjects now, could see that Athens would not negotiate or arbitrate any differences: there was little choice for them other than acquiescence to Athens' greater power.[14]

Naxos, however, was not the only state unhappy with the growing arrogance of power displayed by the Athenians. In 465 another island state, Thasos, broke its association with the League, as the Athenians encroached on its mainland holdings – rich in gold and silver. For some three years the Athenians assailed the island, finally subduing it and forcing it back into the League. Like Naxos, Thasos suffered severe punishment. But there were other casualties as well. Enemies of Cimon, who had commanded the Athenian forces in the campaign, prosecuted but failed to convict him of corruption.[15] Less fortunate were the Athenian settlers later introduced as colonists into the disputed region. Occupying a township known as Ennea Hodoi, the 'Nine Ways', the colonists were attacked by the local Thracian population and virtually annihilated, frustrating Athenian hopes of expansion (Thuc. 4.102.2).

Sometime around 466 the Athenian-led campaign against the Persian menace finally struck a decisive blow. At the Eurymedon River in Asia Minor, the Athenians and their allies led by Cimon destroyed a combined Persian fleet and army, thereby ending any chance of the Persians returning to Aegean waters. Cimon may have reached a settlement with the Persians, but by 460 he was in exile, ostracized, after an abortive expedition to Sparta. The Athenians now began flexing their military muscle throughout the eastern Mediterranean world. An expeditionary force to Cyprus was diverted to Egypt to support the rebellion of the Libyan prince Inarus. Fighting here lasted through several campaigning seasons and the Athenians invested a great deal of money and resources. In the end the Persians scored a major success, diverting the waters of the Nile and marooning the Athenian ships, then destroying them (c. 454).[16]

As these dramatic events unfolded, the Athenian political scene heralded a new arrival – Pericles. Known by name and reputation, his political sympathies were revealed c. 462/1 when he supported the efforts of the reformer Ephialtes to strip the old aristocratic council, the Areopagus, of its authoritative judicial powers.[17] In attacking the Areopagus Council, Ephialtes transferred its power and prestige to other and more popular bodies, the assembly, law courts, and Council of 500. Responses to the reforms were impassioned and cost Ephialtes his life, though the details are far from clear (Plut. *Per.* 10.7-8). These events, however, found their way into the popular imagination through the dramatic medium of Attic drama. In 458 Aeschylus staged the only surviving trilogy in Greek tragedy, the *Oresteia*. In its final play, *Eumenides*, Aeschylus warns of the dangers of civil war and how this worst of political evils must be avoided.

Did Aeschylus make a political statement, and if so who heard his message? While the political nature of the dramatic venue can be over stated, so much so that the rich matrix of intellectual and spiritual ideas and beliefs is overshadowed, it remains that the theater experience was a diverse one with real and contemporary issues sometimes at play.[18] Here the Athenians heard the views and opinions of their best minds, who asked them to think about the world around them and to act as informed citizens. It must also be seen that those who heard these words were almost certainly the minority. The Theater of Dionysus, where Aeschylus' *Oresteia* was performed, as later the plays of Sophocles and Euripides, was apparently not large and may have accommodated no more than the local theater in Thorikos.[19] In many ways, then, the theater experience was an elite experience. It did voice political concerns about the community and its political figures, but those who heard it represented a relatively small portion of the population.

In the turmoil of Ephialtes' reforms and death, and fighting raging in many corners, the Athenians, apparently with Pericles' backing, recalled Cimon from exile (c. 452?). A new Persian fleet threatened Greek communities and Athenian influence in the eastern Mediterranean, and Cimon led an expeditionary force to Cyprus but died not long after arriving (c. 451/0). His death, preceded by the setback in Egypt, led to a settlement between Greeks and Persians. Brokered by Callias, Cimon's brother-in-law, these decade-old enemies signed the so-called Peace of Callias probably in summer 450/449. Three decades of hostilities with the Persians now ended.[20]

As Athens acquired great power so too did it acquire great wealth. Possibly in 454 and because of the failure of the Egyptian expedition, the treasury of the Delian League was moved to Athens. Within a short time, c. 449, the Athenians were rebuilding their city, something they had deliberately delayed since the end of the Persian Wars. In the 'Oath of Plataea' the Greeks had agreed not to rebuild their ruined sanctuaries and now with peace came a great building boom in Athens.[21]

In the decade that followed, the Athenians would have seen their city transfigured from a war-ruined wreck to an architectural showcase reflecting the power of imperial Athens. Pericles, dubbed 'Olympian' by his critics (Plut. *Per.* 8.4), took a keen interest in the designing of buildings and shaping of sculpture, and perhaps sat on a commission that supervised the whole program.[22] His 'Olympian' size ego no doubt prompted many artistic suggestions too. But it appears that his friend, the great sculptor Phidias, acted as the overall director of the rebuilding of the acropolis. Already he had crafted the great statue of Athena Promachos that greeted visitors to the acropolis (c. late 450s). Later he designed the gold and ivory cult statue of Athena Parthenos herself that would be placed in her rebuilt temple, the Parthenon, designed by Callicrates and Ictinus (built 447–432).[23] Later

Phidias got into trouble. Charged with embezzling funds, and despite help from Pericles, he fled into exile (Plut. *Per.* 31.1-5).

Elsewhere Mnesicles built a new gateway to the acropolis, the Propylaea, while below it stood the Odeon, a circular music hall that took its inspiration from the pavilion of the Persian king seized at Plataea some thirty years before. Similar rebuilding took place at the sacred precinct at Eleusis where the important Mysteries of Demeter and Persephone were celebrated.[24]

Not all saw these expenditures as just, since much of the money funding this program came from the allied contributions, now deposited in Athens. Pericles' influence over the city came to be seen by other Athenians as a threat. Chief among these critics was Thucydides, the son of Melesias, a relative of Cimon, who now mounted a challenge to Pericles' leadership. Perhaps for the first time, organized 'party' politics were practiced in the assembly. Thucydides grouped his followers together so that they could present a single voice, literally, in assembly debate. Both men were talented speakers and effective politicians, and their rivalry attracted even the attention of Archidamus, the Spartan king. Once asking Thucydides who the better wrestler was, Thucydides replied that 'whenever I throw him at wrestling, he beats me by arguing that he was never down, and he can even make the spectators believe it'! (Plut. *Per.* 8).

In the end Pericles prevailed. He counterattacked forcefully, arguing that the allies did not contribute men or material to the defense of Greece from renewed Persian attack. Additionally, Athenians from all walks of life were profiting not only from military service but from the many jobs and work springing up from the vast program of public works. The wealth and power that Athens accrued also empowered the democracy, as payments were handed out for jury service as well as attendance at public festivals, making possible the participation of many more citizens in the political process. Against the growing prosperity of Athens, Thucydides could not compete. Pericles secured his ostracism (c. 443/3) and though he later returned, his political influence seems spent.[25]

Thucydides' departure may not have bothered many Athenians who could look around their city and see everywhere the fruits of their labors and their sacrifices made good. Complacent and satisfied, however, the Athenians were not and those like Pericles knew that such hard won gains could be lost just as quickly.

Sparta after the Persians

As Athens grew powerful and wealthy – and just a little cocky – the Spartans watched from their safe haven deep in the Eurotas river valley of the Peloponnesus. Content to remain at home since the Pausanias affair, the Spartans were more concerned with the ever menacing presence of the helots. Critical to this control was their dominance over their neighbors, most of whom were members of the military alliance that Sparta led, the Peloponnesian League.

But in c. 464 disaster struck: an earthquake of tremendous force left virtually every house and building in Sparta destroyed. Striking in daylight, loss of life was severe, including a school full of boys of elite status. Only a few of these survived, having run after a rabbit that appeared moments before the earthquake struck, killing most still inside. Years later remains of the school, now the tomb of those killed, the *Seismatias*, remained a visible reminder of the tragedy (Plut. *Cim.* 16.5).

The Messenian helots, ever dangerous, quickly seized the moment and rose in rebellion, pressing the Spartans hard. Establishing a formidable position on Mt. Ithome, the Messenians repelled successive Spartan attacks. In one of these Arimnestus, Mardonius' killer at Plataea, died with three hundred others in the battle of Stenyclerus, having taken on the Messenians unaided (Hdt. 9.64.2). So severe was the situation that the Spartans appealed to the Athenians for aid. A lone Spartan envoy appeared before the Athenians, a simple and silent suppliant. Moved by this appeal, Cimon led a thousand Athenian volunteers to rescue the Spartans. Soon after arriving, however, the Spartans worried about their would-be saviors. Perhaps afraid that the democratic Athenians might switch sides and help the Messenians, the Spartans told the Athenians that their help was no longer required.

This Spartan volte-face ruined Cimon's stature in Athens and explains the circumstances of his ostracism (c. 461) engineered by his opponents. When fighting with the Spartans flared up and that with the Persians soured in Egypt and the east, Pericles and others called him home, soon sending him off to Cyprus where he died campaigning. But before his death he managed to bring about a five-year peace between Athens and Sparta (c. 452/1). This was only a temporary cessation in the hostilities. Relations between the two states would harden considerably in the following years.[26]

But the Spartans still needed help against the Messenians and called in assistance from other communities, perhaps thought more trustworthy than the Athenians. The struggle with the helots, especially those of Messenia continued for years.[27] Those Messenians holding out in their mountain stronghold on Ithome (as late as 456?) finally agreed to terms with the Spartans, only too happy to grant their safe exit. The Messenians found protection with Athenians who were just as happy to settle these battle-hardened veterans at Naupactus, a port in Ozolian Locris, which guarded the northern approaches to the Corinthian Gulf (Thuc. 1.103.1-3).

After the Persian Wars, Athens and Sparta had taken divergent paths. Sparta remained an old-fashioned tribal community whose goal focused on preserving the status quo – maintaining control over the Peloponnesians to ensure control over the helots. Athens, however, was becoming increasingly a 'modern' state where, as Pericles emphasizes in Thucydides, democracy had reshaped its citizens into lovers of the *polis*.[28] Democratic institutions established at the end of the sixth century continued to be expanded and refined throughout the fifth – magistrates with defined tenures of office, a functioning assembly that wielded real authority, law courts and juries that expressed the will of the people.[29] To maintain this development – and the wealth of empire that came with it – Athens had to stay the course, to exercise power and authority wherever possible.[30]

But this Athenian reality may be expanded. Political scientist John Mearsheimer has argued that democratic states are as driven by power politics as their authoritarian counterparts and practice similar policies of aggression. Such analysis fits democratic Athens in the middle years of the fifth century. In stark contrast to slow and 'conservative' Sparta, as the Corinthians emphasized in an illuminating comparison (Thuc. 1.70), Athens constantly looked for opportunity wherever it could be found. The tensions between these two states were not only between a 'land' power and a 'sea' power, but between two communities that for more than two generations had been heading in opposite directions.[31]

The 'First' Peloponnesian War

By 460 Athens and Sparta were distracted by various problems both at home and abroad. This opened the door to the growing ambitions of Corinth, which now saw an opportunity to assert its wealth and greater strength against neighboring Megara, close on the Attic frontier. Though a member of the Peloponnesian League, Megara found itself isolated. The Spartans, pre-occupied with the helot revolt, had neither the resources nor the inclination to rein in the Corinthians. Moreover, the Spartans usually took notice of the aggressions of their allies only when these threatened their own interests and Megara was far away and small.

Abandoned and threatened, the Megarians appealed to Athens for support. They were not denied. The Athenians quickly saw an opportunity to expand their influence not only close to home but at Corinthian expense. The Athenians helped the Megarians in building their own long walls, connecting their city to its port of Nisaea. Corinth and Athens, one-time friends, now fought in earnest for control of Megara.[32] The conflict soon spread and before long became a wider conflict, now called the 'First' Peloponnesian War.[33]

In 458 a combined Spartan and Boeotian army inflicted a sharp defeat on the Athenians at Tanagra. Soon after the Athenians recovered and defeated the Boeotians at Oenophyta, gaining a foothold in central Greece. The settlements brokered by Cimon and Callias brought some quiet, but some ten years later the Athenians attempted to expand their influence in Boeotia (447/6). Incited by the daring of the impetuous Tolmides, they approved the dispatch of a large expeditionary force into Boeotia, including a thousand volunteers personally recruited by the commander. Pericles warned Tolmides, who bore the ill-omened name 'the daring one', not to live up to his name, but the advice was wasted. Tolmides' force was beaten badly at Coronea. Many brave Athenians fell, including Clinias, an ally and associate of Pericles who now assumed responsibility for raising Clinias' sons Alcibiades and Clinias. That job would not be easy. The Boeotians captured a number of other Athenians, whom they released only when the Athenians agreed to abandon their interests in Boeotia.[34] Now liberated from Athenian domination, the Boeotians created a political union of their own, the Boeotian Confederacy. A formidable rival, and one with a long memory of hostility, now stood on Athens' northern frontier.[35]

Tolmides' defeat sparked a revolt of Athenian allies on the nearby island of Euboea, an important supplier of foodstuffs of all kinds and much more. This setback incited a political coup in Megara that brought the city back into the Corinthian and Spartan orbit. The Spartans, perhaps encouraged by these events, sent the Agiad king Pleistoanax with a large force against Athens. But after ravaging Athenian territory around Eleusis, Pleistoanax suddenly ceased operations and turned his army homewards. Even at the time it was believed that Pericles had successfully bribed the young king's chief adviser, Cleandridas, who engineered the Spartan withdrawal. Later, when submitting his annual report, Pericles reportedly explained a missing twenty talents as expended 'for what was necessary'. Aristophanes later joked of this in his play *Clouds* and a commentator would later explain the line as a subterfuge for 'I gave the money to the king of Sparta'. Word of this leaked out to the Spartan authorities and Pleistoanax's enemies prosecuted him, seizing his property and imposing a hefty fine of fifteen talents.[36] Unable to pay he went into exile and his more malleable son Pausanias, a child, replaced him. Cleandridas, already in voluntary retirement, was condemned to death. Not only are domestic politics involved here, but also attitudes regarding relations between Athens and Sparta. The family of Pleistoanax may have been too well disposed to Athens for some Spartans.[37]

Pleistoanax's convenient change of heart allowed Pericles to return to the suppression of the Euboean revolt, which he achieved. Not long after the warring states negotiated a settlement, the 30 Years Peace of 446/5.[38] While a general calm now swept over Greece, the 'First' Peloponnesian War succeeded in creating lingering animosity for Athens, especially in Corinth: Spartan anxieties were no less.

The Samian War and Athenian Power

There can be little doubt that Athenian ambitions and aggressions worried many, not least the Spartans, some of whom began to fear that control over their own allies might weaken and with dire consequences.[39] The long and brutal fight with the helots was all the reminder any Spartan needed of the importance of the allies. And there seems to be reason for such fears. Not long after the peace was agreed upon, c. 442/1, Athens became involved in a bitter dispute between Samos and Miletus over the control of Priene, a city near both on the Asia Minor coast. The Samians refused an Athenian offer to arbitrate the dispute before an Athenian court and afterwards Athens chose to support Miletus (Thuc. 1.115.2–117; Plut. *Per.* 25.1).

Critics and comic poets alike now had a field day with Pericles and his Milesian born mistress Aspasia. Only a few years before Pericles had divorced his wife and the mother of his two sons Xanthippus and Paralus to live with Aspasia whom he apparently adored – kissing her on leaving and returning home. Rumors now went around Athens that policies were being determined to please her. Perhaps leading the attack was Cratinus who nicknamed Pericles the 'Olympian'. Nastier attacks fell on Aspasia. Pericles' own citizenship law (451/0) would have made legal marriage with her impossible, which meant they could do no more than cohabit. This opened the door to the comic poets to label her a whore and worse. The jokes and innuendo were no doubt crude and funny but they may have backfired – within a matter of months a decree restricting comic ridicule was passed, surely intended to protect the 'imperial' couple.[40]

Pericles intervened on Samos with a large force and dissolved the oligarchic regime, taking as hostage fifty leading citizens along with a like number of children.[41] These were then taken to Lemnos for safe-keeping. The Samians remained defiant. With the help of the Persian satrap Pissuthnes at Sardis and the people of Byzantium, who now joined them in rebellion, they recovered their hostages and prepared for war.[42]

For more than a year Pericles and the Athenians took the fight to the Samians, but it was not easy going. Both sides won several rounds and each resorted to terror tactics: the Samians tattooed Athenian prisoners with the *samaina*, the symbol of their own locally produced coinage now banned, this in retaliation for their own people tattooed by the Athenians with the mark of Athena's owl. Aristophanes possibly joked about this later in his play *Babylonians*, referring to the Samians as a 'many lettered people'.[43]

Pericles pressed a siege of Samos for nine months and in the end the city finally surrendered (summer 439). Sometime later the Samians accepted an Athenian imposed treaty, one extracting complete loyalty and a promise not to rebel against Athens again. While costly, the victory was heady stuff and rumors later went around Athens that Pericles was bragging that he had accomplished in nine months what took Agamemnon ten years. But such bitter fighting left the Athenians in a foul mood and they brutally suppressed Samos. Not only was the Samian pro-democratic regime buttressed, but enemies were eliminated. Pericles also ordered an atrocious punishment: the ships' captains and marines of the Samian fleet were brought to Miletus where they were crucified in the market. Ten days later those still alive were taken down and beaten to death.[44]

The number of men so punished is difficult to estimate: but the Samian fleet numbered at least seventy warships which would yield at least that number of ships' captains plus another seven hundred marines minimally.[45] Allowing for even twenty-five percent casualties (a high figure), this would have placed at Pericles' mercy nearly six hundred men. Their public execution and humiliation – all taking place in an allied city – would have sent a clear message to all the Greeks and not just Athenian allies – beware the power of Athens.

This vicious act may have provided the inspiration for one of the greatest of Athenian dramas, Sophocles' *Antigone*. During the Samian War, Sophocles may have served as general on two occasions, serving with Pericles, who probably acted as 'senior' commander among the Athenian generals.[46] But relations between the two may not have been cordial and for several reasons. Sophocles seems to have had more than a passing interest in good-looking boys and a remark by him about an especially pretty one earned him a Periclean rebuke (Plut. *Per.* 8.8). A few years before the outbreak of war, Sophocles had served as *hellenotamias*, one of the treasurers who handled the finances of empire.[47] His ideas of Athenian conduct regarding the allies may have been more in line with the views of Thucydides, son of Melesias, than Pericles. Sophocles would have found Pericles' hard-line stance with the Samians disagreeable.

Then there is the business of the vicious killings of the Samian officers and marines. This and Pericles' increasing high-handed manner may have energized Sophocles and prompted him to make a not too subtle comment on these events. Drawing from the legendary Theban cycle and lives of Oedipus and his children, Sophocles spun a tale of war's brutalities and the nature of imperial rule producing the *Antigone* probably at the City Dionysia in 438.[48] Attended by Athenians and allies alike, the Dionysia also witnessed the staging of allied tribute and the debuts of war orphans raised at public expense. With its prominent discussion of the dishonored dead and an imperious ruler incapable of wrong, the *Antigone* reflects on the wielding of power and dispensing of justice, all cloaked in the mythology of the family of Oedipus.

Readers of *Antigone* will know that the play begins with Antigone and her sister lamenting the fate of their brother Polynices, whose body is to lie unburied at Creon's order. Within a few lines of this opening scene, Antigone addresses Creon as *strategos*, and surely this would have raised some eyebrows, as it was the same rank that Pericles held in these years and with which he dominated the city.[49] Ironically, Antigone calls Creon 'good' a few lines later.[50] Readers of *Antigone* will also recall that in the drama Creon seems more concerned with his personal authority than with the opinions of his (fellow) citizens as the famous debate with his son Haemon demonstrates: 'Since when do I take my orders from the people of Thebes!'[51]

Figure 1.1 This fragmentary Athenian casualty list preserved not only the memory of these men heroic in death, but also their sacrifice for the wider community, shaping ideas of the common good and even patriotism.

The arrogance Sophocles imputes to Creon matches the unpopular image of Pericles found among contemporaries such as Ion of Chios and Teleclides, who nicknamed him and his cronies 'the new Pisistratids', challenging the 'Olympian' as well to take an oath not to become tyrant (Plut. *Per.* 5.3, 16.1-2). Such criticisms provide a broader context to Sophocles' *Antigone* and make clearer the play's commentary on Pericles, his leadership of Athens, and his harsh suppression of Samos.

Others expressed their disagreement with Pericles' leadership and conduct of the recent war too. Elpinice, Cimon's sister, took advantage of the public funeral of the Athenian war dead the following spring to rebuke Pericles for what she saw was his misguided policies. This funeral took place in the Kerameikos, or 'Potter's Quarter', just outside the walls of Athens. Another of Cimon's relatives, the future historian Thucydides, perhaps just too young to have fought the Samians, later described the

Kerameikos as the city's most beautiful quarter, famous for its beauty and tranquility.[52] Sometime in the early fifth century it had become home to the *demosion sema*, the public cemetery for the war dead, and so in many ways the Athenian Arlington National Cemetery. At the funeral the remains of the dead were gathered, each tribe assigned its own tent, so that families could pay their respects and say goodbye. The remains would then be interred and afterwards came a speech by a prominent citizen. In the years that followed, many monuments listing the names of the honored dead would be found here.[53]

On this occasion, probably in spring 438, it was Pericles who spoke. Afterwards a number of women, surely the mothers and wives of the dead, gathered around him pressing flowers and crowns into his hands, thanking him for his stirring words. Nearby stood Elpinice, waiting for the moment to corner the great leader, unafraid of speaking her mind. Elpinice rebuked Pericles sharply: for his bankrupt policies and leadership, his 'victory' over a Greek city, something her brother, whose victories were over the 'real' enemy, Persians and Phoenicians, would never have done. Pericles' response was hardly gentle or considerate: smiling only, he quoted her a line of Archilochus, 'Why lavish perfumes on a gray head' (Plut. *Per.* 28.7).

The suppression of Samos made the Athenians supreme in the eastern Aegean world, but they were no less active elsewhere. In Italy an appeal for aid from the surviving population of Sybaris, destroyed by its jealous neighbors (c. 510), was accepted. An Athenian organized pan-hellenic settlement at Thurii (c. 443) followed and attracted a number of international settlers: Hippodamus of Miletus, who helped organize it; Herodotus, the Halicarnassian born writer and intellectual; and Lysias, a young Athenian born metic, the son of a prosperous Syracusan merchant living in Athens.[54] But opportunity, economic as well as political, were also motivating factors as the rich lands of southern Italy offered prosperity, sources of food, and allies.

In the northern Aegean, a little later, perhaps c. 437, the settlement at Ennea Hodoi, destroyed by the Thracians some thirty years before, was re-colonized and renamed Amphipolis. This gave Athens access to the rich timber reserves of the region so critical to ship building as well as other natural resources such as gold and silver. Here, however, the Athenians made a costly mistake in alienating a friend. Until now Perdiccas II of Macedon had been friendly, seeing in Athens an ally against his many local rivals. Now imagining himself betrayed, Perdiccas would act against the

Athenians wherever and however he could. Elsewhere in eastern Thrace and in the Black Sea, the Athenian naval squadrons could be found showing the flag in various expeditions in the 430s.[55]

Athens and Corinth

The Samian War and its unrestrained display of Athenian power surely worried the Spartans, dependent as they were on their allies to help check the helot menace. Sometime during the war, the Spartans convened a meeting of the Peloponnesian League, perhaps to hear a plea for aid from the Samians, perhaps to provide the Spartans with a pretext to become involved in the conflict. The meeting's rationale is not known, only that there was a meeting. In the debate, however, the Corinthians spoke against any role in the conflict, arguing that to do so would be to meddle in Athenian affairs.[56] This argument prevailed and it seems clear why: just as the Athenians could do as they wished in their sphere of influence, so too could the other Greeks. For the Spartans this offered some guarantees to their own hegemony over the Peloponnesus and the allies who helped them keep the helots in line. To the Corinthians, who had their own plans of expanded influence, leaving the Samians to the Athenians would offer them the same control over those they planned to rule.

Despite the appeal of the Corinthian argument, the Spartans surely remained wary. Though the helot revolt of 464–456 had indeed been suppressed, the margin of victory was thin and secured only with vital allied support. If Athens could turn on a one-time friend and ally, overturn its political system, and inflict true horrors of war, what might befall her enemies? Such concerns and anxieties were hardly imaginary – Sparta must remain vigilant and protective of her allies.

Quiet vigilance, however, did not appeal to the citizens of 'wealthy' Corinth, as the city had been known since Homeric times (Hom. *Il.* 2. 570). Ever ambitious, Corinth looked in the years after the Thirty Years' Peace to expand her horizons and was in little mood to yield to the greater power of Athens. For the moment the Corinthians seemed willing to put aside their bitter feelings for the Athenians, but this was perhaps a one-concession not to be repeated. Deep down the Corinthians held an old grudge against the Athenians, one that threatened their temporary accommodation.

This abiding dislike of Athens stemmed from the hard fighting of the 'First' Peloponnesian War. Sometime about 458 the Athenians and Corinthians had clashed inconclusively in the vicinity of Megara. Though both claimed victory in the usual fashion, only the Athenians erected a battlefield trophy that marked the other side's retreat. When the Corinthians returned home they were greeted with derision by their own friends and families, ridiculing them for losing to the Athenians. Determined to retrieve their lost honor, the Corinthians returned to the put up their own trophy and while doing so were attacked by the Athenians. This time they were decisively beaten. Fleeing in disorder, a large group of them wandered into a field with no exits and here the Athenians trapped and slaughtered them. Ever after, the Corinthians, as Thucydides says, nursed 'a bitter hatred for the Athenians'.[57] Only a match to this powder keg was missing, and a dispute between the two over Corcyra and Potidaea, two old Corinthian colonies, provided just that.

Notes

1 Thuc. 1.130–131, with Hornblower 1: 216–19. The chronology of the Thucydidean *Pentekontaetia* ('Fifty Years'), the era from the Persian War to the Peloponnesian, is as uncertain as it is hotly debated. See further Badian 1993 and Hornblower 1: 133–93.

2 On the helots, their identity and place in Spartan society see Michell 1952: 36–45, Hodkinson and Powell 1999, and Appendix C. Scheidel 2003: 240–7 discusses helot numbers.

3 Thuc. 1.132.4-5, an accusation seemingly invoked against any Spartan who challenged the social norm. Spartan authorities brought down Cleomenes I, king c. 525-490, on similar charges (Hdt. 6.74, with Huxley 1970: 87).

4 Later rehabilitated and honored (Thuc. 1.134.4), the intrigues that snared Pausanias reflect the tensions of post-war Sparta and Greece.

5 See Plutarch, *Life of Aristides* for details.

6 These treasurers were probably drawn from the elite and prestigious ranks of Athenian society. Another financial committee, the Treasurers of Athena, was drawn from the most elite Athenians, the *pentakosiomedimnoi* ('500 bushel men'). Such qualifications may also have applied to the *hellenotamiai*, making them important officials and citizens.

7 The Athenian tribute lists (= *ATL*) were studied extensively by Meritt, Wade-Gery, and McGregor. In the following years additional decrees regulating coinage, weights and measures (= Fornara 97), methods for the payment of

tribute (= Fornara 98), and other administrative requirements (= Fornara 99, 102, 103) were enacted. A problem here is that the dates for most of these are disputed, largely the result of the fragmentary state of the inscriptions and the letter forms used, particularly the 'three bar sigma'. For discussion see Mattingly 1996: vii–xi (a foreword by M. Chambers).

8 See Sealey 1976: 243–53.

9 Credit for inventing ostracism has traditionally gone to Clisthenes, founder of the Athenian democracy but it may be later (see D.M. MacDowell, 'ostracism', *OCD*[3] 1083 and Sinclair 1988: 169–70). Each year the Athenians voted in the assembly whether or not to ostracize a fellow citizen, literally exiling him from the community for ten years, though this could be rescinded. Only political participation was lost: property and family remained undisturbed.

10 Broneer 1938: 228–43.

11 Plut. *Them.* 22.2-3 (ostracism, with Frost 1980: 187–92), *Them.* 23 (Pausanias, with Frost 194–5), *Them.* 25.3 (confiscated money, with Frost 208–9), *Them.* 26-32 (flight, exile, descendants, with Frost 209–36).

12 Podlecki 1998: 11. Through his mother Agariste, Pericles was also related to Clisthenes, 'founder' of the democracy.

13 Thuc. 1.98.4, Plut. *Arist.* 25.1. Thucydides (1.99.2), surely reflecting Athenian opinion, explains Athenian domination of the allies by the latter's willingness to pay tribute rather than fight like the Athenians – in effect blaming the victim for his plight.

14 Badian 1966: 38–9; cf. Meiggs 1972: 45–6. On arbitration see pp. 29–35.

15 Thuc. 1.100.2-101.1, 3, adding that the Spartans agreed to help the Thasians, an agreement made impossible by an earthquake and helot rising.

16 Sealey 1976: 269, 271–2, Meiggs 1972: 101–8; on Cimon in Sparta, see p. 10.

17 The relationship between Pericles and Ephialtes is uncertain. See Plut. *Per.* 10.6-8, with Stadter 1989: 126–9, [Arist.] *Ath. Pol.* 25, 27.1, with Podlecki 1998: 46–54 (politics) and Sinclair 1988: 18–19 (Areopagus).

18 See Goldhill 1990, 2000, and Griffin 1999a: 73–94 for discussion of the intersection of tragedy and politics; Vickers 2008 argues a more radical view that it was all about politics, but see Dover 2004: 239–49 for critique.

19 Neither is theater capacity clear: the fourth-century Theater of Dionysus held some 14,000, but the fifth-century theater's capacity was smaller, perhaps less than half. Thuc. 8.72.1 notes that never more than five thousand Athenians gathered to decide issues (cf. Hornblower 3: 967). This might give some idea of the largest theater crowd too. See Whitley 2001: 338–40, essentially Wycherley 1978: 207–11.

20 Scholars debate the authenticity of the Peace: cf. Sealey 1976: 278–82, Eddy 1970: 8–14, Badian 1993: 1–72; see Fornara 97–103 for the sources.

21 Done as a reminder of the impiety of the Persians, the act may have been as much for propaganda value as anything. Authenticity of the oath, recorded by

Diod. 11.29.3, Lyc. *Leoc.* 81, has been questioned; see Pollitt 1972: 65–6 and Hurwit 1999: 157 for discussion. Krentz 2007: 731–44 argues for an 'Oath of Marathon', not Plataea.

22 So Philoch. *FGrHist* 328 F121 and Diod. 12.39.1. Stadter 1989: 167 notes that such an office was held only for one year. Like a Medici prince, however, Periclean influence could easily be extended through cronies and allies.

23 Plut. *Per.* 13.6 credits Phidias as 'master builder', but opinion is split: Stadter 1989: 166–7 is skeptical, Podlecki 1998: 101 accepting.

24 Plut. *Per.* 12-13; Meiggs 1972: 152–3. For full discussion on the Periclean building era see Hurwit 1999: 154–221.

25 Plut. *Per.* 9.3 (with Stadter 1989: 114–18), 14 (Thucydides' ostracism), Sealey 1976: 298. Ehrenberg 1954: 84, n.1 remarks that Thucydides returned from his ostracism (c. 433).

26 Plut. *Cim.* 14-16, with Badian 1993.

27 Thuc. 2.27.2, 3.54.5, Xen. *Hell.* 5.2.3 (allied aid for Sparta). On the end of the revolt see Hornblower 1: 156–8.

28 See Thuc. 1.8 ('modernism' in ancient Greece), 2.43.1. See Raaflaub 1994: 130 (lovers of the *polis*) and Shear 2007: 113–15 (*agora* as citizens' domain increasingly after 430).

29 For detailed discussion of the Athenian democracy see Sinclair 1988; note that among its procedures for magistrates, including generals, was an examination of their conduct in office or *euthynai*, which included finances (Sinclair 1988: 78–9). The fundamental text to the democracy is [Arist.] *Ath. Pol.*, with Rhodes 1981.

30 See Raaflaub 1994: 113–18, 130–1, also Raaflaub 1998: 15–41, for a discussion of Athens' rise to 'world power' and its development of political institutions and active participation of its citizens in political and military activities. This is essentially state-building of a modern type.

31 Mearsheimer 2001: 367–8, 406; cf. Doyle 1997: 76–80.

32 C. 490 the Corinthians made available to the Athenians, in an ancient version of lend-lease, warships for use in a bitter fight with their nearby rival Aegina. See Hdt. 6.89, with Lewis 1997: 12.

33 Lewis 1997: 9–21 argues that this war was primarily a conflict between Athens and Corinth, with only minimal participation by the Spartans again fighting their own war with the helots.

34 Thuc. 1.113.3-4, Plut. *Per.* 18.2-3, with Stadter 1989: 212.

35 Plataea had been a bone of contention between the Athenians and the Thebans (in particular) since c. 525 when the Plataeans appealed to Athens for aid, which was granted. The Thebans did not forget or forgive this intrusion into their sphere of influence. The Thebans had also sided with the Persians in 480 and this remained a sore point with many Greeks. For details see Sealey 1976: 144–5.

36 See Ar. *Nub.* 859 and sch., Plut. *Per.* 22.1-3, and other sources in Fornara 1983: 115.
37 See de Ste. Croix 1972: 152. Later Cleandridas' son Gylippus faced similar charges, suggesting not only that the family was notoriously corrupt, but that Spartans already appreciated the value of money.
38 De Ste. Croix 1972: 293–4 lists the terms of the Peace, though his list is not exhaustive.
39 As Thuc. 1.118.2 notes.
40 Plut. *Per.* 24.8-9, with Stadter 1989: 238–9 (Pericles and Aspasia), 25.1 (Aspasia persuading Pericles to support Miletus), Fornara 111 (decree on comedy).
41 Regime change has been debated: Thuc. 1.115.3, 117.3, with Hornblower 1: 192–3; see also Quinn 1981: 17 (against) and Meiggs 1972: 189 (for).
42 Briant 2002: 581 suggests that Pissuthnes acted on the instructions of the Great King. But the distances between the King's court and the Aegean argues against this. More likely Pissuthnes acted on his own initiative, surely aware of what would please the King.
43 Plut. *Per.* 26.4, with Stadter 1989: 249–50, noting Plutarch's error in reversing the tattoos (as Plut. *Nic.* 29 shows: Athenian prisoners tattooed with the Syracusan horse, the device of their coinage); see also Rawlings 2007: 160.
44 Fornara 115 (treaty), 113 (war costs, something like 1400 talents); Plut. *Per.* 25-28.3 (punishments of the Samians). Plutarch rejects the story of Pericles' cruelty, but see Meiggs 1972: 191–2, Stadter 1989: 257–60; Quinn 1981: 69, n.26 downplays the event.
45 Plut. *Per.* 25.5 (Samian warships); Greek (and Athenian) warships carried upwards of ten marines per ship, so the number suggested here is conservative. See Jordan 1972: 184–5 for discussion.
46 Cf. Develin 1989: 89 (Sophocles general in 441/0), Lewis 1988: 41–3 (generalship in 437/6, perhaps also 441/0), and Ehrenberg 1954: 4.
47 In 443/2, so Lewis 1988: 36–8, cf. Develin 1989: 87–8. Holding such an office would place Sophocles among the elites of Athens.
48 The date for the *Antigone* is traditionally 442, but the rationale for this date is not compelling despite its frequent restatement. Lefkowitz 1981: 82 notes that no clear information fixes the play to this year, and Lewis 1988: 35–45 shows why the date of 438 is preferred. Griffith 1999: 1–2 offers no reason to support any date, simply repeating the traditional one.
49 Soph. *Ant.* 8. Thuc. 2.4, 9 notes Pericles' grip on the office of *strategos* and how he virtually ruled Athens through it. Some translations render Sophocles' choice of language, i.e., *strategos,* as 'King' (e.g., Watling in the Penguin edition, p. 126; Grene in the Chicago edition translates as 'commander' [p. 161]) but this obscures what the Athenian audience would have heard and imagined.
50 Soph. *Ant.* 21-32, and so too Lewis 1988: 45, Griffith 1999: 48.

51 Soph. *Ant.* 734, with Griffith 1999: 48.
52 Thuc. 2.34.5. The Kerameikos lay just outside the archaic city of Athens and had been divided when Themistocles rebuilt the walls after the Persian Wars. Here the great festival celebrating Athena, the Panathenaic, began its route to the acropolis and her temple, and here Harmodius and Aristogeiton assassinated Hipparchus, brother of the tyrant Hippias in 514 (Thuc. 6.57.1).
53 Since the Clisthenic reforms of the late sixth century, the Athenians had been divided into ten tribes, and this formed the basis of military and political structures. See Sealey 1976: 147–60 (Clisthenes), Tritle 2000: 155, 166–70 (Kerameikos).
54 Diod. 12.10.3-10-11.4, Plut. *Per.* 11.5, with Stadter 1989: 142, Dion. Hal. *Lys.* 1, and Sealey 1976: 309.
55 Thuc. 1.100.3, 4.102 (Amphipolis), 1.56.2-57 (Perdiccas), also Sealey 1976: 248-9, 312-13.
56 Thuc. 1.40.5-6. Thucydides does not explain the Corinthian argument, but its thrust seems clear enough; see p. 26.
57 Thuc. 1.103.4, 1.106 (slaughter of Corinthian soldiers).

Boeotia-Attica (after B.W. Henderson, *The Great War Between Athens and Sparta,* London, 1927)

2

'GIVE THE GREEKS THEIR FREEDOM'

As the Samian crisis cooled, disturbed only by a diehard oligarchic faction on the Asian mainland at Anaea, the Athenians resumed the normalcy of empire. The acropolis remained a hubbub of activity with work continuing on the Parthenon while the architect Mnesicles began construction of the acropolis gateway, the Propylaea (c. 437/6).[1] The restrictions placed on comic ridicule apparently lapsed, proving incapable of enforcement. But Pericles may not have found much peace. Xanthippus, his older son, chaffed at his father's restrictions, perhaps too his mistress, and gossiped around town about life at home with the 'Olympian'.[2] No less frustrating for Pericles were relations with his two wards Alcibiades and his brother Clinias, sons of his colleague Clinias killed at Coronea in 446. Both were inclined to outbursts of outrageous behavior and even Alcibiades regarded his brother as a madman.[3] While family matters were a distraction for Pericles, worse was about to happen.

A Western Conflict

Half a Greek world away, the Corinthians labored to find new markets and develop their own mini-sphere of influence as the economic and political power of Athens proved increasingly dominant. Since the mid-fifth century Corinth had been expanding its ties in the Greek northwest, where it had old colonial settlements in places like Leucas, Ambracia, Apollonia and Pertum. But these activities ignited conflict with the rich and powerful island community of Corcyra. Also an old Corinthian colony, Corcyra hated her 'mother city' and the sentiment was shared by the mother for the daughter.

This shared animosity boiled over into a major confrontation in 435. The cause was Epidamnus, a city located north of Corcyra on the Adriatic, but which both Corinth and Corcyra long before had co-founded. Local peoples began attacking Epidamnus, which first appealed for aid to nearby Corcyra which declined to help. The Epidamnians then begged Corinth for relief, which willingly provided emergency aid in the form of 'volunteers', soldiers and settlers who rushed in to help. This intrusion into its sphere of influence bitterly provoked Corcyra and with that conflict between these old enemies erupted.

The Corcyreans attempted to solve the dispute by diplomacy, offering arbitration to the Corinthians who refused. The Corcyreans placed Epidamnus and its relief garrison of Corinthians under siege, against which a Corinthian fleet sailed. In a double disaster for the Corinthians, Epidamnus fell while at Leucimme their fleet suffered defeat (435). This success encouraged the Corcyreans who now attacked those Corinthian allies – Leucas and Elis – which had supported Corinth. The Corinthians themselves, furious at the setback, prepared for a new attack on Corcyra, though the fleet dispatched in summer 434 did not engage the Corcyreans.

Afraid that Corinth and its power in the region would overwhelm it, Corcyra – previously a 'non-aligned state' – appealed, probably at the end of 434/3, to Athens for relief. Already expanding its influence westward, an alliance with Corcyra would have struck many Athenians as not only attractive but also potentially useful.[4] After two days of meetings, the Athenians voted to approve a defensive alliance with Corcyra and to send a fleet there. Entrusted with a small command (ten ships) was Cimon's son Lacedaemonius, who received pointed instructions: avoid hostilities, fight only if Corinth attacked Corcyra.[5] In other words, Lacedaemonius' squadron was just big enough to create an incident.

The Corinthian delegates present for these negotiations were unhappy with this Athenian intrusion. They may also have believed themselves betrayed. Only seven years before they had persuaded Sparta and other members of the Peloponnesian League not to intervene in Athens' suppression of the Samian Revolt (c. 441/0), arguing perhaps that it was a 'local' matter (Thuc. 1.40.5–6). Now arguing before the Athenians in 433/2 the Corinthians may have thought that the Athenians 'owed' them the favor of not intervening in Corcyra, and when the favor was not returned, believed themselves doubly wronged.

At the beginning of 433/2, Lacedaemonius' squadron duly arrived on station. When battle broke out between the two old enemies, the Athenians could not stand idly by and rushed to defend their new ally. Attacked on all sides the Corinthian fleet collapsed and fled in defeat. As Corcyra was technically non-aligned, what happened in the battle of Sybota, as it came to be called, did not break any of the terms of the Thirty Years Peace between Sparta and Athens and their respective blocs. But clearly Corinthian ambitions had been blunted, and the culprit without doubt was Athens.

Corinth and Athens continued wrangling over Corcyra when a fresh issue erupted. In the Aegean north lay the city of Potidaea, a member of the Athenian empire, but a city that also respectfully maintained its colonial ties with Corinth, even dutifully receiving their magistrates from Corinth. After the outbreak of fighting between Corinth and Corcyra, Athens decided to discipline this 'pro-Corinthian' member of its empire. Potidaea was told to dismantle a section of its fortifications, surrender hostages, and send away its Corinthian officials.

The Potidaeans, however, refused to knuckle under to Athenian pressure and refused. With little doubt they had received ready encouragement from their Corinthian officials, but the Macedonian king Perdiccas probably incited them as well. The Athenian settlement at Amphipolis had greatly upset him and now he saw a way to hit back. After Samos, Naxos, and Thasos, the Athenian response was surely predictable – large forces invested the city, putting it under siege, probably in spring 432.[6] This at least is what Thucydides tells. It also seems that Athens had been pressuring Potidaea for several years already, having increased the city's tribute from six to fifteen talents – in effect squeezing the city's economic life force.[7] This may be linked to Perdiccas' meddling to which the Potidaeans had responded too favorably. The treatment meted out to Potidaea surely reflects too the lingering fallout of the bitter struggle with Samos.

While the fight between Athens and Corinth over Corcyra had been a peripheral issue, Potidaea was much more complicated. On the one hand, as an Athenian 'ally' or 'subject' it might have been disciplined as the Corinthians had conceded in the case of Samos (Thuc. 1.40.5). But that was ten years in the past and before the full extent of Athenian 'discipline' had been demonstrated – simply, what the Athenians did at Samos was not only horrific but read by many Greeks as a warning. The Corinthians saw Potidaea as family and it seems not much of a stretch to imagine they objected to the treatment being meted out to their own kind. The measures imposed on Potidaea may have seemed to the Corinthians a violation of the spirit of the Thirty Years Peace and that was sufficient to raise a complaint before Sparta and the other members of the Peloponnesian League. While Sparta might not be moved to fight over Corcyra, Corinth with its interests and connections to Potidaea was another matter.

A very loud Corinthian appeal summoned Sparta's other allies to a league meeting. Gathering at Sparta, representatives from Aegina and Megara spoke first to the assembled delegates, setting forth their complaints with the Athenians: Aegina's lack of autonomy contrary to the Peace; Megara's exclusion from Aegean harbors and the market in Attica (Thuc. 1.67.2–5). But these complaints paled before the Corinthian grievances which inflamed both the allies and the Spartans.

Following the Aeginetan and Megarian denouncements, the Corinthians spoke bitterly, complaining of Spartan inactivity which now threatened all of them.[8] More disconcerting to the Spartans was the thinly veiled threat that if Sparta failed to defend allied interests and needs, then the Corinthians, for their part, might be compelled to look elsewhere for a new partner and advocate.[9] Such talk would surely have raised Spartan anxieties, as the allies were always a quick source of aid should the helots rebel.

On hearing of the debate, some Athenians in Sparta on other business asked to speak to the assembled Peloponnesians. With surprising verve and frankness, these Athenians responded to the Corinthian denunciations, arguing that Athens could not be blamed for its actions: that Athenian sacrifices in the Persian Wars entitled them to their successes, that their empire had in part been forced upon them by the Spartan surrender of leadership. Not only did the Athenians not back down, they justified their behavior and actions by appeals to power and its use, not any idea of right: that they only did what anyone would in similar circumstances (Thuc. 1.73–8; cf. 1.99.2).

Two Spartan speakers followed. First spoke Archidamus, Eurypontid king for over thirty years, a veteran of many fights. As he emphasized the costs of war and not to abandon their allies or be blind to Athenian plotting (Thuc. 1.80.4, 82.1), he also argued for continued negotiations and preparations for war. His was a cautionary line, admonishing everyone that wars were easier to start than to win, that all sorts of unexpected things can happen.[10] However, the king's sober comments were perhaps overshadowed by the terse and blunt statement of Sthenelaidas, one of the ephors. Sthenelaidas claimed not to understand the fine speech of the Athenians, but he did see that they were in the wrong now and should be punished twofold: once for having been good in former times, and a second time for being bad now. He argued that Sparta could not allow the allies to be beaten down – a clear allusion to the Corinthian threat to desert the alliance – and that the Athenians could not be allowed to become stronger still (Thuc. 1.86).

Once the speeches ended, the Spartans voted on a simple question: have the Athenians broken the Peace?[11] Spartan procedure called for a simple voice vote, but Sthenelaidas, in charge of the process, claimed to be unable to determine the yeas and nays. He told the Spartans to move to different sides of the assembly area, and in doing so it became clear that those responding yes to the question had prevailed.

The complexity of the Spartan vote, however, has not, it seems, been fully appreciated. On the first, voice vote, those answering no are as vocal – and as numerous perhaps – as those answering yes. But when told to separate the yeas prevail. What has happened? Is it that the yeas actually yelled louder, or is it that in the process of moving about, peer pressure and other forms of intimidation were brought to bear? This can no longer be determined. It seems worthwhile to note that even in Thucydides' text opinion in Sparta was more complicated than some scholars are prepared to admit – that there were more Spartans than Archidamus opposed to war.[12]

Arbitration – A Greek Attempt at Conflict Resolution

Thucydides plainly states that when Athens and Sparta went to war *both* broke the Thirty Years Peace of 446/5. When his account of the outbreak of war in 431 is probed, several factors emerge that shed light on the war's origins. First, perhaps most critically, is the issue of arbitration.[13] He advanced this issue first in the Athenian speech at Sparta at the beginning of the dispute between Corcyra and Corinth. He returned to it in Pericles' first speech to the Athenians in late fall 432 when he urged them to vote for war with Sparta. Pericles stated plainly that the Spartans had refused, or at very least had failed to accept, Athenian offers to arbitrate their differences as called for by the Thirty Years Peace.[14]

But how could such a dispute be arbitrated? Modern political scientists observe that among the features of the international system that prompts states to fear each other is the absence of a central authority that can protect them from the aggressions and ambitions of others.[15] There can be little doubt that as early as Homer the Greeks recognized the same problem.

Homer's classic dispute between Agamemnon and Achilles over Briseis could only be resolved by the gods (Hom. *Il.* 1). But the gods were not always available or sympathetic. In the middle of the Peloponnesian War Aristophanes invokes a similar divine appeal in his play *Peace*. His hero Trygaeus, arriving in heaven to return Peace to the Greeks finds that the gods have turned affairs over to War, sickened by the unending strife of the Greeks (Ar. *Pax* 204–9).

In real life, arbitration could be offered and then refused, as the Corinthians refused Corcyrean offers in 435, and as Elis rejected Sparta's decision in favor of Lepreum in 421, or as the Boeotians refused a Spartan offer to arbitrate in 395. The Athenians themselves also seemed unwilling to arbitrate disputes with their own allies or subjects, preferring simple obedience and if not, war.[16] In the dispute with Samos (c. 442/1), the Athenians offered arbitration, but in Athens before an Athenian jury (Plut. *Per.* 25.1). The Samians rejected this offer, surely right to question the objectivity of any decision. Thucydides strengthens this view, as he adds (1.99.2) that the Athenians had no qualms forcing rebellious allies back into the alliance. Finally, it should be noted that even in the relatively sophisticated Athenian democracy of the fourth century, domestic arbitration was hardly foolproof. Judgments of arbitrators (*diaitetai*) were only final if both parties accepted them, and either party could appeal.[17] The pitfalls of domestic arbitration suggest that inter-state arbitration (particularly in the fifth century) would have been even likelier to fail.

In fact arbitration was neither automatic nor binding. While it is certainly true that the allies swore oaths when the Delian League was founded, their once autonomous standing had eroded leaving them subjects and subject to Athenian discipline. Thucydides makes clear that the alliance was Athenian dominated and that the Athenians were perfectly willing to use force to make the allies 'free'.[18]

Sparta Tries Talking

Routinely the Greeks found the arbitration of disputes difficult. Sparta's purported refusal to arbitrate and its presumed responsibility for plunging Greece into war should not be accepted uncritically. If the Spartans indeed provoked war, they followed a most unusual diplomatic strategy. For on at least four occasions Spartan ambassadors approached the Athenians attempting to find some way to avoid war.[19] Who in Sparta promoted the cause of peace? What did the Spartans hope to accomplish with negotiations? Why did the Athenians refuse to talk?

First, the Spartan effort to try talking to the Athenians flies in the face of the usual image of a military society and state, the image that has dominated perceptions of Sparta since Roman times and into the twentieth century. While the military elements in Spartan society were omnipresent, there were times when ordinary soldiers dissented and challenged their commanders, and significantly on occasion. The reality is that Spartans did not always look for a fight, and that as they never pursued a beaten opponent very far, so too they thought carefully about fighting in the first place.[20]

With little doubt only Archidamus and like-minded Spartans around him possessed the influence to advocate peace and send embassies to Athens. His statements before the Spartans and allies, while guarded, conveyed a cautionary note, that entering into war was a course of last resort. Sometime in late fall/early winter 432, the first Spartan embassy, the 'curse' embassy, came to Athens and opened negotiations. According to Thucydides, the Spartans told the Athenians that war could be avoided if they would drive out the curse of the goddess. This was a none too subtle attack on Pericles. Years before his family had been responsible for the deaths of a number of Athenians who had supported the would-be tyrant Cylon seize power (Thuc. 1.126). The Athenians responded telling the Spartans to drive out the curse of Tainaron and that of Athena of the Bronze House in Sparta. This too was a not very subtle reference to the Pausanias scandal, similarly involving religious pollution (Thuc. 1.128).

Thucydides' intent is not clear. It may be that he is only recording what each side demanded of the other, or that he takes an opportunity to recount old instances of Athenian–Spartan conflict while also revealing the realities of religious pollution in political affairs. Modern readers may well be puzzled by such diplomatic claims, but at the time these would have possessed a reality difficult today to understand.

Within a few months, a second Spartan embassy arrived and this was much more of a diplomatic effort. The Spartans told the Athenians that war could be avoided if they abandoned the siege of Potidaea and restored autonomy to Aegina, an island community the Athenians had subjected twenty years earlier (Thuc. 139.1). [21] At this time the Spartans interjected a new issue – freedom of the Greeks – that they would use with increasing effect in the years to come.[22] The Athenians, however, remained inflexible. They refused to lift the siege of Potidaea.

The Spartans then told the Athenians that there would be no war if they revoked the Megarian Decree (Thuc. 1.139.1), a measure enacted earlier (c. 433?) that had barred Megarian goods from Athenian-controlled markets.[23] This punitive measure had created an economic slump that, if we believe Aristophanes (*Ach.* 535–40), had reduced many Megarians to near starvation. The Athenian response was again unyielding. Pericles justified the ban by accusing the Megarians of cultivating sacred land and providing shelter to fugitive slaves (Thuc. 1.139.2). Pericles added that in any case the decree could not be repealed, as a second decree prevented that. To this Polyalces, one of the Spartan envoys, responded 'well, turn it to the wall. There's no law against that is there'?[24] The simplicity of Polyalces' statement argues for its authenticity – who else but a Spartan could say something so plain and direct? The Periclean stance reflects Athenian intellectual arrogance as well as the unwillingness to enter into meaningful discussions that might defuse the crisis facing now facing the Greeks.[25]

In late winter 432 (?), a third Spartan embassy arrived. Its envoys, Ramphias, Melesippus, and Agesander announced to the Athenians that 'Sparta wants peace. Peace is still possible if you give the Greeks their freedom' (Thuc. 1.139.3). That the Spartans should be imagined as defenders of freedom has been challenged, most notably by de Ste. Croix who dismisses it as 'mere propaganda, except in so far as it happened to coincide with Sparta's own selfish interests'.[26] While in some ways true, the criticism is naive. In the early twenty-first century, US foreign policy has stressed the need to establish democracy in the Middle East, but when societies elect governments or favor political parties unsympathetic to the US, as Hamas in Palestine or Hezbullah in Lebanon, democratic expressions are ignored.

So too with the Spartans: while 'giving the Greek their freedom' may have been dependent first and foremost on what was best for Sparta, there may be more to the Spartan statement than de Ste. Croix and other scholars allow. Namely, the Spartan demand was deliberately sweeping. Even as the Spartans made their proposal, *autonomia* defined a wide range of contemporary political realities: immunity and autonomy could be conditional on the payment of tribute, as in the case of Potidaea; autonomy might exist without complete sovereignty.[27]

Even the Spartans would have had some idea of this. They would have understood that *autonomia* – freedom – was a slogan, a buzzword, a political football as one scholar has defined it. What were they looking for in making these proposals? These were high-stakes political negotiations. The repeated Spartan effort to get the Athenians to talk suggests that the Spartans hoped that the Athenians would give them a way out of an impasse created by Athenian aggressions and Corinthian hostility.[28] They wanted something that they could take back to their allies, especially the Corinthians but their own people too, that would enable them to cool things off and avoid war.

That the Spartans were looking for a way out of the impasse finds confirmation in their handling of an embassy from Mytilene. In the months preceding the outbreak of war, the oligarchic rulers of Mytilene – the strongest *polis* in Lesbos and an old Athenian ally – sent an embassy to Sparta, attempting to win Spartan support for a takeover of the island and a defection from Athens. The Spartans refused even to hear this delegation's offer, which argues that they were not eager for war. Otherwise the Mytilenian embassy would surely have been heard.[29]

The issue of freedom raised by the Spartans and their refusal to listen to the Mytilenian embassy reflects the high-stakes diplomatic initiatives now going on among the Greeks. In this tense atmosphere it seems clear that it is the Spartans who are taking the initiative, trying to avoid war. Many modern scholars determined to absolve Athens of any wrong in starting the war, ignore this.

In response to the Spartan freedom gambit, Pericles responded with a speech intended not only to incite rejection of the Spartan overture, but a vote for war with Sparta. It was in this speech that Pericles claimed the Spartans were plotting against Athens and had refused offers of arbitration. He referred specifically to a clause of the Thirty Years Peace that stipulated the grant of arbitration upon the offer of one party in a dispute and that until a decision, 'each side should keep what it has' (Thuc. 1.140.2, 144.2). This statement would appear to put the Spartans in the wrong in causing a war that the Athenians scrupulously tried to avoid. As shown above, arbitration could easily be offered if it was thought unlikely to be accepted, or if the process could be manipulated. This the Spartans knew just as they knew of the obligation to accept arbitration.[30] In fact the Spartans were probably right to worry about Athenian offers of arbitration, especially regarding Corcyra. Years before Themistocles had ruled for Corcyra in another dispute with Corinth, and his honored status in Corcyra had suggested collusion if not outright corruption (Plut. *Them.* 24.1). In fact arbitration was the rock on which the negotiations between Athens and Sparta crashed: the Athenians unwilling to give an inch, the Spartans unable to persuade them differently.

Many scholars would argue, as Thucydides apparently implies, that the Spartan embassies were only buying time to prepare for war and to gain the moral advantage in the dispute. After all, some Spartans later admitted, Thucydides asserts, to Spartan responsibility in not reining in the Thebans or in taking up the Athenian offer to seek arbitration.[31] But this admission, placed in the context of the Sicilian expedition, comes some fifteen years after the war's outbreak. How well did these *anonymous* Spartans know their own history – of the efforts made by Archidamus, Polyalces and others, most if not all now dead – to stop the march to war? If the statement is genuine and not simply Thucydidean editorializing, it might just as easily reflect the limited understanding of younger men to events of which they had no direct knowledge.[32]

Moreover, Thucydides is silent regarding disaffection in Plataea and the plot conceived there by the ambitious Nauclides to bring Plataea into 'Greater Boeotia', or that in a community with some of the longest ties to Athens there was dissent. In short, Nauclides' conspiracy with the Theban Eurymachus reveals not only the presence of Plataean opposition to Athens, but that the Athenians were as much in the dark as the Spartans about the activities of their friends and allies.[33]

A greater problem seems to be a flaw in the process in identifying an arbitrator that would satisfy each aggrieved party. The Greek city-states by this time had fallen into two armed camps now preparing for war. The only major non-aligned state in Greece proper was Argos, a community that hated the Spartans (and whom the Spartans hated in turn) who would never consent to Argive mediation.[34] In western Greece, Corcyra had been the major non-aligned state, but Corcyra was now party to the dispute and could not possibly act as an arbiter. There were several other non-aligned communities in western Greece, but these – Aetolia and Achaea, for example – lacked the necessary political organization, sophistication, let alone authority to arbitrate the complex issues involving the two Greek superpowers.[35]

The difficulties of implementing arbitration played into the hands of the Athenians. In those speeches Thucydides creates for the Athenians, as well as in the words of the Corinthians and Spartans, the Athenians come across as intellectually quick, able to solve any problem.[36] The Athenians seem to have seized upon a diplomatic technicality that they used to confuse the less sophisticated Spartans. They realized the difficulty in finding and then agreeing on an arbiter and this suited them just fine. It allowed them to assume the role of the injured party in the negotiations, as they could always claim that they were prepared to submit their quarrel to a third party, when in fact they knew it would be difficult if not impossible to settle on one. With such delaying tactics they could put off negotiations and at the same time continue their provocative policies, which were at the root of Spartan fears and anxieties all along. It seemed perhaps a perfect strategy, yet in the end it backfired and brought a war, one that Pericles and many Athenians believed they could win.

Athens Prepares to Fight

While offers of arbitration were diplomatic ploys, it seems clear that Pericles and many Athenians were already preparing for war. As the war broke out, Pericles detailed the manpower resources and financial strength of Athens: 13,000 frontline infantry and 16,000 reservists, plus another 2800 cavalry and archers, 300 seaworthy warships; of material wealth there was more than 6000 talents plus an annual tribute of 600 from the allies – all of this unmatched in the Greek world.[37] Additionally there were the usual revenues that came from the silver mines at Laurium and other taxes and income associated with harbor duties; there were hundreds of talents worth of private and public dedications to the gods which could be made available in an emergency. Such wealth enabled the Athenians, at least at the beginning of the war, to pay their soldiers and sailors rather the extravagant sum of two drachmas per day (one for themselves, one for their attendant): twice the rate of a skilled worker (Thuc. 3.17.4).

For some years before the Athenians had also been constructing and manning fortifications around Attica and other strategic regions such as the eastern Megarid.[38] The building of strategic fortifications and the stockpiling of wealth had been well underway before granting the Corcyreans an alliance. In 434/3 as well several decrees since named for their proposer, Callias, stipulated the consolidation of monies on the acropolis and provision for payments to be made to various gods. More significant perhaps are the provisions for payments toward maintenance of the city walls and docks, both of which point to preparations for war.[39] Such legislation makes clearer the acceptance of the Corcyrean appeal, as well as the renewal of alliances with Rhegium and Leontini in 433/2: Pericles and the Athenians believed that war with the Peloponnesians was only a question of time.[40] Such preparations explain further Pericles' firm position of 'no-negotiations' with the Spartans, which Thucydides elaborates, noting Pericles' 'grand strategy' for winning: look after the fleet, curtail imperial expansion, and keep the city safe (Thuc. 2.65.7).

Going to War in Fifth-Century Greece

The conflict between Corcyra and Corinth over Epidamnus soon entangled Athens and Sparta, each leading a powerful group of allies. As the original dispute worsened and expanded to include Potidaea, the likelihood of a greater conflict gradually increased. Historian E. Badian is surely right that after the war ended there was great discussion over responsibility (who started the war?): an ancient version of the 1919 Paris Peace Conference's 'war-guilt issue', and what Thucydides wrote must be placed within this context. It is also clear that Thucydides gives us his account of how things unfolded and in doing so downplays those events where Athenian responsibility was greater.[41] Yet wars are complex; given the practical limitations of his time and the limits imposed by his own perspective, Thucydides deserves credit for relating as clearly as he does what drove the Greeks to war in 431.

In fact his sophisticated account of the war's outbreak bears an eerie resemblance to Europe in August 1914 and the outbreak of World War I.[42] In discussing the conflicts over Epidamnus and Potidaea, Thucydides identifies what historians today would refer to as 'short-term causes'. He also recognizes 'long-term causes', particularly the growth of Athenian power that so worried the Spartans that, in his view, they saw no alternative but war.[43] Thucydides identifies what could also be defined as the 'necessary' cause, i.e., the type of cause without which a conflict could not begin, in the Theban 'sneak' attack on Plataea (Thuc. 2.1–6). Like the events following the assassination of the Austrian Arch-Duke Franz Ferdinand in 1914, these factors led to the mobilization of the armies after which war could not be stopped (Thuc. 2.7). Moreover, after the failed Theban attack on Plataea, the Plataeans executed 180 Theban prisoners and this undoubtedly hardened hearts. Thucydides makes clear that this sparked the mobilization of the armies of Greece and the war that so many feared became a reality.

Was this war preventable? Or was it, as many translations of Thucydides seem to suggest, inevitable?[44] I would argue that Thucydides understands the reasons behind the actions of individuals and states too well to be satisfied with arguments of inevitability in explaining what happened in Greece between 433 and 431. His reference to inevitability may be no more than a reflection of popular opinion.[45] This finds support in his explanation of the war's short- and long-term causes, the 'necessary' cause in the Theban attack on Plataea, and his own interpretation that the growth of Athenian power led Sparta to conclude that there was no recourse but to fight when their repeated diplomatic overtures failed.[46]

Thucydides' account of the war's outbreak is sophisticated in other ways. In both 1914 Europe and fifth-century Greece other factors gave momentum to war hysteria. Chief among these was the enthusiasm of young men inexperienced with war and thereby drawn to it. There was the willingness of many to imagine that a war would follow a predictable course (an idea common among even modern politicians and statesmen); there was, lastly, the hard 'no negotiations' line assumed by one of the parties – Athens – in the dispute. All this suggests that Thucydides had thought long and hard on what happened in 433–431 and saw war not as inevitable, but rather the result of a series of decisions made by those caught up in the events. The factors just mentioned require further examination.

In discussing the aftermath of the Theban attack on Plataea, Thucydides observes that there was widespread enthusiasm for war. Many Peloponnesian and Athenian young men had never been to war and were thrilled at the prospect – not unlike the youth of Europe in 1914.[47] In Sparta a generation had come of age since the helot revolt (ended not later than 456) and many of these young Spartans would not have understood the apprehensions of their seniors who knew what war was all about. A number of young and old may have feared too that unless they became personally involved the whole effort itself would be handicapped (Thuc. 2.8.1).

Thucydides also notes that support for the Spartans was widespread in Greece. Athenian suppression of Naxos, Samos, and other states had created bitterness and fear, as others worried they might be next (Thuc. 2.8.4). Youthful exuberance for the unknown nourished enthusiasm for war, as did a popular belief that Athens was indeed the 'tyrant city' as the Corinthians said, that those upholding the 'freedom' of the Greeks were the Spartans, as they increasingly proclaimed.[48] Even Thucydides may have succumbed to this line of thought. In Pericles' final speech to the Athenians, he told them that they held their empire *like* a tyranny. Three years later, Cleon would dispense with such pleasantries, simply admitting what the realities were – that the empire *was* a tyranny (Thuc. 2.63.2, 3.37.2).

Enthusiasm for war was matched by the popular belief that it was predictable, though in his own analysis Thucydides had stressed the unpredictability of war.[49] In his speech after the Theban attack on Plataea, Archidamus reminded the allies that war is uncertainty and that too often attacks are made on a sudden impulse. This reference to what is (incorrectly) known today as the Clausewitzian 'fog of war' underlines the idea of popular enthusiasm for war – that people think they can anticipate the sequence of events once war begins – just like so many did on the eve of World War I and often since.

Enthusiasm for war among the Greeks may in part be explained by cultural attitudes that saw war as a way of life.[50] Since Homeric times success in war was the clearest expression of manly excellence; in essence, war brought out the best in man. Herodotus' work on the Persian Wars enhanced this ethos by extending it to the larger community, the *polis*, as demonstrated in Athens' heroic leadership of the Greeks to victory over the Persians. Moreover, not only was war glorious and noble, it also brought power and wealth.

Diplomatic maneuvers, particularly by Corinth, were closely related to these conditions. In explaining how states pressure and influence each other in attempting to balance power, John Mearsheimer identifies one method which he calls 'buck-passing', whereby a state that chooses not to act itself pressures another to act in its place.[51] In this instance, Corinth – unwilling and unable to challenge Athens' greater power alone – maneuvered its leader and protector Sparta to do exactly what it could not. Buck-passing remains a tried and tested diplomatic technique today and its practice among the Greeks supports the suggestion presented above that the Peloponnesian and Athenian conflict 'feels modern'.

It may be too that Thucydides, influenced by the new thought of the day, the era of Enlightenment promoted by the sophists and other intellectuals, recognized that this quest for power drove the 'modern' state that Athens had become.[52] Power brought security, as well as wealth, and power brought the good things in life that the Athenians had fought so hard to win since defeating the Persians. Preserving these accomplishments and expanding them became powerful forces determining Athenian policies and actions.[53] Thucydides saw that states flourish or decay as they are militarily successful and that wielding power allows them to rule others – an experience altogether preferable to being ruled – and to achieve that greatest of political values – freedom.[54] Homer and Herodotus composed their works to keep the deeds of brave men from being forgotten. Thucydides had this in mind too, but he went further in showing how men's exploits in war enabled states to become strong and successful. For the same reason he relates the fate of those states, like Melos, that lacking power, were overcome by the more powerful and had no choice but to accept whatever the strong imposed on them.[55]

What happened then in 433–431? Athens, Corinth, and Sparta, and the lesser states of Greece, had become locked into a way of looking at life that saw conflict as natural, even manly, that the solving of disputes by recourse to war was in the nature of men and states. Kurt Raaflaub has spoken eloquently of the powerful images that conditioned not only Athenians but many others to imagine war as sweet and proper – an image that shows little sign of passing away.[56]

In some ways the Athenians imagined that war would bring out the best in them – it would protect their power and predominance and they would prevail in their adversities as their history demonstrated. One Athenian who suffered no illusions about what was at stake was Pericles. He realized that war brought with it the opportunity to increase Athenian power and wealth and so took advantage of a legalistic interpretation of the arbitration clause of the Thirty Years Peace to disguise an Athenian bid for domination.[57]

For the Athenians to negotiate with the Spartans and Corinthians would demonstrate weakness amounting to a retreat. Any sign of weakness was dangerous and might lead to further conflicts that could deprive the Athenians of their empire. In the debate over Mytilene Thucydides attributes this very idea to the Athenian politician Cleon as justification for imposing a reign of terror over the subjects of the empire (Thuc. 3.37.2, 40.4). In his Melian Dialogue, Thucydides ascribes to the Athenians the same motivation: they must conquer and/or dominate Melos in order not to appear weak or indecisive (Thuc. 5. 91–6). Driven by such perceptions, there was little choice for the Athenians other than to frustrate Spartan overtures. The power that had brought Athens unparalleled prosperity was a two-edged sword, a political straightjacket, limiting options not increasing them.

Notes

1 Quinn 1981: 18–19 (Samian dissidents); Fornara 118 (Propylaea).
2 Plut. *Per.* 36.2–8, with Stadter 1989: 326–9. Laws on comic abuse were vague and made prosecution difficult, so Sommerstein 2004: 205–22; but cf. Sidwell 2009.

3 Sources cited in *APF* 18, see also Ellis 1989: 17–18.

4 Most scholars date the Athenian-Corcyrean alliance to late spring/summer 433/2 (see e.g., Gomme 1: 177, who notes the Athenian squadron went out in the first prytany of the year, which should be late spring; see de Ste. Croix 1972: 67). Sometime later that year, the Athenians renewed earlier alliances (of c. 450) with the west Greek communities of Rhegium and Leontini (ML 63-64, de Ste. Croix 1972: 108). While these diplomatic acts might not be preparations for war, they surely point to the same aggressive acts as directed against Samos only a few years before.

5 Thuc. 1.24–55, 1.45.1–2 (Lacedaemonius' command). Standard studies for the outbreak of the war are Kagan 1969, de Ste. Croix 1972; Sealey 1976: 313–21, notes that the Spartans might have it the 'Athenian War'; Tritle 2007 previews what follows.

6 Thuc. 1.56–65 (Potidaea besieged), 1.56.2 (Perdiccas' role in the region). See also de Ste. Croix 1972: 80–1; on the siege see pp. 52–3.

7 Meiggs 1972: 202, 528 (comments on *ATL*).

8 Cf. Tuplin 1979: 301–7 suggesting an allusion to Athenian economic measures against Megara in Thuc. 1.42.2.

9 Thucydides also attributes to the Corinthians a character analysis of both the Athenians and Spartans, noting the aggressiveness and ambitions of the former, the passivity and complacency of the latter.

10 See also de Ste. Croix 1972: 142–3.

11 Thuc. 1.87.2 shows that the question asked if the Athenians had broken the Peace, not that war should also be declared; in an editorial remark at 1.88, Thucydides adds that the Peloponnesians had decided for war already. But his account does not say that. See also Badian 1993: 147–8.

12 Thuc. 1.88, 79.2. De Ste. Croix 1972: 64–5 claims 'a great majority' of Spartans favored war. But this only becomes clear after Sthenelaidas separated the voters.

13 Beloch 2, 1: 297 is skeptical that it could have worked at all but does not elaborate. Kagan 1969: 353–4 and Badian 1993: 142–4 refer to the issue, but do not discuss how arbitration might have worked. See also Eckstein 2003: 757–74 and Samons 2007: 305, n.43.

14 Thuc. 1.78.4, 1.104.2. Note also 1.28.2 that refers to a Corcyrean offer to arbitrate its dispute with Corinth by bringing in a third party from the Peloponnese acceptable to both. But again there appears no mechanism in place to make this work.

15 Mearsheimer 2001: 3, 32 notes the problems of the lack of mediation and arbitration in the international political arena. While his focus is the modern-day political scene, there should be little doubt that the same factors influenced great powers such as Athens and Sparta, and the less great such as Corinth.

16 De Ste. Croix 1972: 122, seems unable to see that arbitration was automatic, either in its grant or verdict. Badian 1966: 38–9 notes Athenian refusals to arbitrate with allied states.

17 [Arist.] *Ath Pol.* 53.2, with Rhodes 1981: 589–90. Busolt-Swoboda 1920–6: 485-6 refer to other domestic arbitrators from the Hellenistic period. Note also Solon's arbitration of the Athenian land crisis ([Arist.] *Ath. Pol.* 5, 11–12) and his ensuing ten-year absence from Athens to exclude the possibility of over-turning his decisions.

18 Meiggs 1972: 44–5 notes the solemnity of oaths taken when the Delian League was organized. But by mid-century there have been changes in Athenian pro-cedures. The oath then taken by Erythraeans (c. 453/2) states they will not desert the Athenians or their allies (ML 40). Meiggs argues this probably reflects the original oath, but it may be as likely that the phrase follows the revolts of Naxos and Thasos and the Athenians have found it necessary to spell out what was expected of allies. Again the allies or subject states appear to be free and autonomous, but only as free as Athens allows.

19 Badian 1993: 154 notes, after Thuc. 1.139.1, there were 'many' embassies, though Thucydides only comments on those discussed here. These embassies are: (i) the 'curse' embassy (1.139.1); (ii) the 'Potidean and Megarian' embassy of Polyalces (1.139.1); (iii) the 'autonomy' embassy of Ramphias, Melesippus, and Agesandrus (1.139.3); and (iv) the 'last ditch' embassy of Melesippus (2.12.1–3). When these embassies came to Athens is uncertain, but the Theban attack on Plataea at the beginning of spring, probably about February/March 431, helps. The 'curse' embassy should date to late fall or early winter 432, after the Spartan and Peloponnesian declaration that Athens had broken the Peace. The second and third embassies followed in winter 432/1, but before the February/March 431 Theban attack on Plataea. Melesippus' 'last ditch' effort followed that attack, perhaps in March/April 431 (on which see pp. 44–5).

20 Thuc. 1.118.2 (Spartans slow to act), 5.73.4 (short pursuit of beaten enemy only), with Hodkinson 2006: 111–62, and strong arguments against the percep-tion of Sparta as a military state.

21 Rhodes 1987: 160 notes that Thucydides says nothing suggesting that the Aegi-netan complaint was unjustified.

22 Thuc. 1.124.3, 2.8.4, 12.1, 3.32.2, 63.3, 4.85.1, 86.1. See also Lewis 1977: 65, and Raaflaub 2004: 193–202, who notes the emergence of freedom after the Persian Wars and how this became an influential idea in Herodotus' *History*.

23 Cawkwell 1997: 33, argues that the Megarian Decree became an issue after the conflict and debate over Corcyra, that it was an economic measure intended to force Megara back into the Athenian sphere. See also Rhodes 1987: 162.

24 Plut. *Per.* 30.1, confirmed by Ar. *Ach.* 537 (*pace* Stadter 1989: 274); see Lewis 1977: 49, n. 157 with bibliography.

25 Thuc. 1.144.2 notes Pericles' reply: Megarians and their goods would be read-
mitted to Athenian ports, but only when the Spartans agreed not to expel
Athenians and their allies from Sparta. This seems to be a reference to an old
custom whereby 'foreigners' were periodically expelled from Sparta. Thucydides does not explain how this might be connected to the Megarians. If
reported accurately, the argument might be nothing more than an issue raised
by the Athenians to confuse things further.

26 De Ste. Croix 1972: 158; cf. 154–5.

27 On the idea of autonomy and freedom see Raaflaub 2004.

28 Bosworth 1992: 122–6, at 126.

29 See Thuc. 3.2, with Hornblower 1: 382–3.

30 In his first speech at Sparta, Archidamus told the Spartans that it would be
wrong to initiate war while arbitration was pending (Thuc. 1.85.2). Rhodes
1987: 164 notes the ease with which arbitration could be offered but not the
acceptance of a decision (see above n.14).

31 E.g., Gomme-Andrewes-Dover 4: 394, commenting on Thuc. 7.18.2, argue that
the Spartan embassies were designed to provoke refusal; cf. also Cawkwell 1997:
22. This position seems overly cynical. See below and Badian 1993: 125–62 (esp.
143–4) who argues that Thucydides misrepresents Spartan 'plotting and devi-
ousness'. Low 2007: 105–8 also regards arbitration as far from foolproof.

32 See also Thuc. 4.59, broadly addressing the causes of war and how ignorance
and profit influence men in deciding for it. Thucydides also alludes to the
unexpected happening and throwing off the plans of men.

33 Thuc. 2.2.2, 2.5.7 (where Thucydides calls Nauclides' party traitors). Neither
Kagan 1969 nor de Ste. Croix 1972 mention what went on in Plataea before
war erupted.

34 Peloponnesian neighbors Argos and Sparta were enemies from the sixth century
when Sparta's Peloponnesian League began expanding at Argos' expense. C.
494 the Spartan king Cleomenes I destroyed an Argive army at Sepeia (Hdt. 6.
76–80); Argos was so weakened that it played no part in the Persian Wars and
into the later years of the fifth century.

35 Syracuse, the dominant state in Greek Sicily might be considered as an alternative. Yet Syracuse had been founded by Corinth and the two states maintained
the ties appropriate to mother-city and colony, which would have made Syracusan mediation unacceptable to Athens.

36 Archidamus (Thuc. 1.84.3) says that the Spartans are wise because they
are not educated to despise the law, a clear jibe at the Athenians. In his
famous Funeral Oration, Pericles (2.40.2) refers to Athenian daring in taking
on bold, though calculated, ventures and danger. See also Raaflaub 1994:
105–6.

37 Thuc. 2.13.3–6, 8 (cf. 2.31, 3.17), with Akrigg 2007: 30–1 (Athenian numbers),
Rawlings 2007: 115. See also Thuc. 1.141.5, 3.13.6 (wealth of empire).

38 E.g., Thuc. 2.18.1 (fort at Oinoe), with Rawlings 2007: 135, 138.

39 Texts of the decrees in ML 58, with Samons 1996: 91–102.

40 Fornara 125 (treaty with Leontini).

41 See further Badian 1993: 125–63, Rhodes 1987: 161–3.

42 As noted by a number of scholars, e.g., Kagan 1969: 205.

43 Thuc. 1.23.6; for discussion of this famous passage see Hornblower 1: 62–6. Kagan 1969: 345 rejects the idea of long-term causes, but wrongly; cf. also Eddy 1973: 308.

44 The key word here is *anagke*, or 'necessity'; Thucydides (1.23.6) uses its verb *anagkasai*, or 'forced' (so Hornblower 1: 66). The standard translations (Crawley, Lattimore, Warner) render this as 'inevitable', which is close but not quite the same thing: readers need to beware of several nuances that 'inevitable' does not quite convey. See again the sense of Thuc. 4.59 (n. 32 above).

45 Cf. Rhodes 1987: 154–60, who notes that Thucydides took 'pleasure in showing that he knows better than popular opinion'.

46 Kagan 1969: 365–6 discusses the idea of inevitability and the positions taken by scholars on this issue. F.E. Adcock (in *CAH* 5: 182) seems alone in rejecting Thucydidean inevitability.

47 See Thuc. 6.24 on Athenian enthusiasm for the Sicilian expedition – which ended in disaster.

48 Thuc. 1.122.3, 124.3 (Corinth on Athens). For argument that the Spartan drive to 'free' the Greeks was only propaganda see de Ste. Croix 1972: 154–8, a position challenged by Lewis 1977: 108–9; Raaflaub 2004: 197–202.

49 Thuc. 2.11.4 (Archidamus' speech), 1.78.1 (unnamed Athenians at Sparta), and other passages cited in Gomme 2: 13. The argument that war is unpredictable would seem to undercut the idea that war is inevitable – how can that which is changeable be predicted?

50 Havelock 1972: 19–52.

51 Mearsheimer 2001: 156–9.

52 On the Greek Enlightenment see Woodhead 1970: 3–6, Solmsen 1975: 116–22, and de Romilly 1992: 135–7.

53 Raaflaub 1994: 118; cf. the contrast with a very different Spartan state at 121.

54 Havelock 1972: 75.

55 On the destruction of Melos in 416 see Thuc. 5.84–116.

56 See Raaflaub 2001, and the many counter-examples from Tyrtaeus to Wilfred Owen.

57 Kagan 1969: 334, argues that Pericles proposed a 'defensive' war, but with Athenian incursions into the Peloponnese to hurt Sparta and her allies. Not only were such operations offensive in nature, they also served as counter-strokes to the Spartan-led invasions of Attica. Cf. Raaflaub 1994: 130–46 on power, citizens' and leaders' motives.

3

'OUR CITY IS AN EDUCATION TO GREECE'

The war so many expected, and some even wanted, finally came on a wintry night in early March, 431. Some 300 Thebans, led by Pythangelus and Diemporus, Boeotarchs or chief magistrates of the Boeotian Confederacy, entered Plataea and quickly seized control of the town and its sleepy residents.[1] Their task was an easy one. The Plataean Nauclides and some friends, believing war imminent, had decided to empower themselves. To that end Nauclides had made a deal with the Theban Eurymachus: bring Plataea into the Theban orbit and make himself ruler. The Thebans had long coveted Plataea and Nauclides' offer was too good to refuse.[2]

With war fever sweeping Greece, the leadership of the Boeotian Confederacy saw the advantage to be gained here, an outpost on the northern frontier of Attica. It might be a bit extreme to credit Nauclides for starting the Peloponnesian War. But it remains just as true that his Theban initiative did not involve Athens or Sparta but rather influential figures in two allied communities thinking to take advantage of a diplomatic crisis. It seems doubtful too that either Nauclides or Eurymachus remotely considered that what they agreed upon would launch a long and bitter war.

As the surprise wore off, the Plataeans realized they had been betrayed and that their Theban enemies were few. Most Plataeans were well disposed to the Athenian alliance and rejected Theban overtures to join 'Greater Boeotia'. They moved quickly to regain control of the situation. Tunneling through the walls of their houses, they concentrated their forces and took control of the city gates. Spears were shoved into the locks and then broken off, the butts effectively disabling the mechanisms. The unsuspecting Thebans were then attacked. A few managed to escape, but most were rounded up and placed under arrest.

The escapees met up with the main force now advancing on Plataea, arriving late on account of the night and poor weather. A Theban plan to take hostages from the country population and exchange them for their friends failed when the Plataeans threatened to kill their prisoners if the country people were harmed. The Thebans complied and withdrew. Relieved, the Plataeans evacuated the countryside. Then they killed the Theban prisoners – 180 in all – the first of many atrocities to come.[3] Report of these events had reached the Athenians who instructed the Plataeans not to do anything rash. But the message came too late, the Thebans were already dead. Soon after Plataea became a fortress as the women, children, the old, and even the slaves, were sent to Athens; eighty Athenians joined 400 Plataeans, determined not to give up their city without a fight.[4]

The final Spartan attempt to avert war now came. Archidamus, moderate and not eager for battle, sent Melesippus back to Athens in a last-ditch measure to avert war. He hoped that the Athenians might now talk as they could see that the Peloponnesian allies had not only mobilized but were preparing for action.[5] The Athenians would not budge. This was largely the work of Pericles, who had persuaded the Athenians to enact a decree that Peloponnesian mobilization would terminate negotiations. Refused entry to Athens and escorted to the borders of Attica, Melesippus went home. As he departed, he said to those present, 'This day will be the beginning of great misfortunes for Greece'.[6] Hardly the words of a war-mongerer, Melesippus' words were prophetic.

Summer came and with it the first of the nearly annual Spartan and Peloponnesian invasions of the Attic countryside – burning fields and crops, taking away whatever livestock and property.[7] As said of US Army operations in Vietnam – really any army throughout history – smoke pointed out the line of march, the path of destruction. This the Spartans could do because the Athenians had abandoned the land and retired behind their city walls. This produced a wave of anger and frustration in Athens, especially among those who lived in the rural *deme* of Acharnia, the area most affected by the Spartan raids (e.g., Ar. *Ach.* 86–7).

While the Spartans and Peloponnesians attacked into Attica, the Athenians did not sit back and simply take it. Responding with equal force, Pericles led a major land and sea operation into the Megarid (autumn 431), ravaging that land as the Spartans did the same to theirs (Thuc. 2.31). This seemingly was the Periclean strategy: to attack the Spartans by sea using the superior power of the Athenian fleet as well as its manpower reserves (see Thuc. 1.143.4).

In Athens, however, the refugee population soared, mostly Acharnians, but others too. Many Athenians wanted to march out and fight, just what the Spartans hoped for, but Pericles used his authority and position to put off meetings of the assembly.[8] As losses and anger grew, the Athenians blamed Pericles for the crisis, forgetting altogether how they had gotten into the war in the first place. More telling, the Athenians now attempted to renew negotiations and stop the war, but now it was Sparta's turn to refuse.[9] Over the next twenty-six years, Athenians and Spartans would take turns offering a settlement, usually when, as the god Hermes joked in Aristophanes' comedy *Peace*, one side thought it had the upper hand (Ar. *Pax* 211).

Pericles believed that he had found in his naval campaigns a key to a winning strategy – hit the Spartans and the Peloponnesians where and when they were vulnerable and hold fast behind the walls of Athens and exhaust their enemies. But was this strategy viable? Later in the war the Athenians would stage one spectacular success – that at Sphacteria where they captured nearly 300 Spartans – but there was also the greatest defeat, that of the great armada that sailed to Sicily in 415. John Mearsheimer has analyzed the nature of sea power and noted the 'stopping power' of water, how amphibious operations are not able to inflict enough damage on enemies to make them hurt. Naval strategist Sir Julian Corbett argues further that since most men live on land and not water, wars have always been decided by what your army can do against your enemy's territory.[10] A brilliant yet brief success at Sphacteria and a great failure in Sicily stand in sharp contrast to the eventual Spartan decision to hold Athenian terri- tory in Decelea (412), revealing the inherently fatal assumptions of the Periclean naval strategy.[11]

War and Plague at Athens

In the winter of 431/30, at the end of the first year of fighting, the Athenians gathered, as they had so many times in the past, to remember those who had died defending their lands against the Peloponnesian raids, as well as in distant campaigns. Assembling in the Kerameikos where they said their last goodbyes to fathers, son, and brothers, they waited again for Pericles' words of country, honor, and devotion as they had in the aftermath of the Samian War (Thuc. 2.34–46). As reported and phrased by Thucydides, his speech would assume iconic proportions, not only for later generations of Athenians, but for those in the distant future. As historian Garry Wills has shown, Lincoln's Gettysburg Address owes much to what Pericles now said and how he said it.[12]

It was the city – Athens – that Pericles first praised. Calling attention to their ancestors, Pericles noted the sacrifices and accomplishments of the past and how these led to the current democracy: how in Athens there were equal rights under the law, where poverty was no bar to public service and distinction (Thuc. 2.36–7). This democratic way created an open community – not one closed like the Spartan – and one that promoted education as well. In an additional rebuke to the Spartans, Pericles reminded the Athenians that in attacking them the Spartans required help from their allies while the Athenians had not yet even mustered theirs. In this Pericles tried to undercut the Spartan mystique that intimidated all the Greeks – of an army so courageous that no one could stand up to it in battle, of a society no less virtuous.[13] In fact Pericles argued that the Spartans were actually inferior to Athenians in courage, arguing that in reality their training was compensation for natural shortcomings. The Athenians did not need to train as they naturally possessed courage in ample doses. Pericles did not make any false claims, as the Athenians would demonstrate repeatedly during the war.[14]

Courageous and law-abiding as any, the Athenians have amassed wealth and wisdom. These, Pericles emphasizes, stimulate action in both private and public spheres, and perhaps in another critique of the Peloponnesians, the citizen who remains aloof from politics is not simply apolitical, he is in fact useless. All this together creates a society that confers good, acquiring friends by giving, not receiving benefits. In short, Pericles proclaimed that 'our city is an education to Greece' and has achieved so much that the songs of a Homer will not be needed to sing its praises – its own accomplishments will do just that (Thuc. 2.40–1).

Finally, Pericles turns to the courageous dead. These he claims were heroes, men who did not shrink from their duty, who lived up to the deeds of their forebears. The whole earth is their tomb. It is for this reason that Pericles offers comfort and not pity: parents of fallen sons might still have others who will in some way take their place as they add to the city's future security; brothers and sons of the fallen must realize that the dead will always outdo them in reputation; and wives now widows must remember their place and reputation (Thuc. 2.42–6).

Within a few months of Pericles' funeral speech, the war's second campaigning season began, and again Peloponnesian forces led by Archidamus invaded Attica (Thuc. 2.47.1). The Athenians retaliated as they had the previous summer, Pericles again leading another major operation into the area around Epidaurus and neighboring cities, reaching even into Spartan territory.[15]

As the fighting raged, Athens had become a giant fortress whose walls included the port of the Piraeus. Supplied by the sea, Athens was like an island and immune to Spartan attack. It was not immune to disease.[16] Beginning in summer 430 and lasting intermittently into 427, a plague struck hard at the masses of Athenians crowded behind the city walls. The plague took many. Perhaps a third of the population would die including thousands of men of military age. One Athenian who survived was Cimon's relative Thucydides. With great attention to detail, he took notes of the course of the disease, in part to occupy himself as it struck him too, but also out of scientific interest and curiosity. He left behind a description that remains a model of clinical precision, one that later generations would imitate and investigate.[17]

Thucydides suggests that the plague originated in Africa and first appeared in the Piraeus, seemingly arriving with one of the many ships that pulled into the harbor. Thucydides relates how the disease struck those suddenly who seemed to be in perfect health. Eyes became red, tongues swollen, to be followed by prolonged fits of violent coughing and retching. But this was only the beginning. A burning fever broke out, so fierce that people could not bear to be touched and only wanted to immerse themselves in water.[18] Sometimes this abated but soon worse followed: uncontrollable diarrhea that would lead to dehydration, weakness, and death. Survivors often suffered severe after effects: paralyzed extremities, blindness, and loss of memory (Thuc. 2.49.6–8).

Many have tried to identify this terrible illness, and explanations have ranged from influenza to toxic shock to typhus.[19] While certain identification seems unlikely, the plague surely resulted from the crowded conditions in the city and poor hygiene, but no one including Thucydides would have understood this. More certain and terrifying were the social consequences of the plague. Thucydides tells how established social mores simply broke down. People became terrified that by coming into contact with the sick they too would become ill, and so many died from neglect. Bodies piled up around the city – in the fountains where the dehydrated and thirst-crazed sick fell in their desire to drink and cool off; in the temples where they went hoping for divine intervention. In this horror, people became indifferent to religion and law: funeral rituals were no longer observed and the dead were disposed of however possible – mass graves and whatever funeral pyre was handy (Thuc. 2.52.4).

Modern-day construction and forensic archaeology has confirmed what Thucydides relates. Recent construction of the Athens metro has uncovered mass graves dating to the late fifth century, surely victims of the plague. In a common grave in the Kerameikos, 150 skeletons were found and it was clear that this was a hurried burial: bodies lying on top of one another, some in outstretched position, the number of grave offerings few for so many. The picture is both tragic and disturbing, particularly in view of the premium the Greeks put on observing proper burial rituals.[20]

Such a breakdown in something so fundamental as funeral rituals points to a deeper issue and Thucydides notes this too: a growing state of lawlessness. Death appeared so indiscriminate – rich and poor, good and bad – that many of the survivors adopted a new and different attitude: live today for tomorrow you may die. Neither the laws of society nor those of the gods imposed any sort of restraint – life itself seemed to have passed such a death sentence that nothing more than enjoying the moment seemed important.

Among the items found in the Kerameikos grave was one white *lekythos* (probably of the Reed Painter), the oil flask commonly left as an offering to the dead (Figure 3.1). Painting on the older black *lekythoi* had featured mythical scenes of maenads and satyrs, but the new white form in the mid fifth century depicted real people in real scenes – the heroic dead, ladies with their maids, visits to tombs. A work of the Group R Painters (c. 425–400) provides a good illustration of the new depiction of the dead. On this vessel a young man sits before a grave, another young man to his right, a young woman holding a helmet on the warrior's left. The colors are vivid, especially the dark brown hair of the young men, and the eyes are treated in rich detail, giving some idea of what the original colors would have been like. What we have here is the memorialization of a dead young soldier, but the scene conveyed seems to evoke the sorrow of war, not the glory. The dead soldier gazes ahead, seemingly lost in thought, as the young man to his right gazes on him with outstretched hand, at once directing the viewer to the dead but also in a gesture suggesting loss.[21]

That the plague struck the Athenian psyche hard is also evident in increased cult activity. Statues to Apollo and Heracles *Alexikakos* ('Averter of evil') were set up in the agora and new gods also appeared. In the Piraeus, cults to Asclepius (imported from Epidaurus) and Bendis (from Thrace)

Figure 3.1 A soldier at his tomb. Attic white *lekythos* of the Reed Painter, late fifth century.

arrived in the aftermath of the plague, perhaps signaling that this district of Athens was hit especially hard.[22]

War in a Time of Plague

Left reeling by the plague, the Athenians vented their anger on Pericles. Now in (late) summer 430 they voted his dismissal from the board of generals and fined him. But they soon repented and begged him to take up his burdens of leading them again. An unrepentant and undeterred Pericles chastised the Athenians. Boldly he told them that he never doubted his own resolve, or their lack of it, or that the course of action he had advised was anything other than correct. No one knew better than he what was best

Figure 3.2 A relief honoring the Thracian goddess Bendis. Wartime violence and plague popularized non-traditional cults, as people turned to the spiritual for comfort, as in Europe in World War I.[23]

for Athens, and no one loved Athens more or money less. Pericles admonished the Athenians to remain true to the actions and achievements of their forebears and not to give an inch to the enemy. Their spirits lifted, the Athenians voted Pericles general once more and entrusted the city and their hopes to him (Thuc. 2.60–4).

The Athenians did not let something like a plague stop them. Some early successes by Phormio, a gruff but brilliant tactician, may have inspired Pericles and others to hope that the naval strategy would pay off. Like Pericles, Phormio may also have been punished by those Athenians angry at the war's cost, fining him for mishandling the siege of Potidaea.[24] Hardly wealthy and unable to pay the fine, Phormio simply retired to his farm. But the war did not stop and the fickle Athenians changed their minds. Worse, the Spartans responded favorably to a plea for aid from the Ambraciots, Corinthian colonists, and organized a major expedition to the west. In the line of fire were the Acarnanians, Athenian allies, who now arrived in Athens (perhaps autumn 430) and pleaded to give them Phormio as their commander. Phormio, however, reminded them of the fine, which the Athenians themselves paid. Within months, Phormio was off with a small force of twenty ships to aid the Acarnanians and deal with the Peloponnesian threat.[25]

From the Athenian–Messenian naval base in Naupactus, Phormio inflicted several crushing defeats upon the Peloponnesian fleets: each a victory of superior Athenian seamanship over superior Peloponnesian numbers. On one occasion forty-seven Peloponnesian ships adopted a circle formation, leaving gaps in their ranks for a few fast ships to attack. Phormio simply sailed his ships around them, moving ever closer, waiting for favorable winds and currents to attack. Pressed by the wind and the Athenians, the Peloponnesians became rattled – then the Athenians attacked: quickly several Peloponnesian ships, including a commander's, were disabled, then the whole force collapsed in a panic. Twelve Peloponnesian ships were captured. The Peloponnesians soon increased their forces, hoping to defeat Phormio before he received reinforcements. An attempt to draw him away from Naupactus failed and in the end even more Peloponnesian ships were captured. The Athenians, however, may have drawn the wrong conclusions from Phormio's dual victories: they withdrew their Corinthian Gulf squadron, perhaps thinking the area secure.[26] A better decision would have been to maintain a powerful presence from Naupactus and from there raid into the Peloponnese. Their failure to do so suggests that the concept of a 'Periclean naval strategy' might be a bit exaggerated.

As for Phormio, he may have retired from active service after these spectacular successes. Over the next ten years, the comic poets Aristophanes (e.g., in *Babylonians*, *Knights*, *Peace*) and Eupolis (e.g., *Draft-Dodgers*, *Officers*) mention him in their plays and always in a positive light – a soldier's soldier, a soldier's general. In Eupolis' *Officers*, Phormio's success in training soldiers and sailors provides the comic setting for his training of Dionysus who flees Hera by entering navy service. The play's story was funny and famous enough to be replicated on pottery and illustrates the popularity of the story as well as Phormio's legendary reputation.[27] This is borne out by another Acarnanian request, probably in 428/7, that the Athenians send them Phormio again, and if not him then a relative. By now too old for service, the Athenians sent them his son Asopius, certain evidence not only of Phormio's abilities but his reputation and leadership too.[28]

In the northern Aegean, Athenian forces continued to press the siege around Potidaea, established some six months before the Theban surprise on Plataea and the formal outbreak of war.[29] Through the following winter and next year the Athenians persisted and tried in every way possible to take the city, bringing in rams and similar types of siege engines (Thuc. 2.58.1). Finally, by winter 430/29, the Potidaeans, starving and even resorting to cannibalism, surrendered to the Athenian generals Xenophon, Hestiodorus, and Phanomachus. The Athenians allowed the starving survivors to depart the city, the men with one garment, the women two, and some travel money (Thuc. 2.70). While the Athenians could find some satisfaction in taking the city, later settled with colonists, the costs of the operation were steep – at least 2000 talents spent and hundreds of men lost. In one forty-day period, some 1500 hoplites died from the same plague then ravaging the Athenians at home.[30]

The Athenians, however, had little time to savor final victory at Potidaea. Now in summer 429 and after delaying for two years, the Spartans and their allies advanced on Plataea and put it under siege. But this did not deter the Athenians from consolidating their victory over Potidaea. They advanced in a punitive campaign against the people of the Chalcidice who had been too helpful to the Potidaeans. Some 2200 Athenian troops commanded by the trio of Potidaea commanders, Xenophon, Hestiodorus, and Phanomachus, marched on Spartolus and began ravaging the land. What followed was a running engagement that in the end left all three generals and more than 400 other Athenians dead – twenty percent of the force engaged.[31] While the Athenians fought bravely, they could not defend against the hit and run tactics of cavalry and light infantry thrown at them. Such a combination of arms would become more common as the war progressed.

Not long after the fall of Potidaea and the disaster at Spartolus came an incident that revealed all too clearly the hardening of hearts brought by the war. In late summer a Peloponnesian embassy of six – the Corinthian Aristeus, three Spartans, and envoys from Tegea and Argos – set out to meet the Persian king Artaxerxes I to negotiate a wartime alliance. While at the court of the Thracian king Sitalces asking for travel aid, they were observed by the Athenian envoys Learchus and Ameiniades present on a similar task. The Athenians persuaded Sitalces to arrest the envoys and surrender them, which he did. The Peloponnesians were taken to Athens where they were promptly put to death without benefit of trial. Thucydides claims this was in retaliation for the Spartan summary killings of sailors taken at sea and this may have been true, at least in part. But the Corinthian Aristeus had distinguished himself in the fighting at Potidaea, and his summary killing now makes clear this was a case of payback. What Thucydides also leaves unsaid is that envoys were customarily regarded as inviolable and this the Athenians simply ignored in their rage and desire for vengeance (Thuc. 2.67).

Socrates – Soldier of Athens

Among the soldiers in the Athenian ranks at Potidaea was Socrates whose feats of endurance and self-discipline not only amazed his comrades, but thanks to the efforts of his protégé Plato, students ever since. The Platonic Socrates was physically tough: barefoot and clothed in summer cloaks in winter, surviving on meager rations. This Socrates was also physically brave: in one clash he stood over a wounded Alcibiades, the impetuous ward of Pericles, and saved his life. On this occasion Alcibiades won a prize for valor, one that by all rights should have gone to Socrates, but the generals made the award to Alcibiades, his elite status and social connections taking precedence.[32]

The Kat and Paul like relationship that Socrates and Alcibiades enjoyed, whatever the problems with the details, must be true to some degree, though these will likely remain a subject of debate. Socrates' military service, however, provides a glimpse into the socioeconomic status of those Athenians who served as hoplites or heavy-armed infantry. These are the men Euripides and Aristophanes called 'manly men', those from the countryside who owned small homesteads and worked the land themselves (Eur. *Or.* 918–22; Ar. *Eq.* 1373). Both writers contrast these rock solid 'soldier-farmers' with the urban loafers hanging out in the agora, dodging service however they could, sometimes with the intervention of influential friends (Ar. *Eq.* 1369–71, *Pax* 1181–8).

But the contrast should not be taken too rigidly. Socrates was of the city and was as brave and hardy a soldier as any from the country. As a soldier from the city, his service profiles the urban ranks: like his father Sophroniscus, Socrates worked (at least at some point) as a stone mason, a vocation that included sculptors too.[33] Like Phidias, and artists and craftsmen of the Renaissance, Sophroniscus and Socrates belonged to circles including social and intellectual elites, and fought alongside them.

At Potidaea Socrates would have been about thirty-seven years old (forty-five when he fought at Delium in 424), a bit old for one to fight as a foot soldier. His age, certainly so at Delium, may point to how hard pressed the Athenians were to meet their obligations after the plague, taking older men to do young men's work.[34] And fighting is young men's work. Hoplite equipment – shield (bronze over wood, 13.5 pounds), spear (ash or oak, 3 pounds), sword (*kopis* or 'chopper', 2 or 3 pounds) – are heavy items to carry around, not to mention wield in battle.[35] Perhaps his deme Alopeke (from the tribe Antiochis) was short-handed and to meet its call-up obligations had to recruit older men for service; it is also possible that for various reasons (adventure, escape the wife and kids), Socrates may have volunteered for duty.[36] In battle Athenian infantry fought alongside fathers and brothers and fellow tribesmen: at Syracuse in 415 one tribe, with cavalry support, routed Syracusan cavalry in heavy fighting (Thuc. 6.98.4).

To serve as a soldier, Socrates would have spent at least 75–100 drachmas, the equivalent of three months' pay for a skilled worker, on his equipment, and that would have gotten him only the basic gear. Elites would spend much more: Alcibiades carried a shield emblazoned in gold and depicting a lightning bolt armed Eros (Plut. *Alc.* 16.2). Defensive protection (corselet, greaves, for example) would have cost more, but also were cumbersome and impeded movement and speed, and many soldiers, perhaps Socrates too, would not have bothered with these.[37]

Figure 3.3 A warrior's farewell. This *lekythos* of the Achilles Painter depicts one of war's sorrows – the soldier going off to war. In addition to the soldier's helmet, shield (and device), and clothing, note that his wife affectionately rests her foot on his.

On departing for a campaign, Socrates would have taken along some rations but these would not have lasted long. Provisions would have to be acquired locally and these Socrates would have bought with his own money and that which he received from the state. Athenian soldiers were paid (*misthos*, pay; *siteresion*, *sitos*, provisions), and the phrase *tetrabolou bios* – the 'four obol-life' – was bandied about in a later comedy of Theopompus.[38] At Potidaea, Socrates would have received a daily pay of two drachma, one for himself and one for an attendant, almost certainly a slave, who would have helped carry his gear and in other ways around the camp. Such pay may have been extraordinary, intended to recompense soldiers far from home and for an extended period. The rate may also reflect a full Athenian treasury, as pay later in the war, as in Sicily, appears to have been less.[39] But pay for service offered little compensation for the hardships and horrors seen in military service. Plato's picture of those hardships faced by the Athenian soldiers at Potidaea, allowing even for a little exaggeration, suggests that it was a hard life for those ordered to implement policy facing the sharp end of the spear.

Death of Pericles and a Poetic Message

As the war wore on, so did the plague in Athens. Like many families, that of Pericles also suffered dearly. Friends and relatives including a sister died, followed by his older son Xanthippus; father and son had quarreled bitterly over finances and domestic issues and now Xanthippus died before any reconciliation. Not long after Paralus, Pericles' younger son, also died and for the first time Pericles broke down and wept – something no one had seen him do before. Not long after, as Pericles himself lay sickened with the disease, he pleaded with the Athenians to legitimize his son Pericles, the child of his mistress Aspasia, but this meant overriding his own law. More than twenty years before, Pericles had proposed a law restricting Athenian citizenship to the children of two Athenian parents. Now Pericles asked for an exemption which was granted. So it was that Pericles died in autumn 429 leaving behind one son only, the child of a courtesan.[40]

In the midst of this traumatic event, perhaps about 427, one Athenian made an attempt to ease at least the mental sufferings of his fellow Athenians.[41] The dramatist Sophocles staged a play that remains an intellectual icon today, thanks largely to Sigmund Freud and his foundational work in psychology. *Oedipus Tyrannus*, better known to most students and readers as 'Oedipus the King', begins with as sharp an attention-getting device as ever crafted, a plague-ravaged city. Dramatically set in Thebes, Sophocles' words surely struck the Athenian audience like a slap across the face: 'a deadly pestilence, is on our town, strikes us and spares not', [the land] 'is emptied of its people'... 'black death grows rich in groaning and lamentation'.[42]

Oedipus and the people of Thebes grapple with their plague and try too to understand their suffering. While Sophocles explores many issues, the one that surely deserves mention is that which the Athenians themselves must have desperately wanted an answer to – why? In the end Sophocles offers an answer which in its simplicity remains true today – because we are humans, and suffering is the nature of the human condition.

The plague hit the Athenian population hard. By the winter of 427/6 some 4400 men eligible for service as foot soldiers, plus another 300 wealthier Athenians who served in the cavalry, had died. These figures Thucydides may have deduced from a military roster, the *katalogos*, which listed the names of men able to serve on expeditions. As the plague wore on, commanders and tribal secretaries simply struck the names of the dead. In this manner an accurate roster of available resources could be kept. Thucydides also notes that the number of citizens taken by the plague was unknown. This contrasts with the specific number of dead citizen-soldiers, which argues for the existence of military record-keeping in democratic Athens.[43]

Plataea Besieged

In summer, 429 a Spartan and allied army led by Archidamus advanced not on Attica, but Plataea. Since fending off their Theban enemies, the Plataeans knew their enemies would be back. After all, they had summarily executed their Theban prisoners and this was an act that demanded payment.

Upon arrival the combatants agreed to a parley at which the Plataeans reminded the Spartans that their own Pausanias, commander of the Greek armies that had defeated the Persians a generation before, had given over to them their land: in part for their sacrifice, but also to look after the graves of the heroes who had died for Greece. This Archidamus acknowledged. He then attempted to persuade the Plataeans to remain neutral in the present conflict. He even came up with a novel option that would allow the Plataeans to sit out the war: hand over their land to the Spartans who would manage it and then return it at the war's end. But the Plataeans were anxious and with good reason: not only were their families now in Athens, but there were also the Thebans and their thirst for vengeance. Archidamus allowed time for the Plataeans to consult with their Athenian allies, but the response of the Athenians was not encouraging: they had not acted contrary to their alliance and now expected no less from the Plataeans (Thuc. 2.71, 74–5).

So began a two-year siege of Plataea. In the course of the struggle both sides resorted to amazing ruses and devices: the Spartans built a stockade around the city and then a ramp, and the Plataeans answered with first a counter wall, then opened a breach in their own wall to take away the dirt being piled up for the ramp! Back and forth for seventy days the measures and countermeasures went. Finally, seeing that their efforts were gaining little, the Spartans departed, leaving behind a small force to keep the Plataeans busy and in place.[44] Months later, in winter 428/7, the defenders were running low on food and conceived a daring escape plan. In a brilliant night-time operation, 212 out of 220 men succeeded in breaking out, fooling the besieging Peloponnesians by first making for Thebes, then changing direction and reaching safety in Athens (Thuc. 3.20–24).

By the following summer (427) there was no more food in Plataea. The Spartans attacked and the weakened garrison could only make a token defense. The Spartans accepted the garrison's offer of surrender, primarily so that the claim could be made later that Plataea had not been taken by storm, but had instead freely given itself up. The remaining garrison, some 200 Plataeans and twenty-five Athenians, placed themselves in the hands of their enemies.

By now four years of war had passed and the Spartans and their Theban allies were in no mood to play the role of the noble victor. The captured garrison paid a fearful price. Forced to come before the Spartans one by one, they were asked what good they had ever done for Sparta. Lacon, the son of Aeimnestus, named after the glories of the Spartans in a long ago battle, attempted a response.[45] He argued that Plataea had always done rightly by Sparta and that they were entitled to the protection of suppliants. But no answer, however well argued, could have swayed the vengeful Thebans, or explained away the wrong done the Theban prisoners four years earlier. Not only the siege but four years of war had now embittered everyone – the hardy survivors were taken out and killed while the women, including certainly some wives and mothers who had remained behind to cook, were sold into slavery. Plataea, as loyal an ally as Athens could ever hope to find, was razed and its lands were eventually placed into the hands of individual Thebans. Historian Donald Kagan remarks, 'the Athenians had not lifted a finger', but one wonders what else they could have done.[46] In fact Athenian ambitions were outstripping not only Athenian resources, but those of an empire.

The Spartans demonstrated little sympathy for their Plataean and Athenian prisoners, sacrificing them to their revenge-minded Theban allies who demanded blood (Thuc. 3.68.4–5). The Thebans had lost some 200 of their friends and kinsmen, most of them killed out of hand. That demanded payback – not getting even but getting back. Not so much an excuse as an explanation – the simple reality is that when fighting men see the bodies of their friends, anger and pain frequently take over and will lead to excess. Homer tells this of Achilles and Patroclus and the same forces now impelled the Thebans in pushing the Spartans to give up the Plataeans.[47]

But Theban anger created Athenian outrage. What would have happened to the bodies of the slain Athenians and Plataeans? Thucydides says nothing of this, but given Greek values and attitudes toward burial, we might expect that a Theban or Spartan herald appeared in Attic territory (the Plataean refugees were here too) and announced where the bodies might be found. Recovery of these, especially after lying exposed for several days would not have been pleasant work. In moving bloated and disfigured corpses the Athenians and the Plataeans now would have shared in the anger.

None of this was apparently lost on Euripides who about this time wrote *Andromache*. While seemingly a post-Trojan War drama, the hostility shown to the Spartans suggests that the killings at Plataea provide the drama's background.[48] Throughout the play the Spartans appear evil and wayward: their men like Menelaus lie and are inclined to acts of cruelty (*Andr.* 445–54), their women like Helen and Hermione are whores, running around half-naked and wrestling with boys (*Andr.* 594–606). Of war's horrors Euripides has more to say: easy talk of the killing of a child, here Andromache's son Astyanax (*Andr.* 68–9, 316–19, 339–40); Menelaus stating the madness of letting your enemy escape death (*Andr.* 519–22); the ambush of Achilles' son Neoptolemus whose body is then mutilated (*Andr.* 1118–20, 1149–55). The trauma of a real war woven into a mythical one provides the context to these scenes and statements. These give us today some idea of what people were thinking as they learned of shocking incidents as the killing of helpless prisoners of war.

The *Andromache* of Euripides and its wartime violence contrast with his earlier more introspective dramas of *Medea* (c. 431) and *Hippolytus* (428). Now in his mid-fifties, Euripides would have been no stranger to war, though we have no idea of what his real-life experiences might have been. As a dramatist and observer of the human condition, he might have been content to explore issues found in *Medea* and *Hippolytus* as these were in some ways 'safe' topics detached from the reality of war. But the outbreak of extreme violence in 431 may have energized Euripides. As in the case of other veterans turned authors, Euripides may have turned his thoughts now to analyzing and processing the horrors that he had seen as a young man and what he was now seeing as an older one. Speculation? Perhaps, but later in his *Helen* (lines 1151–4) Euripides will write 'Madmen are you who seek glory in combat, among the spearshafts of war, thinking in ignorance to find a cure for human misery there'. This, I think, is the sentiment of one who has stood in the line of battle and having survived, realizes what folly it is.

Financing War

Written off as expendable, little Plataea had served Athens well as a pawn, distracting the Spartans and their allies at a critical time. While the plague had certainly deprived the Athenians of the steadying hand of Pericles, other threats presented dangers no less worrisome. Wartime expenditures were running up fast: not only had the siege of Potidaea cost the Athenians hundreds of lives, it had also consumed 2000 talents, a vast sum of money.[49] While tribute from the allies could be increased, there were limits to what they would and could bear without creating even more problems. In these circumstances with money running short, the Athenians voted a war tax on themselves, the *eisphora*, and sent out ships to collect more money from the allies.[50]

At home, however, there were other allies willing to contribute to the Athenian war effort. Among these was Pulytion, a member of the resident alien population in Athens, the metics. Businessmen and entrepreneurs, the metics supported the Athenian state in many ways with their taxes and active military service.[51] But they had no voice in affairs, and perhaps to this end Pulytion wanted to ingratiate himself with Alcibiades, the flamboyant and erratic ward of Pericles.[52] Wartime service at Potidaea had made Alcibiades a hero and this only added to his reputation. Now on Pericles' death, he must have imagined himself Pericles' successor. This status attracted the attention of many would-be friends and admirers and Alcibiades was not one to shun attention or ignore a possible benefit.

Pulytion was no less ambitious and driven to win favor with Alcibiades and join his circle. After selling all his property and possessions, he came to Alcibiades' house, announced himself and told Alcibiades what he had done. Alcibiades' reaction may have surprised his would-be friend – he laughed in his face, but invited him to dinner anyway. Afterwards Alcibiades returned his money but told him that the next day he should go into the agora and make the highest bid on the public contracts being offered for sale. Pulytion protested that he lacked the supporting capital for such a venture, but Alcibiades threatened to beat him if he did not agree, and Alcibiades' reputation was sufficiently intimidating.

In the morning Pulytion did exactly as instructed. On hearing his bid, the other bidders angrily surrounded him, demanding to know the identity of his guarantor, suspecting that he had none and was simply trying to drive up costs. Suddenly, from the corner of the market came Alcibiades' voice: 'Put my name down – he's my friend and I guarantee him'. Quickly the other bidders realized that they were threatened with financial ruin: usual practice was to pay the amount due from the profits of the preceding year. With the Pulytion's bid they would not be able to do this and stood to lose considerable sums of money. The only way out for the contractors was to persuade him to withdraw his bid and they offered him money to do so. Alcibiades remained on the spot and would not allow his 'friend' to accept any offers: finally, on receiving an offer of a talent, Alcibiades allowed him to accept and so withdraw his bid.

Cited most often as evidence for Alcibiades' character, the story reveals as well the inner workings of wartime Athenian society, particularly its finances. In a defense speech after the war (c. 400), Andocides provides a similar story of bidding on contracts to collect taxes for the state and to create a livelihood in the process. This was done by syndicates or groups of Athenians who basically pooled their resources, did the work (with the assistance of slaves that is), and then paid what they owed to the state, keeping the rest as profit.[53]

Like other societies in other times, citizens engaged in financial wheeling and dealing to make a living. What both Andocides and Plutarch describe is the financial activity called tax-farming, an economic practice found not only in Greece but Rome too. It provided the funds necessary to cover the ordinary expenses of running the state such as salaries for jurors, wages for the Scythian archers, the police force of ancient Athens. Such revenue also provided the money essential for fighting a war. Soldiers and sailors received daily wages up to a drachma as living expenses; when campaigning, armies, as at Potidaea, built siege engines and technicians for these had to be paid; the building and maintaining of warships and city walls demanded skilled workers and money for these had to be found; public support for war orphans and invalids (established in the sixth century perhaps) grew steadily.[54]

While allied tribute certainly helped defray these and other expenses of war, still more money was needed. For this reason the Athenians assessed themselves the *eisphora*, which fell upon Athenian elites already subject to the many liturgies with greater impact than the working population in the Piraeus. Such burdens may have antagonized more than a few who saw that the democracy expected and demanded more from them than their more humble fellow citizens. Their discontent might have been anticipated, especially as the war dragged on without resolution.

Notes

1 Sealey 1976: 270, 325, 404–5 discusses the background to the Boeotian Confederacy.
2 Thuc. 2.2.1–2, with Hornblower 1: 239–40. On the outbreak of fighting see Kagan 1974, Lazenby 2004, Hanson 2005. On Theban desire to control Plataea see p. 21, n. 35.
3 Thuc. 2.2–6, all of this happening the same night and into day; among the Theban slain was Eurymachus (2.5.7). See de Ste. Croix 1972: 20 for a list of Peloponnesian War massacres.
4 Thuc. 2.68.2 (size of the Athenian/Plataean garrison), 2.78.3 (their losses: twenty-five Athenians killed, 200 Plataeans).
5 Thuc. 2.12.1. Lewis 1977: 48 questions Archidamus' authority in Sparta, but Thucydides says that it was Archidamus who sent Melesippus on this mission, which clarifies both his views on the imminent war and his ability to influence politics. Sealey 1976: 321, argues that the Spartans miscalculated here, thinking that invasions would force the Athenians to yield as in 446. Yet that occasion ruined Pleistoanax and gave Euboea to the Athenians – not much of a victory it would seem.
6 Thuc. 2.12.1–3, and Hornblower 1: 250, who considers the statement genuine.

7 Month-long invasions into Attica occurred in 431, 430, 428, 427; that of 425 lasted about fifteen days only as crops were not yet ripe. Plague cancelled the invasion of 429, as did an earthquake in 426. The Athenians threatened to kill Spartan POWs (mostly the men captured at Sphacteria, see further below) held in Athens and this spared Attica of invasion after 424. In 429 the Peloponnesians campaigned against Plataea. See further Ober 1996: 75, n.5; Rawlings 2007: 73, 82.

8 Thuc. 2.22.1, with Hornblower 1: 275–6.

9 Thuc. 2.59.2 (Athenian negotiations rebuffed), 65.3, with Diod. 12.45.4, Plut. *Per.* 35.4, with Hornblower 1: 341.

10 Mearsheimer 2001: 86. Critics might point to the amphibious operation conducted in the Pacific by the United States in World War II. But many islands were bypassed, while others, e.g., Peleliu and Tarawa, were needlessly attacked at great loss; Okinawa might well have been sufficient after Guadalcanal.

11 A Messenian garrison holding the fort built at Pylos abandoned it under truce to the Spartans in 409 (Diod. 13.64.5–7); on the Spartans and Decelea see pp. 165–7. Cf. Ober 1996: 72–85, Cawkwell 1997: 44, and Lazenby 2004: 32, 37, all more enthusiastic of the Periclean strategy.

12 Wills 1992: 41.

13 Noted too, grudgingly, by Eur. *Andr.* 724–6, and at about the same time.

14 Thuc. 2.39, with Miller 2000: 73. Notable examples of Athenian courage occurred at Delium and Amphipolis, see pp. 99–104, 112–13.

15 Thuc. 2.47.1 (Archidamus' campaign), 2.56 (Pericles').

16 Lazenby 2004: 38 claims Pericles should have known better than to crowd the city with refugees. Even in World War II, American GIs washed out their mess kits in communal tubs of water and ended up suffering diarrhea.

17 In the sixth century AD another plague would strike the late Roman empire of Justinian. Procopius of Caesarea would report that event and model his account after Thucydides. See Rosen 2007: 217–18.

18 In building the new Athens metro, workers uncovered fifth-century clay water pipes running from the Theater of Dionysus to the Phaleron Gate and from the aqueduct that brought water into the city from the Hymettus hills. Elsewhere archaeologists have uncovered a maze of waterpipes under the agora dating to the sixth century. All this confirms Thucydides' reference to the availability of water to the urban population of Athens. See Parlama and Stompolidis 2001: 58–9, 154–5, Ratto 2006: 307.

19 Cf. Kolata 1999: 35–7 and Whitley *et al.* 2007: 7, the latter arguing for typhus on the basis of forensic study of DNA recovered from skeletons excavated in 1994/95. Littman 2006: 12 notes the unreliability of ancient DNA.

20 See Parlama and Stompolidis 2001: 271–3, 352 including photographs (c. 1994) from this grave and another found near Pireos Street, the latter bare of offerings; see also Mitchell-Boyask 2008: xii–xiii.

21 See Oakley 2004 for full study.
22 Camp 2001: 124. Xen. *Hell.* 2.4.8 mentions the shrine of Bendis in the Piraeus, placing it near the scene of fighting between the Thirty Tyrants and the 'Men of Phyle' in 403. On Asclepius see pp. 115–16.
23 See further Winter 1995: 54–77.
24 The Athenian siege of Potidaea began in late spring 432 and before the Theban attack on Plataea. See Thuc. 1.56–68, with Gomme 1: 222–4, Hornblower 1: 99–107.
25 Thuc. 2.69.1. See Hale 2009: 160–70 for detailed discussion.
26 Thuc. 2.79–92, with Lazenby 2004: 41–7.
27 See Storey 2003: 246–60 for study of the fragments of Eupolis and description and photos of the pottery, and Hale (above, n. 25).
28 Thuc. 3.7.1, with Hornblower 1: 387–8.
29 Thuc. 1.60–6, 2.2.1, 31, 58, 70. Operations lasted into winter 430/29 when the people of Potidaea finally surrendered. See also Kagan 1974: 78–80, 97–100 and Lazenby 2004: 40–4, 99–100. Among the Peloponnesian commanders, Aristeus of Corinth distinguished himself, surely contributing to his later death at Athenian hands. See Westlake 1969: 74–83 and below.
30 Thuc. 2.30, 58, with Lazenby 2004: 40–1.
31 Thuc. 2.79, with 2.70 (for the generals commanding), Diod. 12.47.3. Such losses in killed alone are high. Usually the wounded outnumber the dead by a factor of two or three to one which means that this Athenian force got more than just a bloody nose.
32 Pl. *Apol.* 28e, *Symp.* 219e–220e, with Ellis 1989: 24–7, who notes various problems with these stories, chronological and other.
33 Pl. *Euthphr.* 11b, *Alc.* I 121a, with Guthrie 1971: 58–9.
34 For military manpower see Akrigg 2007: 30–1 and van Wees 2004: 241–3. There may have been occasions when 'reservists' joined the frontline troops, especially if tribes were understrength. This might explain Socrates' service in his late thirties and forties.
35 Sekunda 2000: 12–13, 16–17, 21, with photographs and drawings of these.
36 Demes were the local units into which Athenian citizens were organized (see further Sinclair 1988: 51–2). On tribal call-up and service see Christ 2001: 398–9.
37 Sekunda 2000: 10–12; Rawlings 2007: 46–7, 158.
38 In Kassel-Austin 1984: 7, 734 (fragment 56), with Pritchett 1: 18–19. Thuc. 7.82.3 tells that when Demosthenes' men surrendered in Sicily, they were forced to surrender their money. Some 6000 men filled four shields with coin. Kallet 2001: 174–6 estimates this yielded ten to twelve talents.
39 Thuc. 3.17.4, with Hornblower 1: 402; Thuc. 6.31.3, with Gomme-Andrewes-Dover 4: 293–4, Thuc. 8.45.2, with Gomme-Andrewes-Dover 5: 97–8; Ar. *Ran.* 718–37, with Dover 1993: 281–2 refers to debased coinage. See also Pritchett

1: 3–29 (pay), 30–52 (provisions), 49–51 (attendants). Thuc. 7.27.2 notes that 1300 Thracian mercenaries were recruited on the basis of a daily wage of one drachma, which complicates the picture of reduced pay owing to treasury shortfall. But these were elite 'specialty' troops and may have commanded higher pay than ordinary Athenian hoplites.

40 Plut. *Per.* 36–8, with Stadter 1989: 325–41.

41 Mitchell-Boyask 2008: 56–7, argues for 426/5, or 'slightly earlier.' Cf. Vickers 2008: 37, who suggests a date of 425, tying the drama to a burning summer in 426 and an Athenian-financed purification of Delos in winter 426/5. But he pays too little attention to the trauma of the plague and the play's opening scene of desolation and even panic. C. 428/7 remains the most likely setting for the drama.

42 Soph. *Oed. Tyr.* 25–30 (D. Grene trans.)

43 Thuc. 3.87, with Hornblower 1: 494–5 and Gomme 2: 388–9. The subject of the military *katalogos* has been debated by scholars; cf. Burckhardt 1996: 21, n.31 (for) and Christ 2001: 400–1 (against). Argument focuses on the difficulty of record keeping, but these were kept for building expenditures on the acropolis, which argues the same for other records.

44 Thuc. 2.75–8; see Lazenby 2004: 42–3 for some details.

45 See p. 2 for the origin of Lacon's name.

46 Thuc. 3.52–68, with Gomme 3: 357 (status of the women); see also Low 2007: 230 and Kagan 1974: 174. Afterwards the Plataeans, as well as Megarian exiles, served with the Athenians as light-armed troops. See Rawlings 2007: 51.

47 A beginning place for discussion is Shay 1994. A sampling of war literature over the ages will reveal the truth of this idea of payback, as well as its corrosive force on the human psyche. See also below on the debate in Syracuse on the fate of the Athenian captives, pp. 156–7.

48 The date and occasion of the play are uncertain, but most agree that it was staged c. 430–426; see Nims 1958 for discussion.

49 Thuc. 2.70.2. How much would this represent? Such calculations are famously difficult to estimate. But this sum was one-third of the cash reserve held on the acropolis at the outset of the war; a daily wage for a skilled worker at this time was one drachma. Two thousand talents would yield 12,000 drachmas (one talent = 6000 drachmas), or the daily wages of 12,000 skilled workers. See *APF* xx–xxiv for additional facts and figures.

50 See Thuc. 3.19.1. Details regarding *eisphora* during the war are poorly known and it seems possible that earlier levies were made, e.g., 434/3 (see ML 58).

51 See generally D. Whitehead, 'metics', *OCD*[3] 969.

52 Plut. *Alc.* 5; the date of this unknown, but likely to be c. 431–415, i.e., during the war and when Alcibiades is in Athens. See also Plut. *Phoc.* 9.5 for another Plutarchan example of Athenian finances. Ellis 1989: 19 suggests that the

unidentified metic in Plutarch's story was the same Pulytion later caught up with Alcibiades in the scandal involving the Mysteries.

53 Andoc. *Mys.* 134, with MacDowell 1962: 158–9; see also [Arist.] *Ath. Pol.* 47.2 on the *poletai*, the sellers of contracts, with Rhodes 1981: 552–3.

54 Military expenses might have been covered by a military fund like that mentioned at [Arist.] *Ath. Pol.* 47.2; Plut. *Sol.* 31.3–4, [Arist.] *Ath.Pol.* 49.4, with Rhodes 1981: 570–1 (war orphans and invalids). On the finances of the Athenian state, including liturgies, see Cohen 1992.

4

'WAR IS A VIOLENT TEACHER'

At Mytilene, the wealthy elite chafed under Athenian dominion. Though they had prospered from their alliance and association with the Athenians, they had also observed at firsthand, as Athenian helpers, the fates of other Greeks who had dared challenge Athenian power. During the debates leading up to the war these same Mytilenean elites had secretly contacted the Spartans, attempting to win their support in a plan to break away from the Athenian orbit. In a telling response, the Spartans declined.[1]

So in spring 428 most of the Lesbian communities seized the moment and broke with Athens and hoped that the Spartans would aid them. Though disheartened by the news of the Lesbian rising, the war and plague weary Athenians assembled a fleet and prepared a surprise attack on Mytilene, diverting a force preparing for operation in the Peloponnese.[2] Tipped off by scouts or spies that the Athenians were coming, the Mytileneans were ready and beat off the Athenians when they arrived. At this point an armistice was arranged so that the Mytileneans could negotiate with Athens, but envoys also traveled to Sparta to seek help there. While the Athenians would not negotiate a settlement, the Spartans were now more than willing to grant an alliance to the Mytileneans.[3]

Armistice over, the Athenians sent out additional forces commanded by the general Paches and by fall Mytilene was besieged. Preoccupied elsewhere and now burdened by allies already tired of campaigning, the Spartans were unable to provide much support – in fact only a single officer, Salaithus. But he must have excelled in the *agoge's* stealth lessons as he successfully infiltrated Mytilene where he attempted to raise morale and encouraged the Mytileneans to fight on. He made one fatal mistake however. Knowing that a Spartan relief fleet would not be coming, Salaithus persuaded the elites to arm the people for an attack on the Athenians. Now possessing real arms and not the light weapons they had held earlier, the commons demanded an equal sharing of the food, threatening that if this were not done they would surrender the city to the Athenians. Frightened that they would be left out of any negotiations should this happen, the elite Mytileneans surrendered the city (summer 427).[4]

After nearly a year-long struggle, the Athenians had finally suppressed the rebellious Mytileneans and their neighbors, Pyrrha and Eresus, which had joined them. Paches sent the Spartan Salaithus to Athens along with a number of Mytileneans whom he thought responsible for the rebellion. Embittered and vengeful, the Athenians were little inclined to show mercy. Though he offered to broker a settlement on Plataea, still under siege at this point, Salaithus was quickly put to death. A debate in the assembly followed, at which the Athenians voted not only to kill the Mytilenian prisoners now in custody, but all the adult citizens of Mytilene, their one-time dutiful ally – while the women and children were to be enslaved (Thuc. 3.35–36.3). In short Mytilene would suffer the fate of Troy.

Few sections of Thucydides' *History* exceed the 'Debate over Mytilene' in power and drama. Thucydides also introduces a new Athenian leader, Cleon, whom he clearly dislikes, describing him as the most violent man of the day.[5] In the debate Thucydides gives the purported speeches of Cleon and his rival Diodotus, in which the issue of democracy's ability – or inability – to rule an empire is discussed. Mixed in with their rhetoric are representative sophistic ideas, most notably self-interest and expediency.[6] While evidence is absent, there should be little question that other Athenians participated in this debate. Cleon and Diodotus represent vehicles used by Thucydides to explore ideas regarding the nature of power politics. These include the notion of institutional power, that sometimes the exercise of power clashes with justice, and the view that power is not static but dynamic.[7]

In the Thucydidean setting, Cleon and Diodotus argued the fate of the Mytileneans before the assembly of their fellow Athenians. While they spoke to persuade the Athenians to adopt a course of action each saw proper, it was for a decision of the assembly that they competed. This is, as A.G. Woodhead notes, an example of institutional power that is no less important to understand than the roles of prominent individuals such as Cleon, Pericles, and later Alcibiades.[8] Just as in the case of world events in the modern era, popular institutions influence events no less than individuals. In this setting Thucydides analyzes the nature of the Athenian democracy.

Cleon began his speech not condemning the Mytileneans as much as the Athenians, particularly those who favored reopening discussion when it had been resolved the day before. Just as quickly he attacked the nature of democracy, arguing that it was incapable of ruling others, that the empire the Athenians held was a tyranny (Thuc. 3.37.1–2). This attack Diodotus countered, arguing that the greatest obstacles to good counsel were haste and anger, as well as speakers who tried to intimidate their opposition (Thuc. 3.42.1, 2). Cleon's speech, however, expands the attack on democracy by comparing its deliberative functions to a theater performance where fine words and fancy speeches are the only things admired. Not only do Athenians regard the assembly as the best show in town, issues that actually that affect their lives and futures are ignored, not to mention sound advice (Thuc. 3.38.2–4).

In these speeches Thucydides reveals a dimension to the nature of power and power politics that is entirely new: the role of society in determining matters of policy that affect not only themselves but others. As Cleon and Diodotus debate, it is as much for the minds of the Athenians as it is for the lives of the Mytileneans; it is as much for determining the course of the Athenian empire as it is over the life or death of Mytilene. In this context it is interesting to observe that in the end the Athenians rejected the brutal measure recommended by Cleon and supported the only slightly milder recommendation of Diodotus. While not much in itself, this decision suggests that, at least on this occasion, a majority of Athenians realized that vindictive acts of oppression were not just shortsighted but counter-productive.

While Cleon's concern is with the exercise of power, he is yet aware that justice and a sense of right conduct are also at issue. The Mytileneans, he tells the Athenians, should be punished as their crime deserves, that all are equally guilty, both those who instigated the revolt and those who changed their minds later and opened the city to Athenian forces.[9] At the end of his speech Cleon returned to this point: punish them as they deserve and show the allies that death will be the penalty for anyone who revolts (Thuc. 3.40.7).

This harsh definition of justice Diodotus answers in perhaps the earliest attack on the death penalty: men will always be driven by poverty, abundance, and hope in taking risks or in breaking the law.[10] Because of this Diodotus argues that the Athenians must look at what is best or useful for themselves and act accordingly. In this Diodotus rebuts Cleon's claim that punishing the Mytileneans is both just and expedient, arguing that such a policy is impossible. The Athenians were neither the first nor the last to discover the problems and dangers of ruling others. Other empires and occupiers have been confronted with revolts and acts of defiance and have made decisions that differ little from those of the Athenians in 427.

In his closing remarks, Cleon tells the Athenians, paradoxically, that it was both just and expedient to punish the Mytileneans, and, if they did not, they were condemning themselves.[11] Why? Because if the Mytileneans were right to revolt, the Athenians were wrong to rule. Cleon went on to say that if the Athenians voted not to punish their former allies, they should give up their empire so that they could live in peace.

Thucydides anticipated the nuances of imperial power and justice in several places before exploring them in detail in the debate over Mytilene. In a speech in Sparta before the war, an anonymous Athenian speaker boldly stated that the Athenians had acquired their empire not by force but because the Spartans had handed it to them. He claimed that it was unsafe to risk letting it go now that they were detested and that the Spartans were no longer friendly as before, and that the allies would abandon Athens for Sparta.[12] Two years later and amid a decline in Athenian morale owing to losses incurred in battle and to the plague, Pericles confronted the Athenians with the grim reality that the empire could not be surrendered, that it was held like a tyranny and while unjust to have acquired it, letting it go was too risky (Thuc. 2.63.2). As Woodhead notes, this points up the problem of power as well as its intrinsic nature and the inherent dangers in wielding it. Power is not static but in fact possesses its own dynamic inducing a powerful state to act with force and arrogance.[13]

In the end the Athenians voted to rescind their first decision, one that would have brought the deaths of all the men of Mytilene and the enslavement of the remaining population. Instead only a 1000 of those most responsible for the revolt would die, while the rest of the population would soon see the arrival of Athenian cleruchs to take their land and watch over them. In a passage of true drama and hype, Thucydides relates how the second ship dispatched to countermand the order carried by the first, rowing and eating without pause, arrived just as Paches was reading his orders to kill and enslave the Mytileneans.[14]

Mercy for the Mytileneans was as far removed from these discussions as was any notion of Athenian popularity among their allies. While modern scholars have debated the degree to which the Athenians and their empire enjoyed the favor of their allies, the question seems a little misguided. Imperial and foreign rule is not about popularity, but rather utility: for those who hold an empire it is about power, holding it and keeping it. For those who are ruled, it is also about power, but to an inferior degree. The quest for power attempted by both Nauclides of Plataea and the Mytilenean oligarchs hardly differs from the acts of their more powerful patrons.[15]

The treachery of Mytilene claimed one last victim – the Athenian general Paches himself. In sources from as late as the fifth century AD/CE, we learn that the Athenians ordered an investigation of Paches' generalship and his conduct of the operations in Mytilene. While the cause of the investigation is unknown, it ended with brutal clarity. Hauled into court, Paches responded to the charge by drawing his sword and taking his life before the astonished jury.[16]

Arguments have been offered for and against Paches' guilt and innocence, but the affair will likely remain a mystery beyond resolution. Possibly Cleon brought charges against Paches for being too soft on the Mytileneans. It may have been that the Athenians were simply enraged by the late arriving Spartan–Peloponnesian fleet of Alcidas supporting the Mytilenean rebels (Thuc. 3.36) and blamed Paches. The late writer Agathias asserts that Paches' crime was personal, namely the murder of two Mytileneans and the rape of their wives. Whatever the charges, Paches' dramatic suicide gives some idea of the potential treatment of women in a fallen city, and the vulnerability of Athenian commanders to political enemies at home.[17]

The Athenians in the West

Spartan aid to the Mytileneans arrived too late to help. Under the command of Alcidas, the Spartan and Peloponnesian ships arrived on station and quickly backed away, pressured by the Athenians. No losses were inflicted and Alcidas successfully brought his ships home where he received a new assignment. A revolution or *stasis* had broken out in Corcyra and Alcidas was to intervene before the Athenians could react (Thuc. 3.69; cf. 3.29–32). Brasidas, already famous for wartime heroics, joined him as co-commander.[18]

Some months before the Corinthians had returned to the Corcyreans on payment of a ransom some 250 prisoners captured in a series of naval fights early in the war.[19] The Corinthians treated these prisoners well and won over many. Most belonged to the Corcyrean elite, and many would have held conservative or oligarchic views: this may have made them susceptible to Corinthian persuasion (and bribery?). While it seems unlikely that all could have been so persuaded, there might have been a group dynamic at work, peer pressure that united these men into a coherent faction. Social clubs, what the Greeks called *hetairiai*, also provided cells around which these men could organize.[20] Whatever transpired in Corinth, once home these Corcyrean quislings set out on a secret mission: to subvert their own city.

The formation of this faction reinforces the view that what the Greeks called *stasis* was essentially about gain and profit (*kerdos*) – taking and getting more than others – and this also led to the formation of groups, in effect parties, to achieve such goals. Profit margins and survival were never easy. In times of peace, or what passed for peace in the Greek world, competition would realize itself in politics and politicking. War now endangered the likelihood of gain and turned competition sharp and cruel.[21]

On the return of the quislings the Corcyrean people held an assembly attended by Athenian and Corinthian representatives to discuss their city's relationships with the 'great' powers and the future course that Corcyra would take. After debate the decision was made to maintain the treaty made with the Athenians, the original source of conflict with Corinth, but to act friendly toward the Peloponnesians (Thuc. 3.70.2).

But the quisling faction was not for any compromise. They forced a prosecution of the pro-Athenian and democratic leader Peithias, claiming he was enslaving Corcyra to Athens, but failed to win. In turn he successfully prosecuted five of his most outspoken opponents who were assessed heavy fines. Peithias decided to follow up this success with another, namely a fully fledged alliance with Athens. On learning of this the quislings struck and struck hard: breaking into the council chambers, Peithias and sixty others were killed. They then attempted to seize power and persuade their fellow citizens to break with Athens and return to their pre-war neutral status. Envoys were sent to Athens declaring the new Corcyrean position, but these the Athenians placed under arrest on Aegina. The arrival of a Corinthian ship and Spartan envoys energized the quislings. They now attacked their opponents who held on to those parts of the city that they could. This was the first act in a violent political upheaval that would see far worse. It was also the first of a series of political revolutions that rocked the Greek world during this time of 'total' war.[22]

The vicious street fighting that erupted after the murder of Peithias intensified. Women joined the fray as did slaves whose support both sides solicited – most joined the democrats. The quislings brought in mercenaries and soon there was street fighting complete with women throwing roof tiles, injured and dead lying around, and fires breaking out all around the city. In this hellish situation the small Athenian squadron from Naupactus arrived and its commander Nicostratus managed to cool passions and stop the fighting. While his arrival owed more to his own initiative than to orders from Athens, it might also be seen as the first move by the Athenians to take a direct role in the internal affairs of the island, supporting their friends in suppressing the quislings. The truce brokered by Nicostratus soon broke down as the democrats feared that the quislings would not honor their agreement and would attack at the first chance. Some 400 of the quislings surrendered and were taken across to the mainland and kept under guard (Thuc. 3.73–5).

The 'great' power intervention that had begun with Nicostratus' arrival now took an ominous turn. The Peloponnesian fleet commanded by Alcidas and Brasidas moved toward Corcyra. As it moved to attack, the Corcyreans hurriedly assembled their fleet in response, ignoring an Athenian suggestion to allow the Athenians to take the lead so as to relieve pressure on their allies. The Athenians were ignored. As the Corcyreans began to engage, several ships deserted to the Peloponnesians, while aboard others the crews could be seen fighting among themselves. The small Athenian squadron managed to defend itself against the more numerous Peloponnesian ships, superior seamanship saving them. The Corcyreans, losing thirteen ships, barely survived (Thuc. 3.77.3–5).

At this point the democratic leaders resolved to solve the crisis. Negotiating with the quislings they concluded a pact to put the defense of Corcyra first and resolved to defend against an expected Peloponnesian attack. But that same night a large Athenian squadron of sixty ships arrived and on learning this, the Peloponnesians hurriedly withdrew. The democrats then wasted no time in attacking their opponents. They seized all that they could, including those previously placed in detention, as well as any thought disloyal on the surviving ships. Then the slaughter began (Thuc. 3.80–1).

Thucydides reveals not only the vicious nature of these political uprisings, but also the brutality that now became commonplace. In his analysis of the civil war that erupted in Corcyra, he brings out two principal ideas: how the violence of war leads those who have been experienced in its ways to commit atrocity;[23] and the extent to which those who desire power will go. This can be seen first in his statement that in the fighting every form of death was seen. Fathers killed sons and while he does not say so explicitly, his statement implies that sons too killed their fathers; men were dragged from temples and shrines where they had sought sanctuary and then were killed, while others were simply walled up in such places and allowed to die (Thuc. 3.81.5).

Behind this great blood-letting was, as Woodhead notes, the quest for power.[24] In this instance it was political power that was at stake. The quislings released by the Corinthians aimed at the group led by Peithias and replacing it with their own oligarchic and pro-Corinthian regime. In the turmoil and bloodshed that followed there was a total breakdown of civil society of which the above noted murders are only a few examples. Not only were traditional mores ignored, but also any sense of law and justice, what might also be called 'due process,' as those bent on seizing power would allow no impediment in stand in their way. This calls to mind political scientist Ned Lebow's analysis of the relationship of justice to power: that which is done outside the language of justice equates to the use of power, which in turn leads to more extravagant expressions of force and excess.[25] Thucydides relates how all this was to be seen in the inversion of language that emerged from the political struggle, where old norms of conduct – restraint, moderation – were seen as the acts of a coward or simpleton, while new norms of conduct and political violence were seen as those of the bold, clever, and perceptive.[26]

Woodhead argues that these displays were the product of envy and rivalry, which Thucydides expresses in the word *phthonos*, and enmity or *echthos*.[27] But what causes these passions to emerge in the first place? Woodhead offers no suggestion. In fact what Thucydides has related has emerged out of the horror of war. He makes plain that the 'excesses' that became the norm in the Corcyrean civil war followed from war's violence – that this had become a 'teacher' of men and led them into atrocity (Thuc. 3.82.2).

This may sound like so much circular reasoning, but those who have not experienced war's violence – who do not know how war can and will change your very character – will not be able to understand or recognize the process at work.[28] Thucydides' account of the *stasis* that destroyed Corcyra came after the events and reflects his analysis of these events. But contemporary comment from the sophist and intellectual Gorgias confirms Thucydides' observations. In his *Encomium of Helen* written about this time, Gorgias refers to the traumatic responses of men confronted by war's violence: how even if men survived the experience of battle, many were left useless, unable to work, while others suffered from physical or psychic disorders.[29]

These responses are but the other side of the coin to Thucydides' picture of events in Corcyra. The Corcyreans who overthrew their own community ignited a bitter conflict that instilled in them a sense of *echthos* or enmity: what we in the post-Vietnam world know as 'payback', where finding vengeance at any cost becomes the 'good'. Woodhead's notion of *phthonos*, envy or rivalry, emerges from the same environment of violence and refers to an extreme sense of competition, but one in which the stakes are high – literally a matter of life and death. Underneath all this are the many forms of war's violence, which has shaped these forces in the minds of men and driven them to extremes in their quest for power and vengeance.

The Call to Sicily

As affairs in Corcyra descended into chaos and worse, a new storm swept Athens. Not a storm of arms but rather one of dazzling oratory the likes of which the Athenians, not easy to impress, had seldom seen. Gorgias of Leontini arrived in Athens in 427 (perhaps late spring or early summer) as a member of a diplomatic mission negotiating with Athens. Out west in Sicily the most powerful of the Greek cities, Syracuse, was expanding its influence and the smaller surrounding cities such as Leontini were feeling the pinch (Thuc. 3.86). Gorgias' reputation as a speaker had preceded him and he took time out of the business of diplomacy to deliver lectures and samples of his rhetorical brilliance. At private symposia and in public gatherings Gorgias gave epideictic speeches and it is not difficult to imagine the likes of Sophocles, Thucydides, and other elites not only hearing these but engaging Gorgias in conversation.[30] After his initial visit to Athens, Gorgias traveled extensively in Greece, giving speeches and lessons at Olympia and Delphi among other places.

Gorgias' visit was exciting and his stylized rhetoric with its antithetical structure, balancing clauses, and other rhetorical flourishes exerted tremendous impact on Athenian oratory.[31] His speeches were noteworthy for their reflections on the power of words and moral responsibility.[32] This influence has been questioned since several contemporary plays of Euripides – *Alcestis*, *Medea*, and *Hippolytus* (II) – also display impressive examples of rhetorical technique including point–counterpoint arguments.[33]

But there can be little doubt of the impact of his visit, as seen perhaps in the dialogue Plato would later name after him.

The golden tongue of Gorgias was beguiling. Athens, already committed to Leontini as a friend and ally since the alliance of 433/2, had looked upon the green fields – and grain – of southern Italy and Sicily wistfully. The outbreak of full-scale war now meant that these resources must be controlled. Accordingly, the Athenians dispatched two generals, Charoeades and Laches, with a small force in summer 427. The next summer (426) left Laches in sole command as Charoeades was killed in combat (Thuc. 3.90). Later (winter 426/5) another general, Pythodorus, succeeded Laches and continued operating in Sicily, though this was in the face of growing Sicilian and especially Syracusan resistance (Thuc. 3.115.3).

While the declared aim of this activity was to secure Leontini from Syracusan aggression, there was the strategic plan. Not simply to deny the Sicilian food basket to the Peloponnesians, but to see if it might be possible to bring Sicily under Athenian control (Thuc. 3.86.4). Over the course of the next three years the Athenians and their allies worked to counter Syracusan aggression while winning friends among the island's Greek and native peoples. The region's rich resources drew the Athenians like a moth to the flame.[34]

Gorgias' visit to Athens and the Athenian Sicilian gambit that followed probably attracted the interests of another Greek thinker with Athenian connections. Herodotus of Halicarnassus had been working on his storied account of the Persian Wars for some time when the war with Sparta broke out, even referring to at least one early event, the killing of Spartan and Peloponnesian envoys in summer 429. It is also possible that he won honors and financial gifts from the Athenians: Eusebius' *Chronicle* (AD/CE 445/4) states that Herodotus read some of his *History* to the Council and was honored by it for his work.[35]

In all likelihood, it was not until about 424, or even a little later, that the final version of Herodotus' *Histories* were published.[36] This would have enabled Herodotus to observe not only Gorgias' embassy of 427, and all the hoopla attending that event, but also what the Athenians debated and then decided upon in regard to what became their first Sicilian expedition. There is good reason to think that this influenced his account of the Persian war, particularly the attention given to Persian imperial expansionism and its accompanying arrogance of power. As historian Kurt Raaflaub has concluded, Herodotus' idea of history, his interpretation of the past, emerges from a dialectical process that brought together past and present.[37]

Gorgias and Herodotus may also have witnessed the foundation of a new festival to Apollo. Since the outbreak of war Apollo's international center at Delphi, owing to its pro-Spartan inclinations, had been unfriendly to Athens. Other festival sites of the Greeks – Isthmia, Nemea, Olympia – would have been no less uncomfortable as they lay in 'enemy' territory. These reasons, as well as the impact of the war itself, prompted the Athenians to inaugurate, actually restore, a festival to Apollo, the Delia, on his island home of Delos.[38]

In winter 426/5 the Athenians sailed to the island and while no reference is made to any leading Athenian political figures – Cleon and Nicias for example – they may have been associated with the event. A plausible case has been made for some role by the historian Thucydides himself.[39] On arrival the Athenians went about the rituals of purification. All graves were removed and it was announced that henceforth there would be no births or deaths on the island. Though Thucydides is vague regarding the rationale behind this act, it appears that thanksgiving for an end to the plague might explain why the Athenians now undertook this measure.

Established with the festival were various athletic contests including equestrian (i.e., chariot races) events, as well as poetic and dance contests. Among the latter would have been the *pyrrhiche* or war-dance, a dance that prepared men for battle, teaching them how to duck blows and get at their enemies (see Athen. 628e–f, Pl. *Leg.* 815a). Such dances and contests also possess a certain cathartic power, which suggests that the festival and games provided the Athenians with an emotional release from the plague and wartime conditions.[40] The institution of the Delia then provides additional insight into the impact of war and plague upon the Athenian population.

An Athenian Hero Born

The resilience of the Athenians knew no bounds. With forces committed in Sicily and in the Aegean against Melos, a small but recalcitrant Spartan colony, yet another was sent out into western Greece under Demosthenes and Proclus in summer 426 (Thuc. 3.91.1). The Spartans had only lately founded a stronghold and colony at Heraclea in Trachis in central Greece from which they could easily threaten the Athenian 'protectorate' of Euboea (Thuc. 3.92–93.1). A response here now seemed critically important.

Sailing around the Peloponnese, Demosthenes first brought his forces into action against Leucas which Athens' Acarnanian allies were keen to eliminate. But the pro-Athenian Messenians holding Naupactus had ideas too. They believed themselves threatened by their Aetolian neighbors whom they saw as a major nuisance. A rough and tumble rustic people accustomed to raiding and robbing their neighbors, the Aetolians still walked around armed (Thuc. 1.5.3). As Naupactus was a key to Athenian interests in the west, Demosthenes had to listen to the Messenian complaints. But he seems to have had his own ideas too and seen an opportunity in the Messenian argument. Through the Aetolians Demosthenes could find an avenue directly into central Greece: he could not only get behind the Boeotians but also the Spartans in their new stronghold in Heraclea (Thuc. 3.94–95.1). With the manpower and resources he now held, he could make things very difficult for Athens' enemies.

Demosthenes moved against the Aetolians with a strong force composed of elite Athenians and allies, though without the Acarnanians still smarting from his refusal to reduce Leucas. Urged on by the Messenians, who kept telling him that the Aetolians posed little threat, Demosthenes found it easy to invade their land but not to bring them to battle. Near the Aetolian settlement of Aegitium, Demosthenes finally got what he wanted – a fight to settle the issue. But he got more than he bargained. The Aetolians did not fight a straight-up battle but preferred hit and run which gave the allied Athenian army all it could handle. The fighting was in rugged terrain, but the advance–retreat–advance maneuvers employed by the allies, along with steady work by the archers, kept the Aetolians contained. But then the archer's captain was killed and the counter-tactics employed by the Athenians and their allies simply exhausted them. The Aetolians closed in for the kill – with the Messenian guide dead, the Athenians and their allies lost their way and the retreat became a slaughter. Of 300 Athenian infantry, 120 – forty percent – were killed along with Demosthenes' colleague Proclus, and the allies suffered equally heavy losses.[41] On returning to Naupactus, the Athenian ships and the infantry survivors returned to Athens. Demosthenes remained behind afraid to return: the example of Paches, perhaps, looming large in his mind (Thuc. 3.96–8).

This Athenian debacle opened the door to the Spartans. Immediately on learning of Demosthenes' planned invasion, the Aetolians appealed to the Spartans for relief, which was granted. Soon a combined force of 3000 allies, under the command of the Spartan Eurylochus, arrived to intervene (by autumn 426), with plans mostly for seizing the Athenian stronghold at

Naupactus. The Ambraciots also began pressuring him to take action against their enemies in Acarnania and Amphilochian Argos to which he agreed. Demosthenes, however, was able to organize a defense, thanks primarily to the Acarnanians whom he persuaded to stand with him. With Naupactus secured and denied him, Eurylochus realized that another plan would be needed (Thuc. 3.100–2).

A major struggle for control of western Greece was now taking shape. The stakes were high not only for the Athenians and the Spartans, but also their respective allies. The Messenians had invited Demosthenes to help them beat back the Aetolians but this had misfired. Similar feelings sparked resentment between the Acarnanians and Ambraciots and the people of Amphilochian Argos. The time had arrived for a settling of scores. This began with an Ambraciot attack on the Amphilochian Argives, allies of the Acarnanians, who seized Olpae, a stronghold close to the sea.

At Olpae Demosthenes would not only smash his assembled enemies and so clear his name and record, but establish himself as a brilliant tactician, successfully combining lightly and heavily armed troops. From the heights overlooking Olpae, Demosthenes lured the Peloponnesians into a trap and the two sides clashed in the rugged terrain. In a running daylong engagement, Demosthenes and his Messenian allies swept the field clean as the Ambraciots did on their side.[42] In the fighting the Spartan commanders were killed or incapacitated and the Spartan-led army disintegrated; matters were made worse when the surviving Spartans and Peloponnesians negotiated a separate truce with Demosthenes and then abandoned their allies (Thuc. 3.107–11).

As the fighting wore on, the Ambraciots sent out the whole of their remaining forces, more than 1000 men, who rushed to join the action. Reaching the height of Idomene in early evening, they stopped for the night, unaware that Demosthenes had beaten them to the high ground and had placed an advance force above them. Just before dawn Demosthenes hit the sleeping Ambraciots from below and above, getting past tired sentries with allies speaking the Ambraciot dialect. The result was a slaughter. Those not killed on the spot, tried to flee but only into the arms of waiting enemies. Few escaped (Thuc. 3.112).

The next day the Acarnanians commemorated their victory in typical fashion: the dead were stripped naked, a humiliation made clear in the Greek word for shame, *aidoios*, from which stems genitalia, *aidoion*, and their weapons and armor were piled up.[43] When the Ambraciot herald arrived to ask for the return of the dead, the vast quantity of arms shocked him. He asked if these were of the Ambraciots who had fought two days before. When told that these arms were those of the Ambraciots killed at Idomene the previous day, the herald nearly fainted, as he realized that the relief army had been destroyed. Overwhelmed and numb at the great loss, the herald left without asking for return of the dead (Thuc. 3.113).

Knocked out of the war, Ambracia suffered losses such as no other city. The scope of the Ambraciot loss is made clear in the subsequent division of spoils. Dividing them up, Demosthenes received one-third, some 300 sets of arms, which he took back to Athens where they were later placed in various temples as thank-offerings (3.114.1).[44] This should mean that at least 900 Ambraciot men had been killed, a staggering loss for a small community. These gifts, along with his incredible victory, made it possible for Demosthenes to return home, his earlier defeat overlooked. Before his departure, Demosthenes urged the Acarnanians and Amphilochians to seize Ambracia, but they hesitated, happy enough that their mortal enemies had been so badly beaten.[45]

Demosthenes – General of Athens

Philip of Macedon once quipped that while the Athenians could find ten generals every year, he had only known one, Parmenion (Plut. *Mor.* 177C). As king and commander himself, Philip recognized that not every soldier was a leader or commander, so where did Demosthenes learn the arts of war, how did he win election to the office of *strategos*?

Election to the office was not a simple matter. While in the office's early history the Athenians had probably chosen one general from each of the ten tribes, by late in the fifth century this result was fading away and there were years in which one tribe had multiple representations, other tribes none.[46] But there were other obstacles to winning office too. Among these were wealth and name recognition. Xenophon reports a conversation between Socrates and a veteran soldier Nicomachides in which the latter complains that for all his service and wounds, the Athenians still chose Antisthenes, a man better known for his wealth and success as a *choregos*.[47] Sophocles may well have owed his generalships to his plays, as there are hints that his strategic talents were not especially remarkable (Ion of Chios,

FGrHist 392 F6). This points to a truism of democratic realities, namely winning election in Athens depended no less on name recognition than in any other democratic society.[48]

A case in point may be seen in another literary construct of Xenophon, who records a conversation between Socrates and the younger Pericles. Their discussion gives some idea of how generals learned the art of war as well as the problems they encountered in leading Athenian soldiers into battle. The younger Pericles did win election to the *strategia* and his election surely owed much to his famous name.[49] Unlike Antisthenes, however, Pericles wanted to be a military man and had prepared for his role as *strategos*. Socrates suggests that Pericles had inherited from his father a collection of stratagems and had access to other sources of military lore as well, and Pericles implies agreement.[50]

Most generals, as Xenophon/Socrates observes, learn the art of war by doing and possessing a certain aptitude for military affairs and life. How Demosthenes achieved sufficient name recognition to win election to the *strategia* is unknown, but it might well be explained by battlefield losses and those to the plague.[51] In such circumstances as these, the Athenians might have been grateful to anyone willing to take up the challenges of command.

As demonstrated by his conduct of the campaign in Acarnania, Demosthenes clearly possessed a basic understanding of tactics and recognized that combining different types of troops (peltasts, hoplites, and archers) and the weapons they carried could produce striking results.[52] He recognized the advantage of high ground, as seen in taking the height of Idomene and setting an ambush for the Ambraciots there, in tricking them with men who spoke their own dialect. Even the unsuccessful engagement with the Aetolians demonstrates the same tactical skill. In that fight, Demosthenes enjoyed success until the commander of his archers was killed and it was only then that things fell apart, making clear the importance of subordinate officers and the role that they played in battle. In the end, Demosthenes triumphed and his subsequent victory over the Spartans at Sphacteria made clear again his tactical skills.[53]

Notes

1 Thuc. 3.13.1 and Hornblower 1: 382–3. Telling, as the refusal shows the Spartans were not looking for a fight. See pp. 30–5.

2 Thuc. 3.17 reports that the Athenians now manned 250 ships: 100 raised from both citizens and metics for the Peloponnese; 100 guarding the area around Athens; some 50 stationed at Potidaea and elsewhere.

3 Nothing is said of arbitrating the dispute, which supports Badian 1966: 38–9 that Athens did not negotiate complaints with the allies.

4 Thuc. 3.27–28.1, with Gomme 2: 290–1.

5 Thuc. 3.36.6; it is sometimes thought that Cleon played a part in Thucydides' later exile. Plut. *Gr.* 2 notes Cleon's oratorical style suggesting that enough was known of this to analyze.

6 Thuc. 3.37–49. For discussions of this debate see e.g., Hornblower 2: 420–39. While the authenticity of these speeches might be disputed, it is not really a relevant question. A more important and telling issue is what the speeches reveal of ideas current at the end of the fifth century, ideas certainly explored by Thucydides.

7 See e.g., Woodhead 1970: 7, 13–16 who notes these issues.

8 Woodhead 1970: 7–8.

9 Thuc. 3.39.6. Here Cleon argues against any special consideration for those Mytileneans who helped the Athenians by turning against the ruling elite and opening the gates allowing the Athenians to take the city. See Thuc. 3.27–28.

10 Thuc. 3.45, and noted also by Hornblower 1: 435.

11 Solmsen 1975: 38–9, refers to this as 'Cleon's Paradox'.

12 Thuc. 1.75.4. The speaker is unknown, but the speech is, as Hornblower 1: 117 notes, a lucid and harsh exploration of the philosophy of imperialism.

13 Woodhouse 1970: 13, 47.

14 Thuc. 3.49.4–50, with Hornblower 1: 440–1 and Gomme 3: 325–6.

15 See, e.g., Bradeen 1960, Cawkwell 1997: 92–106, and Morris 2009.

16 Plut. *Nic.* 6.1, *Aristid.* 26.5, *Anth. Pal.* 7.614, and, e.g., Gomme 3: 332.

17 Cf. Westlake 1975 and Tuplin 1982.

18 Brasidas had nearly single-handedly repulsed an Athenian attack in the Peloponnese early in the war and his reputation had grown from that. See further p. 88.

19 Thuc. 1.54–5 (number of prisoners), 3.70.1 (payment of ransom), with Gomme 2: 359 and Hornblower 1: 466–8.

20 Thuc. 3.82.5–6, with Hornblower 1: 484–5, notes the division into clubs, something that would happen too in Athens.

21 On *stasis* see Finley 1982: 80–2 and Loraux 2002: 24–5.

22 For the background see Thuc. 3.70–81, with Gomme 2: 360–82, Hornblower 1: 468–91. Lattimore 1998: 168, note, argues that it was the first rather than 'among the first'.

23 Thuc. 3.82.2, with Tritle 2000: 12831.

24 Woodhead 1970: 21.

25 See again Lebow 2003: 122.

26 See in particular Thuc. 3.82. The passage, both its translation and meaning, are both complex and highly debated. See e.g., Wilson 1982: 18–20, Loraux 1986: 103–24, and Tritle 2000: 128–31.

27 Woodhead 1970: 21.

28 See, e.g., Shay 1995 and Tritle 2000 for discussion.

29 On Gorgias see next note and pp. 158–60.

30 Kerferd 1981: 44–5, with Gorg. No. 82 B11, 16–17 Diels-Kranz 1961 (trans. G. Kennedy, in Sprague 1972: 53–4).

31 See, e.g., Wills 1992. Ar. *Vesp.* 421, *Av.* 1701–5 attack Athenian disciples of Gorgias.

32 D.A. Russell, 'Gorgias (1)', *OCD³*, 642–3.

33 Solmsen 1975: 24, Whitehead 2004: 161–2.

34 Thuc. 3.86. Thucydides' narrative of Sicilian affairs in these years is not continuous. By 324 the Sicilian Greeks and Sicilians were tired of the fighting. At the Congress of Gela (424) they came to terms and pressed the Athenians to leave the island, which they did for some eight years (Thuc. 3.103, 4.2.2, 24–5, 58–65.2).

35 Hdt. 7.137.1 (Spartan envoys killed); cf. Thuc. 2.67.1, and West 1999: 110–11.

36 Raaflaub 2002, notes 'publication' should not be construed in the modern sense. Rather it is a complex affair of oral presentations or recitals of speeches or lectures that over time were written down.

37 For further discussion see Raaflaub 2002.

38 Thuc. 1.81, 3.104, with Gomme 2: 414–15, Hornblower 1: 517–31, Diod. 12.58.6–7. Restoration, as Thucydides notes an earlier festival which at some point had been discontinued.

39 Thucydides does not directly connect either Cleon or Nicias with the new festival, but see Hornblower 1: 517–19, who suggests that Thucydides himself may have had a part in the purification and establishment of the festival (on the basis of 1.8.1 and the account of the excavation of bones and weapons, though it seems just as possible that Thucydides learned this from others like so much else in his work).

40 See McNeil 1995: 6–8, Tritle 2000: 189–91 for further discussion on these phenomena.

41 Thuc. 3.98.4, with Hornblower 1: 514, claims that these Athenian dead were the best men lost by the city during the war (perhaps meaning the Archidamian War?). When the number of wounded (unstated, but likely another thirty or forty percent) are factored in, it would appear that this force of Athenian infantry would have been left incapable of further combat, which explains its return to Athens.

42 Thuc. 3.108 makes clear that the battle lasted all day. While not a 'traditional' hoplite battle, its duration gives some idea of how long such engagements could last.

43 On this see Soph. *Ant.* 409–10, a literary but real description of battlefield dead, and Tritle 1997.

44 On battle spoils see Pritchett 1: 53–92.

45 Acarnania and the Amphilochians made a 100-year non-aggression pact with the Ambraciots, a clear sign of their great defeat (Thuc. 3.114.1–3). Later 300 Corinthians arrived to garrison their town, surely indicating that only very old men and boys were to be found there (Thuc. 3.114.4).

46 [Arist.] *Ath.Pol.* 22.2, with Rhodes 1981: 265–6, Sinclair 1988: 17–18.

47 Xen. *Mem.* 3.4.1–12, with *APF* 39 and Develin 1989: 226, 291. The occasion is post-Peloponnesian War but more than that is obscure; the situation Xenophon relates remains exemplary, however.

48 Note the role played here by commemorative statues, as those of Pericles, his father Xanthippus, and other mid-fifth century generals, Phormio, Tolmides. These appear to have been private dedications, the first public statue for a general being that of Conon in the fourth century. See further Shear 2007: 108.

49 Pericles the younger seems to have been a courageous soldier but unlucky. As co-commander of the fleet that won at Arginusae, he was executed by the Athenians for failing to save the crews of damaged warships. See pp. 208–9, 210–12.

50 Xen. *Mem.* 3.5.21–3, with Gomme 3: 638.

51 See Hansen 1988: 14–28 for population losses, including casualty tables, but cf. Akrigg 2007: 30–1.

52 See Roisman 1993 for full discussion of Demosthenes' generalship.

53 See pp. 88–9 and treatment of Demosthenes' grasp of strategy.

5

'SPINDLES WOULD BE
WORTH A LOT'

With western Greece now secure, thanks to Demosthenes, the Athenians could refocus on affairs in the west. In winter 426/5 Pythodorus had replaced Laches, soldiering on alone in Sicily since the death of Charoeades, but neither seems to have accomplished much (Thuc. 3.115.1–2). The next summer (425) the Athenians sent out a much larger force, some forty ships, commanded by the generals Eurymedon and Sophocles. Instructed first to assist the struggling pro-Athenian faction in Corcyra, the generals were then to continue on to Sicily and assist Pythodorus. Tagging along in a private capacity with the two generals was Demosthenes. Absent fighting in the west the previous year, he had missed the elections for the general-ship. Anxious to get back into action, Demosthenes asked to join the expedition as a volunteer. A hero now, the Athenians granted his request.

Eurymedon and Sophocles probably regretted the decision. Intent on following their orders to relieve Corcyra and move on to Sicily, they were for pushing on even when a report arrived that a large Peloponnesian fleet had gotten there ahead of them. Demosthenes, without rank but lots of experience, tried persuading them to lay over in Pylos where he wanted to try out an idea. He had sailed this way before, he may have told them, and had noticed the isolated yet sheltered bay and the quiet surrounding coun-tryside. It was a perfect place, surely, to establish a base of operations that could create big problems for the Spartans.[1] The generals, resentful perhaps of his reputation and dismissive of his private status, apparently resisted. But then a storm blew up and decided the issue, forcing the fleet to put in to the bay of Pylos.

Scouts quickly determined that there were no Spartan military forces nearby. While Demosthenes debated with Eurymedon and Sophocles to secure the place and take advantage of the Spartan absence of mind, bored Athenian sailors and soldiers took matters into their own hands and began building a fort. The two generals decided to leave Demosthenes in place with a small force and from this base raid into the surrounding country-side, to carry the war to the Spartans as they were to the Athenians.[2]

The Athenian raids threatened not only the fields, but more so the deli-cate social balance in Sparta, the authority of the Spartan elites over the helots. Pylos was in Messenia, home to the most hostile of Sparta's servile population: the same Messenian helots who had rebelled in 464 and kept the Spartans occupied for eight years before finally yielding. Demosthenes would have known this and imagined that a strong Athenian base in Pylos had the potential to undo Sparta. In reality, Pylos was too far from Athens and maintaining a base here posed many problems for the Athenians. But as so often in war, what often happens is neither planned nor anticipated.

A festival briefly delayed the Spartan response to the Athenian occupa-tion, but they seemed unworried, thinking that little effort would be needed to drive the Athenians away. However, in their confidence, they might have miscalculated: forcing the Athenians to abandon their base would not be easy. Athenian naval forces remained superior to Spartan and the entrance to the bay of Pylos could be easily blocked, as indeed it was. The Spartans landed a force of 420 hoplites commanded by Epitadas on Sphacteria island (see Figure 5.1) opposite Pylos.

The Spartans may have thought that this force would give them a base from which to harass the Athenians and force their withdrawal. In landing these men on the island, however, the Spartans only succeeded in making them hostages to fortune. Soon these men were marooned, then food and water began running low. With the help of helot volunteers, Spartan authorities were able to re-supply the trapped men with essential supplies, but daily the situation became more critical. Keeping these men supplied was difficult, but getting them off the island was another thing: the battle for the island, as the Spartans would call it, was shaping up.[3]

Epitadas – Soldier of Sparta

Of the 420 men that Epitadas commanded, many were not Spartiate or full citizens, but Laconian allies or *perioikoi* who now filled out the ranks of the Spartan army. Epitadas himself was the son of a prominent Spartan, Molocrus, perhaps among those Spartans who had secured financial con-

Figure 5.1 The island of Sphacteria lying opposite Pylos and the Bay of Navarino. The main Spartan camp lay in the center of the island just below the high ground.

tributions to Sparta's war fund.[4] In assigning troops to the island, Spartan commanders may have detached a section (chosen by lot perhaps) from each of the battalions now present, a procedure often followed in other situations. Many (all?) hoplites would have come with a helot attendant. Thucydides makes no distinction in these, but some were perhaps *mothakes* (shield-bearers, or squires) who could be expected to fight in a pinch as they were raised with the Spartans they served. Other helots might have been only attendants who mostly provided the typical functions of camp laborer and batman, though these could also serve as light-armed fighters.[5] Each soldier would also have carried his own provisions, the Spartiates drawing from their own lands and the contributions they made to the common messes (the *syssitia*). The other soldiers would have made similar arrangements.

Where the life of the Spartan soldier stands out is in the structure of the military organization, in modern terms the chain of command. Thucydides calls attention to how in effect every Spartan soldier was potentially an officer: from king to *polemarchoi*, to the *lochagoi* (battalion commanders), to *pentekosteis* (company commanders), to *enomotarchoi* (platoon commanders), the job of every soldier was to pass on orders and obey. Each man was potentially a leader, the execution of orders the responsibility of all.[6] The discipline this chain of command created would be plainly revealed in the fight for the island. Hemmed in by superior numbers with no chance of relief, Epitades' unit broke only under a massive assault.

The Island Battle – A Spartan Defeat

Demosthenes acted to close the noose around the entrapped Spartans on the island and Spartan attacks increased as the situation became more desperate. The Spartans brought in extensive forces and began attacking the Athenian position by land and sea. In this curious reversal of war's fortunes, the Spartans were attacking the Athenians from the sea, attempting to seize enemy land actually their own. The Spartan assaults were determined as seen in the amphibious landings they attempted. Brasidas, already famous for earlier heroics at Methone, won even greater fame now.[7] Forcing his ship's pilot to land on the rocky shore of the island, Brasidas charged down the gangplank and into the Athenians. The fighting was ferocious and in the end Brasidas' men dragged him away semi-conscious bleeding from many wounds and shieldless.

Despite their efforts the Spartans could make no headway and asked for a truce which the Athenians accepted.[8] It was agreed that the men on the island could be re-supplied while Spartan envoys negotiated in Athens for terms to end the stand-off and even the war itself. The impatience of the Athenians matched the desperation of the Spartans. The Spartan ambassadors came before the assembled Athenians and presented their case: the release of the trapped men on the island and an end to war and an alliance (Thuc. 4.15–22). As in the debate over Mytilene, Cleon came on strongly in answering the Spartan envoys. He argued that the Spartans on the island should be surrendered and brought to Athens, that the Spartans should return a number of lost places, Nisaea, Pagae, and others, before any truce were made. He also attacked the Spartans charging them with duplicity and accusing them of seeking private negotiations away from the Athenians where they might get a better deal. Under this rhetorical onslaught, negotiations broke off and the Spartan envoys returned home.

On returning from a fact-finding mission to Pylos, Cleon challenged the competence of the generals in command at Pylos, telling the assembly that if the generals were men they could mop up the Spartans and if he were in charge there would be no question that this would happen. [9] On this bold claim, Nicias, a veteran commander and statesman, took Cleon at his word and agreed to yield his generalship to Cleon so that he could make good on his claims. Quickly Cleon backpedaled, but the more he did so the more Nicias insisted that he take command. The Athenian assembly watching the debate joined in the scene, some laughing at Cleon's bravado, others thinking that if he went he might get killed and that would be end of his trouble making. In the end Cleon accepted the command rather than humiliation (Thuc. 4.28). He made his way to Pylos, bringing with him a number of light-armed troops, where he joined forces with Demosthenes, awaiting the outcome of the truce.

Within a short time the Athenians made an all-out assault on the island. Before dawn forces were landed on both the north and south ends of the island, trapping the Spartans between them. Brutal hand-to-hand fighting followed throughout the day. As the Athenians tightened their ring around the Spartans, they set fire to the island. The Spartans, thirsty and hungry, tired and under constant attack from an enemy they could not close with, suffered many casualties. At last with their senior officers, Epitadus and Hippagretus, dead or seriously wounded, Styphon, the officer now in command, asked for a truce in the late afternoon. The Athenians allowed him to send a dispatch to his superiors requesting instructions. These responded only that the survivors should exercise their own judgment, and do only what was honorable (Thuc. 4.31–5). Styphon then surrendered. In the end two factors explain the Athenian victory: light-armed troops able to maneuver more easily over rough terrain than their heavy-armed opponents, and the skill of Demosthenes in commanding these. Of the Spartan force, 128 were killed, some thirty percent; 292 men, including 120 Spartiates, chose surrender over a fight to the death. Much to the surprise of everyone, perhaps himself most of all, Cleon had made good on his promise – his political stock in Athens soared.

The Spartan surrender sent shock waves through the Greek world. The prevailing belief that Spartans would die before surrendering, either to hunger or an opponent's spear, was shattered, and the Spartan mirage dimmed. It may have been now (424/3) that the Athenians concluded an

Figure 5.2 A captured Spartan shield later displayed by the Athenians: it reads, 'The Athenians from the Lacedaemonians at Pylos'.

alliance, the Peace of Epilycus, with the Persians.[10] In Argos, however, the 'island' had much greater impact. The Thirty Years Peace with Sparta would soon end and the Argives began sending out signals that they would welcome as allies any Greeks willing to join them in what they anticipated would become their hegemony over the Peloponnese. For years afterwards some Athenians claimed that Spartan confidence remained shaken even after their decisive victory at Mantinea (418).[11]

Cleon's victory touched off a storm of controversy in Athens too. Demosthenes, the architect of the Pylos strategy and of the tactics employed to defeat the Spartans, saw that Cleon had cheated him of his victory.[12] The Spartans themselves did not think much differently, referring to what had happened as 'a theft of war', though there were some in Sparta, in particular Brasidas, who saw the sense and utility of such tactics.[13]

Cleon brought his Spartan captives to Athens where their lives were dangled before the Spartans as bait on a hook. Whenever there was a threat, whenever the Spartans tried to force concessions from the Athenians, the prisoners would be held as hostages to Spartan policy and good behavior. Some of the Spartan survivors were either politically or socially connected. One of these may have been Clearchus, the son of Ramphias, one of the ambassadors sent to Athens before the war.[14]

The Spartan prisoners were evidently lightly guarded and probably held in some sort of house arrest. On one occasion a visiting Athenian ally met a prisoner and taunted him, asking if the 'real' Spartans had not died on the island. The survivor responded, 'spindles (i.e., arrows) would be worth a lot if they could pick out the brave'.[15] In other words the Spartans had not been beaten in a fair fight manfully, but shot down from afar with arrows and javelins. Echoes of this sentiment are heard in Sophocles' play *Ajax* and the disdain shown by the Spartan Menelaus to Teucer, Ajax's heroic archer-brother (Soph. *Aj.* 1120–2) and represent the model of the heroic warrior.

The capture and imprisonment of 120 citizens not only embarrassed the Spartans, it also complicated their war plans. During the fighting at Sphacteria the Spartans had offered terms of peace but these the Athenians had rejected. After the debacle the Spartans continued attempts at negotiation, but the Athenians repeatedly refused (Thuc. 4.41.3). Athenian confidence, stimulated by Cleon's arrogant leadership, made peace seem a distant hope.

Already during the struggle at Sphacteria the frustration, anger, and malaise of some Athenians provided a subject for the comic wit of Aristophanes, a brilliant young writer and social-political critic. In his first extant play, *Acharnians*, staged at the late winter festival of the Lenaea in 425 (nearly simultaneous to the first fighting on Sphacteria), Aristophanes exploited the wartime malaise of many Athenians. Aristophanes focuses on this through his chorus of embittered Acharnians, the rural population that had borne the brunt of the Spartan invasions. Aristophanes' comic hero Dicaeopolis makes a separate peace with the Spartans and as the play unfolds, Aristophanes has much to say of the causes of the war, soldiers who want only to fight, all in a context of peace now! Aristophanes won first prize with this play, beating out his rivals Cratinus and Eupolis for top honors.[16] While the play's humorous situations and images help explain its victory, the appeal for peace subtly wrapped into it cannot be ignored.

Clearly Aristophanes touched on a nerve with his cry for peace. At about the same time the Athenians heard a similar call from Euripides. Some years earlier, Euripides had attacked the Spartans in his *Andromache*, while also addressing war's brutal realities.[17] Now in another Trojan War themed play, *Hecuba*, he reminds the Athenians of the fate of a fallen city, of decisions made in assembly that lead to the death(s) of children, and the human – even feminine – potential for violence.[18]

On the heels of mass executions carried out in Mytilene, *Hecuba* would have challenged those thinking members of the audience. Euripides describes in detail the plight of young Polyxena, her death decreed by an assembly of men not very different from that Athenian assembly that authorized the killing of so many in Mytilene (Eur. *Hec.* 206–8, 220). More thought provoking still was his account of the revenge of Hecuba. In mythology Hecuba had been driven mad by her losses at Troy, but in Euripides' drama she is very calculating as she plans the destruction of her one-time friend Polymestor who had betrayed her and Priam by killing her sole surviving son Polydorus. Luring Polymestor into her tent on the promise of more wealth, he is seized and bound and forced to watch the deaths of his own young sons – then his eyes are gouged out (*Hec.* 770–1170). The *Hecuba* is more than a play of Troy – it is really a play about Greece in a real war. With its theme of revenge or payback, it is about the cycle of violence and how, as Thucydides later wrote, war is a violent teacher, bringing people down to the level of their circumstances.

Spartan Populations

Even before the final Athenian victory on the island, the crisis revealed increasing manpower shortages that drove the Spartans to approach the Athenians and attempt their release. The lives of these men now hung in the balance as the Athenians made it clear that they would be forfeit for any new invasion of Attica. In 479 an army including 5000 Spartiates had been sent to Plataea. Now a half-century later the capture of 120 of them became a matter of grave consequence for the Spartan regime. What had happened to cause this near panic? While some of the 120 were the sons of elite Spartans, not all could have been. Some other pressure must have been driving Spartan anxieties and the simplest answer is that the Spartans were simply running short of fully franchised citizens and the loss of 120 of them was serious business. Two factors explain this social crisis: the losses suffered in the great earthquake of 464 and the ensuing helot revolt; and the system of inheritance whereby the division of the ancestral lots were leading to smaller plots of land and a decline in the wealth necessary to qualify for full citizen status.

As battle losses and the unfolding social decline continued to take its toll, helots became increasingly a fixture of the Spartan military. In the summer of 424 Brasidas led an army into the north with a plan to disrupt

Athenian interests there. This force included many helots, and his choice of these men as soldiers argues that he and the few Spartiates with him trusted these men.[19] But did all in Sparta? Thucydides claims that the Spartans assembled 2000 helots on the pretense of offering them their freedom, only to put them to death (4.80). His placement of the 'Great Helot Massacre' after the battle at Sphacteria raises a number of questions. Many modern writers accept the account, but the story is troubling in several details.[20] Thucydides notes that this happened, 'as it is said', which does not inspire great confidence – it could be so much gossip and maligning of the Spartans, a famously secretive society. The story may also be an example of bias in Thucydides. Despite his reputation for objectivity, he was biased as his portrait of Cleon shows, and in this case he is an Athenian telling a Spartan story.

Thucydides admits that no one knew how these men were put to death. In itself this is no obstacle, as there are enough modern-day examples of such massacres, e.g., the Katyn Forest where 15,000 Polish officers were killed by the Soviets in 1941. The larger problem is that if no one knew how it happened, then the question that should be asked is did it happen? Some modern authors admit that the story is timeless, which suggests that, if true, the Peloponnesian War is not the only possible context.

A likelier occasion might be the helot revolt that followed the earthquake of c. 464. In suppressing the Messenian helots, by far the most rebellious of the helot population, the Spartans could easily have recruited soldiers from other helot communities to fight with them. Helots typically fought alongside the Spartans and now, in this emergency, it seems likely that they would use them even more extensively. Moreover, they did, after all, ask the Athenians for help, and the helots already there and many with wartime experience makes them a natural recruiting pool. When the revolt ended, the Spartans perhaps remained anxious about the helots and might have decided that even those who had fought for them were no less dangerous and resolved to eliminate them. But forty years and a new war had dimmed memories and brought new attitudes. This is made clear in the recruiting of helots to swim across the bay of Pylos bringing rations to the trapped soldiers, and later the grant of freedom and land to those helot veterans of Brasidas' campaign on their return home.[21] Wartime propaganda, whether or not it was Thucydides', and the continued service of Brasidas' helots after his death, suggest extreme caution in accepting Thucydides' tale of the Great Helot Massacre.

Trouble in the West

During the fight for the island, affairs in the west had taken some ominous turns. Debate in Athens over policy and goals had continued and on one occasion, Hyperbolus, a controversial, some would have said despised, popular leader, argued for an even greater effort – sending 100 ships against Carthage (Ar. *Eq.* 1303–4). While this might be comic distortion, it does reveal unchecked Athenian passion for the west.

Closer to home, Corcyra remained a hotspot and a distraction for the Athenians. Eurymedon and Sophocles, dispatched to support the struggling Corcyrean democratic regime, now arrived (summer 425) as the in-fighting between democrats and the quisling oligarchs was nearing its brutal and fatal conclusion.

The quislings had established themselves across from Corcyra town. Now supported by the Athenians, the Corcyrean democrats attacked, forcing the quislings to terms, namely to let the Athenians solve their collective troubles. But the Corcyrean democrats feared that such intervention would be too merciful, and struck first. Messengers were sent telling the quislings that the Athenians would kill them on arrival and that they should get away as quickly as possible. Transportation to Corcyra was provided and the quislings unwittingly placed themselves in the hands of their bitterest enemies. In fact Eurymedon and Sophocles abetted the plot as they were eager to sail on to Sicily and did not want others to get credit for ending the crisis.

A massacre followed soon. Shut up in a large building, the quislings were brought out in small groups and forced to run a gauntlet in which they were stabbed, beaten and killed. When the others realized what was happening they barricaded the doors. At one point the quislings yelled out to the Athenians that if they wished to kill them they should, but they were not coming out of the building. At this the democrats and Athenians proceeded to attack, breaking through the roof, attacking with missile weapons and throwing tiles, until the men inside were either dead or had committed suicide. The next day the Corcyreans piled the dead into wagons 'like lumber' and carted them away for disposal. Those women who had been in the quislings' fort were taken captive and enslaved. Thus came a vicious end to a brutal civil war. As one scholar rightly notes, this was a revolting affair. Yet it reveals with utter clarity the depths of violence in not just the revolution in Corcyra, but the war itself.[22]

Arriving in Sicily, Eurymedon and Sophocles found a rapidly evolving situation. A truce had ended fighting between Camarina and Gela and the latter had provided a venue for a general conference among the Sicilians and Sicilan Greeks to discuss the ongoing war. The Syracusan Hermocrates delivered a speech in which he promoted Sicilian unity and warned against outright Athenian imperialism which threatened them all. He called for unity against the foreign invaders – the Athenians – and urged all the Sicilians to shun outside allies or mediators. His speech struck a responsive chord. There was agreement that each city should keep what it held and that the Athenians should be sent packing, which they were. On returning home, the Athenians dealt harshly with their generals: Pythodorus and Sophocles were exiled, while Eurymedon was fined, all ostensibly for taking bribes. While such charges were the usual response to anything that went wrong, the punishments meted out to the generals reflects too Athenian disappointment at ambitions denied.[23]

A Spartan Napoleon

There were those in Athens and Greece who believed that the defeat at the 'island' demonstrated that the Spartans could be beaten on the battlefield. But the supposed lesson in Cleon's victory would seem misplaced. Rather what it revealed was the effectiveness of light-armed troops when placed under an innovative commander like Demosthenes. Soon the Athenians would be confronted by a commander no less talented than Demosthenes – Brasidas.

As gifted a military commander as the Spartans ever produced, Brasidas presented a plan to Spartan authorities that would strike back at the Athenians. Authorize an expedition to the northern Aegean, he claimed, and he could achieve such results that Athens would sue for peace and the prisoners held in Athens could be safely recovered. The plan was bold. Supported it could hurt Athens, especially its presence in Macedonia, its access to timber and other material resources, as well as the lifeline to the Black Sea.[24] But the plan entailed some risks and the Spartans, not accustomed to such innovative ideas, gave Brasidas little more than token support. In 424 he began to march north with a small force totaling some 1700 men, composed mostly of mercenaries and helots (Thuc. 4.70.1, 78–81). But the mercenaries were paid and the helots were probably *motho-*

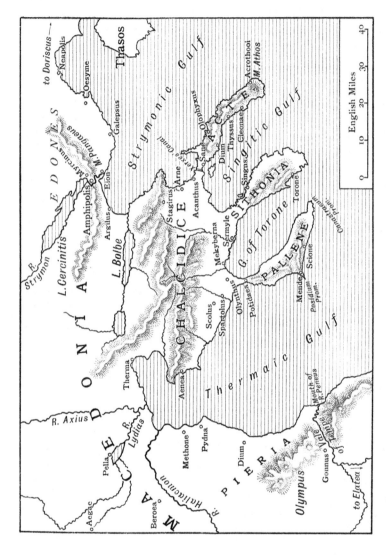

Macedonia-Chalcidice (after B.W. Henderson, *The Great War Between Athens and Sparta*, London, 1927)

nes: helots educated in the Spartan *agoge* as 'brothers' to elite Spartiates, or Spartiates whose families had sunk into the social ranking of the 'Inferiors'. In either case they were not only trained soldiers but loyal too.[25]

Brasidas not only talked a good game, he delivered. While preparing his northern march around Corinth, he learned that the Athenians had made a major effort to retake Megara. For some time Megara had been in turmoil. Rival groups of exiles and democrats were negotiating a truce, which frightened some democrats. These secretly met with the Athenians and asked for help which was readily provided – recovery of Megara would be a major coup.

Athenian forces under Demosthenes and Hippocrates attempted a night-time operation to retake both Megara and Nisaea, its port, but in the confused fighting, managed only to get Nisaea. On learning the situation, Brasidas rushed to intervene. With the aid of Boeotian troops he pushed the Athenians back, keeping Megara within the Peloponnesian camp. Later Megarian extreme oligarchs took power. Most democrats had already slipped away, but a number suspected of being too friendly to Athens were rounded up and killed. Megara became again a staunch oligarchic stronghold. The Athenians, however, retained control of Nisaea, which continued to give them a naval facility from which to harass the Peloponnesians.[26]

Within a short time, Brasidas set off on his northern campaign, quickly reaching the Spartan base in Heraclea Trachis. Once here Brasidas contacted his many friends in the area to secure a safe passage north. A whole entourage of friends and allies from Pharsalus in Thessaly, as well as Niconidas, a friend of Perdiccas of Macedonia, joined him in Melitia (Thuc. 4.78.1–2). Brasidas' expected arrival raised hopes in the region: the Greek cities of the Chalcidice, fearful of Athenian aggression, and especially Perdiccas, the Macedonian king. Long unhappy with the Athenian presence in the north, Perdiccas had been working against the Athenians for years.[27] He saw in Sparta and Brasidas not only an opportunity to weaken the Athenians, but to expand his power, especially at the expense of his neighbors (Thuc. 4.66–79).

Brasidas' march through Thessaly was unhindered thanks to the support of elite friends in Pharsalus. Escorting him as his small force rapidly pushed through Thessaly, they persuaded their countrymen that Brasidas posed no threat to them and urged restraint.[28] Brasidas knew that there were limits to the local support he could expect owing to the long friendship between the Thessalians and Athenians. For this reason he pushed his troops hard and by the time his opponents could even think of organizing resistance he had safely reached Macedonia (Thuc. 4.76–8).

On arrival Perdiccas welcomed Brasidas throwing out the red carpet in the process. While the northern campaign that Brasidas proposed to the ephors was largely his conception, Perdiccas and the Greek cities in the north, particularly those in the Chalcidice, welcomed it (Thuc. 4.79.1). But from the beginning the alliance between Perdiccas and Brasidas was tenuous. In Perdiccas' view, he had invited Brasidas to the north not so much to harm Athenian interests as those of his local enemies, particularly Arrabaeus, chief of the Lyncestian Macedonians. Upon his arrival Perdiccas expected that Brasidas' troops would lead the attack against Arrabaeus to Perdiccas' advantage. Brasidas had other ideas. He intended to create a great coalition of allies in the north with which to attack the Athenians. To Perdiccas' disbelief, Brasidas ended the feud between the two Macedonian kings. This proved costly as Perdiccas reneged on the financial subsidy he had promised Brasidas, who now received only a third of that promised. Moreover, according to Thucydides (4.83), Perdiccas believed himself poorly treated, which may mean that he realized that Brasidas was not impressed by a Macedonian king, that it was the Spartan, unsurprisingly, who would dictate affairs.

Delium – The First Big Battle of the War

Brasidas' successes at Megara and in the north posed real threats to Athens, but closer to home Thebes posed an even greater menace. The two cities had long disputed several border areas, particularly Plataea, which by now had paid the ultimate price for its loyalty to Athens – captured and turned into a part of 'Greater Boeotia'. This longstanding animosity at last resulted in a full-scale battle, that at Delium in 424, the first major hoplite fight of the war.[29]

Two previous campaigning seasons had produced little, and now in early November 424 Demosthenes, the victor of Pylos, and a colleague, Hippocrates, planned a three-pronged attack on Thebes and Boeotia.[30] From the port of Naupactus, Demosthenes would sail with forty ships and a force to seize the port of Siphae, belonging to Thespiae, which would be betrayed to him. Inland Chaeronea and the surrounding area would be seized by prospective Athenian allies creating yet more problems for the

Thebans. Lastly, a large Athenian army would descend on Delium lying near Tanagra and there establish a base of operations as well as a refuge for local Athenian friends.

Successful execution of such a plan would have been a challenge even if everything worked: coordinating the operation of forces coming from different start points, even in modern armies, is not easily done and here the Athenians failed: Demosthenes arrived at Siphae prematurely, while Hippocrates had not even begun moving out of Athens. No less critical than timing is intelligence, and here too the Athenian plan failed. A spy learned the details of the plan, and passed them on to the Spartans who informed the Thebans. When Demosthenes arrived at Siphae, a Boeotian garrison was in place forcing him to sail off, mission failed. Similarly, Athenian friends in Chaeronea and elsewhere were compromised and dared not lift a finger. When Hippocrates reached Delium there were no friends to be found – he and his army were entirely on their own.

We are left to conjecture if Demosthenes attempted to get a dispatch to Athens with report of the plan's failure.[31] In any case, with the operation completely bungled, Hippocrates should have returned to Athens where the plan's many failures could be analyzed. Instead he stuck with his orders and proceeded to spend nearly three days fortifying the temple of Apollo and its precinct, in effect trespassing on sacred ground and violating religious scruples. As completion neared he sent back to Athens a number of his light-armed troops, probably as an escort for the crowd of workers brought along as a labor force. The main body of his troops, some 7000 hoplites and a force of cavalry, also retired to a position just inside the Attic–Boeotian frontier where they stacked arms and waited for their commander, who remained at the temple site supervising final touches to the defensive works. Here too Hippocrates made a poor decision: a general's place is with his army, not performing a subordinate's task.

While the Athenians dawdled at Delium, the full force of the Theban army was descending on them. Led by Pagondas, Boeotarch of the Boeotian Confederacy, an army of some 18,000 infantry (both light and heavy) and cavalry was about to hit the Athenians standing by their arms, clueless to their imminent danger. Hippocrates could not have reached his troops much before the arrival of the Thebans and when he did he would have (or should have) made a horrifying discovery. His men had taken position not on the high ground to their front where they could observe potential enemy movements, but below the ridge where they could see nothing.[32] This failure has to be counted again as Hippocrates' responsibility – not being present to position his men properly. The battle's site – literally on a hillside – weakens the models of some historians that hoplite armies sought out level ground on which to fight.[33] In reality, armies then as in later times often make mistakes in taking up positions and fighting on poorly chosen ground.

The battle that followed became a black day for Athens. In hoplite warfare the right was the post of honor, always going to the bravest and strongest. The reason for this lay in the rightward drift of hoplite armies as they approached their opponent, a drift caused by men sliding sideways as they moved forward, trying to cover their unshielded side under the shield of the man on their right (Thuc. 5.71.1). At Delium Hippocrates had arranged his men in a standard formation, eight ranks deep occupying a front perhaps a half mile in length with a depth of up to 100 yards as an interval separated each rank[34] Pagondas dispersed his troops differently. His right consisted of the Thebans, excellent soldiers now standing in ranks twenty-five deep. The remainder of the Theban force, comprising the Boeotian contingents, extended to the left of the Thebans and in the same depth as the Athenians.

As both sides formed ranks, the two generals spoke to their troops. Pagondas reminded his of how only thirteen years earlier they had beaten the Athenians at Coronea (Thuc. 4.92.6–7), as effective a pep talk any general can give his men. On the other side Hippocrates must have been in a near panic. Caught unaware, he had to hurry everything and could only say a few things before the Boeotians began moving rapidly – downhill – toward them (Thuc. 4.95–96.1). Outpositioned and outnumbered, though they probably would not have realized this, the Athenians gamely advanced – at the run – toward the oncoming Thebans. In this they demonstrated great courage and discipline.

The crash of two quickly moving formations of heavily armed soldiers must have been terrific and a number of men must have gone down at once.[35] Moreover, not all of them would have been equally strong or brave in resisting an opponent's shield – some would have given way more than others. And some would not have been brave at all and would have begun quickly looking for a way out, some way of disengaging as soon as possible. What all of this points to is a mass of men fighting, pushing, shoving with spears and shields, with the pre-battle ranks breaking down rather quickly.[36]

The sights and sounds of this fight – like any battle ancient or modern – are nearly beyond the comprehension of the inexperienced. The battle-

Figure 5.3 The clash of hoplites: here an Athenian tramples over a fallen enemy who attempts defense. The Athenian's raised arm reveals the sword he also carries.

ground itself would have become, as Thucydides suggests, littered with bodies of the wounded, dying, and dead making it difficult to walk and fight at the same time. Blood and lots of it would have made the ground slippery and the air foul. The noise and confusion would have been bewildering and disorienting all at once, a reaction known too in modern combat. Thucydides remarks that in battle no one knew much more than what happened right in front of him (Thuc. 7.44.1). But this remark should not be pressed too far. In fact Epizelus at Marathon saw the man next to him killed, while a few years after Delium, Brasidas' men would observe his mortal wound and carry him from the field at Amphipolis. Hoplite battle was much more than simply pushing and shoving like some rugby scrum and some modern historians fail to understand this.[37] In fact men die, and horribly: spears into the chest and groin, heads crushed by swords.[38]

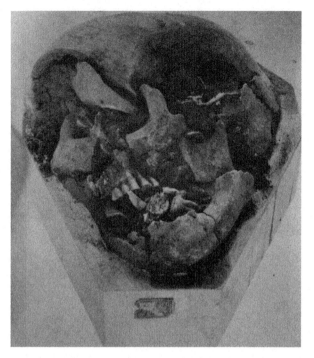

Figure 5.4 This Theban soldier died from massive head trauma, perhaps caused by the downward stroke of a cavalryman's sword. Though after Delium, such wounds in the Peloponnesian War were little different.

In the fighting that followed the initial clash, the right wings of each army prevailed, the usual outcome in a fight where the best fight those inferior to them: the Athenian right routed the men of Tanagra and Orchomenus, and closed viciously around those of Thespiae who, like their forebears at Thermopylae in 480, fought tenaciously suffering severe casualties.[39] In the fighting some Athenians got turned around and mixed up with them, and were struck down by their own men, an early example of 'friendly fire'. This confusion in the ranks also points to chaos that was hoplite battle and how the notion of nice, neatly ordered ranks is but an academic novelty.

But on the Boeotian right, the Thebans had the advantage: formed more deeply than the Athenians opposite, the Thebans steadily pushed them back. Yet even now and despite so many Athenian mistakes, the battle remained in doubt. At this critical moment Pagondas ordered up his cavalry, who delivered a flanking attack hitting the Athenians from behind and causing a panic as they believed a second army was now falling upon them.

An Athenian rout followed as a near contemporary source tells. In the *Symposium*, Plato relates how Socrates, who fought this day at Delium, finally gave way with the rest of the Athenians. Many blindly ran for their lives only to be cut down by the Boeotian cavalry, speared in the back. Socrates, however, calmly marched off in the company of Laches the general and Alcibiades, who later claimed that of the two, Socrates was much the more forbidding.[40] With his spear and shield ready in defense, Socrates stood ready to sell his life dearly. As Alcibiades tells, any opponent will avoid someone like this, preferring instead those panicked and blindly running away.[41]

Delium took the lives of at least 1500 men – nearly 1000 Athenians including the unfortunate Hippocrates, and some 500 Boeotians, mostly the men of Thespiae and Tanagra. For the Athenians, the losses were staggering. These 1000 men proportionally represented nearly ten percent of available hoplite strength: Delium was like the first day of the Somme 1916, or as if in 2009 Iraq, US forces lost 14,000 men in a single day. In the case of the latter, even with the vast population of the United States, such losses would be catastrophic, certainly to the politicians and to the public at large.[42]

Victor Hanson has suggested that Delium 'appears to have lasted not more than a few minutes', but that so many men could die in so little time seems unrealistic.[43] Killing with spears and swords is not easy – many more men would have been wounded than killed – and with thousands of men fighting, and pushing their way forward to replace the fallen, the duration of the hoplite battle would have been an affair that lasted hours rather than minutes. At Delium, for example, Thucydides relates that the Theban right even with its deep ranks could only push the Athenians back slowly, and it was while this happened that Pagondas observed his left reeling from the Athenian attack. At this point he ordered up his cavalry who, attacking, broke the Athenian resolve and turned them to flight. All of this would take some time to happen, not a matter of minutes.[44] Thucydides does not tell us how long the fighting lasted, when it began or when it ended. This sort of information is seldom found in ancient accounts of battles, but occasionally references are made to the duration of a hoplite fight. Opposing armies fought at Tanagra (457) over the course of two days, and in 423/2 the armies of Mantinea and Tegea fought at Laodicium until nightfall and even then issue remained in doubt.[45]

Delium was a disaster for the Athenians, but worse was to come. In hoplite battle, traditionally the vanquished could approach the victors, usually the next day and ask to recover their dead. This request was formulaic and signaled an admission of defeat. On this occasion, however, the Thebans refused the Athenian request – something that hardly ever happened. The Theban pretext was that the Athenians had trespassed on sacred ground, had turned a religious precinct into an armed camp and were guilty of sacrilege. The Athenians denied the Theban accusation and claimed that there was no violation of sacred law, that there was even a law permitting such action.[46] But the resulting impasse left the Athenian dead on the ground for some seventeen days exposed to the ravages of animals and the elements. A passage from Menander's *Aspis* (69–79, third century but relevant here) makes clear that what the Athenians finally collected was not pretty: bloated, blackened bodies, virtually unrecognizable. This horror left a mark in the literary tradition as Euripides' *Suppliant Women* makes clear. While the play, dating from c. 420–415, probably refers, among other things, to the momentary fling with democracy in Argos, it also makes prominent mention of the rituals given to the war dead, as well as an instance of the refusal of burial of such rites. Euripides' reference to Thebes makes clear that it is the Thebans he has in mind and their conduct after Delium provides the context.[47]

A disaster for the Athenians, Delium was a spectacular success for the Thebans. Not only did the Athenians lose 1000 men, there was also the loss of much wealth that the Thebans exploited. Stripping the dead, again naked, meant taking everything of value – weapons, defensive armor, shields, and whatever personal items there may have been including money. From all this the Thebans collected enough wealth to build a colonnade in their marketplace which they adorned with shields, armor and bronze statues. Today in the small municipal museum of Thebes five funeral stelae of men killed at Delium – those of Mnason and Athanias among others – are still to be seen.[48] The Thebans also inaugurated a new festival called the Delia which commemorated the victory for years to come.[49] Victory in war brought not only glory and civic pride to Thebes, but wealth too. In Thespiae there was less in the way of celebration – losses had been heavy, and these the Thespians honored with a monument naming the names of the fallen.[50]

An Athenian Defeat in the North

Brasidas worked to expand his alliance and soon an opportunity arose with Acanthus, a colony of Andros and a member of the Athenian empire. Timing is often everything, and at Acanthus Brasidas' was impeccable. As he approached the city with his army the Acanthians had not yet brought in their harvest, and they surely knew what a Spartan army could do to the countryside – the news of eight years of Spartan invasions in Attica had certainly preceded him. But Brasidas did not act rashly and instead asked only to speak with the people and tell them of his plans and hopes for them all. Thucydides notes that he was not a bad speaker 'for a Spartan' and the speech attributed to him was seductive (Thuc. 4.84.2–87). He emphasized freedom and autonomy from Athenian oppression, adding that he had no interest in becoming involved in the city's internal politics. While his oratory may have been smooth, it was the prospect of burning orchards and vineyards that dazzled the Acanthians, who voted to break with Athens and embrace Brasidas' call to freedom.[51]

While winter often delayed or caused the postponement of military operations, Brasidas remained active. His success with Acanthus and elsewhere in the north gave him the strength and whetted his appetite for more, and so he moved against the strategic city of Amphipolis. The foundation of Amphipolis had not been easy for the Athenians. A colonial venture in the 460s, it had been nearly wiped out. But the Athenians persevered as Amphipolis' location gave access to all kinds of natural resources – gold, timber, and much else – making it a valuable place which the Athenians would not yield without a stubborn fight.[52] Brasidas, however, had many friends in the nearby city of Argilus and these and others elsewhere became a fifth column that allowed him to move against the city easily.

Eucles, the Athenian general given responsibility for defending the city, sent for relief to a colleague, Thucydides, who was stationed at Thasos with a small squadron of ships. Upon hearing of the dangers facing the city, Thucydides immediately set sail, hoping that he could relieve Amphipolis, at very least its port of Eion. But Brasidas appealed to the great majority of Amphipolis' inhabitants, offering unhindered withdrawal from the city to the Athenians within (who were the minority), while the political rights of everyone remaining would be respected. Thucydides could not counter the political rhetoric and by the time he arrived in the area, Amphipolis had fallen. Eion was rescued, denied Brasidas who came within a breath of taking it, but this did not save Thucydides. The general would go into exile rather than return home to report a failure to an unhappy Athenian audience. Thus relieved of his military and political career, Thucydides returned to the writing of his account of the war, something he tells he had begun from its beginning.[53]

The loss of Amphipolis, coming on the heels of the defeat at Delium, alarmed and disheartened the Athenians: not only were there economic and material losses, they also could see that Brasidas was becoming popular in the region with his talk of freedom and the Athenians feared even more defections among their allies. This in fact happened: a number of small towns near Amphipolis embraced his cause, and then he moved against Torone, an Athenian foundation, which also fell to him.

Brasidas' successes cost the Athenians much and lifted Spartan spirits, and encouraged many in Sparta that the prisoners held in Athens might be freed. A one-year truce, sometimes called Laches' Truce, was arranged in 423. It stipulated that each side was, basically, to remain in place while negotiations were conducted to arrange for a longer and more durable peace.[54] But Brasidas' fame and personality, as Thucydides would have it, scuttled the negotiations. Scione, a city in the Chalicdice, broke away from Athens and took up the cause of freedom that Brasidas had so effectively announced. This was discovered when Athenian and Spartan representatives arrived in the area to announce the truce, and the Athenians were furious at what they saw as Brasidas' and Scione's treachery. Brasidas objected, arguing that Scione had come over to him before proclamation of the peace. Now that he held it, he refused to surrender it and Spartan authorities backed him up (Thuc. 4.120–3). Thucydides supports the lead Athenian negotiator, who calculated that the peace was in place when Scione revolted. Brasidas and the Spartans refused to budge, however, and in fact it was now the Athenians who refused to arbitrate the dispute. Athenian losses were further compounded when Mende, another local community, also broke free and joined Brasidas.

But not everything went Brasidas' way. Perdiccas of Macedonia still desired to eliminate Arrhabaeus, his Lyncestian rival, and Brasidas had little choice but to cooperate at last. In the campaign that followed the reluctant allies defeated Arrhabaeus. As they celebrated their victory, the mutual antagonism of Perdiccas and Brasidas again surfaced. Perdiccas had recruited Illyrian mercenaries to add to the allied army and with these he hoped to complete the destruction of Arrhabaeus. Brasidas, however, was more concerned about the allied communities he had left behind, especially Mende, which was exposed to Athenian attack. But the Illyrian mercenaries decided the issue. They betrayed their alliance with Perdiccas and joined his rival Arrhabaeus and this terrified the Macedonians and the other local troops composing Perdiccas' army. Panicked, they fled in the night abandoning Brasidas and his troops to face alone the onslaught of the Illyrians and Lyncestian Macedonians.

Surrounded, Brasidas kept a cool head. He organized his troops into marching squares and proceeded to fight his way out of Lyncestian territory and back into lower Macedonia. Upon reaching safety, the suppressed fury of Brasidas' troops bubbled up. As they marched the soldiers slaughtered any livestock they encountered and appropriated the abandoned baggage left behind by Perdiccas' fleeing army. This was the final straw for Perdiccas, who now broke with his ally and began to consider how he might come to an arrangement with the Athenians.[55]

Notes

1 Thuc. 4.3.1 implies that Demosthenes had a plan; Thucydides would still have been in Athens at this time and may have gotten this information directly from Demosthenes. While campaigning in the area the previous year he may have noticed the quiet bay of Pylos and thought that it offered the Athenians a strategic edge if they would only take it.

2 Lazenby 2004: 82 overlooks the 'stopping power of water' in assessing the Athenian success at Pylos (and at Methana and the Corinthiad), though he acknowledges that Sparta's 'heartland' lay too far from the sea for raiding to affect it.

3 Thuc. 4.8.9. Thucydides adds that the Spartans had helots with them, which would mean that Athenians may have faced nearly 1000 fighters on the island. On the helots and their military roles see below; Thuc. 4.19.1 notes the phrase, 'men of the island'.

4 See P-B 52, 94, with Hornblower 2: 160–1, Loomis 1992: 53–4.

5 Thuc. 4.8.9, 38.5, with Hornblower 1: 193. See also Cartledge 1987: 41–2 (on the duty assignment) and Hunt 1998: 56–62 (helot soldiers).

6 Thuc. 5.66.3–4. See also Xen. *Lac.* 11.5–10, Hodkinson 2006: 130, for further discussion of Spartan military organization.

7 In the war's opening campaign, the Athenians attacked the unguarded but walled town of Methone in the Peloponnese. Brasidas learned of this and led a 100-man counter-attack that drove off the Athenians, earning him the war's first honors (Thuc. 2.25.1–2).

8   Thuc. 4.15, and 5.15.1, which adds that the Spartan force isolated on the island included prominent and well-connected Spartans. See also Lazenby 2004: 73, 79.

9   Thuc. 4.21–2, with Hornblower 2: 174–6 and Low 2007: 224.

10 See Andoc. 3.29, with de Ste. Croix 1972: 108 and MacDowell 1962: 144–5 (with bibliography); Briant 2002: 591 concludes that these negotiations may argue that Athens and Persia desired to avoid hostilities. Thuc. 4.50.3, however, suggests that nothing came of the Athenian efforts to discuss an alliance with the Persians.

11 Thuc. 4.40 (Greek amazement at the Spartan surrender), 5.28 (Argive confidence, with 5.14.4, and Gomme-Andrewes-Dover 4: 658), 6.16.6 (Spartan self-doubts in 415: but the speaker is Alcibiades, the remark self-serving. Thuc. 5.75.3 states just the opposite of what Alcibiades claims).

12 Cawkwell 1997: 50–5 argues that Thucydides does not assess Demosthenes' military talents at all justly, suggesting that Demosthenes was just lucky.

13 Paus. 1.13.5 (Sphacteria as theft), Thuc. 5.9 (Brasidas and wartime stratagems).

14 As in the case of Epitadas; on Clearchus see Tritle 2004. There is no evidence for any of the prisoners' identities. Clearchus, however, later refused to accept the orders of Spartan authorities, breaking away and following a mercenary life. Both might be expected from one who believed himself dishonored by his own actions as well as those of his own state. See also Thuc. 5.34.2 and pp. 92–3.

15 Thuc. 5.34.2, with Gomme-Andrewes-Dover 4: 36; Thuc. 4.40.2, with Tritle 2000: 65–6 where it is placed in a context of survivor's guilt.

16 Ar. *Ach*. See the introduction in Sommerstein 1980.

17 See pp. 59–60.

18 Eur. *Hec*. The date is uncertain, but 425/4 seems to fit best; see Arrowsmith 1958 for introduction and translation.

19 On this campaign and the helots see pp. 95–7.

20 Hornblower 2: 264–7 and Gomme 3: 547–8 discuss the passage. See most recently Harvey 2004: 199–217 and Paradiso 2004: 179–98, discussing the incident in the same volume. Harvey argues for a massacre of helots, while Paradiso rejects, rightly in my view, the historicity of the event.

21 Thuc. 4.26.5 (helots swimming to Sphacteria, receiving freedom), 5.34.1 (Brasidas' helot veterans receiving freedom and land).

22 Thuc. 4.46–8, with Hornblower 2: 204–5, who calls Thucydides' narrative 'revolting'.

23 Thuc. 4.58–65; Westlake 1969: 174–202, suggests that Thucydides regarded Hermocrates as a hero, a man of integrity and principle.

24 On Athens and the north see de Ste. Croix 1972: 48.

25 Suggested by Michell 1952: 40, who concedes there is no evidence, but he is surely right. Thuc. 5.34.1 refers to the freedom and land later given to Brasidas'

helot veterans. A distinction is drawn between these men and the freed helots known as *neodamodeis*, which argues that Brasidas' helots were probably *mothones*. *Mothakes* may refer to the helot squires or 'shield-bearers' who went into battle with the Spartiates (so Michell 337), but Cartledge 1987: 28 suggests that the terms are interchangeable.

26 Thuc. 4.66–74, with Gomme 3: 528–36 and Hornblower 2: 230–44.

27 See p. 27 and Perdiccas' support of Potidaea against the Athenians.

28 Brasidas' rapid march through Thessaly demonstrates his instinct for speedy and decisive action. Note too his advice, rejected, to Alcidas on arriving at Corcyra in 427 (Thuc. 3.79), demonstrating the same principles.

29 See Lazenby 2004: 86–91 for discussion.

30 On the date see Gomme 3: 558.

31 Roisman 1993: 50 seems to fault Demosthenes for leaving Hippocrates in the lurch, not informing him of the operation's failures. But given the distance separating the two commanders and the lack of communications, Hippocrates should have taken some initiative in responding to a changing situation. On the other hand, the Athenian *demos* did not take failure or disappointment lightly.

32 Noted clearly in Henderson 1927: 234 (map).

33 E.g., Hanson 2005: 142, 153. Short of fighting on prepared parade grounds, the idea that Greek hoplite battles took place on nicely even ground should be dismissed. Cf. Plut. *Aem.* 20.7 and the description of the battlefield at Pydna where the Macedonian phalanx stumbled over broken ground before the Roman legions, this after initially pushing the Romans back.

34 The seventh-century Chigi vase depicts hoplites advancing with an interval between ranks. While it is difficult to estimate the space between ranks, an interval of several yards plus another for each rank seems conservative. See Ratto 2006: 78 (photograph of the vase); cf. van Wees 2004: 170–2.

35 Hanson 2005: 129–30 obscures the Athenian response to the Theban advance: Thuc. 4.96.1 makes clear that the Athenians ran uphill to meet the Thebans, no mean feat given the equipment they carried.

36 The nature of hoplite battle is among the more contested subjects in Greek history. The picture suggested here is similar to that of Pritchett 4: 1–93, at 91–3; see also Rawlings 2007: 81–103, van Wees 2004: 188–95.

37 Cf. Sabin 2000 with Cawkwell 1997: 10, the latter imagining there is a difference between 'a well-directed spear' and 'a random bullet'. But as American soldiers in World War II and Vietnam, commonly said, 'Don't worry about the one with your name on it – worry about those addressed 'To whom it may concern'.

38 See Xen. *Ages.* 2.14–5 for such a picture as that described here. Salazar 2000: 233–5 describes various fatal wounds. These would not include men who later died from sepsis, those who became permanently incapacitated either physi-

cally or psychically. On the latter see the discussion on Gorgias' *Helen* and the Spartan *tresantes*, pp. 163–4, nn. 38–9.

39 This was the second time since 480 that the men of Thespiae lost heavily in battle. See Hanson 1999 for discussion of their fate at Delium.

40 Develin 1989: 133 suggests that Laches was not *strategos* on this occasion. Perhaps, but the size of the Athenian army argues for the assignment of several generals, the sources just do not identify them.

41 Pl. *Sym.* 219e–221b.

42 Rubincam 1991 discusses battlefield casualties but without noting what these figures represent to the populations. See p. 57 for Athenian military manpower.

43 Hanson 2005: 128; cf. Pritchett 4: 46–51, who argues that battles lasted a 'long time'.

44 Cf. Hanson 2005: 19.

45 Tanagra: Thuc. 107.2, Diod. 11.80, Paus. 1.29.6; Laodicum: Thuc. 4.134.1–2; Demosthenes' battle at Olpae also lasted daylong (Thuc. 3.109.1).

46 See Low 2007: 224–6 for discussion.

47 Eur. *Supp.* 10–19, 24–7, 60–3, 75–87.

48 See Ratto 2006: 250 and Tritle 2000: 176 for photographs.

49 Diod. 12.70.5 provides the details, unmentioned by Thucydides; see also Thuc. 7.82.3 and Pritchett 1: 53–92.

50 See Hanson 1999, Low 2003: 104–9.

51 Thuc. 4.84.2–87, with Gomme 3: 551–8. See also Raaflaub 2004: 149–50, 225–6 for discussion of Brasidas' speech and his use of freedom in this speech.

52 Thuc. 4.102.1, with Hornblower 2: 319–45.

53 Thuc. 4.106.3, with Hornblower 2: 337–8.

54 Thuc. 4.117–19, with Gomme 3: 593–607 and Hornblower 2: 356–75. See also Cawkwell 1997: 65, Lazenby 2004: 96.

55 Thuc. 4.124–8, with Gomme 3: 612–19. Again this is not the kind of thing to interest Thucydides, but the killing of the animals expresses relief at survival and rage at the loss of friends. See O'Brien 1990: 78–80.

6

'WEEPING FOR JOY'

The break with Perdiccas left Brasidas between two enemies whose common interests would surely bring them together sooner rather than later. The Athenians, perhaps energized by what they regarded as yet another example of Spartan treachery – Brasidas' obstinate refusal to give up Scione – resolved not to give up without a fight. Soon large forces – more than fifty ships and 3000 troops – arrived in the area of the Chalcidice under the command of Nicias and Nicostratus. The fighting was protracted, but the Athenians recovered Mende and then turned their attention to Scione. Their resolve here knew no bounds as a motion had already been enacted condemning the Scioneans to death. Cleon had proposed the motion and the Athenians were determined to carry it out (Thuc. 4.129–31).

Brasidas' successes had turned the north into a primary battleground and both sides moved to improve their chances of victory. The Spartans sent out a new force commanded by Ischagoras to join Brasidas; also included in their number were some senior men, Ameinias and Aristeus, who had come to assess the situation (Thuc. 4.132.2–3). Athenian naval power forced them to take the overland route through central Greece, and here the Athenians moved to block them. Nicias informed Perdiccas that proof was needed of his loyalty to the newly made Athenian alliance. He responded by persuading his Thessalian friends to oppose Ischagoras' relief force, but in the end these failed to deliver: Ischagoras duly arrived. Brasidas established several of the younger men in Amphipolis (Clearidas) and Torone (Pasitelidas).

While the truce expired in the following summer (422/1), the previous year's struggle around Scione and Mende reveals that it was a truce in name only.[1] The Athenians dispatched additional forces into the area, making an all-out effort to accomplish their aims. In command of this new force was Cleon, whose earlier success on Sphacteria had perhaps convinced him that he possessed talent as a soldier.[2] Thucydides does not seem to think so. On his arrival, he added to his command some of the Athenian forces in the area and moved against Torone. Brasidas, he had learned, was away and Cleon seized the moment to attack the city which was weakly held. As it turned out, Pasitelidas, the newly appointed commander, could not mount an effective defense and not only lost the city to Cleon, but along with a number of his troops was captured. Pasitelidas soon joined the other Spartan prisoners in Athens (Thuc. 5.2–3.2).

Cleon then turned his attention to Brasidas and Amphipolis. He established a base at Eion and sent word to Perdiccas and Polles, a Thracian king, that they should make good on their alliances with Athens and send him troops. While he waited for them to comply, Brasidas consolidated his defenses and forces around Amphipolis. Unlike Cleon (and Hippocrates at Delium), Brasidas understood the tactical value of high ground and established his base at Cerdylium. From this base not far from Amphipolis he could observe Cleon's every move.

Brasidas recognized Cleon's lack of strategic sense. He also apparently thought, or at least Thucydides attributes to him, that Cleon would become overconfident once he learned that Brasidas' forces were inferior to his own in number. But as the two armies waited, a malaise began to form in the Athenian, as soldiers began grumbling about the greatness of Brasidas and the ineptitude of Cleon.[3] Perhaps learning this, Cleon moved up to Amphipolis with the idea of putting his soldiers to work and also seeing how he might exploit a development. In any case he played into Brasidas' hands. Brasidas had moved his troops into Amphipolis where Cleon would not really be able to determine his strength, but Brasidas could see his numbers and dispositions clearly. Rather than give Cleon the opportunity to establish a siege, Brasidas prepared to attack an unsuspecting and overconfident opponent. His success would be complete.

Cleon brought his forces up to a vantage point which provided commander and troops with a distant look into the city. Brasidas could be seen conducting sacrifices as his men stood at arms, waiting orders and the pronouncement of the will of the gods. His pre-battle warm-up speech probably came now too. But scouts also brought word that behind the city gates, feet and hooves could be seen – clear signs that an assault was imminent.

Not prepared for battle, Cleon was unwilling to engage until the hoped-for reinforcements arrived. As he did so, an observant Brasidas turned to his men and told them that the Athenians would not stand and fight – he could see their heads and spears bobbing and sensed that on being attacked they would break ranks (Thuc. 5.10.2). As he spoke, Cleon gave orders to withdraw. But in doing so he endangered his own men and played into the hands of Brasidas: the left wing of his army had to lead the retirement and as they withdrew the right wing followed. As the Athenians turned and moved, they exposed their unshielded right sides. At this point Brasidas and a picked force charged out of one gate and pounced on the retreating Athenians. This unexpected charge unnerved and panicked them just as Brasidas had predicted. A few moments later the rest of Brasidas' army charged out of other gates and hit the Athenians on all sides.

Outnumbered, Brasidas' troops fought well, as most Athenians thought only of escape. Early in the fight, Brasidas was mortally wounded, but as he was quickly carried from the field this was hardly noticed. Cleon, as Thucydides notes, 'had no intention of standing his ground' and took to flight immediately. Not quick enough, one of Brasidas' peltasts chased him down and, unheroically, Cleon died.

The Athenian right wing, perhaps some 600 men or more including Athenians as well as allies, maintained its formation. Brasidas had been wrong about these men. Led now by their junior commanders, these men closed ranks and fought courageously. Clearidas, assuming command for the fallen Brasidas, reorganized his forces and with the Chalcidian cavalry and allied peltasts made several determined assaults. Finally, under a hail of spears what was left of the Athenian right at last gave way and the rout was complete (Thuc. 5.10.9). The 'last stand' made by the Athenian right wing would have taken some time, again demonstrating that Greek infantry battle was not a simple affair measured in minutes.

The Athenians lost some 600 men, the Spartans seven. But one of these was Brasidas, who like Wolfe at Quebec and Epaminondas at Second Mantinea (362), lived just long enough to learn that his men had won a spectacular victory (Thuc. 5.10.11). Militarily, it was an unqualified success for the Spartans. Amphipolis had been successfully defended and despite many efforts in the future, the Athenians would never recover it. As for Brasidas, the people of Amphipolis honored him as the real founder of their city, dedicating a hero's shrine at his tomb. All visible ties to Hagnon, the Athenian who had founded the city, and to Athens were destroyed wherever possible (Thuc. 5.11.1). Such honors reveal equally the reputations enjoyed by Brasidas and the Athenians.

The Peace of Nicias

Cleon's death at Amphipolis enabled his adversary Nicias to advance his more moderate ways and ideas. Perhaps eight or nine months later, Aristophanes staged at the Athenian City Dionysia in spring 421 his play *Peace*. In a mad, farcical comedy featuring flying dung beetles, sarcastic labeling of war-mongering generals, like Lamachus, and stupid politicians, like Hyperbolus, capped off by the seduction of Peace, Aristophanes takes time to make some serious comments. He labels the lately dead Cleon and Brasidas the 'pestles' in the 'sauce bowl' of war (Ar. *Pax* 270–82), asserting that their provocative acts stirred up the Greeks to continue fighting: each side offering peace only when it held an advantage like the Athenians buoyed by their success at Sphacteria and capture of Spartan POWs. He rebukes everyone for their betrayal of Greece, fighting each other all to the benefit of the 'barbarians' or Persians – a theme to which he will return in the future. War profiteers were not ignored either: greedy Argives taking money from both Athens and Sparta and arms merchants making a killing from their sales were both rebuked. Aristophanes seems to take special delight in showing their unhappiness at losing so much business (*Pax* 1209–64). But as the prospects for peace loomed large, the Greeks began jumping with joy as the reconciled cities could see an end to the fighting (*Pax* 538–40). Happiest of these were the farmers who joined the play's hero Trygaeus in restoring Peace. Not only thrilled by the prospect of returning to their fields unmolested by invading armies, these men jumped for joy at their release from military service, a burden that fell on them with greater frequency than the socially connected urban loafers.

As Aristophanes wrote his drama and critique of wartime Athenian and Greek society, Athenian and Spartan leaders were stumbling toward a settlement that would in fact bring the peace that Aristophanes' play reflects. On the Athenian side, Nicias, an experienced leader, and cautious general, now emerged as the leading political voice in Athens. Taking advantage of prevailing war weariness in Athens, made worse by defeats (and losses of life) at Delium and Amphipolis, rebellion in Mytilene and chaos in Corcyra, Nicias was able to inch the Athenians to the conference table.

For its part Sparta may have had an even greater desire for peace. Uppermost in the minds of many Spartans was the safety, literally the survival, of more than 300 of their friends and relatives held as POWs in Athens, their lives totally dependent on Spartan good behavior.[4] This may explain the return to Sparta of Pleistoanax, exiled on charges of bribery the last nineteen years, and his resumption of his kingship (probably c. 426). From the beginning he faced great hostility, as his enemies blamed him for all the setbacks the Spartans had recently suffered (Thuc. 5.16.2–3).

Pleistoanax may have been more a believer, first, in what was best for Sparta, rather than any sense of pan-hellenism or love for Athens. Once some Athenian was running down the Spartans saying how uneducated they were. Pleistoanx replied, 'Yes, you're right – we're the only Greeks who have learned nothing from you Athenians' (Plut. *Mor.* 231D). Still, he may have been more willing than many Spartans to deal with the Athenians and such views were now timely.[5] Athenian raids from bases in Pylos and Cythera were disrupting the rural economy of Sparta and providing safe havens for fleeing helots. Lastly, an Argive–Spartan truce was due to expire soon, and the Spartans were not eager to fight a two-front war (Thuc. 5.14). Pleistoanax was the right man at the right time for Sparta.

The settlement that Athens and Sparta reached just a few weeks after the performance of Aristophanes' *Peace* (which placed second) came in March 421. While ten commissioners from each side worked out the details, the agreement reached has since been called the Peace of Nicias. It secured a peace on the basis that everyone should keep what they had before the war, but this did not quite happen. Thebes retained Plataea (which had surrendered voluntarily, so the Thebans claimed) and in compensation Athens kept Nisaea, the fortified Megarian port and several Corinthian territories in western Greece.[6] The Plataean reaction to all this wheeling and dealing is unrecorded.

In their eagerness for peace, and return of their men, the Spartans abandoned to the Athenians a number of communities in the north won over by Brasidas. These Athens recovered, but concession of certain freedoms guaranteed these states made their return incomplete. Scione, however, suffered the full fury of Athenian wrath: once the town was taken, the men of military age were killed and everyone else sold into slavery (Thuc. 5.32.1). The land was then given over to the Plataeans, survivors of yet another, this time Theban, massacre. The peace ended what the Greeks called the 'Ten Years' or 'Archidamian War', and even Thucydides, the war's historian, seems to have thought that it was over.[7] But the battles and horrors only appeared to have ended.

Athenians and Greeks greeted the apparent return of peace with tears of joy and dance. An Athenian, more likely an Epidaurian resident in

Athens, Telemachus, went further. He traveled (home) to Epidaurus in the Peloponnese and returned to Athens with the healing god Asclepius and his daughter Hygieia ('Health') and founded a new shrine for the god, probably first in the Piraeus and then later at the foot of the acropolis. For some time, some sources claim, the god's earthly manifestation, a snake, resided in the home of the dramatist Sophocles, who received the honorific *Dexion* or 'receiver' and after his own death a hero's shrine.

Asclepius took Athens by storm. A healing god, many of the cult offerings dedicated to him are associated with fertility, votive breasts and genitalia, but the god could answer any appeal for a cure. While his arrival in Athens may be explained by its intrinsic appeal – the sick want to get well in any time or place – the trauma of war surely attracted the Athenians to Asclepius too. In the Epidaurian miracle inscriptions several texts relate the healing of the war wounded and such calls were surely made in Athens too, explaining again the cult's rapid growth and popularity.[8]

Over the next ten years and at his own expense, Telemachus built a sanctuary for Asclepius at the foot of the acropolis. This included an Ionic stoa with rooms for priests, pilgrims, and suppliants, as well a small temple for the cult statue (and altar) and a small pool, perhaps a home for the sacred snake or a pool to treat ailing men (kidney stones) and women (nursing difficulties). So popular was the new cult that dedications to the older cult of Athena Hygieia on the acropolis all but ceased. Attention now focused on an unofficial healing god located just below the ancient gods of Athens.[9]

Art in a Time of Violence

As Nicias, Pleistoanax, and like-minded Greeks hammered out their agreement, work of another kind was going on in a remote corner of Greece. In pastoral Arcadia a new temple dedicated to Apollo *Epikourios* – 'the Helper' – was going up in a place now called Bassai. Dedications of armor argue that the money funding this temple came from soldiers, the tough and much sought after Arcadians, and that the temple's cult name *Epikourios* refers to those helpers who are in fact mercenary soldiers.[10] Just as the Thebans renovated their city with the spoils taken from the Athenians at Delium, the Arcadians also found a profit in war and were able to hire some of the finest artists and builders in Greece to erect this new temple.[11]

Figure 6.1 Detail of the Ionic frieze of the temple of Apollo *Epikourios*: here Heracles and the Amazon queen Hippolyte fight, but violence dominates elsewhere in the frieze.

While the temple's architecture is of some interest thanks to the influence of its designer, the same Ictinus who assisted in the building of the Athenian Parthenon, it is the art that is of special interest. The Ionic frieze reliefs are filled with scenes of violence: the violation of sacred precincts, centaurs attacking fleeing women, Amazons attacking men (see Figure 6.1). Such scenes had been seen in art before, but here the violence is more intense. In one scene a woman clings to the statue of a god as a centaur tears at her clothes as a young man attacks the centaur. In a metope fragment a disembodied hand grabs the neck of a young woman: while the sculpture is fragmentary, the violence is not in doubt. The scenes depict an orgasm of violence that seems almost helter-skelter – Greek soldiers fighting, their opponents seemingly looking to the spectator for help.[12] Moreover, a strong sense of individualism pervades the scenes and this makes sense: the Arcadian soldiers who funded the temple regarded themselves as individual contractors of violence, fighting for themselves and the money they earned.

Across the Peloponnese the Argives began rebuilding the Heraeum, the sacred precinct to Hera which had burned down in 422 (Thuc. 4.133.2). The Heraeum would become the home of one of the great statues of the classical era, Polyclitus' *Hera*, a work if not inspired by Phidias' Athena reflects the impact of its Athenian predecessor. Known only from poor quality images preserved on coins, the ivory and gold Hera evidently sat on a throne nearly eight meters high. Though neutral, the Argives had still profited from the fighting, as Aristophanes tells, and could afford such a

Figure 6.2 Paeonius' *Nike* descending – the accompanying inscription made clear that this was a wartime victory monument over the Spartans.

magnificent statue. The Athenian connection reveals further the nature of inter-city contacts amid the fighting.[13]

Contemporaneous to the temple of Apollo *Epikourios* and Polyclitus' *Hera* is the *Nike*, or 'Victory' (see Figure 6.2), sculpted by Paeonius of Mende and dedicated in Olympia by the Messenians of Naupactus (c. 420). In this instance an inscription records that the sculpture commemorated the role played by the Messenians in defeating the Spartans at Sphacteria in 425. The place chosen for the dedication is instructive: Olympia, the major pan-hellenic site, and a gathering place where visitors could see this Messenian celebration of their victory over the hated Spartans, oppressors for hundreds of years.

While the politics and propaganda of the *Nike* of Paeonius is unmistakable, the emotional appeal and sexual allure of the statue is no less apparent. The *Nike* descends onto her pillar and as she does, the wind blows her

Figure 6.3 The *Dying Niobid* mixes sexual allure with wartime death, making clear the Rich Style of the Peloponnesian War era.

garments back leaving a rich trail of clothes behind and a sensuous body for the observer to behold. Sexual allure then symbolizes victory and, as the *Dying Niobid* shows, death too (see Figure 6.3).

The earliest large female nude statue surviving, the *Dying Niobid* may have been designed originally for a temple pediment (c. 430). The *Niobid* is shown being cut down by an arrow; she reaches to pull it from her back and as she does her dress slips from her shoulders revealing the delicate feminine features underneath. A date contemporary with the *Nike* of Paeonius and the Bassai frieze, c. late 420s, seems certain in a literary reference of the same date. In his drama *Hecuba*, Euripides vividly describes the heroic death of Polyxena, Hecuba's daughter, sacrificed at the tomb of Achilles. About to be slain, Polyxena rips her own gown, opening it to her waist, and as Euripides says, exposing her naked breasts like a sculpted goddess.[14] Not only does Euripides apparently draw for inspiration from contemporary art, but also from a world in which women could be put to death as an act of wartime necessity or simple vengeance.

These same exotic scenes also began to appear in Athens. At the same time the Arcadian mercenaries were funding their temple at Bassai, the Athenians began construction of a small temple of Athena Nike on the acropolis (c. 420–410). The frieze relief depicted a series of combat scenes, some involving the Athenians and Persians at Marathon (south panel), but others depict Athenians fighting other Greeks. The inspiration from contemporary events seems unmistakable. Perched rather precariously on a corner of the acropolis, it was surrounded by a waist-high balustrade or parapet. Among the figures in the frieze here were a series of *Nikai*, winged victories, leading animals to sacrifice, and in one scene, a bull is slaughtered. Robin Osborne suggests the significance of this scene: it is a paeon to victory in battle.[15] Construction beginning soon after the Peace of Nicias suggests that these scenes surely have a political as well as military significance.

But like the *Nike* of Paeonius, the Athenian *Nikai* also convey a strong aura of sexuality. One *Nike* shows this clearly – as she reaches down to remove her sandal as she enters sacred ground, her gown slips off her shoulder bearing it and outlining her breast, just like the *Dying Niobid* and just like the scene in Euripides' *Hecuba*. Men viewing this *Nike* would perhaps imagine Victory sexually – desirable and fleeting – but also worth fighting for. As classicist Steven Lattimore observes, the *Nikai* are unreal in their beauty and sensuousness and stand in sharp contrast with the subject matter – war and violence. But they show the emotional and sexual appeal of the 'Rich Style' and its escapist message.[16]

The pressure exerted on Greek culture and society by war has led some art historians to argue that there occurred in art a wartime expression that reflected this era of stress. Art historian J.J. Pollitt has likened developments in art at the end of the fifth century to the kind of entertainment Americans watched during the era of the Great Depression in the 1930s – movies with heroes and heroines tap-dancing 'their way with unfailing elegance through a series of soothing, inconsequential episodes to an inevitable happy, if never very believable conclusion'.[17]

Not all agree with this view, but Steven Lattimore adds that the sculpture of this so-called 'Rich Style' is at once pretty and softer and tends to be viewed from one angle. This technique he sees as rhetorical, something that again reflects the intellectual climate of the era and Greek fondness for oratory.[18] Artists and intellectuals of the Renaissance and the Age of the

Sun King argued, debated, and exchanged views on all matters of art, literature, philosophy, and aesthetics.[19] Greek artists and intellectuals of the fifth century were no different. The Roman writer and scientist Pliny the Elder tells of the rivalry and artistic competition between Zeuxis and Parrhasius. Xenophon relates the same issues in a conversation between Socrates and Parrhasius. Asked by Socrates if he could imitate nature right down to the hostile expression on a man's face, or emotions like happiness or displeasure, Parrhasius responded emphatically that he could.[20] This Euripides dramatically confirms in his depiction of Polyxena's death, which only makes sense if the audience made the connection between what they heard on stage and could see in the art and imagery around them. It seems certain that in a time of great stress and anxiety caused by war and violence, artists would not only pick up on these but bring them to life as well.

A Diplomatic Revolution

The peace agreed upon was to last fifty years, and its final clause made clear that Athens and Sparta imposed acceptance of the peace upon their allies. Aside from Athens and Sparta, there was little joy in Greece over the recent settlement. Thucydides relates that nothing was settled and that there was little 'peace' to be found: terms prescribing the return of land were ignored, violations of all kinds by all parties occurred (Thuc. 5.26.2). Corinth, Megara, Thebes, to name the most prominent, disliked the settlement: Corinth and Megara were denied recovery of strategic sites; Thebes saw that peace meant an end to greater power. Frustrated these states refused to sign the agreement. This in turn worried the Spartans who then secured a defensive alliance with Athens. The Athenian–Spartan agreement to a separate defensive treaty only increased anxieties, as the two 'superpowers' appeared to be looking after their own interests as they denied the other Greek states similar arrangements. In 420 came a series of diplomatic moves that reshaped traditional alliances, which at the same time heightened tensions all around in this era of phony 'peace'.[21]

Corinth played a key role in this diplomatic shuffle. Particularly annoyed at Sparta, Corinth made overtures to Argos for a separate alliance, basically following the example of Athens and Sparta. This could only antagonize and worry Sparta, as Argos and Sparta had a centuries-long history of bad blood. A Corinthian agreement with Argos could only weaken Spartan leadership of the Peloponnesian League and increase Spartan fears, particularly over the helot problem. Before long there were even more diplomatic overtures: Athens allying with Argos, Mantinea and Elis, the latter two old Spartan allies now abandoning their one-time leader.[22]

While Corinth successfully concluded its defensive alliance with Argos, the Argives, still anxious and desiring a little extra security, decided in summer 420 to renew their 'non-aggression' treaty with Sparta. The lingering dispute over the border area of Kynosouria threatened to disrupt negotiations, and the Argives even offered to settle the matter by a trial by combat as in olden times. The Spartans were shocked at such an offer, replying, 'you're joking'. But Sparta had no desire to open a new front and so reluctantly agreed to terms settle the matter by arbitration, though the disputed region remained Spartan.[23]

But Spartan diplomacy was walking a fine line and it soon tripped. A pact with Argos was bound to worry the Athenians and now the Spartan envoys, Andromedes, Phaedemus, and Antimenidas, proved unable to make good on their obligations to control the Boeotians. Holding Athenian POWs and the strategic city of Panacton, the Boeotians handed over the former to the Spartan envoys (who did get them to Athens), but destroyed the latter, contrary to terms of the Peace. The Athenians became more furious when a Boeotian–Spartan treaty became known, again contrary to the Peace which Athens with Sparta had agreed to dictate to the other Greeks (Thuc. 5.36–42).

These provocations played into the hands of a rising star – Alcibiades of Athens. Since Pericles' death in 429, Alcibiades had probably been looking for an opportunity to take center stage politically and claim the leadership role that he perhaps believed his as Pericles' heir and as one possessing old diplomatic ties of proxeny to Sparta.[24] Angered that the recent Peace had been brokered without him and eager to find an opportunity for political center stage, Alcibiades invited an Argive embassy to Athens (Thuc. 5.43). On learning of this and fearing there might be trouble, the Spartans sent an embassy of their own to keep the peace. The negotiations that followed were open and politic, secret and treacherous, with most of the latter Alcibiades'. The Spartan delegation in fact had a difficult task: to defend as benign their alliance with Boeotia, derail a feared Athenian alliance with Argos, and trade Panacton for Pylos. As skilled a con man as there could be, Alcibiades schemed to detach them from their alliance with Nicias while discrediting them before the Athenians. This achieved, Alcibiades secured an alliance with Argos, much to the disappointment of Sparta which failed to block it. With Argos came Mantinea and Elis, all three possessing democratic constitutions, and all three enemies of Sparta in her own backyard.[25] As for Alcibiades, he succeeded in making fools of just about every one, though time would reveal the wisdom of his duplicity.

Mantinea – Spartan Honor Reclaimed

This diplomatic shuffle solved nothing, merely creating the illusion of peace. In summer 419, the Athenians and their new allies conducted operations into the Peloponnese: the Argives went after Epidaurus while the Athenians strengthened their position in the Corinthian Gulf, persuading the people of Patrae to abandon their Spartan ties. The Spartan response was muted. Typically slow to act, they only moved now as they saw their allies in Epidaurus threatened.[26] In the following summer, 418, the confrontation that might have been expected from such botched diplomatic activity finally came.

The new Athenian confederation began to organize in summer 418, in part responding to a Spartan effort on Argos. Agis brought together a number of allies from the Peloponnese as well as Boeotia and met the Argives around Nemea. To this point only minor skirmishing had taken place. Just as the two armies were about to engage, several Argive officers asked for an impromptu peace conference which Agis granted. After discussion a truce was agreed upon and both sides disengaged and went home. On the return march there was considerable grumbling in the Spartan ranks at the wasted opportunity: the Argives had been surrounded and without cavalry, in other words trapped. Once home there was more criticism of Agis: fined and threatened with the demolition of his house, the ephors decreed that henceforth Agis would have to take the field with advisers to supervise his actions. The Argive officers were rebuked no less.[27]

A threat soon after this fiasco gave Agis a second chance. Tegea, one of Sparta's most trusted allies, seemed on the brink of defection and the Spartans hurriedly reassembled their army to save it. Leading his army against Mantinea, Agis found the Argives and their allies holding a strong defensive position. Agis formed up and gave the order to attack when out of the ranks came a voice, yelling that one bad move would not redeem another (Thuc. 5.65.2). Much to the surprise of the Argives, Agis halted the attack and withdrew, spending the rest of the day spoiling the water system of Mantinea, hoping to provoke his enemies into battle.

The next day Agis led out his army, some 11,000 men composed of Spartans, other Peloponnesians and Boeotians, stiffened with the Brasideans, (or 'Brasidas' Boys') veterans of Brasidas' northern campaigns.[28] Much to his surprise he found to his front the allied army drawn up and ready for battle – Spartan scouts and intelligence had certainly failed (Thuc. 5.56.3–66.2). The allied coalition army Agis faced was larger than his own – 1000 Athenian hoplites and 300 cavalry, joining some 6000 Argives, 3000 Elians, and 6000 Mantineans, and these now stood facing him, ready for battle. Thucydides later described Agis' army as the finest ever assembled, while the coalition they faced, although not Spartan, would have been hardly less impressive (Thuc. 5.60.3).

As the two armies advanced against each other, the right-hand drift typical of hoplite armies became acute. Agis realized this and at the last minute attempted to correct it by ordering to the left two battalions to fill the gap now opening in his ranks. Aristocles and Hipponoidas, the two commanders, receiving these orders only minutes from engaging the enemy, refused to move.[29] Not only were they about to make contact, but to maneuver left would have meant exposing their unshielded sides to the onrushing enemy.[30] As the Athenians under Cleon had found at Amphipolis, this was an invitation to disaster.

In fact the Argives and their allies were coming on quickly, perhaps at a run.[31] As in the case of the Boeotians and Athenians colliding at Delium, the resulting crash of two lines meeting must have been thunderous. Again differences in strength and courage would have meant that ranks would have been pushed back to varying depths and the fighting would have resembled a brawl. The elite Argives and Mantineans, holding the right of the allied line, plunged into the gap created by the disorganized Spartan advance, and they shoved aside the elite Skiritai and Brasideans whose flank had been uncovered. A number were killed and the Argives and Mantineans penetrated to the Spartan camp where some of the older men on guard were also killed. As they rushed forward, their laughter may have been heard over the din.[32]

On the Spartan right and in the center where Agis and his elite Spartan guard stood, all was well.[33] In the center, the Peloponnesian and Athenian troops facing Agis and his guard put up little fight, in many cases not even bothering to make a stand but turned to flight. On the far right of the Spartan line, the Tegeans and Spartans swept the Athenians before them and then wheeled left to engage the victorious Mantineans and Argives. Taken in the flank, these now reeled under a new Spartan attack and also began giving ground. This was not the first time such a flanking maneuver swept the other side from the battle. Few students of hoplite fighting seem to have noticed the limitations imposed by human anatomy on the Greek way of war. Humans can only act effectively in the direction of their hands and eyes: as soldiers move and fight their way forward they are vulnerable to lateral attacks.[34] For this reason soldiers through the ages – from battle-fields like Mantinea to those of Vietnam – have attempted to envelope or flank their enemies, to hit them quite literally in their blind spots.

The flanking movement also argues for a more fluid style of fighting than is usually imagined. Those who argue that hoplite battle consisted of an initial clash of spear and shield followed by the 'push' or mass shove have not taken sufficiently into account, like the limitations imposed by hand and eye movements noted above, the human obstacles to such a movement. Quite simply, as soldiers in the front ranks fell either slain or wounded, their bodies would become obstacles to those behind. In his classic study *The Face of Battle*, John Keegan notes that prostrate bodies make poor fighting platforms and are stumbling blocks to the heels of a man trying to defend himself against an attack to his front.[35]

As a formation of men begins to suffer casualties, gaps in its ranks will open. As they do the limitations imposed by their weapons – shield, spear, sword – and their close order will contribute to a formation's weakening. Most academics, not being experienced brawlers or fighters, will little understand that in such situations two men will gang up on one, five on three and so on.[36] What follows then is that as more men fall a formation will slowly begin to lose its integrity: the more this happens the weaker it becomes, the more ground it gives. Finally, it will give way and will turn to flight as happened at Mantinea and so many other fields of battle.

Thucydides believed that Mantinea was the greatest battle that the Greeks had fought for some time (Thuc. 5.74). It restored the prestige of Spartan soldiers and for them at least, wiped away the dishonor of Sphac-teria. But Agis' handling of the battle does not warrant the claim that the Spartan king was either a great commander or strategist, not to mention tactician.[37] Surprising too is the silence of commentators over the subse-quent condemnation of Aristocles and Hipponoidas, clearly scapegoats for Agis' bungling.[38] Moreover, too much has been made of Spartan 'profes-sionalism' and the supposed 'amateurism' of the other Greeks whom they faced in battle.[39] As Woodhouse notes in his study of the battle, one-third of the Spartan force consisted of men from Arcadia and their skill and courage were no less than the Spartans.[40]

A soldiers' battle, Mantinea was won by the courage of the individual Spartan – and allied – soldier, something noted by Thucydides (5.72), and not skill in maneuver or tactics.[41] Clearly the elite Argives and Mantineans gave the Spartans and the Peloponnesians a good fight, in fact all that they could handle. But the Spartans probably did possess an edge in skill at arms and discipline and this in the end proved decisive. Mantinea cost the lives of some 1100 allies in the new coalition. Among these were 200 Athenians – twenty percent killed in action, at least an equal figure wounded – high by any standard. Both their generals, Laches and Nicostratus, two experienced commanders, also died fighting.[42] On the Spartan side some 300 were killed (Thuc. 5.74).[43]

Mantinea was a crushing defeat for the new coalition. In the following winter, Argives friendly to Sparta launched an attack on the Argive democracy and, aided by peaceful Spartan overtures and a strong military presence, broke with Athens. Woodhouse suggests that Sparta's moderation and self-restraint was deliberate policy – that at the battle the Spartans allowed the elite Argives to escape the slaughter in order to pull off a political coup at home.[44] But the heat and conditions of battle argue against this and it seems more likely that the battle's result created new political opportunities. In any event, the Argive–Spartan alliance called for a fifty years' treaty and alliance and the return of various prisoners held by democratic Argos. Moreover, the treaty attempted to secure the Peloponnese against outsiders, namely the Athenians, who were expected to leave the Peloponnese and the forts they had established there, especially that at Epidaurus. Soon after Mantinea, now isolated, also returned to the Spartan orbit (Thuc. 5.76–81.1).

But democracy was not yet dead in Argos. Timing a rising to coincide with the distraction of a Spartan youth festival, the democrats attacked the oligarchs and after some street fighting, prevailed. Alerted by the now exiled Argive oligarchs, the Spartans marched against Argos but found that the people were in control of the city. They were also hard at work building walls to the sea to bring in aid from Athens, and in this they were not alone. Not only did women and slaves join the work, so too did Athenian workers brought in for the effort as also local volunteers – Peloponnesians unhappy with Spartan domination. A Spartan attack dismantled what wall had been built, followed up by the capture of an outlying Argive town, Hysiai. But the Argive democrats were back in control of their city and there was little the Spartans could do. In the next spring, Alcibiades arrived with a relief force from Athens. Argives of questionable loyalty were placed under arrest on nearby islands friendly to Athens (Thuc. 5.82–84.1).

End of Hope?

Not long after Mantinea Euripides addressed issues of war and reconciliation in his drama *Heracles*, the story of the greatest of Greek heroes. Euripides' play is most comfortably placed in the era of 'phoney peace' that followed the Peace of Nicias.[45] Early in the drama, Heracles' wife Megara tells her sons how their father will marry them to brides from Athens, Sparta, and Thebes (*Her.* 477–8). Members of the audience would have associated the reference with the current political climate in Greece as the formerly warring states struggled to find peace.[46]

Euripides casts Heracles as a soldier/hero who upon returning home from 'the wars' loses control and in a fit of madness, kills Megara and their children.[47] The madness is divine, the intervention of Iris and Lyssa ('Madness') unleashed by Hera to get back at Heracles. On coming to, Heracles' father tells him, to his horror, what he has done and this nearly drives him to suicide. Shortly Theseus, king of Athens, arrives on scene. Theseus persuades Heracles not to take his own life in pain and shame, but to suffer and endure his grief, and come to Athens for peace and purification (*Her.* 815–1426).

Discussions of Heracles focus on his heroic status, looking at the drama as a treatment of a cultural hero or individual ethos. But any notion that Euripides might be reflecting his own times, the killing then going on in the Peloponnesian War, and what this might be doing to his fellow Athenians does not find much favor.[48] Attempts to argue this away, dismissing it as 'historicist' is in fact ahistorical and itself ignores contemporary literature that confirms the reality of what Euripides relates in this drama – a crazed soldier going off and killing those nearest and dearest to him.[49] The madness of Heracles, staged after fifteen years of war, may be Euripides' reflections on the realities of war in Athens and Greece: men returning home from war who could not stop the violence. In the nearly contemporary *Encomium of Helen*, Gorgias refers to men who had gone into battle, seen horrific things and then, having survived, were left physically and psychically damaged, mad in some cases.[50] Writing about the same time too, Thucydides states plainly that 'war is a violent teacher' – that it brings people down to the level of their circumstances. The violence that Thucydides witnessed and Gorgias reflected sometimes became the same madness that drove Heracles to kill his own family.

Efforts to explain away Heracles as some sort of manic-depressive in fact reflect the world of modern-day academics.[51] These have little understanding of what happens to people caught up in the trauma of war, who are subjected to its violence and who are changed by it. There is mental illness hidden in the pages of Euripides. But it is not the illness suspected by scholars, but rather another kind, that which in the post-Vietnam world has come to be associated with wartime trauma and now known as posttraumatic stress disorder. What Euripides ascribes to Heracles happened in 2003 at Fort Bragg, North Carolina, as in the space of six weeks four wives were killed by their husbands returning from war.[52]

Notes

1   Thuc. 5.1.1, with Gomme 3: 629–30 and Hornblower 2: 421–2. Laches' Truce of 423 had been renewed though the circumstances of that are unknown.
2   Thuc. 5.8.2 reports that armies of Brasidas and Cleon were roughly equal in number, each side fielding some 2000 infantry and 300 cavalry. But the Athenian force included 1200 of their own hoplites and contingents from Imbros and Lemnos of equal quality.
3   Thuc. 5.7.2. How does Thucydides know this? It might be the result of a source (a spy in the Athenian camp) or perhaps more likely, told him by Athenian survivors of the battle that followed.
4   In addition to the 292 men captured at Sphacteria, other captives had joined them in Athens, including Pastelidas captured at Torone (Thuc. 5.3).
5   De Ste. Croix 1972: 152 attributes a 'pro-Athenian' policy to both Pleistoanax and his son Pausanias, but such views may have been influenced as much by domestic Spartan politics as any concern for Athens, not to mention the rest of Greece.
6   Thuc. 5.18–19 provides a transcribed text of the treaty, perhaps from an Athenian copy (Gomme 3: 666; for full discussion see 666–82).
7   Note Thucydides' second introduction to the war at 5.26.
8   Parker 1996: 175–85, Hurwit 1999: 219; LiDonnici 1995 (Epidaurian miracle lists).
9   See Hurwit 1999: 221–2, with photographs of the precinct's layout and orientation.

10 Construction of the temple dates to c. 429–400; it was virtually forgotten until the eighteenth century when modern travelers found it. See Osborne 1998: 205–10.

11 On Delium see p. 104. On offerings from booty see Pritchett 1: 53–100.

12 See Jenkins 2006: 140–7 for discussion of the Ionic frieze and metope fragments.

13 On the statue: Paus. 2.17, Stra. 8.6.10 (=C 372). Polyclitus, creator of such famous pieces as the *Doryphoros* and *Diadoumenos*, was one of the great fifth-century sculptors; see Pollitt 1972: 108–10; Ar. *Pax* 475–7 (profiting Argives).

14 Eur. *Hec.* 559–60, and a similar line in fragment 125 of *Andromeda* (ed. Collard-Cropp 2008).

15 Osborne 1998: 184; Hurwit 1999: 213–15 suggests that the sculptures may date c. 415 or even 410 and associates them with such sculptors as Agoracritus, Paeonius, and Callimachus, but resists attribution to any.

16 Lattimore 2006: 468–72.

17 Pollitt 1972: 125.

18 Lattimore 2006: 468–72.

19 For example, see Baynham 2009: 294–312 for discussion of the intellectual milieu of the court of Louis XIV.

20 Osborne 1998: 209 (Zeuxis and Parrhasius); Xen. *Mem.* 3.10.1–4 (Socrates and Parrhasius).

21 See further Thuc. 5.17–48, *IG* I³ 83, with Clark 1999: 116–19; Lazenby 2004: 106 (phony peace).

22 There was also the question and problem of Perdiccas of Macedonia. Argos and Sparta now separated him from his Athenian alliance (Thuc. 5.80.2, 83.4) and by early 415 the Athenians are campaigning against him (Thuc. 6.7.3). But by 414 he has changed sides again, now joining the Athenians in attacking Amphipolis (Thuc. 7.9, with Gomme-Andrewes-Dover 4: 386.

23 Thuc. 5.41.1–3, with Hornblower 1: 483; see also Hanson 2005: 147.

24 This connection explains the origins of Alcibiades' name and several of his relatives. See further Rhodes 1984 and Ellis 1989.

25 Negotiations were complex. But it is clear that Alcibiades not only deceived the Spartan envoys, made to look like fools as well as liars before the Athenian assembly, but also Nicias. See Thuc. 5.44–8.

26 See Lazenby 2004: 111–13 for full discussion based on Thucydides; Thuc. 1.118.2 (Spartan deliberation).

27 Thuc. 5.57–63. Hodkinson 2006: 146 notes the political dimensions of Spartan society, again showing that to see it only in military terms distorts the true picture there.

28 Hanson 2005: 155, thinks the helots were untrained. But this is unlikely. Thuc. 7.72 identifies them as 'the troops who had been under Brasidas', which argues that they were battle hardened and hardly inferior to those they faced. Were

they *mothones* too, as Michell suggests, then they were as trained in war as any elite Spartan (see p. 87).

29 Thuc. 5.71. Surprisingly, Lazenby 2004: 125, takes no position on the refusal of the two officers to move.

30 Apparently not noticed by Woodhouse 1933: 87–8, Hanson 2005: 156–7, and Hodkinson 2006: 134.

31 Thuc. 5.70.1 says eagerly and with violence, in contrast to the Spartan slow steady pace to the tunes of pipes. This suggests that the Argives were coming on at a run.

32 A fragment of Sophocles *Eurpylus* (date unknown; ed. Lloyd-Jones 1996: 90.47–8) tells of Argives trampling over the bodies of the slain, laughing. Poetic, yes, but the occasion is little different from that here.

33 Note above the discussion on Delium and the sources cited there.

34 Perhaps so obvious, the point has seldom been appreciated. Thanks to Rosen 2007: 86 for noting it.

35 See Keegan 1976: 101 and Sabin 2000.

36 See Keegan 1976: 100, and Hom. *Il.* 5.1–24, 144–7, 151–6, 11.101–10, 255–60, 419–24, 543–6 – a selection of passages that attest 'team-fighting' My own experience and that of some friends confirms this picture.

37 Cf. Woodhouse 1933: 106–25.

38 More than battlefield discipline may be involved in the condemnation of the two polemarchs. It seems likely that Aristocles is the brother of Pleistoanax, the exiled king recently restored (Thuc. 5.16.1–2); Thucydides makes the relationship clear in the dealings with Delphi that brought Pleistoanax back to Sparta and the condemnation of Aristocles could easily be seen as an attack on his brother. As Hornblower 2: 465 notes, Pleistoanax had many enemies who were always stirring things up. For discussion see P-B 27–8, Kagan 1981: 128, and Gomme-Andrewes-Dover 5: 120. Hanson 2005: 157 seems not to notice the connection, so too Lazenby 2004: 123, 125. See now Hornblower 3: 188–9, who questions the identity of Aristocles the polemarch with the royal brother. But the evidence is unclear.

39 Lazenby 2004: 9. The skill of the Athenians at Marathon in facing the Persians, their envelopment of the Persians, argues against a Spartan monopoly on courage and skill. On many occasions during this war, Athenian commanders and soldiers alike demonstrated skill and ability; so too Hornblower 1, 303–4 and Hodkinson 2006: 118–19. Demosthenes' handling of troops at Sphacteria suggests that the Athenians made the wrong assignment for the Mantinean campaign.

40 Woodhouse 1933: 67, who then contradicts himself, asserting that those the Spartans fought were 'half-trained civic militia'. While some Greeks were surely better soldiers than others, it goes too far to dismiss all but the Spartans as simply inept.

41 On Spartan courage see Miller 2000: 15–23.

42 Rubincam 1991: 184 suggests the number may be conventional. But the number could also be determined by simply counting names on a casualty list.

43 Pritchett 4: 143–4 tentatively identifies an inscription from Mantinea as a casualty list naming some of the Mantinean dead from the battle; see also Hanson 2005: 157, 355. Thuc. 5.61.1 and Diod. 12.79 (with Develin 1989: 144) identify the two Athenian generals, both long-serving commanders.

44 Woodhouse 1933: 84–5.

45 Neither the occasion of the play nor its date is recorded. On the basis of internal evidence and metrical analysis Arrowsmith 1956: 57–8 suggests a date c. 418–416; so too Bond 1981: xxxi, Barlow 1996: 18; contra Papadopoulou 2005: 141, n.42. This date seems to make the most sense of the internal references as argued here.

46 Not noticed by Bond 1981: 188, Barlow 1996: 146, Papadopoulou 2005: 79; cf. Arrowsmith 1956: 57–8.

47 Multiple references, e.g., to *polemos* – war – at ll. 1135, 1273, and with variations to *doru* – spear – at 1176.

48 For an exception, see the remarks in Konstan 2007.

49 Exemplified by Papadopoulou 2005: 141–2, so too Michelini 1987: 243, n.54.

50 On Gorgias see pp. 158–60.

51 So Papadopoulos 2005: 82–3.

52 On the modern homecoming experience, not much different when one reads the *Heracles*, see Shay 2004 and Gibbs 1920: 447. Officer friends report to me that today in the US Army, domestic abuse – wife-beating – is endemic.

7

'THE STRONG DO WHAT THEY HAVE THE POWER TO DO'

Alcibiades had commanded the Athenian forces that had intervened in the suppression of the opposition party in Argos in the aftermath of Mantinea (Thuc. 5.84.1). Now in the following summer 416/15 he evidently pushed hard for a decision that would tighten the grip on the empire and demonstrate that opposition to Athenian power, whether real or imagined, would not be tolerated.[1] The target in question was the small island *polis* of Melos, an old Spartan colony, which had so far played only a bit role in the war, mostly, it appears, in the form of monies contributed to Sparta's war fund.[2]

Ten years earlier (426) Nicias had campaigned on the island but had accomplished nothing, perhaps in part because the island was not really the aim of his campaigning.[3] Now the Athenians returned with a composite force drawn from their own troops plus a large contingent of allies from Chios and Lesbos, altogether some 3000 men against a small city that could field perhaps 500.[4] In command were two generals, Cleomedes and Alcibiades' friend Tisias. Such a large commitment of force demonstrates the reality of Athenian power and the intolerance of opposition. But why would the Athenians bother with such a small community?

The answer may be found in the continuing drain of monies owing to the war. Either in 428, or perhaps after Cleon's victory at Sphacteria (c. 425), the Athenians set up a financial commission or taskforce to enhance revenues. It is possible that Alcibiades, still a young man and not a major player politically, sat on this commission as *taktes*. Though not a member of the Athenian empire, tiny Melos was still assessed fifteen talents but evidently never paid the assessment.[5]

It has been suggested that Alcibiades took the obstinacy of the Melians personally and now pushed for the assault on the island. While personalizing the Athenian response is attractive, real factors like the need for money and the need to assert imperial power argue that the Athenian decision was impersonal.[6] The Athenian generals met privately with the Melian leadership to discuss the situation, but the Melians remained firmly defiant. Reports and gossip of what was said in this meeting did get out, and with it Thucydides constructed a damning indictment of the pursuit and use of power. This statement has since become known as the Melian Dialogue.

The Melian Dialogue

In the David vs. Goliath confrontation that played out on Melos, Thucydides provides a none too subtle commentary on the nature of power and democracy in Athens. Next to the Periclean 'Funeral Oration', the 'Melian Dialogue' composed by Thucydides is perhaps the most famous part of his *History*.

Melos and what happened there in 416/15 was but a minor swirl in the vast landscape of the Peloponnesian War, a mere footnote of an event. But the speeches and the exchange of ideas between the two sides have attracted attention and study from historians and political scientists alike. The language and words are clearly those of Thucydides. But the statements he reports preserve at least some information revealed by his sources, either or both Athenian and Melian, of what each party said.[7] It may be true that the Dialogue is not much of a dialogue, as the Athenians brusquely tell the Melians what they must do in order to survive.[8] The exchanges made by the two sides also give some idea of the nature of political debate among the Greeks, whether it be the Athenian assembly or peace negotiations as those leading to the Peace of Nicias: speakers making statements or giving responses to each other.

In the reported negotiations with the Melians, the speeches that Thucydides attributes to the Athenians explore the nature of raw, unadulterated power. He makes the case that in war, the strong do what they have the power to do, and the weak suffer as they must (Thuc. 5.89). As he makes abundantly clear, Athens exercised the power, and the Melians suffered its consequences. Political scientist Ned Lebow has defined power as that which is applied unjustly, and this definition resounds throughout the Athenian statements.[9]

From the beginning, the Athenians make clear that the very survival of the Melians is at stake and this is tied in to the sophistic idea of self-interest:

that it is in the interest of the Athenians to persuade the Melians to acquiesce peacefully and without a fight, as it is in the self-interest of the Melians,
quite simply, to survive (Thuc. 5.87–8, 92–5). This position has inspired
the argument that the Athenian demand of the Melians was actually
humanitarian – that the Athenians really would have preferred the Melians
simply to acquiesce enabling them to move on to bigger and better things.[10]
But this is a half truth at best. Such argument overlooks the powerful force
that political ideas like freedom and autonomy exerted on Greek society,
how dying on your feet was preferable to living on your knees. The heroic
defense of Greece against the massive Persian invasion in 480 is just the
greatest example of this powerful drive. While it may seem that the fool-
hardy Melians committed suicide in their stubborn act of resistance to the
Athenians, their decision was by no means unusual. And the argument of
hope they throw out to the Athenians in the course of the debate would
have been on many Greek lips in 480.

As Thucydides brings up the role of self-interest early in the debate, it
quickly becomes apparent that what the two sides are discussing is really
about power. The Athenians state candidly that they will not resort to 'fine
words' and 'unconvincing speech' (Thuc. 5.89.1). These, as A.G. Woodhead suggests, are typical reactions of those confronted by a powerful
individual or state, who 'will cover their own enmity and envy by saying
that they stand for justice, equality before the law, peace, humanity, [and]
morality itself'.[11]

Rather the Athenians declare their intent to be a simple revelation of
what constitutes power and justice. Justice, they declare is a matter to be
decided by forces or powers that are equal in strength – when this is not
the case, as clearly between Athens and Melos, it is simply a matter of raw
power, that the strong impose and the weak accept.[12] This passage, which
has an echo in 5.101 where Thucydides refers to an 'evenly' matched
contest, illustrates perhaps perfectly Lebow's argument that power is that
which is applied unjustly. What is also revealed in these passages is the
argument that the essence of power is the extent of military force that can
be brought to bear, and the wealth that backs it up. As the Athenians make
abundantly clear, they possess superior might, which the Melians cannot
hope to match, and which the Spartans, inclined to look after their own
interests first, will not strengthen (Thuc. 5.89, 101, 106–10).

Power is that which is decided by opposing, and in the eyes of the Athenians, equal force(s) (Thuc. 5.89). But does it not also happen, the Melians

suggest, that sometimes the underdog wins? The Melians note that occasionally the fortunes of war swing to those who are smaller in number and less in strength, and in this they find hope (Thuc. 5.102). The Athenians quash this argument, noting that 'hope' is the comforter of those in danger, who find additional solace in prophecy and oracles and in doing so only hasten their own destruction (Thuc. 5.103).[13] Here the Athenians conveniently forgot their own history and how 'hope' was the slender thread to which they clung in the midst of the Persian invasion.

Thucydides' analysis of power is based on observations of not only what happened at Melos, but from similar events that occurred throughout the entire course of the war.[14] During this time he saw that the failure of diplomacy, as in the events of 433–1 and the breakdown of the Peace of Nicias, forced the Greek states to resolve their differences by resort to raw military power. Sometimes inspired generalship, as seen in Brasidas' campaigns in Macedonia, or the superior soldiering of the Spartans at Mantinea (who redeemed Agis' botched orders with their blood) decided the issue. On other occasions the ostensibly powerful lost: the 'unbeatable' Spartans surrendering at Sphacteria, the mighty Athenian expedition completely destroyed in Sicily, are the best examples of this.[15]

But how is Thucydides' fascination with power to be explained? Why does he compose a literary fiction such as the 'Melian Dialogue' that explores in such blunt fashion the nature of power and empire? He does not give us the answers to these questions and we are left only to surmise his reasons for the harsh language and ideas. It would not be the first or last time, however, that such cynical *Realpolitik* would come from a disappointed soldier and politician reflecting on a life time of war and violence and realizing that military force is man's preferred solution to conflict resolution.[16]

Death of a City, and a Peace

Unable to persuade the Melians to yield, Cleomedes and Tisias invested Melos with a wall and established a siege. A garrison of Athenians and allies remained to press the siege, but the two commanders left the island with most of their forces. Teisias for one had other more pressing business to attend to – the Olympic Games were soon to begin. The Melians, however, refused to cooperate: one night they sallied out and attacked an inattentive Athenian garrison, killed some of them, and gathering what food and other items they could quickly find, retired. In the following late winter or early spring (416/5) Athenian reinforcements arrived and the siege – aided by treachery within – brought victory. The Melians yielded unconditionally, accepting Athenian terms, but nothing more could have been possible. A decree, possibly moved by Alcibiades, called for extreme measures: men of military age (16–45) were killed and the rest of the population was enslaved. The killing of the Melian men was not the sort of detail Thucydides liked to report, but presumably the men were bound, walked to some convenient place, and then dispatched.[17] Alcibiades apparently took advantage of the sale of Melian women to buy one whom he made his mistress: she later bore him a son.[18]

Later the Athenians settled the island with cleruchs(?) 500 strong, a figure that gives a good idea of the number of Melians either killed or driven into exile (Thuc. 5.116.4; some did escape the Athenians and returned home after the war: Xen. *Hell.* 2.2.9). Thucydides takes care to identify the Athenian commander who carried out the final reduction of Melos: Philocrates, son of Demeas, unusually adding the patronymic, or father's name. The meaning of this name to the Greek reader, 'lover of power, son of the people',[19] suggests a Thucydidean editorial comment: a clearer indictment of an Athenian abuse of power would be difficult to find.[20]

The Summer Olympics, 416

As the Athenians pressed the siege of Melos, undeclared war continued around the Greek world. The Peloponnese was the hotspot and here the Corinthians resumed military actions against Athens. More troublesome was the Athenian base at Pylos. Too difficult to resolve in peace talks, Pylos remained Athenian much to the consternation of the Spartans who badly wanted it back.[21] In the months that had followed the Peace of Nicias, Spartan diplomacy had proved increasingly inept. Efforts to acquire control of Panacton from the Boeotians so as to trade it for Pylos failed and succeeded only in antagonizing both the Boeotians and Athenians. Athenian operations continued unchecked from the base at Pylos, ravaging Spartan territory and encouraging helots to defect. With diplomacy at an end yet fearing to break the Peace, the Spartans allowed their citizens to take up arms against the Athenians, privately (Thuc. 5.115, 7.18). Open war was just around the corner.

But with summer 416 also came the Olympic Games and with them a pause in the fighting. Amid peaceful surroundings in the plush glens and valleys of Zeus' sanctuary, the Greeks could assemble in peace though sometimes tensions ran high. Controversy of all kinds had characterized the Games of 420. The shuffling of alliances after the Peace of Nicias (421) had increased tensions and Elis, guardian of the Games, would not allow the Spartans to participate. Allegedly the Spartans had campaigned against the Eleans after the Olympic truce had been proclaimed though the Spartans denied this. Contingents of troops from several states including Athens stood by to guard the sanctuary from a Spartan incursion that never materialized. The 'Olympic truce' held even when the Spartan Lichas, having entered the chariot race under Boeotian colors, was flogged on discovery – he had boldly presumed to crown his victorious charioteer (Thuc. 5.49–50).

During the Games Greeks were free to mingle and among them almost certainly was Thucydides, the exiled Athenian general now historian. Confirmation of his presence at the Games seems clear in his citation of the treaty of 420 that brought together Athens, Argos, Mantinea, and Elis. The text of this agreement was set up in Olympia, presumably to inform the other Greeks and the gods of what these communities had agreed. Not only would Thucydides have been able to read and copy this document, but also discuss the issues with those it concerned.[22]

The Games of 416 were no less spectacular and as in 420, Thucydides may have been present once more to witness the competition and to learn what he could of the war's recent events as, for example, what had happened in the campaign and battle at Mantinea. As he notes, the Games of 416 were made extraordinary by his own countryman, Alcibiades, who had entered seven racing chariots in that contest. No one, not even kings, had ever done this. As he also notes, Alcibiades' teams were sensational, placing first, second, and fourth. But even this did not satisfy Alcibiades and he later hired Euripides to write odes singing his praises (cf. Thuc. 6.16.2, Plut. Alc. 11).

No less remarkable was the attention and favors showered on Alcibiades by some of the Greek communities. The people of Chios provided animals for the sacrifices as well as fodder for the teams of race horses, while those of Lesbos supplied wine and other provisions for him and his entourage, lording it over everyone in a great tent supplied by the Ephesians. These were the same allies who had only recently participated in the opening round of the siege of Melos. Their presence now at Olympia showering gifts on Alcibiades gives some indication of the influence and prestige of perhaps the most powerful of the Athenians, and how the allies went about winning (his) favor and staying out of harm's way.[23]

With this glory, however, also came fraud and deceit. Tisias, co-commander of the Athenian forces first dispatched to Melos, and ostensibly Alcibiades' friend, was dying to win Olympic glory for himself. Tisias learned that a fast chariot was to be had at Argos and since Alcibiades had many friends there, asked him to intervene and make a purchase on his behalf. Alcibiades agreed, bought the chariot and then entered it in the contest in his own name. Furious at the deceit, Tisias screamed loudly to gods and men alike that he had been cheated.[24] More than fifteen years later, Isocrates, the most talented speaker and legal mind money could then buy, defended Alcibiades' son against charges of theft. Nowhere perhaps are Alcibiades' values plainer than in this story of double-cross and fraud – and this was how he treated a friend.[25]

Olympic glory may also have saved Alcibiades from political defeat at home. Politics in Athens had always been sharply contested, especially so after the death of Pericles and the absence of a dominating figure. Yet there had been no ostracism since that of Thucydides, son of Melesias in 444/3. Now in the aftermath of Mantinea and Melos, the diplomatic turmoil of the Peace of Nicias, political rivalries intensified. Among the social elites, Alcibiades and Nicias dominated, but the more popular figures of Hyperbolus and Androcles also figured in the debates. Probably in 416 the Athenians voted to conduct a formal ostracism. When they later assembled and voted, it was the less influential (and more despised?) Hyperbolus who lost the vote and suffered the ostracism. How this happened has been debated at length, but in the end Athens would remain in the hands of two dominating and divisive figures, Alcibiades and Nicias.[26]

Tale of a City's Death?

Not long after the destruction of Melos, probably at the City Dionysia in early spring 415, Euripides explored the sufferings of a dead city in his drama *Trojan Women*.[27] The captive women of Troy, assigned to their captors, await departure to Greece to begin new lives as slaves. Euripides paints a bleak picture of a destroyed city, one made emphatic by an opening statement delivered by the god Poseidon: 'That mortal who sacks fallen cities is a fool, who gives the temples and the tombs, the hallowed places of the dead to desolation. His own turn must come' (*Tro.* 95–8). War's cruelties are made even more explicit in the debate by the Greeks in assembly to kill Astyanax, the young son of Hector. That such a discussion could take place reveals the depths to which war's violence can take a community. Euripides sees this as so much foolishness, something he expresses through the voice of Cassandra, who delivers a stunning indictment on the waste of war (353–405).

Is *Trojan Women* an anti-war play? It has been argued by classicist Peter Green that it is not, that it is rather 'a grimly pessimistic survey of a society's religious and ethical bankruptcy, the tawdriness of its myths, the jungle mentality governing its conduct. ... [O]ne has no confidence that Euripides' point goes beyond a grim reminder that overreaching brings retribution'.[28] Additionally, Green denies any linkage between Euripides' play and the recent events at Melos.

What the Athenians did at Melos, however, does seem to have weighed upon them, at least by the end of the war. Barely ten years later, they found themselves at the sharp end of the spear and with no shield. Defeated, the enemies of Athens demanded payback for Athenian atrocities: massacres at Scione, Torone, and Melos (among others), and the Athenians worried that such retribution might be visited upon them (Xen. *Hell.* 2.2.3). Fears like these did not arise overnight. What Euripides writes of in *Trojan Women* argues that he reflected, and surely others in Athens too, with concern over the various excesses they had committed during the war.

But Green is probably correct in arguing against any immediate impact of the destruction of Melos and the writing of *Trojan Women*. For one thing, Euripides had been commissioned by Alcibiades to write odes celebrating his spectacular Olympic victories and while the timing of these compositions is unknown, Alcibiades was not the sort to wait patiently! Composition of a tragic drama was a complex affair and for Euripides to have written and staged the play in spring 415 demands that it was already in the works when the Athenians sailed into Melos and demanded its surrender. Moreover, there were more than enough instances of wartime atrocity to provide Euripides with adequate inspiration to relate the plight of a sacked city, for its women and everyone else. Finally, what Euripides writes finds an echo in Thucydides' assessment of the civil strife that destroyed Corcyra ten years before. As he noted war is a violent teacher, one that brings people down to the level of their circumstances. In his drama Euripides makes the very same observation, as Green states. When the comments of both Euripides and Thucydides are placed in contrast to prevailing perceptions of the glories of war, as Thucydides does in the debates leading to Athenian approval of the Sicilian expedition, the assertion that *Trojan Women* is not critical of prevailing Athenian attitudes, in short an anti-war piece, can only be seen as special pleading. Moreover, it just might be that it was the massacre at Melos that made *Trojan Women* famous, not the other way round.

Tragedy may also be found hidden in comedy and the next year, at the City Dionysia of 414, Aristophanes produced *Birds*, a fantastic and escapist tale of democratic life stressed by war, empire, and corruption. Two characters, Euelpides ('hopeful') and Pisthetaerus ('trusting') abandon Athens and its ills, incessant litigation, ignorant juries, corrupt politics and politicians, to found a new city in the sky, what is sometimes called 'Cloud-cuckoo-land'. Such escapist fare allows Aristophanes to make a number of comments about contemporary Athenian society, particularly as Euelpides and Pisthetaerus found their new city in the sky: priests, poets, and sooth-sayers all come in for ridicule, but so does the *episkopos*, the Athenian inspector whose appearance Athens' allies would have dreaded.[29]

In the course of the drama Pisthetaerus jokes about blockading the gods to keep them from interfering in the creation of Cloud-cuckoo-land and starving them just like the hungry Melians.[30] Peter Green argues that the intent of this line was to raise a laugh, just like the starving Megarians that Aristophanes mentions in *Acharnians* (Ar. *Ach.* 729–835). Green adds further that 'the cruelty of Mediterranean humor has seldom been better documented', but is this ancient Mediterranean humor, or 'humor' of another kind?[31]

Aristophanes is a comedian and his aim is to entertain and win first prize. But his comedies also have an edge to them and he comments seriously about war, politics, and the real enemy of the Greeks – the Persians – throughout his plays. As a young Athenian, he would have been caught up in all the violent and crazy things that were happening in the war, just like his contemporary and rival Eupolis.[32] This too influenced the 'humor' that he wrote, which also explains its edge. Wartime comedy, as veteran and author Paul Fussell notes, is not simply 'humorous' as commonly understood, but darker, more bitter expressions of what is 'funny'. Wartime humor is cynical and expresses vividly and clearly the tragedy of war. Journalist Michael Herr tells that in Vietnam, 'a sucking chest wound is Nature's way of telling you that you've been in a firefight': no doubt Aristophanes would have appreciated the 'humor'.[33]

Notes

1 Plut. *Alc.* 16.5–6 tells that Alcibiades was largely responsible for the decree that ordered the deaths of the Melian men and the enslavement of the rest of the population. His culpability for initiating the campaign is more obscure. See also Andoc. 4.22, with Ellis 1989: 49, Vickers 2008: 125–6.
2 This most likely occurred in the 420s, possibly following Nicias' campaign against the island in 426, but the inscription on which this information rests is fragmentary. See pp. 86–7 and Loomis 1992: 63–4, 74.
3 See Gomme-Andrewes-Dover 4: 156, n.1 suggesting that the campaign to Melos in 426 was a feint, the real target of Athenian operations being Boeotia.
4 Thuc. 5.84.1 (Athenian force), 5.116.4 (number of Athenian colonists who replaced the Melians killed and enslaved: this should represent, approximately, Melian manpower). On the allies see Quinn 1981: 42–3.
5 Develin 1989: 131 and Ellis 1989: 31 accept Alcibiades' membership on this board, but Andrewes in Gomme-Andrewes-Dover 4: 49 doubts it. On Melos and the tribute see Meiggs 1972: 327–8 and Gomme 3: 503, Gomme-Andrewes-Dover 4: 156 for details.
6 Vickers 2008: 125–6.
7 Full analysis of the Dialogue itself exceeds my aims here. For discussion see Andrewes in Gomme-Andrewes-Dover 4: 182–8. See also Vickers 2008: 126–32 who suggests that Thucydides covertly identifies 'the Athenians' of the Dialogue with Alcibiades, in some way accusing Alcibiades of the Melian massacre as earlier authors did Pericles of the Samian campaign (see pp. 15–16).
8 Hussey 1985: 126, and Bosworth 1993: 38, n.43.
9 Lebow 2003: 122.
10 Bosworth 1993.
11 Woodhead 1970: 21.
12 Thuc. 5.89. Readers of Plato will recognize the similar sentiment expressed by Callicles, which suggests that there is a sophistic influence at work here. See Solmsen 1975: 48, 118.
13 This idea of hope is one Thucydides also explored in the debate over Mytilene. See p. 69.
14 See Thuc. 5.91.1, and its reference to the potential end of the Athenian empire, and Gomme-Andrewes-Dover 4: 166–7 for discussion.

15 Here it helps to keep in mind that when Thucydides wrote the Dialogue, the war had ended and he had the advantage of hindsight.

16 It has long been observed that cynicism is the hallmark of the veteran combat soldier, which Thucydides certainly was. See Tritle 2000: 128–36, and for another example, Duncan and Klooster 2002, and the (US) Civil War writings of Ambrose Bierce.

17 Plut. *Alc.* 16.5–6 and [Ps.] Andoc. 4.22 (Alcibiades' role), Thuc. 5.116.4 (the Melian sentence).

18 Reported by [Ps.] Andoc. 4.22; see Gomme-Andrewes-Dover 4: 190–1 for discussion.

19 Noted by Lattimore 1998: 301, n., as 'Lover of Might, son of Populace (or Democracy)'. My rendering may not be quite as literal but the difference seems slight.

20 Cf. Bosworth 1993: 42, who sees no such expression of sympathy.

21 Thuc. 5.14.3, 39.2, 44.3 makes clear that the Athenian base remained off the table during negotiations. That this happened points perhaps to the desperate search for peace at the time.

22 Thuc. 5.26.2 (Thucydides in the Peloponnese after exile), 5.47, with Clark 1999: 115–34.

23 Other than Alcibiades' grandstanding at Olympia, calculated so he claimed to impress upon the Greeks that Athenian power was undiminished (Thuc. 6.16.2), the Games of 416 were otherwise unremarkable and so not discussed by Thucydides. But see also Plut. *Alc.* 12.1–2 (and the next note) for incidents that did occur but which were of little 'historical' concern to Thucydides.

24 Plut. *Alc.* 12.2–5, with *APF* 302 and Vickers 2008: 124–5 discussing the evidence. Tisias may have been still in Melos: but Alcibiades' character was such that he could have committed the fraud before an unbelieving Tisias.

25 On the later history of the chariot case, see Whitehead 2004: 151–85, at 170–1.

26 Thuc. 8.73.3, Theopomp. *FGrHist* 115F96b, and Plut. *Ar.* 7.3–4, *Nic.* 11.3–7, *Alc.* 13. On the ostracism see Gomme-Andrewes-Dover 5: 257–64 (extensively), Ellis 1989: 45–9.

27 The play's date is uncertain but probably after the destruction of Melos. Cf. Morwood 2000: lii, with Green 1999: 100, who places it before the final reduction.

28 Green 1999: 107.

29 Noted by Meiggs 1972: 583–7.

30 Ar. *Av.* 186. Gomme-Andrewes-Dover 4: 189 argue 'from this [it would not] seem that the Athenians felt any remorse' [i.e., for their actions]. See below and Fussell 1975: 203–4 for discussion.

31 Green 1999: 103.

32 Wartime service for Eupolis is certain, but the argument that he died in battle is unpersuasive; cf. Storey 2003: 378–81, with Sidwell 2009. Little is actually known of Aristophanes' life; see Sommerstein 1980: 2–3, Dover 1993: 3–4. Unless he was physically unable, military service is virtually certain, and his numerous comments on generals such as Lamachus, Nicias *et al.* suggests a typical soldier's disdain for the 'brass'.

33 Herr 1978: 226.

8

'WHAT OF US THEN WHO FOR OUR CHILDREN MUST WEEP?'

In late spring 415, as the last Melians were sold into slavery, the Athenians began debate on a resolution to embark on an ambitious campaign to the Greek west – the conquest of the island of Sicily. Two speakers – Alcibiades for, Nicias against – dominated the discussions though surely others participated. Some eight years before, the Greeks of Sicily had solved their disputes in a congress held in Gela obliging the Athenians to leave the island. But Athenian ambitions and strategic goals, namely that the island's rich resources should not fall into the wrong hands, never dimmed. Agreement, however, did not suit the Sicilians and within a few years the Gela accords began to break down.[1]

By winter 416/15, powerful Syracuse reverted to form and renewed its expansionist ways. A quarrel between Egesta and Selinus allowed Syracuse to become involved and support Selinus; Leontini and Syracuse had a history of dispute and their quarrel revived as well. As in earlier instances of Syracusan aggression, Egesta and Leontini appealed to Athens for help as both communities possessed diplomatic ties. In the following spring of 415, Athenian ambassadors returned from their mission to Egesta with tall tales of Sicilian wealth.[2]

In fact the Athenians were tricked by their Egestaean hosts who collected all the silver plate and gold cups in town, sharing these with those entertaining the visiting Athenians. Wined and dined in luxury, the ambassadors came to believe that the whole town possessed great wealth. These marvelous tales moved the Athenians to approve the dispatch of a sizable force, some sixty ships, to Sicily to defend their allies against Syracusan aggression. Three generals, Alcibiades, Nicias, and Lamachus, commanded jointly, holding full powers to manage everything as they saw best for Athens (Thuc. 6.8.2). This decision the Athenians evidently reached quickly. Five days later they convened another assembly meeting to discuss the equipping and

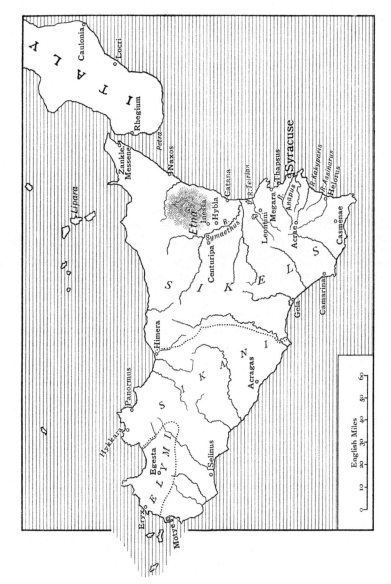

Sicily (after B.W. Henderson, *The Great War Between Athens and Sparta*, London, 1927)

provisioning of the fleet now being assembled. Nicias, unhappy with his assignment and thinking the campaign a bad idea, attempted to persuade the Athenians to change course. On the other side, Alcibiades was wildly enthusiastic about the expedition's prospects. In the speeches that Thucydides wrote for their purported debate, he explores ideas of power and power politics, and what the course of empire should be.[3]

Debate at Athens

The debate that Thucydides relates was fiercely contested and shows just how heated exchanges could be in the Athenian assembly. The debate also illustrates A.G. Woodhead's observation on the nature of 'institutional power' and how the Athenian assembly may be seen as an instrument of power.[4] Though his account alludes to the participation of various speakers, Thucydides constructs the debate around Alcibiades and Nicias, the leading political figures of the day. Nicias, known for his luck and caution, had negotiated the Peace that took his name and was unenthusiastic about the planned invasion. In the debate he did everything he could to derail it, as well as give the Athenians opportunity to replace him as one of its commanders. On the other side was the flamboyant and charismatic Alcibiades. A few years before he had successfully concluded the alliance with Argos, an agreement that, if Thucydides is read carefully, failed to deliver all that had been anticipated or promoted. Thucydides adds to the contrast between the two, noting not only an age difference (embodying an idea of old versus new), but also a sense of caution and foreboding versus a spirit of adventure bordering on recklessness.

In his first speech on the proposed expedition (Thuc. 6.8.4–14), Nicias argued that the Athenians were entering into a conflict that did not concern them: they were being swayed by foreigners begging for help, who would say anything to get the Athenians to do their fighting. Dispatch of even the moderate-sized force then being debated struck him as shortsighted in view of the precarious situation at home. The recent Peace was hardly stable. Sparta had accepted it only to get back the men captured at Sphacteria and now surely planned ways to trip them up. Nicias told the Athenians they might be able to maintain their rule if they prevailed over their enemies. But Sicily, so far away, was a different situation, and maintaining rule over such a faraway place would be much more difficult.

Interestingly Nicias observed that sometimes a power was all the greater because it remained at a distance, allowing its reputation to intimidate potential enemies. A failed attack, even a partially successful one requiring reinforcements, could have severe repercussions as enemies would imagine the feared power to be a paper tiger and would join others in attacking it (Thuc. 6.11.4). Far better, Nicias suggested, to let people think you were powerful and so remain feared, than demonstrate otherwise. What Nicias argued to the Athenians then was a policy of restraint, to keep what they possessed and not to exceed their limits. His argument is of interest as it echoes points made by the Athenians in the Melian Dialogue, particularly the explanation for their demands on the Melians: that they must act so as to make others aware of their power (5.92–5).

The restraint and caution proposed by Nicias found its opposite in Alcibiades. In his response he told the Athenians that they had nothing to fear in Sicily: that the many cities there were disorganized by internal unrest and lacked military strength (Thuc. 6.17.2–3). Syracuse, the island's great power, was so hated that once the Athenians showed up, it would face a general rising of the island's native population who would rally to the Athenians. With even fewer resources than what they now possessed, their fathers, Alcibiades claims, had achieved even greater things against the Persians, and so now they should not hesitate to act. Empire over all the Greeks – from those in Sicily to those at home – was the prospect, and the very least that they would achieve was the elimination of Syracusan power and arrogance.

In making this extravagant claim, Alcibiades also talked about empire. He argued that the Athenians had an obligation to aid the Egestaeans, with whom they had allied in order to defend themselves against attack closer to home. Alliances such as these strengthened the empire the Athenians now ruled, but more to the point, an energetic response to an ally in need was crucial to keeping that empire. Empires survive, he said, because when they see danger coming, they strike first rather than wait to be struck. A 'moderate' sized empire, or 'just enough' empire is not a reality. Instead empires must grow and expand if they are to survive. For this reason, he told the Athenians, an aggressive policy was needed not only toward Sicily, but also in suppressing any defections or challenges to Athenian imperial power.

On this point there could be no question of Alcibiades' sincerity. Many of those present in the assembly hearing these words would have known that it was his support, if not proposal, that had led to the destruction of

Melos. Now listening to his hard rhetoric of power, Alcibrades told them others will rule you if you do not rule them (Thuc. 6.18.3). It will be clear that in this speech, Thucydides makes observations on the nature of power and empire that he has touched previously. A point made earlier in his *History* is that power is not static and that letting it go is a dangerous thing. This Pericles and Cleon had both observed on various occasions and now Alcibiades reaffirms.

Alcibiades speech was electric. The pleas of the Egestaeans and Leontinians present for the debate only reinforced what he said and fixed the resolve of the Athenians to embark on the expedition. Nicias made one final effort to stop what he clearly regarded as folly (Thuc. 6.20–3). He attempted to frighten the Athenians by telling them that great military forces awaited them in Sicily and so they must increase their own accordingly. An unnamed Athenian challenged him to state what his requirements were there and then. With these approved Nicias had no option but to accede to popular opinion.

Thucydides paints a scene of popular support for the campaign. By now some ten years had passed since the plague had ravaged Athens. Overall, people were stronger and for many of the young coming of age, this was the first big exciting thing that had happened to them. Things had been quiet too since Nicias' peace and material losses had been made good. Older Athenians, Thucydides tells, thought with satisfaction of the places that would now be added to the empire. The young looked forward to traveling to a far-off place and the exciting experiences they would have – an enthusiasm that finds counterparts in all eras of history, in virtually every army ever assembled. Poorer Athenians, the men who would man the fleet of ships, looked at the expedition as a means of making a living wage, both now and later as a result of an even greater empire (Thuc. 6.24.3–4). To meet manpower needs, some 700 of these poorer Athenians were pressed into service as marines, their equipment coming from the state (Thuc. 6.43).

This is what Thucydides reports. Reality might well have been different. In his *Lysistrata*, written some five years later (411), Aristophanes refers to the rants of the democratic leader Demostratus, who railed at the assembled Athenians, 'We must sail for Sicily!' 'Enlist hoplites at Zakynthos'! (Ar. *Lys.* 391–4). But others were less confident of the plan and its promises. Meton, an astronomer better known as a mad scientist from Aristophanes' *Birds*, pretended to suffer from a nervous breakdown. Disabled, he persuaded the Athenians to dismiss his son from participation in the expedition so that he could remain at home and care for his father. Another Athenian who had misgivings was Socrates. Students and friends later claimed that his inner *daimon* warned him of impending disaster.[5] A survivor of the siege of Potidaea and the defeat at Delium, Socrates had already seen death on a large scale and had little reason to think that things would go better in far-off Sicily.

The decision to embark on an expedition that seemed greater than Agamemnon's energized Athens. In the Piraeus and in the city, the business of outfitting ships for sailing and recruiting of soldiers and sailors reached fever pitch (see Ar. *Ach.* 544–54). Lamachus sailed first for Sicily with an advance party: as the 'real' soldier among the expedition's commanders, he had gone ahead to contact prospective Sicilian allies and secure a beach-head.[6] But then two incidents rocked the city. One night the herms (*hermai*) or phallic charms that stood before most homes in the city were mutilated. This may have been no more than drunken revelry, the acts of some young men.[7] But revelation of worse soon followed. In a meeting of the assembly it was claimed that at a private party some young men had not only mocked the sacred Mysteries of Demeter and Persephone, they had done so in the presence of those uninitiated in the cult. Worst of all, informers implicated Alcibiades in both, and while he proclaimed his innocence, many were prepared to believe the worst.[8]

Informers and politics turned these disturbing events into a political nightmare. Since the plague public mores had been stressed and this seemed only another example of the social malaise affecting Athenian society. Among the informers was Andocides, descendant of a well-placed democratic family with links to Pericles, his family and politics. Caught in the snare of conspiracy and granted immunity, Andocides sang like a canary. He identified the alleged perpetrators of these incidents while absolving himself of any blame. Along with other informers, both slaves and metics, many were named and among these was Alcibiades and Critias, another Socratic friend. In the course of his defense, Andocides alludes to an anti-democratic conspiracy, particularly in regard to the incident of the herms. Some 300 men, according to informers, had gathered in the area of the Theater of Dionysus and then set out in small parties to mutilate the herms. In the end, between fifty and 100 Athenians, mostly young and rich, would be expelled from Athens.[9]

Amid the inquiry and freely flowing accusations, Alcibiades maintained his innocence and the events do not appear to be his style. Yes, his personal conduct was impulsive, brazen, and fully egocentric. Making fun of the

Mysteries privately would seem to be the sort of thing he might do, and while in bad taste perhaps, it was a private affair without political connotation. But no, he was on the eve of leading a powerful military force on a great expedition – he had secured the following of the mass of people who would man the ships. Why would he do anything that would throw away everything he had worked so hard to achieve? In short there is some reason to think that the affair of the Mysteries involved Alcibiades, that report of it leaked, but that it had no political purpose. The mutilation of the herms, however, was directed against the sailing of the expedition. It might well have aimed to overthrow, if at all possible, Alcibiades' position in Athens and before the people.[10]

But powerful forces were pushing to keep the expedition's sailing date firm. Alcibiades, denying his role in these affairs, demanded an immediate trial, offering to pay any penalty if found guilty – to be put to death even – and to keep command if innocent. His enemies, however, feared that his popularity with the people would save him. They pushed for the fleet's sailing and postponement of a trial, thinking to prosecute later when he was more vulnerable. Amid this turmoil, the expedition – including Alcibiades – sailed west for Corcyra, the jumping-off point for Sicily (Thuc. 6.27–9).

To make matters worse, when the expedition finally sailed, it did so under a bad sign. As the fleet weighed anchor and the wind caught the sails, Athenian women, or at least those in the Piraeus, were celebrating the Adonai festival at which miniature images of dead youth were carried about to the accompaniment of dirges and chants. This cult, an eastern import, reveals not only new attitudes in religion then current in Athens, but also how the strain of war was causing Athenians to look elsewhere for comfort in a time of stress and anxiety.[11] The last words many Athenian soldiers and sailors heard as they left home were women crying out, 'Woe for Adonis', 'Weep for Adonis' (Ar. *Lys.* 389–93).[12]

The fleet's voyage west was uneventful perhaps except for an incident involving Alcibiades and the comic poet Eupolis. In his comedy *Baptae*, Eupolis had made some fun of Alcibiades, mocking perhaps his famous lisp. Now at sea and at Alcibiades' not so tender mercies, the general retaliated. Sailors grabbed the playwright and tossed him over the side: while being dunked, Alcibiades hollered out, 'you gave me a dunking on the stage, I'll soak you in the sea'![13] Eupolis probably got just that, as he appears later in Athens still writing comedy.[14]

Unmoved or unconcerned with either emotions or high jinks, Thucydides focused his discussion and analysis on the grandeur of the expedition's sailing and its tremendous display of power and wealth. He calculated that no other expedition could compare, not only in terms of size and armament, but also in terms of the daring and the hopes planned by the enterprise (Thuc. 6.30–2). His picture is, as A.G. Woodhead notes, one of a 'manifestation of power in action' and so underlines John Mearsheimer's definition of power as consisting of the wealth and military forces of a state.[15] But also revealed is the nature of 'institutional power' and how a people, in this instance the Athenians, have decided in a formal, organized political organ of state to use their wealth and military power to acquire still more wealth and thereby more power. Power is not static: as Thucydides makes clear, use it or lose it.

The War with Syracuse

Arriving in Sicily the Athenians soon found they had been duped. Their Sicilian allies had promised great sums of money and ready support, but all this was so much wishful thinking. The three commanders discussed their options. Nicias, ever cautious, suggested they try to find allies and if unsuccessful, return home. Alcibiades thought this an admission of failure, and proposed that they recruit allies among the local Greeks and native Sicilians and then attack Syracuse. Lamachus, the soldier, proposed an immediate attack on a still unready Syracuse, the target of their campaign, as the likeliest way to win. While risky, Lamachus' strategy held the best chance for success – the Athenian force was fresh and in high spirits while the Syracusans were disorganized.[16] The views of his colleagues prevailed, however, and with that decision the best chance for a quick victory – and the initiative – was lost.[17]

Athenian efforts to find local support generally failed and except for local Sicels and the communities of Naxos and Catana, there was little sympathy for the Athenian cause. As Lamachus had perhaps feared, as the Athenians dallied, the Syracusans, under the leadership of Hermocrates, prepared. Even worse, word arrived from Athens (summer 415) that Alcibiades was to return home to face charges for his alleged participation in the acts of religious vandalism of the past summer (Thuc. 6.53).

Rather than return to a certain condemnation, Alcibiades fled Sicily, eventually reaching Sparta where he revealed Athenian plans and strength to his hosts. He may also have suggested to the Spartans that they could inflict greater damage and distress on the Athenians by establishing a permanent presence in Attica.[18] While the annual invasions had certainly disturbed the Athenians, what was now proposed would hurt far more. A garrison in Attica would inhibit the movement of troops as well as civilians, it would make the flight of slaves possible, and it would demonstrate to the allies that the Athenians were not invincible. These very things the Athenians demonstrated from their base in Pylos and the Spartans could easily have decided to return the favor. It is impossible to know if Alcibiades persuaded Thucydides that the fort in Decelea was his idea. But it surely appealed to Athenian conceit that the cause of their later defeat came not at the hands of the sluggard Spartans, but from a brilliant plan conceived by one of their own.[19]

Alcibiades' departure did not long delay Nicias and Lamachus. A reconnaissance of Sicily brought in money, allies, and recruits, some of the latter including Etruscans from northern Italy (Thuc. 6.62, 7.57.11), and with that they moved against Syracuse. A hard-fought battle followed in which the Athenians and their allies, especially the Argives, succeeded in turning back a large and enthusiastic but inexperienced Syracusan army. As the Syracusans broke off and returned home, the Athenians found that the numerous and well-equipped Syracusan cavalry was very effective (Thuc. 6.63–71).

The winter months (415/14) allowed the Syracusans to reorganize while the Athenians found it difficult to bear up under the weather and with short supplies. The Athenians also sent word to Athens requesting money and cavalry reinforcements (Thuc. 6.74.2). In the following summer (414) the first serious fighting began as the Athenians began closing in around Syracuse, laying the groundwork for a siege. Walls and stockades were built, and the struggles were fierce around such places as the circular fort and the height of Epipolai. A fierce fight broke out around Epipolai and when Lamachus saw his Athenians and Argives giving ground, he rushed in to help. But his brave action miscarried – attacking with only a few men he was cut off and killed (Thuc. 6.103). Now Nicias commanded the expedition alone and he was sick, as he reported to Athens late that summer, asking again for relief (Thuc. 7.82).

Lamachus' death notwithstanding, the Syracusans remained hard pressed by the Athenian assault. News of the Athenian successes had reached as far as Leucas where the Spartan commander Gylippus now arrived with a small expeditionary force (mid-summer 414), dispatched perhaps at the suggestion of Alcibiades. Not even twenty ships strong, this Spartan and Corinthian aid was dismissed by Nicias as of no consequence.[20] What Nicias failed to appreciate was that such aid, no matter how small, was bound to raise the morale of the embattled Syracusan defenders, while Gylippus' role as military adviser would prove no less beneficial. In short, Nicias misjudged the impact of what Gylippus now brought to Syracuse.

As Gylippus was about to turn the tables in Sicily, the Athenians departed from their previous disengagement with Sparta and now joined their Argive allies in invading into Spartan and allied territory. Such operations provided the Spartans with all the provocation needed to claim that the Athenians had broken the Peace of Nicias and to take up openly the cause of aid for Syracuse.[21]

War without Mercy

The trireme bringing Nicias' dispatch arrived in Athens in early winter 414 and set the Athenians into action with their customary energy. His letter read to the assembly, the reaction was speedy: two generals, Menander and Euthydemus were appointed to join him (at once?) in commanding the expedition and new levies were also approved with two more generals, Demosthenes and Eurymedon, given command of these.[22] By early summer 413 this force was ready for sailing and Demosthenes led it out, along the way collecting additional Athenian and allied forces. Speed was essential and diversionary operations were minimal (Thuc. 7.26).

Soon after Demosthenes sailed with the relief force, some 1300 Thracian peltasts arrived in Athens, just missing the fleet. After some deliberation, the Athenians decided that they should return home, but in doing so should punish the enemy en route. Escorted by the Athenian general Diitrephes and a small contingent of Athenians, the Thracians headed north.[23]

On entering Boeotian territory, the Thracians came upon sleepy Mycalessus, a small town that was had pretty much bypassed. That soon changed. Charging in through broken-down gates, the Thracians fell upon the unsuspecting town with unparalleled fury. They burst into a crowd of boys assembling for school and slaughtered them. Neither were animals spared, nor the adults, men and women alike. Amid the carnage someone managed to escape and go for help. This arrived but only after the worst of the slaughter was over. Some of the Thracians, overloaded with loot, were tracked down and killed, but most made good their escape, as did their Athenian employers. While the actual killing must be laid at the door of the Thracians, this was an Athenian-conceived operation and makes clear the kind of war Athens was now willing to fight.

The slaughter that Thucydides relates at Mycalessus merely anticipates a much greater slaughter soon to come in Sicily. While Nicias' plea to be relieved had been ignored and he was still sick, he did have help in commanding the expedition. Four more generals, including Demosthenes, the hero of Sphacteria, now shared the command. Though unwell, Nicias knew the lay of the land and had the Sicilian (and Syracusan) contacts, and this experience, alongside his seniority, no doubt gave him a louder voice in the decisions to be taken. This gives some idea of the nature of joint command for Athenian generals who were technically equal in authority.[24] The forces that Demosthenes brought had in effect doubled the resources available to the Athenian commanders. The Athenians might have had reason for some optimism, guarded though it may have been. In reality they had lost the initiative, though they seem not to have noticed.

The arrival of Gylippus and the Corinthians had boosted morale at just the right moment (Thuc. 7.1–3) and several acts of indecision by Nicias surrendered the offensive to Gylippus and the Syracusans. What followed in the summer was a 'battle of the walls' in which an Athenian effort to encircle Syracuse failed as the Syracusans were able to build counter walls that denied the Athenians their aim.[25] A final effort, a night battle on the critical point of Epipolai failed, leaving Nicias and Demosthenes to ponder their diminishing opportunities for victory (Thuc. 7.43–5). At this critical moment, and just as Nicias mulled over a retreat, an eclipse of the moon brought Athenian action to a halt for nearly a month. As the Athenians sat, Gylippus and the Syracusans tightened the ring around their opponents (Thuc. 7.50–1).

In fact Athenian options were limited to what their naval forces could now achieve. Destruction of the Syracusan fleet might just make possible the final defeat of their enemy. Despite the declining seaworthiness of their fleet, the Athenians challenged the Syracusans and their Peloponnesian allies in an all or nothing gamble in Syracuse's Great Harbor.[26] In a hard-fought battle, the Athenians suffered heavily as the Syracusans had strengthened the bows of their ships in order to ram head-on. The shoreline was

Figure 8.1 Syracuse's Great Harbor, looking south to the site of the great battle between Athenians and Syracusans.

lined with the armies of both sides, who, Thucydides tells, watched as spectators at a game, cheering their team on – the Athenians lost (Thuc. 7.59–72).

Defeated, Nicias and Demosthenes attempted to rally their sailors and soldiers and try again, but the survivors were totally demoralized and refused. The decision was made then to disengage and abandon the campaign. In a dramatic and poignant account, Thucydides relates how the Athenians broke camp leaving behind their sick and critically injured as well as their unburied dead. Dividing their men into two columns, Nicias and Demosthenes led out the defeated remnants of their forces with the cries and jeers of those abandoned ringing in their ears.

The Syracusans were not about to let the Athenians get away. They gathered their forces and devised an elaborate strategy and ruse to delay the Athenian withdrawal. Gylippus also spoke to the Syracusan soldiery and incited them, telling them of the indecent things the Athenians had planned for their women and children had they won (Thuc. 7.68.2). Images of wailing and raped women, murdered children drawn so powerfully in the plays of Euripides are given substance in this rousing pep talk which later drove the Syracusans to acts of frenzied violence.

In a few short days the Athenian retreat became a rout, the Syracusans harrying their enemies as prey on a hunt. With little in the way of food and especially water, the Athenians and their allies lost all semblance of order. The army broke in half and separated with Demosthenes' part being caught and surrounded first. Realizing that resistance was pointless, Demosthenes surrendered himself and his men. Isolated, Nicias tried to keep his men moving ahead, but it was difficult as the Syracusan cavalry – always so effective – harried them relentlessly. Finally, on reaching the Assinarus River what little discipline was left dissipated. Men crazed by thirst fought their way forward thinking only of water, and in the process were cut down as they drank. Not battle but slaughter, Thucydides described the killing with language drawn from sacrifice *sphazo/sphazein*, a verb used to describe sacrificial slaughter as in the cutting of throats. The water turned red with blood as the Syracusans and especially the Peloponnesians shot the Athenians and their allies down (Thuc. 7.84.2–5). Nicias finally found Gylippus with whom he pleaded to stop the killing and allow his men to be taken captive. This happened at last, but it is silly to imagine that a ceasefire was ordered quickly – bloodlust was up and there were scores to settle.

The Athenians had retreated like rabbits and only a few showed any coolness. One group of about 300 hoplites with Nicias managed to break free of the Syracusan encirclement, but these were later rounded up. A detachment of cavalry led by the Athenian Callistratus did make good its escape; seeing his men safe in Catane, Callistratus turned back to the scene of the disaster. As he approached the last Athenian camp, he charged into the looters, killing half a dozen before being overcome and killed, his heroic horse dying too (Paus. 7.16.3).

The survivors would have envied Callistratus his noble death. A Sicilian source relates a Syracusan debate over fates of the Athenian rank and file as well as their generals. One popular leader, Diocles, proposed that Nicias and Demosthenes should be tortured to death, and the rest thrown into the quarries. Hermocrates, whose leadership had led to victory, challenged this proposal but he was shouted down. At this point an old man, Nicolaus, came forward. As he sadly told of his sons' deaths in battle, leaving him to face a bleak future alone, he surprised all arguing that the prisoners should be spared. At this point Gylippus supposedly intervened and challenged Nicolaus' appeal, arguing that such consideration was hardly appropriate for people who caused the deaths of so many. After this debate Diocles' original proposal was approved and Nicias and Demosthenes were executed, the rest of the Athenians thrown into the quarries (Diod. 13.18.4–34.1).

The sinister image of Gylippus in this western Greek account is probably fabricated and may reflect later anti-Spartan propaganda.[27] In reality Gylippus saw the value in returning Nicias and Demosthenes to Sparta as living trophies of victory – this was especially so for Demosthenes to avenge his defeat of the Spartans at Sphacteria. But a number of Syracusans feared Nicias might betray them as they had secretly negotiated with him, while the Corinthians feared that both men might somehow get free and live to fight another day. In the words of Thucydides, the Sicilian expedition 'turned out to be the greatest connected with this war and, at least in my opinion, of Greek affairs we have heard of. It was the greatest victory for those who won and the worst of defeats for those who were ruined' (Thuc. 7.87.5).

Athenian and allied rank and file may have envied Nicias and Demosthenes their quick deaths. Some 7000 were herded into the quarries outside Syracuse where they were left to the elements and short rations – a daily cup of water and two of food.[28] After seventy days the Sicilian and Italian captives were sold – going to their new masters with the Syracusan horse tattooed on their foreheads (Plut. Nic. 29). Some six months later those still living – Athenian and their Greek allies – were sold too.

Details are scare, but the Syracusans were confronted by guerrilla activities carried out by some of the Athenians who escaped the final disaster. One Athenian survivor told later how he had continued fighting the Syracusans, first with other survivors and then with the Catanians. Their resistance allowed them to rescue some of the captives. It may have been this resistance that prompted the Syracusans to sell off the surviving captives so as to end the fighting.[29]

Some of these survivors managed to get home after a journey that Odysseus would have appreciated. What they told their friends and neighbors seemed beyond belief, but slowly more news arrived confirming the rumors (Thuc. 8.1). One such story tells of a sailor arriving in the Piraeus whose first visit is to the barber. As the barber worked, the sailor calmly remarked, as if it were common knowledge, how tragic it was that so many Athenians had died in far-off Sicily. Dropping what he was doing, the barber raced off to city hall in Athens with the sailor's news of the catastrophe (Plut. Nic. 30). A story yes, but reality may have been little different.

The Horror

The disaster cut the Athenians deeply. Even eighteen months later the Athenians were still sensitive to the word Sicily. In perhaps his best-known comedy, *Lysistrata*, Aristophanes writes a scene in which Lysistrata, the play's protagonist, debates an arrogant magistrate over women's knowledge of war. She rebukes him, 'what of us then who for our children must weep?', causing him to beg her not to remind him of those lost in Sicily.[30] Another story tells that news of the disaster coincided with the performance of a comedy by the dramatist and parodist Hegemon of Thasos, *The Battle of the Giants*. As news of the disaster spread through the crowd, none of the Athenians in the audience left, but instead remained in their seats laughing and enjoying the show.[31] What explains this apparent callousness to the great loss of life that so many families would have suffered? The answer lies in part to the presence of Greeks from the allied cities also attending the play. The Athenians present could not show any emotion, any fear, in such a setting. To do so would amount to a display of weakness to those whom they regarded as subjects.

But there is something else going on in this supposed expression of Athenian joy at a time of sorrow and profound loss. What is revealed here is a sense of deep personal as well as communal shock, the devastating impact of traumatic loss upon a people in a time of war. A modern counterpart to such reactions is told by correspondent and author Dexter Filkins talking to families of sons killed in Iraq, 2003–8. With smiles on their faces, they say, 'he died doing what he wanted'. Filkins describes this as 'a front, a Potemkin thing, and one whose construction had come at no small effort'.[32] The full measure of the shock of such loss and the human attempt to cope with it is illuminated in an unexpected contemporary text, Gorgias of Leontini's rhetorical exercise on the innocence of Helen.

When Gorgias arrived in Athens in 427 he evidently had so many invitations for speaking and lecturing that he remained in Greece for a time, traveling and giving sample speeches at Olympia and Delphi among other places.[33] Among these showcase performances was the *Encomium of Helen*, his speech designed to absolve Helen from blame in abandoning Menelaus for Paris, a work described as 'an essay on the nature and power of logos'.[34] Like the composition of Herodotus' *Histories* (and the articles and books of modern scholars), the writing of the *Helen* was a long process and Gorgias probably gave many presentations of the piece before finally getting it into final and polished written form. A date of 414 for this has been proposed and this finds confirmation in a reference pointing unmistakably to the wartime conditions of the Peloponnesian War.

In the course of this speech Gorgias notes how sight takes in images and passes them on to the mind (or soul) remembering them. In the case of soldiers experiencing the sights and sounds of battle, these images and their memories are not forgotten and induce in them unending terror. Panic and fear are not heroic reactions, as Gorgias knows all too well, but this is what happens to many men who are then driven to break the law and run from obedience as well as victory. So destructive are these images of war and violence that some are unable to think clearly or otherwise function. As Gorgias concludes, many of these men are unable to work, they have become chronically sick, physically, and suffer as well from what can only be described as psychic trauma.[35]

What should amaze the modern reader is the perceptiveness that Gorgias demonstrates in this observation. Even today in the early twenty-first century, few people seem to grasp the essential fact of war – that when men are sent into battle they return different. Some are more deeply changed than others, but there is an undeniable change that has occurred and Gorgias may well be the first in the western tradition to recognize this.

Gorgias' reference to the trauma of war comes up incidentally in a context of debate and thought analyzing Helen's actions in abandoning Menelaus for Paris. It is an oblique reference and as such ranks as the 'purest' form of primary evidence that scholars can hope to find.[36] Additionally, the emphasis on sight that Gorgias makes finds a parallel in similar imagery used by Euripides. In his *Suppliant Women* (c. 420), Euripides also combines the power of sight and the terror of battle; in a speech to Adrastus on standing in the battle line and facing the enemy, Theseus says 'when you stand against the foe, it is hard enough to see what must be seen (*Supp.* 855–6). What Gorgias and Euripides tell provides literary parallels to the real-life cases of the Athenian soldier Epizelus at Marathon who in the midst of battle becomes blind, suffering what modern medicine knows as hysterical blindness (Hdt. 7.224). Similar cases of hysterical blindness and battle trauma are recorded on the Epidaurian miracle inscriptions and these provide further evidence of wounds received but long remained unhealed.[37]

Athenian stories of war and survival tell a similar tale as does Gorgias, but those of the Spartan *tresantes*, 'cowards' or 'tremblers', reveals even more of war's trauma upon its combatants.[38] Perhaps first used by Herodotus in the 420s in telling the story of Aristodemus, the Spartan survivor of Thermopylae (480), *tresantes* or 'cowards' came to be applied to those Spartans who ran away in battle and who, as a consequence, lost their citizen rights and were subject to other forms of social abuse.[39] It is difficult to know how many of these men were simply runaways or cowards and how many were 'shiverers' and 'tremblers', men who had seen the horror of battle and had broken down. But without question, the condition points to the stress of battle being as much a Spartan reality as for any other Greek, all the training notwithstanding.

Gorgias' testimony and the story of the Spartan *tresantes* are valuable as they put a human face on the terror of the Peloponnesian War, and so complement those given by Thucydides, as in the Athenian retreat from Syracuse, his account of the terrible *stasis* in Corcyra. But what Gorgias tells is actually richer in that it makes a connection between the effects of going into battle, seeing and experiencing horrific things, and how this affects the mind (or soul insofar as Gorgias could tell) and changes the man – something that today is defined as post-traumatic stress disorder.[40] Such horrors are universal and a striking parallel can be found in the post-World War I experience, as told by Philip Gibbs, a war correspondent who had seen it all:

> After the trouble of demobilization came Peace pageants and celebrations, and flag-wavings. But all was not right with the spirit of the men who came back. Something was wrong. They put on civilian clothes again, looked, to their mothers and wives, very much like the young men who had gone to business in the peaceful days before the August of 1914. But they had not come back the same men. Something had altered in them. They were subject to queer moods, queer tempers, fits of profound depression alternating with a restless desire for pleasure. Many of them were easily moved to passion when they lost control of themselves. Many were bitter in their speech, violent in opinion, frightening.[41]

Another Comment on Helen

The defense of Helen that Gorgias offers, as well as his reflections on the trauma of war, were followed up in other ways by Euripides. The result appeared on stage in the spring 412 as news of yet another slaughter began to be known. In his drama *Helen* Euripides tells of yet another reason why Helen could not be blamed for leaving Menelaus or the great Trojan War that followed – she was in Egypt the whole time – whisked away by Hermes (*Hel.* 36–55)! In the course of this escapist fantasy, Euripides attacks the very stupidity of war, how the greatest war among the Greeks was fought for a mirage – men died for nothing (*Hel.* 608–15).

Euripides returns to this theme twice more: a servant of Menelaus and Menelaus himself, both survivors of Troy, refer to war as a waste. Euripides adds further comment from a depressed and mentally exhausted Menelaus stating his readiness to die – a sure expression of war-induced trauma.[42] Toward the end of the drama, Euripides delivers a further indictment of war in a choral song: 'mindless, all of you, who in the strength of spears and the tearing edge win your honors by war, thus stupidly trying to halt the grief of the world. For if bloody debate shall settle the issue, never again shall hate be gone out of the cities of men (Eur. *Hel.* 1151–5).

The thrust of these passages is that war is not only a vain exercise, but idiocy. Yet some scholars continue to resist the idea that in the *Helen* Euripides makes an anti-war statement, arguing instead that at the play's end, Menelaus saves Helen and escapes the scheming of the Egyptian king Theoclymenus by resorting to violence.[43]

Such argument misses the forest for the trees. In fact Menelaus' use of violence makes perfect sense within the context of war and survival. A war-exhausted veteran, Menelaus arrives lost in Egypt and suddenly finds Helen – the cause of so much suffering – gone in an instant, her divinely created phantom snatched away by the gods. On finding the real Helen and learning that she is not the cause of such great loss of life, Menelaus at last finds something worth fighting for. There is a propensity for violence in many, if not most, veterans, though it is mostly self-directed and inflicted. On finding a reason to fight again, and surely finding a long–lost love counts as this, many veterans will fight to keep that which is dear to them.

Notes

1 See Chapter 4 for discussion of Athens in Sicily, c. 424.
2 Thuc. 6.1.1, 6.1–26 (Egestaian plea for aid); Thuc. 6.46.3–5, Diod. 12.83.3.
3 See Thuc. 6.8˙26, with Gomme-Andrewes-Dover 4: 223–64, for the speeches.
4 See pp. 68–71 and Woodhead 1970: 7.
5 Plut. *Nic.* 13.5–6, Ar. *Av.* 998.

6 Andoc. *Mys.* 11.

7 Thuc. 6.28.1 delicately notes that the heads of the statues were knocked off. But it appears that this was done to the statues' phalluses as well where there was one. See Gomme-Andrewes-Dover 4: 288–9 for discussion; Andoc. *Mys.* 62 claims only one herm was left intact but this may be exaggeration.

8 Andocides' speech *On the Mysteries* provides much of what is known of these incidents (on which see MacDowell 1962), but the speech is post-war, c. 400, and is self-serving (see Lattimore 1998: 336, n. and Todd 2004: 87–102 for discussion). Thuc. 6.27–28, 60 also relate these events; it is helpful to recall that Andocides was caught up in the events while Thucydides was in exile.

9 Andoc. *Mys.* 36–7, with MacDowell 1962: 87–8; Todd 2004: 89–97 discusses Andocides' place in these events. Thuc. 6.60.2 notes that these events, and what actually happened was essentially beyond knowing. Gomme-Andrewes-Dover 4: 276–88 lists the alleged participants and their associations.

10 See Dover in Gomme-Andrewes-Dover 4: 264–90; MacDowell 1962: 193 and Ellis 1989: 58–62 suggest that Alcibiades had a hand in profaning the Mysteries but not the mutilation of the herms.

11 Plut. *Nic.* 13.7. See also Parker 1996: 196–7 and pp. 115–16 on the arrival of Asclepius in Athens.

12 Aristophanes is writing a comedy and is unconcerned with ordering correctly the sequence of events; Plutarch, who would be following a source, associates the festival with the fleet's sailing and should be followed here.

13 See Sutton 1990: 81–2 and Sidwell 2009 for discussion. Cf. Storey 2003: 56–60 who prefers a death in battle for Eupolis based on *IG* I³ 1190, l. 52, a casualty list for the battle of Cynossema (411/10); but the name is common and Eupolis appears active after the battle.

14 Sidwell 2009 dates Eupolis' *Demes* to 410; cf. Storey 2003: 112 for a date c. 418–411/10, but see previous note. On the later activities of Eupolis see pp. 171–7.

15 Woodhead 1970: 7, Mearsheimer 2001: 56.

16 For discussion of Athenian strategy and which should have been adopted see Lazenby 2004. Thuc. 6.72 notes the anxiety that gripped the Syracusans after their first fight with the Athenians, calmed by Hermocrates' counsel. His leadership was instrumental to the eventual Syracusan victory.

17 Thuc. 7.42.3 suggests that Thucydides shared this view; see the discussion on Demosthenes' arrival and decision to act quickly and decisively – just as Lamachus now. See also Cawkwell 1997: 83, Lazenby 2004: 138–40.

18 Thuc. 6.61 (Alcibiades' flight), 6.88.10–93 (Decelea, on which there is considerable debate; cf. Hanson 2005: 64, Ellis 1989: 66).

19 It may be worth noting that Alcibiades and Thucydides, both exiled elites, might well have met at some point and talked about the war and its course.

20 Thuc. 6.93.2–3, 104. In the following year, Thuc. 7.19.3–4 reports the arrival of another Peloponnesian relief force, some 1600 hoplites (and light-armed troops omitted?) in Sicily to aid the Syracusans.

21 Thuc. 6.105, with de Ste. Croix 1972: 113.

22 Thuc. 6.74.2, 7.10–15 (Nicias' dispatch, reporting on various problems with the fleet, its ships and sailors, as well as deserting mercenaries).

23 Thuc. 7.27.1–2, 29–30. Thucydides names only the Athenian general with the Thracians, but it seems unlikely that Diitrephes would travel without an Athenian escort, here omitted.

24 See the discussion pp. 80–1 on the *strategia* and Sinclair 1988: 17–18, 80–2, 138–9.

25 See Rawlings 2007: 136–7.

26 So-called after the map in *CAH*² 5, 454.

27 The source is probably the Sicilian Greek writer Timaeus whose authority and reliability are suspect. A similar rhetorical exercise, a defense speech by Nicias in this debate, is credited to Lysias. See Gomme-Andrewes-Dover 4: 461.

28 The number of prisoners is difficult to reconstruct. Thucydides notes that 'all Sicily' was full of household slaves now taken, so it is clear that there was a good deal of profiteering (Thuc. 7. 85.3). The 7000 that Thucydides reports may also have included servants, the slaves of the Athenian troops also taken. In the quarries, however, they were all treated the same (Thuc. 7.87.4, with Plut. *Nic.* 29).

29 Lys. 20.24–5, a speech usually dated to c. 410.

30 Ar. *Lys.* 587–8, hinted at l. 524–8; see Henderson 1987: 145, and below.

31 Athen. 407a-b, other sources in Kassel-Austin 5: 546–7. See also Green 1970: 351; Lesky 1966: 417 notes that the play would have been performed at the Panathenaic festival at which allies would have been present both as spectators and competitors. As the disaster in Sicily occurred sometime in September 413 (after the Panathenaea of that year), it would not have been until the next year's festival, that of summer 412, that news would have arrived. Given the circumstances and the distances involved, this seems about right.

32 Filkins 2008: 342.

33 On Gorgias' diplomatic mission see pp. 75–6.

34 Sources cited in Guthrie 1971: 192.

35 Gorg. F11.16–18 (Sprague).

36 In terms of primary source material, it is well known that unintended evidence, that which is an unconscious reference to an idea, argument, or anything else, is the 'purest' and consequently, most valuable. For discussion see, e.g., Burckhardt 1998: 5.

37 See passages and discussion in Tritle 2003: 130–4.

38 *Tresas* (coward, runaway) evidently appears first in Hdt. 7.231 (related forms in Tyr. 11.14 and Plut. *Ages.* 30.2) in reference to the infamous Aristodemus,

but this should date c. 420s (see p. 76 for Herodotus' date). How and Wells 1912: 2, 231, translate *tresas* as coward. The first modern discussion is that of V. Ehrenberg, 'Tresantes' *RE* VIA (1937): 2292–7. A World War I combat soldier (see Audring *et al.* 1990), Ehrenberg translated *tresantes* as *gezittert* or 'shiverers', the same term then applied to post-war veterans in Germany (see E.M. Remarque, *Der Weg zurück*, 1931 [= Frankfurt, 1984]: 148–9; *The Road Back*, trans. A.W. Wheen [New York, 1958 = Boston, 1931]: 269), and seen in Otto Dix's *War Cripples* (1920). It is this translation and interpretation that has found its way into the literature and history today, exemplifying the present's influence on the past.

39 Plut. *Ages.* 30.2 notes they could be beaten with impunity on the streets, could not marry, and had to shave half their beards, yet Hdt. 7.231 only notes of Aristodemus that no one would talk to him or give him light for a fire. Yet he fought at Plataea in 479 and was up for honors as Herodotus notes (9.71), so clearly the terms of the condition were complicated. It would appear that as time progressed (and the number of Spartiates declined) the status was defined more restrictively and punitively. Note how such penalties were relaxed for the Sphacteria survivors (Thuc. 5.34.2). See also the discussions of Cartledge 1987: 179 and Ducat 2006, the latter filled with useful information but without appreciation of the psychic dimension or Ehrenberg's wartime service. Finally, *pace* Ducat, the penalties for *tresantes* were surely incremental, increasing as manpower losses grew in Sparta.

40 Tritle 2000.

41 Gibbs 1920: 447.

42 Eur. *Hel.* 703–5, 1113–21 (war for nothing), 765–79 (Menelaus worn out by war).

43 So Allan 2008: 6–9, in the most recent edition of the play. Too often analysis of plays occurs in isolation. For example, Aristophanes' *Lysistrata* and Euripides' *Helen* appeared within a span of some eighteen months or two years and after catastrophic loss. Each in its own way points to war exhaustion and war idiocy and not to see this is to imagine that these playwrights were not sensitive to their own times and the issues that concerned their own contemporaries (on which see Ehrenberg 1954: 7).

9

'THE WHOLE OF GREECE
AGAINST ATHENS'

As news of the Athenian disaster swept the Greek world, friends and foes alike greeted the reports with undiminished joy (Thuc. 8.2.1). Enemies now saw the chance to close in for the kill. The allies, subjects really, saw the opportunity for revolt. The unaligned realized that action against Athens would save them from what Syracuse had escaped. Such expressions make clear the depths of Athenian unpopularity and the methods by which they ruled and dominated the rest of the Greeks. The legacy of Melos and Scione, only the worst demonstrations of Athenian power and excess, now struck home with a vengeance.

News of the disaster in Sicily shook Athens to its foundations too. In an editorial-like comment, Thucydides sarcastically rebukes the Athenians now angry at the orators and politicians who persuaded them to approve the expedition, as if they had not voted for it themselves (Thuc. 8.1.1). But there was a sense of panic in the air, evident in the creation of a ten-man executive committee, the *probouloi*, who would now work alongside the Council. Two of these advisors are known, Hagnon and the tragedian Sophocles, the latter some eighty plus years old. The apparent conflict of oligarchic and democratic ideals seems best explained by the impact of wartime tragedy and an unsettled population.[1]

But the Athenians scarcely had time for recriminations or mourning. Closer to home an even greater threat loomed. In the previous spring/ summer offensive (413) Agis had led another Peloponnesian force into Attica to conduct the by now usual burning of crops and destruction of property. This time, however, Agis did not withdraw. He established a permanent base of operations at Decelea, located near the Boeotian border. From this base he could intercept the shipment of food and material into Attica and Athens from nearby Euboea via the port/transit hub of Oropus. The Spartans could now strike much of the Athenian countryside whenever and wherever they chose.[2] Not only did the Spartans command the greater part of Attica, even to the walls of Athens itself, but Athenian movements could be observed and threatened, even those to Eleusis and the sanctuary of Demeter where the famous Mysteries were celebrated.[3]

This rare example of Spartan initiative threatened Athens and its inhabitants. Word went around that escaping slaves would find sanctuary in Decelea, and in the years to come more than 20,000 slaves fled: most were handed over to the Thebans who cashed in, reselling the fugitives. Even some Athenian citizens now panicked and defected to the Spartans, seem-

Ionia (after Henderson 1927)

ingly making their own truce much like an Aristophanic hero. Such traitor-ous conduct did not go unnoticed: a decree was enacted pronouncing a death sentence on any Athenian who did so. The agrarian economy suf-fered and shortages began to appear in the markets, forcing the Athenians to bring in food and supplies from more distant sources. All of this made control of the eastern and northern Aegean even more critical to the Athenians.[4]

The Ionian War[5]

At Decelea Agis held court and entertained embassies from various com-munities exploring opportunities as they abandoned Athens. The most notable of these were from Euboea and Lesbos, both loyal Athenian friends of old, while at Sparta a delegation from Chios, another Aegean state and Athens' last major ally, arrived with a representative of the Persian satrap Tissaphernes (Thuc. 8.5–6). The potential defection of these Greek allies along with the Persian overture did not bode well for Athens, as loss of the Aegean was now threatened from north to south, along with the Asian coast.

The Spartan investment at Decelea soon paid a major return. An Athe-nian naval success (Thuc. 8.10–11) in the waters around the Corinthian coast near Epidaurus was tempered by an Athenian realization that their Chian allies could not be trusted. Worse was to follow. Alcibiades, still in league with the Spartans though not with Agis (the matter of his sleeping with Agis' wife still rankled!), arrived in Chios with the Spartan Chalcideus and a small squadron. Despite his problem with Agis, Alcibiades retained the favor of high-ranking friends in Sparta, particularly the ephor Endius. An old family friend, Endius blessed his efforts to bring about the defection of whatever Athenian allies he could, and this he did. His primary goal, as he ostensibly convinced Endius, was to win over Tissaphernes for Sparta, bring about a revolt of Athens' allies in Asia, and with Persian aid defeat Athens.[6]

A meeting with Chian oligarchs had been pre-arranged and with this local support Alcibiades and Chalcideus brought about the defection the Athenians feared. With its wealth, manpower reserves, and strong fleet, the loss of Chios to Sparta was not good news. But the Athenians refused to give in. A cash reserve held on the acropolis, the 'iron fund', was opened and new ships were built, new crews recruited and paid (Thuc. 8.15.2, 2.24.1). Clearly the Athenians were determined not to go quietly – and Alcibiades moved on to pick off more disaffected Athenian allies.

As the Athenians dug in their heels and prepared to answer the Chian defection, the Spartans continued to make gains in the eastern Aegean. The communities of Lesbos soon became the focus of the Spartan and Athenian duel. Though Lesbos was lost to the Spartans, Clazomenae, an important transit point opposite on the Asian mainland reverted to Athenian control (Thuc. 8.17, 22–6). Alcibiades continued to exploit opportunities for both himself and the Spartans at Athenian expense and toward the end of summer 412, he brought about the defection of Miletus. The Athenians quickly organized a response and counterattacked, their forces stiffened by hundreds of Argive volunteers whose Athenian alliance Alcibiades himself had forged only six years before. In fierce fighting around the city Alcibiades joined the Milesians in fighting his former countrymen. Though the Athenians prevailed, some 300 Argives were killed.

The arrival of a joint Peloponnesian–Syracusan fleet, however, blunted the Athenian success. Urged on by Alcibiades, the Peloponnesians and Syracusans took up positions around Miletus, challenging the Athenians who now balked at further military action. Opinion among the Athenian generals commanding was mixed, some pushing to fight on, others for tactical withdrawal. In a debate that reveals clearly the functioning of the Athenian *strategia*, Phrynichus persuaded his colleagues that the risks were too great at a time when Athens needed to husband every ship and soldier. At this the Athenians disengaged and withdrew home, having accomplished little. The Argives, who had suffered severely in a now meaningless fight, sailed home too, bitterly (Thuc. 8. 25–7).

Enter the Persians

Successes in Sicily and Decelea sparked a flurry of diplomatic activity unmatched perhaps since the aftermath of the Peace of Nicias. Not only did Greeks petition the Spartans for aid in breaking away from Athenian control, but envoys from Persia now arrived looking to make a deal. Among these was an envoy from the Persian satrap Tissaphernes. Several years before and as events in Sicily unfolded, a revolt in Asia first by the satrap Pissuthnes, then taken up by his son, Amorges, brought the Athenians into conflict with the Great King, Darius II (c. 413). Athenian intervention in Persian affairs enraged the king, and drove him to the Spartans.[7] Tissaphernes had been able to suppress Pissuthnes, but Amorges aided by the Athenians remained a threat. After the defection of Miletus and the fight for the city, Tissaphernes and the Spartan officer Chalcideus agreed to terms (summer 412). As equal allies, they agreed to cut off the Athenians from local Asian revenues and not to come to terms separately with the Athenians.[8] Most ominously perhaps, the Spartans implicitly recognized Persian claims to possession of lands ancestrally held by the Persian kings. This would place in jeopardy the Greek cities of Asia and undermined already, if anyone noticed, Spartan claims to be fighting for the freedom of the Greeks.

But Tissaphernes was not the only Persian notable to open negotiations with the Spartans. On the heels of Tissaphernes' overture came a second from Pharnabazus, satrap of Hellespontine Phrygia, who urged the Spartans to come north, promising them support.[9] Military action would soon return to the northern Aegean, site of intense action in the Archidamian War. Brasidas had recognized in this region an Athenian Achilles' heel as the sea lanes from the Black Sea and through the Hellespont kept the Athenians fed: block these and Athens starves. Brasidas' death and the Peace of Nicias had ended hostilities here, but in the months following the Sicilian disaster and the defection of Chios the area once more became a battleground. The entry of the Persians, however, now complicated the issues and raised the stakes considerably.

Persian overtures soon paid dividends. Perhaps toward the end of summer 412, Persian and Peloponnesian forces stormed the Carian city of Iasus. The rebel leader Amorges was captured alive and turned over to Tissaphernes, who sent him to the Great King for surely a hard death. Iasus became an open city and suffered the full scourges of war – sack, rape, killing, enslavement – and delivered great wealth into the hands of the victors. Amorges' Greek mercenaries, mostly Peloponnesian, were not enslaved but now found employment with their former enemies.[10]

Putting an end to Amorges perhaps put Tissaphernes in a good mood, as in the following winter he came forward with the money he had previously promised the Spartans (412/11). Initially he attempted to cheat them, cutting sailors' per diem from one Attic drachma to three obols.[11] But the Syracusan Hermocrates, now in the fight with the Spartans commanding twenty-two ships, refused this, arguing for a full payment of three talents per month per five ships.[12] Tissaphernes relented and yielded to

Hermocrates' demands. Tissaphernes also agreed to Spartan arguments made by Therimenes for revising their prior agreement.

This second treaty (Thuc. 8. 36–7) enlarged upon the first by agreeing to provide financial support to the Spartans operating in the king's lands, whether lands he now controlled or those that had once belonged to his ancestors and which he claimed by right of succession. The treaty also created a fiction that the king had summoned the Greeks to fight on his behalf and recover his lands. Subsidies now became part of the agreement between the allies. With Persian gold, the Spartans now possessed the resources to build a fleet and recruit sailors and challenge Athens for control of the sea.

During this same winter (412/11), the Persian–Spartan alliance convened in Cnidus to review their earlier agreements and strategy for the coming campaigning season. In attendance were eleven Spartan delegates and Tissaphernes. The discussions turned rancorous when Lichas, a prominent Spartan – Olympic winner and diplomat – spoke up and condemned the two agreements for depriving the Greeks of Asia their freedom.[13] A veteran diplomat, Lichas clearly recognized that the agreements mocked Spartan rhetoric – that Sparta stood as the defender of Greek freedom from Athenian tyranny – and now fought to make that a reality. Tissaphernes angrily departed the conference, but the agreements made with the Persians remained in place.[14]

Perhaps Tissaphernes' anger and disappointment with the Spartans resulted from Athenian tampering, namely Alcibiades'. Supported by his influential Spartan friends, Alcibiades had provided useful services in bringing about the defection of Chios followed by Lesbos, Miletus, and Rhodes. His primary goal, as he evidently had persuaded Endius, was to win over Tissaphernes for Sparta, and with Persian aid defeat Athens. In the Spartan–Persian negotiations that followed into the late fall and winter of 412/11, Alcibiades did just this, urging Tissaphernes to support Sparta. Perhaps this was only a ploy on Alcibiades' part, as he told Tissaphernes that unending war would simply wear out Athens and Sparta and make possible the reestablishment of Persian supremacy in the Aegean.

The material support Tissaphernes provided the Spartans, however, was only just enough, so Alcibiades later explained to his fellow Athenians, to allow the Spartans to put up a good fight but not to win.[15] Among these Athenians were a number of elites serving as trierarchs, ship commanders, with the fleet at Samos. These men had sacrificed considerable personal wealth in the war and like their elite counterparts in Corcyra were concerned, perhaps driven, by material gain and loss, key factors behind the *stasis* that destroyed communities.[16] A number of these men, now tiring of their burdens, were susceptible to the cynical solutions and plots of others.

Once these wealthy Athenians may have been persuaded by what their leaders, Pericles above all, had told them of what they were fighting for and what their sacrifices would bring – that Athens was and would be the school of Greece. But after twenty years of war, plague, and a good deal of death, with no end in sight, the rhetoric and the cause were increasingly seen as little more than a lie.

War is not only a violent teacher, but a producer of cynicism on a vast scale, as any survivor of violence can confirm if he (or she) only will. The comedies of Aristophanes, for example, replete with their jokes of corrupt and misguided politicians, leaders, and intellectuals, only confirm and relate the cynicism that swept wartime Athens. Cynicism is like a cancer for a democracy and will slowly eat away at democratic resolve and democratic values. When trust and respect for law-makers and policy-makers erodes, there is a risk of collapse in the trust and respect for the law and the political system too.[17] Attacked on all fronts and pressed hard by their enemies, the Athenians were as vulnerable now to their own internal malaise as they were to the Spartans. Into this crisis intervened Alcibiades and his polarizing persona, forces that would lead to political turmoil and a bitter division of Athenian society.

Revolution in Athens: the Four Hundred, the Five Thousand[18]

The defection of Chios prompted the Athenians and their democratic allies in Samos, the last of Athens' three powerful Aegean allies, to take preemptive action. Striking first in summer 412, the Samian democrats rounded up some 200 elite citizens and killed them. Another 400 were exiled and those remaining suffered a range of civic penalties (Thuc. 8.21). In the fall and winter that followed (412/11), Samos became a staging area for Athenian forces now engaged in combating the growing threat posed by Sparta in the eastern Aegean. Thucydides does not report much on conditions on the island, but there would have been something like seventy-four ships and some 15,000 men preparing for battle.[19] There would also have been time apart from the preparations for battle when these men, many of them now at war for two decades, could reflect on the desperate circumstances facing them and their city.

Among these were those wealthy and alienated trierarchs noted above (Thuc. 8.47.2). Some of them now began thinking that their troubles could be solved by overthrowing the democracy.[20] With a more moderate form of rule, a peaceful solution with the Spartans might be found. Into this bed of discontent came Alcibiades, confident in his many talents, his never satisfied ego, and his overweening desire to return home and restore his tarnished reputation. Losing no time in playing up his Persian connections, his influence with the Great King's man Tissaphernes, Alcibiades spread word that he could make things right, but that the democracy would have to go, that an oligarchy should be created in its place. Not all, however, were taken in by his talk. Phrynichus, a general and influential speaker (he had persuaded his colleagues not to attack the Peloponnesian–Syracusan fleet at Miletus), attempted to undermine Alcibiades by informing the new Spartan commander, Astyochus, of Alcibiades' double-dealings, but to no avail (Thuc. 8.47–51).

While Alcibiades continued his efforts to win over Tissaphernes, a delegation from the Samian fleet traveled to Athens to negotiate a regime change. Led by Pisander, these men argued to the people that only a change in the democratic form of rule could now save them by making the Great King their friend and so beating the Peloponnesians. The recall of Alcibiades was essential to this plan – only he possessed the personal connections that would bring about this reversal. Many were opposed to any political change and as many resisted Alcibiades' restoration – arguments were made concerning his sacrilege, his violation of the Mysteries, his breaking of the laws. Pisander replied to each charge by asking who other than Alcibiades could provide the money, ships, and men necessary to defeat the Peloponnesians. Pisander apparently gave the impression too that a change to the constitution was only a temporary expedient, that the proposed changes could be nullified later. Hints were made also that the Persians would look more favorably upon such changes and this would help secure their support against the Peloponnesians.

Worried by the prospects of what a Peloponnesian–Persian alliance might accomplish, the opposition grew still. Mollified, appeased, or frightened, the Athenians voted to dissolve their democratic constitution. The silence of the opposition might also have come about through outright intimidation. Pisander met with the political clubs, the *hetairiai*, and won over their support for his cause (Thuc. 8.53–54.1–2). Later groups of young men armed with daggers intimidated opponents of Pisander and his allies and their armed participation in events at this stage seems likely. Through fear and intimidation then Pisander won approval for a resolution authorizing him to negotiate however he might with Alcibiades and Tissaphernes and do what was best for Athens (Thuc. 8.52–54.1). Though it had not yet been organized, an oligarchic faction was about to rule war-torn Athens.[21]

But if the opposition could have anticipated what happened next they surely would have regretted any concessions. Alcibiades disrupted a meeting between Pisander and his fellow oligarchs and Tissaphernes, advising them in succession to seek more and greater demands in any alliance. The Athenian delegation now realized that Alcibiades had duped them: Tissaphernes, for his part, negotiated a third treaty with the Spartans, calling for a joint effort against the Athenians. Additionally, it was made clear that the funds now being given to the Peloponnesians were not gifts but rather loans which, on the successful conclusion to the war, would be repaid (Thuc. 8.56–9).[22]

On returning to Samos, Pisander and his fellow envoys had better luck. Assembling the sailors and soldiers, they announced that decisions had been made in Athens to revise the democracy, though just what had been decided seems not to have been made too clear. They also made certain that Alcibiades was no longer one of them. Efforts were made as well to persuade the Samians to adopt a similar political arrangement even though the democrats there had only lately overthrown their own ruling oligarchy in favor of democracy (Thuc. 8.63.3–4).

Pisander and some others now returned to Athens to establish what would in fact be an oligarchic regime. On their way home they overthrew democracies of whatever allied communities they could. Ironically, these Athenian revolutionaries played into the hands of the Spartans and their allies. Diitrephes, *strategos* in Thrace, perhaps the same general responsible for the massacre at Mycalessus, brought about such a revolution in Thasos.[23] In fact he saved the oligarchs there the trouble of doing it themselves. After arranging affairs there he left Thasos in the hands of oligarchic allies who simply handed the city over to the Spartans (Thuc. 8.64). Thucydides notes that this happened elsewhere in the Aegean as numerous oligarchic regimes embraced the Spartans.

Once home the Pisandrian faction began to plan sweeping political reform in Athens. The groundwork for such reforms were already in place: even before arriving home Pisander found that youthful associates belonging to oligarchic clubs had carried out several assassinations of prominent democrats including Androcles, who had been among those responsible for Alcibiades' exile.[24]

A climate of fear gripped Athens, people were afraid to say or do anything, and so the oligarchs were able to act with little resistance. Word of what was coming also began making the rounds in Athens: the only public pay authorized would be that for military service – all the payments handed out to the people since the time of Pericles – for jury service and attending meetings of the assembly – would be banned. Sailors' rule too was about to end, as Theramenes and others were proposing to put in charge only those Athenians who could fight with shield and spear (Xen. *Hell.* 2.3.48). It was announced too that the new constitution would rest upon 5000 citizens of wealth, property, and standing (Thuc. 8.65). But as Thucydides notes, this was a phony gesture. In reality those who shaped the state would be those to control it (Thuc. 8.66.1). What was announced as a 'moderate' constitution founded on 'Five Thousand' of means was in reality a narrow oligarchy of Four Hundred.

While the assembly and the Council had continued to meet since the Sicilian disaster, its deliberations were supervised by the *probouloi* as well as the oligarchic conspirators (Thuc. 8.66.1). Pisander and other leaders of the movement – most prominently Antiphon, Phrynichus, and Theramenes – now changed all this.[25] Meeting in Colonus, the assembly approved a resolution creating a board of commissioners who would introduce measures for ruling the state. Again a tense atmosphere intimidated dissent and even Sophocles, one of the *probouloi* when later asked if what was done was not bad, agreed but said there was nothing else to be done.[26] Moving into the council house, the Four Hundred ruled Athens, claiming that they ruled for the Five Thousand.[27]

The agenda of the new regime became known quickly. Envoys went to Agis at Decelea to offer peace to the Spartans (Thuc. 8.70–1), but these he advised should seek out Spartan authorities at home and deal with them directly. Envoys were also sent out to the fleet at Samos to assure it that all was well at home (Thuc. 8.72). Events there, however, were already taking place and would not be to the liking of the oligarchs.

The Samian oligarchy that Pisander had created planned to strike against their democratic opponents who detected the plan. Rather than suffer attack, these appealed to a number of Athenians present – the generals Leon and Diomedon and two others, Thrasybulus, a trierarch, and Thrasyllus, a hoplite soldier – whose democratic sympathies were certain. The crew of the *Paralos*, one of the Athenian state triremes and staunch democrats, also threw in with the Samian democrats. An agreement was struck, and so were the Samian oligarchs – attacked before they themselves could strike. Some thirty were killed and several others exiled, but the majority was not punished (Thuc. 8.73).

The men of the fleet then dispatched the *Paralos* to report on these events to the unsuspecting Four Hundred. On board were several prominent Athenians including Chaireas, who had initially supported Pisander in displacing the democracy. Again the Four Hundred were not of the same mind politically and some, like Chaireas, joined to improve Athenian democracy, as he saw it, not destroy it. Now on arriving in Athens several of these men were arrested, while the remaining crewmen were immediately sent out to sea on a meaningless guard detail. Chaireas, however, managed to escape and returned to Samos where he revealed the overthrow of the democracy and current political crisis, adding lurid details of murder, imprisonment of families, and worse (Thuc. 8.74.3).

This report sparked a counter-revolution of the fleet at Samos that Thrasybulus, Thrasyllus, and Chaireas guided. Not only did they announce their determination to restore democracy to Athens, but also that there would be no peace with Sparta and that they would bring about the restoration of Alcibiades (Thuc. 8.75–7).

Recalled by the fleet, now representing a sort of 'government in exile', the men of the fleet elected Alcibiades general and he quickly took action. The sailors and soldiers wanted to move on Athens and the Piraeus immediately and suppress the Four Hundred and restore the democracy (Thuc. 8.81–3). But Alcibiades prevailed on them to wait – they could not turn their backs on their enemies so close to hand in Miletus. Instead he persuaded them to trust him to bring over Tissaphernes to the Athenian side along with the Phoenician fleet that Tissaphernes advertised was so near at hand. This the Peloponnesians feared and dissension between the supposed allies worsened: Sicilian sailors nearly lynched the haughty Astyochus when he refused to pay them (Thuc. 8.84) but the arrival of a new Spartan commander, Mindarus, helped ease the crisis. Tissaphernes, concerned that the Spartans believed him to be playing a double-game, sent an envoy to Sparta to assure them of his support (Thuc. 8.85).

In this murky world of intrigue and double dealings, Tissaphernes sailed for Aspendus where he expected, so he claimed, to find the Phoenician fleet. The Spartan envoy Lichas accompanied him, while Alcibiades made his way there separately to make good on his promise of delivering the Persians and their gold to Athens. Thucydides' comments and assessment make it clear that even contemporaries were unsure of what the principal players in this drama hoped to accomplish: for Tissaphernes, to exhaust the Peloponnesians and/or the Athenians, or extort money from the Phoenicians; for Alcibiades, to detach Tissaphernes from the Spartan alliance (Thuc. 8.87–8, 108).

The truth is unlikely to be known. But the subsequent arrival of the Persian prince Cyrus (408/7), and his assumption of control over Persian activities in the eastern Aegean, effectively marginalized Tissaphernes. This suggests that Tissaphernes was playing, at very least, a double-game to his own profit, if he had not succumbed to some degree to Alcibiades' charms.

Alcibiades found as much success with his fellow Athenians as he may have had with Tissaphernes. The fleet at Samos remained highly agitated and eager to settle scores with the Four Hundred in Athens. Again succeeding in holding the sailors back, Alcibiades brokered a deal at Delos between the fleet and the oligarchs. With a crowd of angry soldiers and sailors behind him, Alcibiades held the upper hand and he knew it. He told the envoys from the Four Hundred that the Five Thousand who they claimed ruled Athens should be empowered and that the Council of 500 should be reinstated as before.[28] In a telling comment, Thucydides comments that this was the first time that Alcibiades had performed a good deed.

The restoration of democracy in Athens, however, did not come quickly or easily, despite Alcibiades' efforts. While some of the oligarchs were only too happy to escape the dilemma they had created, others acted to accelerate a settlement with the Spartans. Among these were Pisander, Antiphon, and Phrynichus. They now dispatched envoys to Sparta and began building a fortified stronghold in Eetionea, right at the entrance to the Piraeus (Thuc. 8.90). Though it was called a defense against the fleet at Samos, some among the Four Hundred suspected that Eetionea was there to enable a Spartan fleet to enter Athens. With this unity among the Four Hundred collapsed.

The death of Phrynichus, just returned from his mission to Sparta, was the beginning of the end for the radical oligarchs. As he entered the agora in broad daylight he was assassinated, the assassin making good his escape. A Megarian accomplice, though tortured, revealed nothing except that there were many other like-minded men in Athens.[29] Hoplites at work on the fort at Eetionea, led by Aristocrates, arrested another of the radical oligarchs, Alexicles who had good contacts with the clubs. All-out civil war nearly followed. During the next day radicals and moderates confronted each other with charges and counter-charges of who was the 'true' patriot or citizen, while an outsider, the Thessalian Thucydides, *proxenos* of Pharsalus, pleaded with the Athenians to remember who the enemy was (Thuc. 8.92).

The struggle to restore democracy at Athens did not come cheaply. Distracted by the in-fighting, the Athenians had not paid close enough attention to the important island of Euboea and its cities, particularly Eretria. Dissidents here had already brought about the defection of Oropus and now with Spartan aid they brought about the defection of the entire island with the exception of Oreos which the Athenians occupied themselves (Thuc. 8.60, 95).

The loss of Euboea shook the Athenians badly, more so than even the defection of Chios or the Sicilian disaster, as now the city was open to attack. But as Thucydides points out, the Spartans were gentle opponents, not eager, or too dull, to exploit an opportunity.[30] But the blow was enough to bring reconciliation in summer 411. A series of measures were passed: the Four Hundred were deposed and the Five Thousand, those who could afford to outfit themselves as hoplites, were entrusted with the running of affairs. Alcibiades' old friend Critias led the way in authorizing his recall. In Thucydides' view, this was the best regime the Athenians ever had in his lifetime.[31]

The die-hard radicals refused to give way: some, Pisander and Alexicles among them, joined Agis at Decelea; another, the general Aristarchus, approached the frontier fort at Oinoe and told its garrison that a settlement with the Spartans had been reached, that the place was to be turned over to the Boeotians. The garrison believed him and left it in his hands.[32] A few of the Four Hundred remained in Athens unrepentant. The Council, perhaps that representing the Five Thousand, gave orders for the arrest of Antiphon, a key player in bringing the revolution about, and Archeptolemus. Both were quickly rounded up and placed on trial. Taking the lead in their prosecution were Theramenes and several other former associates from the Four Hundred who may have been driven more by self-interest than justice. Antiphon, a brilliant orator, delivered one of his best speeches on this occasion, but still he was convicted and soon after executed along with Archeptolemus. That passions ran high as the democracy recovered may be seen in Critias' posthumous prosecution of Phrynichus. Convicted, his remains were dug up and thrown out of Attica.[33] Some nineteen months after the assassination (410/9), his killers, among them Thrasybulus and Apollodorus, were honored with citizenship and other rewards.[34]

A Call for Peace

In the spring of 411, and amid the struggles of the Four Hundred and Five Thousand, Aristophanes produced one of the best-known comedies ever written, *Lysistrata*.[35] Often regarded as his third 'peace' play, *Lysistrata* is dominated by women – in fact the women of Greece, who have come together to demand that their men end the war and make peace.[36] To accomplish this goal, the women unite and swear to abstain from sex with their husbands until they agree to stop the violence and bring peace to Greece. This comic vehicle creates some hilarious scenes that were surely as amusing to Aristophanes' audience as to modern readers. But what does the play say about men, women, and war?

Lysistrata's name means 'Dissolving armies', and the contemporary priestess of Athena Polias, Lysimache ('Dissolving battles'), may have inspired Aristophanes in the choice of his heroine's name. More than simple wordplay may be at work here however. The cult of Athena Polias was an ancient one, and its priestess always came from an equally ancient family, the Eteobutadae, who claimed to be present at the beginning of Athenian history.[37] Moreover, the priestess of Athena Polias performed important rituals in Athens, particularly those of the Panathenaic festival, the annual celebration of Athena as depicted on the Parthenon frieze. The real-life Lysimache, then, not only occupied a high-profile position in Athenian society, but also one in which her public image was paramount. When the Athenian audience saw Lysistrata on stage, they would have seen not only a fictional equivalent of a real-life person, but also one who was an organizer of the most important ritual celebrated in Athens. Organizing a sex strike to end the war was only a little more complicated than organizing the great celebration honoring Athena.

These organizational talents first appear as the women of Greece come to Athens in response to the summons sent round by Lysistrata. This, too, would have supplied great comic relief to the audience, especially when the Spartan representative Lampito ('Shining one') walked onto the stage. Lampito is tanned and muscular, so much so that even Lysistrata comments that she could strangle a bull! Spartan women, the Greeks knew, spent a good deal of time outdoors exercising nude and competing in various athletic contests, activities unknown to the other women of Greece. Aristophanes makes other comments appropriate to the Boeotian and Corinthian women who have accompanied Lampito. These women are unnamed and only referred to generically (e.g., 'the Boeotian woman'), as they accompany Lampito just as real-life Peloponnesian and allied soldiers accompanied Spartan armies.

Lysistrata's leadership of the women of Greece would have occasioned yet more humor as it shows her acting assertively like Athenian men, convinced they have a right to lead any group. The women seize the Athenian acropolis which provokes a clash with the authorities. A commissioner sent out to find out what the women are doing there is aghast to learn they intend to stop the war by denying access to the money that fuels it.[38] Lysistrata debates the issue of money, budgets, and war with the commissioner, which enables Lysistrata to make the point that women know something of this too as they control their household budgets. She also refers to women suffering at the foolish decisions made by their husbands in the assembly, noting that if a wife said something, she would likely hear the words of Homer's Hector to his wife Andromache, 'War's man's work'! accompanied with the threat of a beating (Hom. *Il.* 6.492).

Lysistrata asserts that war could be a 'women's affair' too, and proceeds to debate the issue with the commissioner (*Lys.* 506–614). Jokes about arrogant generals on parade, handsome young cavalrymen, and wild Thracian mercenaries terrifying civilians provide humorous distraction, but then Lysistrata gets serious (*Lys.* 557–64). She tells the commissioner that her plan to end the war is no more complicated than weaving, a household occupation of Greek women as old as Penelope.

That Lysistrata could reduce the complexities of war to the simple chore of weaving amazes the commissioner, who tells Lysistrata to explain (*Lys.* 565). She first tells how the yarn or wool has to be washed to get the dirt out. So too in Athens, she explains, the plague of corrupt officials must be purged, and then those Athenians living in distant colonies should also be brought home and made part of the whole community (*Lys.* 567–86). The commissioner reacts to this foolish plan with the remark that only a woman could reduce war and military planning to something so simple as weaving. Lysistrata responds harshly, reminding him 'what of us then who for our children must weep'? (*Lys.* 588–9). This muted reference to the losses of the Sicilian Expedition silences the commissioner, who begs Lysistrata not to mention the matter further (*Lys.* 589–90).

Lysistrata concludes her argument for the authority of women to pronounce on war and its effects by noting that the time lost when men are away fighting is hardest on them. Not only do they suffer in the absence of their husbands, but they grow older and grayer and so less attractive with each passing day. The commissioner attempts to argue back that men age too, but Lysistrata will not hear it. She tells him that even an old man bald and toothless can find a pretty young girl easily, while the women left at home become old with the first gray hair (*Lys.* 591–7). Aristophanes' comments are timeless and have been the reactions of many women enduring other wars and long periods of separation. What Aristophanes provides is probably the earliest literary portrayal of the 'waiting wife' and the difficulties that women face when their men have gone off to war.[39]

In the scenes that follow this debate, Aristophanes creates the vividly (and wildly) funny situations for which this play is famous: the returning Athenian soldier Cinesias Paeonides (whose names are slang words for sexual intercourse) attempts to bed his wife Myrrhine, who frustrates his every move; the arrival in Athens of Spartan ambassadors who have been put off by their women and who conceal their enormous erections under their famous scarlet cloaks. In the end, Lysistrata and her allies force a settlement on their men, and in doing so Aristophanes makes the point that while the Greeks have been so busy fighting each other they have scarcely noticed that the Persians – the ancient enemy – have been watching and waiting to take advantage of the warring Greeks (*Lys.* 1133–5). The drama ends amid great celebration and Spartans dancing before the temple of Athena of the Bronze House, the cult temple at Sparta. Aristophanes' point could not be clearer – Athenians and Spartans are one and should stand against the barbarian enemy.

Is this drama about peace? Aristophanes builds into it all kinds of jokes and situations to entertain and make the audience laugh; he is, after all, writing comedy and hoping to win the prize. So there are jokes about how women love to drink and how sex-crazed they are, views that many men in the audience pretty much shared. Early in the play, for example, Lysistrata raises the idea of a sex strike to stop the war, and one of her Athenian friends responds, 'I couldn't. No. Let the war go on', a sentiment echoed quickly by another (*Lys.* 129–30). Lampito's support for the plan, however, overcomes initial resistance and Lysistrata proceeds with her plan.

In doing all this, Aristophanes also mentions the long absences of the men fighting in various places and throws in jokes about how women responded to this with sex toys and drink (*Lys.* 102–10). It should not be thought that masturbation is a modern invention, and in fact scenes on Greek pottery earlier in the fifth century depict women using the dildos that Aristophanes jokes about. But the women shown on pottery are prostitutes, not citizen wives, and so the Aristophanic humor appears again to reflect male fantasies and ideas. While the use of sex toys cannot be entirely discounted, most Greek women endured the long periods of separation doing whatever they could to pass the time. Hector's notion that war was man's affair tells only half the story. Mesmerized by the glory and the trauma, he overlooked the fact that war was woman's affair too, and countless other men both before him and after have made the same mistake. But Aristophanes was not one of them.

There is more than enough serious matter in this play to support the view that *Lysistrata* is a 'peace' play and that Aristophanes realizes and conveys in the drama the hardships of war that women endure. This is seen most clearly in those passages discussed above when Lysistrata and the commissioner argue: clearly she is the level-headed one who makes sense, while the commissioner is full of male arrogance and bluster. What Lysistrata says about cleaning house on corruption – that women knew too well the sorrow of war – were all sentiments that would have struck a resonant chord in the more thinking members of the audience, which was as much Aristophanes' goal as to make them (and the dullards in the audience) laugh. Aristophanes knew the difficulties of making peace with the Spartans. However hard that might be, he saw it not only important in itself but necessary in order to defend all Greece against the growing menace of Persia, waiting in the wings, to move against the Greeks states weakened by unending war.

An Athenian Success

The shock of the Euboean defection prompted a timely though not always gentle reconciliation in Athens, for in the eastern Aegean Mindarus, the Spartan commander, moved a large fleet of some eighty-six triremes into the Hellespont. His plan was simple - take control of the Hellespont and deny Athens the vital link to Black Sea grain. But the loss of Euboea and the recent political turmoil seemingly energized the Athenians or, perhaps more likely, gave them the strength of desperation.

In the narrow straits of the Hellespont, near the site known as Cynossema ('the Bitch's Tomb', i.e., Hecuba of Trojan War fame), a smaller Athenian fleet gamely offered battle.

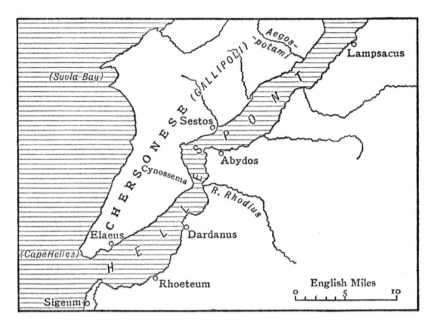

The Hellespont (after Henderson 1927)

Commanded by the democratic heroes of the Samian fleet, Thrasybulus and Thrasyllus, the Athenians demonstrated that they remained the better sailors as they first repulsed Mindarus' flanking movement (designed to keep them from escaping his trap) and then proceeded to rout the remainder of the Spartan fleet. At the end of the day, the Athenians had taken some twenty-one enemy ships at a loss of fifteen, but more importantly, were able to recover the strategic city of Cyzicus and return it to Athenian control.[40] Thrasybulus and inspired Athenian seamanship – and valor – saved Athens, at least for the moment. Had Mindarus prevailed, the war that concluded in similar but reversed circumstances six years later might have ended now. For the moment the Athenians lived to fight another day.

For one Athenian family, the victory came at a cost. One of the trierarchs killed this day was Phocion, the son of Phocus, who would not see the birth of his namesake grandson in 402/1. That Phocion was destined to become one of the great Athenians of the age of Alexander, and a martyr second only to Socrates.[41]

Notes

1 Thuc. 8.1.3, 8.67.2, with Gomme-Andrewes-Dover 4: 6–7 and 164–5.
2 Thuc. 6.91.6 (Alcibiades' advice to fortify Decelea), 93.2 (Spartan fortifying of the place), 8.3.1 (Agis using it as a base of operations).
3 Thuc. 7.19.1–2. Occupation of Decelea hurt Athens, but the city could still be supplied by sea. See pp. 193–5 for the next stage in the Spartan campaign to strangle Athens.
4 Andoc. *Mys.* 101 and Lycurg. *Leoc.* 121 refer to Athenians fleeing to Decelea. Thuc. 7.27.2–5 describes the economic impact of Agis' occupation of Athenian territory.
5 Thuc. 8.11.3 notes the name for this phase of the Peloponnesian War.
6 Thuc. 8.12, 14–15. On the Spartan connections of Alcibiades' family see p. 251.
7 Miller 1997: 28. Cf. Briant 2002: 592 who suggests that Tissaphernes acted independently (or semi-independently) of the King, but Thucydides suggests that in his negotiations he represented the King.
8 Thuc. 8.18. Thucydides appears to be citing from a document, which makes no mention of Persian subsidies, but the passage may be only a summary of the document. See Lazenby 2004: 176, though he does not mention how the treaty undermined the Greeks of Asia.
9 Thuc. 8.5–6 notes the arrival of envoys from Pharnabazus.
10 Thuc. 8.28; cf. 8.53 (Athenian aid for Amorges).
11 Thuc. 8.29, with Gomme-Andrewes-Dover 4: 70–2 (on the confusing pay calculations). When Tissaphernes agreed to the subsidy is not clear, as it is not noted in the first treaty or in initial discussions conducted by the satrap with the Spartans.
12 Thuc. 8.2.3, 26.1, 29.2: the Syracusans (twenty ships) and Selinuntines (two) had come east to join the fight in gratitude for what the Spartan alliance had done for them.
13 On Lichas' Olympic victory at the games of 416, see p. 137.
14 Thuc. 8.43. Not long later the Milesians seized a fort in their territory belonging to Tissaphernes, turning out his troops (Thuc. 8.84). Lichas reprimanded them, telling them that until the war was won they would have to curry the King's favor. This statement and Lichas' outburst to Tissaphernes suggests that he regarded the treaties with Persia as expedients: that after the war further negotiations would be needed to safeguard the freedoms of the Asian Greeks.
15 So Thuc. 8.45–7 tells, Alcibiades' credibility is questionable, his so-called plan debatable.
16 As noted again by Finley 1982: 80–2 and Loraux 2002: 24–5.
17 Cynicism in political life is a topic of current study; see e.g., Wills 2002.

18 [Arist.] *Ath. Pol.* 33.1 provides the date: 411/10, the archonship of Theopompus, taken over by Mnasilochus for ten months.

19 Suggested by Ostwald 1986: 345, after Thuc. 8.30.2.

20 Ostwald 1986: 385 notes the range of views among those who would now seek to overthrow the democracy.

21 See the discussion below and Thuc. 8.65–9, [Arist.] *Ath. Pol.* 29–33, with Lazenby 2004: 191–4 and Taylor 2002, the latter discussing why the *demos* ceding its freedoms to the oligarchs.

22 Thuc. 8.60 should date this treaty to about February 411.

23 Thuc. 8.64.2, with Gomme-Andrewes-Dover 5: 156–7.

24 Thuc. 8.65.2 notes the murders. See also Edwards 2004: 79; the basic study of the clubs remains Calhoun 1913.

25 Thuc. 8.68, with Gomme-Andrewes-Dover 5: 169–78, provides rather positive mini-biographies of these oligarchic leaders. See also Edwards 2004: 75–86, somewhat more favorable to Antiphon.

26 Arist. *Rh.* 1419a, the question comes ostensibly from Pisander, but this seems odd given his role in the affair. Some sort of textual error seems likely.

27 Thuc. 8.67–70; see also Ostwald 1986: 367–86 for full discussion.

28 Thuc. 8.86 refers generally to 'the council', which should probably be the Council of 500.

29 Thuc. 8.92.2, with Gomme-Andrewes-Dover 5: 309–11.

30 Thuc. 8.96.3, perhaps ironically.

31 Thuc. 8.97, with Gomme-Andrewes-Dover 5: 323–40, Andoc. 1.98; Plut. *Alc.* 33.1 (Alcibiades' recall); see also Loraux 2002: 131.

32 Thuc. 8.98. Among those caught up in the politics of the Four Hundred and who possibly lost civic rights was Eupolis, the comic poet. See Sidwell 2009.

33 [Plut.] *X orat.* 833A, with other sources in Edwards 2004: 82–3. On the speech see Arist. *Eud. Eth.* 1232b7; Lycurg. *Leoc.* 112–16 (Phrynichus).

34 ML 85; Shear 2007: 100, notes that the decree stood on the acropolis not in the agora, the domain, she claims, of the Athenian citizen.

35 Aristophanes produced two plays at the festivals of the Lenaea and Dionysia, *Lysistrata* and *Thesmophoriazusae*, but the sequence of their staging is unknown.

36 On the 'peace' theme, cf. Dover 1972: 158–9, and (e.g.) MacDowell 1995: 248.

37 Parke 1977: 17.

38 The commissioner's inquiry suggests that normally women did not frequent the acropolis other than at festival times.

39 Men absent on campaign also disrupted the normal social rhythms for women in other ways. Gamelion, for example, was the traditional wedding month. With fathers and other male relations away, not to mention prospective grooms, women would have assumed new responsibilities here. Thanks to my friend and colleague for this observation Catie Mihalopoulos; she plans to investigate this more fully elsewhere.

40 Thuc. 8.98–107, Diod. 13.45.8–10 (skill of the Athenian pilots); see also Kagan 1987: 217–25. Soon after the account of Cynossema, Thucydides' text breaks off. The narrative continues with Xenophon, though his account, called the *Hellenica*, dates c. 370s (see Appendix A).

41 *IG* I² 950, l. 3 (Phocion the trierarch), and Tritle 1988 (Phocion, the grandson and martyr).

10

'SHIPS GONE ... DON'T KNOW WHAT TO DO'

The defection of Euboea tempered whatever joy the Athenians may have found in their victory at Cynossema. While the losses in Sicily had taken place far away, Euboea could be seen from Attica and its defection was all the more troubling as so many other Greeks could see it too and recognize Athenian vulnerability.[1] Moreover the recovery of Cyzicus and its important naval base was fleeting. As the Athenians withdrew after briefly occupying the place, Pharnabazus apparently moved his forces into the city and nearby countryside, providing sanctuary for the beaten but not defeated Mindarus.[2] A second round in the struggle for the Hellespont was about to begin, one in which Alcibiades would play a decisive role.

Athenian and Spartan forces soon reassembled and the sparring in Hellespontine waters continued. After inconclusive fights at Abydus and Sestus, Alcibiades and the other Athenian commanders were forced to interrupt their pursuit of Mindarus and break off to find money wherever they could and to get more help from Athens (Xen. *Hell.* 1.1.5–8). Alcibiades continued his diplomatic pursuit of Tissaphernes. An arranged meeting with the satrap suddenly soured and Alcibiades found himself under arrest and on his way to Sardis, the Persian capital in Asia. The Great King, so Tissaphernes claimed, had decided for war against Athens and Alcibiades was prisoner number one. But Alcibiades managed an escape and made his way first to Clazomenae and then Cardia. While clearly his standing with Tissaphernes was bankrupt, he made more trouble for his rival by telling everyone that Tissaphernes had engineered his escape.[3]

From Cardia Alcibiades made contact with his colleagues and within a few months he had brought together the fleet at Sestus. The reassembly of several squadrons totaling eighty-six ships suggests that all the Athenian movements – Alcibiades to Tissaphernes, Thrasybulus to Thasos, Theramenes to Macedonia – were coordinated (Xen. *Hell.* 1.1.12).

Alcibiades' mission had been to win Persian support, while the others were detailed to find supplies and money for their crews. The combined Athenian fleet now moved to Proconnesus: its mission, to locate Mindarus and bring him to battle and recover Cyzicus.[4] At a pre-battle assembly, Alcibiades told his men that they would be fighting by sea, land, and against walls. In doing so they would be up against an enemy well provided with money, of which they had none. Clearly the recent measures taken by their commanders had yielded them little (Xen. *Hell.* 1.1.14).

The next day Alcibiades led his fleet into action and managed to catch Mindarus unawares: drilling part of his fleet at sea, he allowed the Athenians to separate his forces and destroy them in turn. Mindarus attempted to save the day by taking refuge on land, but in the action that followed he was killed and his forces, including those of Pharnabazus, routed. The next day, the Athenians reoccupied Cyzicus and were welcomed into the city by its citizens. The Spartan defeat was crushing, every ship lost. Hippocrates, Mindarus' surviving deputy, sent a dispatch to Sparta with its laconic message, captured by the Athenians: 'Ships gone. Mindarus dead. Men starving. Don't know what to do'.[5]

The 'back to the wall' rhetoric employed by Alcibiades worked, as the Athenians inflicted a crushing defeat on the Spartans, which surely provided them with significant spoils. More importantly, the twin victories at Cynossema (411/10) and Cyzicus (410) boosted the sagging morale of Athenian sailors and soldiers. The Athenians had also recovered some momentum and now quickly consolidated their gains, seizing Chrysopolis opposite Byzantium, only a little less strategically important. A sizable force – thirty ships and perhaps as many as 6000 men – was positioned here, behind a stockade, and under the command of two generals, Eumachus and Theramenes. Their assignments were financial as much as military: to collect a ten percent tax on all cargo sailing out through the Bosphorus, and hurt the Spartans in any way possible (Xen. *Hell.* 1.1.22).[6]

In effect a toll station, this measure confirms, as even Aristophanes' Lysistrata knew, that wars required money and lots of it. Both Athens and Sparta required vast sums of money to equip and man their fleets. This necessity explains to some degree the conniving and intrigue that drove Alcibiades and his Spartan counterparts in their negotiations with the Persians. Extravagant pay for a sailor in this last stage of the war would have been an Attic drachma per day (skilled workers in Athens such as masons received such pay, while Athenian jurors, many of them retirees, received two later three obols, or half a drachma for their daily service), or roughly a talent per day.[7] At this rate a fleet of thirty ships then, as the Athenian squadron at Chrysopolis, would have required something on the order of 30 talents every month (as the Attic month ran twenty-nine or thirty days). For both sides the war was also a struggle to find ever greater sums of money.

A Bitter Struggle

At Cyzicus Spartans and Persians lost heavily. Pharnabazus tried to encourage the Spartans offering them timber from around Mt. Ida and elsewhere to enable them to rebuild their fleet (Xen. *Hell.* 1.1.24–5). The Spartans again offered to end the fighting, this time sending an embassy led by Endius, Alcibiades' old friend. Endius had represented Sparta in the negotiations that resulted in the Peace of Nicias and it is tempting to see in this mission not only the influence of a Spartan 'peace' faction, but also that of Alcibiades. Endius offered the Athenians a settlement based on three key points: each would hold what it currently possessed; garrisons would not be manned in the territory of the other; and prisoners would be exchanged one for one. But the Athenians were heady with victory. As Aristophanes had sarcastically commented before, negotiations for peace always followed someone's setback, only to be refused by the other's rejection. This time was no different. Buoyed by the hopes that Alcibiades would save them they succumbed to the militant rhetoric of Cleophon, the most noisome of the current crop of demagogues, and rejected the Spartan overtures.[8]

Rebuffed by Athens yet again, the Spartans returned to the attack. For good reason the Athenians had concentrated their forces and efforts in the eastern Aegean, but this left them vulnerable elsewhere. Decisively and opportunely the Spartans now hurt the Athenians. First in the Megarid and close to home, the port of Megara, Nisaea, fell to a sudden Megarian coup (409/8). The Athenians responded vigorously, rushing in a taskforce of some 2000 men commanded by Leotropides and Timarchus to recover it. Hard fighting followed, and while the Athenians fought bravely and beat up the Megarians, recovery of Nisaea remained beyond their grasp.[9]

Loss of Nisaea with its port facilities was a blow, but on the other side of the Peloponnese worse was about to befall. The Spartans attacked the Messenian garrison holding Pylos by land and sea. Hard pressed, the Messenians appealed to the Athenians for relief to which the Athenians responded, dispatching a force of some thirty warships, twice the size of the attacking force. But bad weather made sailing impossible and forced the fleet back to Athens. Anytus, the taskforce commander, now found himself in the earlier predicament of Paches and so many other unlucky (or incompetent) officers. Opportunistic demagogues, looking to curry favor with the people, prosecuted him for treason. Only by bribing the jury, reportedly the first time this occurred, was Anytus able to secure acquittal. His escape from popular punishment underlines the challenges faced by democratic leaders and the shortcomings of Athenian justice. It may explain too why at the war's beginning the Spartans were suspicious of Athenian offers of arbitration. Meanwhile, the embattled and now abandoned Messenians, starving and suffering heavy casualties, finally surrendered at Pylos. So eager were the Spartans to recover the place, they allowed the Messenians to leave unmolested.[10]

Though important, the struggles around Nisaea and even Pylos were sideshows for the Athenians compared to the ongoing struggles in the eastern Aegean. In early summer, 409/8, Thrasyllus campaigned into Asia with a large force newly authorized by the Athenians. A few minor successes on Samos and then against Miletus perhaps made him overconfident. He decided to take action against Ephesus, which had broken with Athens along with so many others in 412. Unfortunately, he walked into a trap. Tissaphernes had gotten wind of his plan and had brought up his own cavalry to support the Ephesians and their Sicilian Greek allies.[11] Forewarned, the Ephesians and their allies pounced on the unsuspecting Athenian soldiers and marines and killed hundreds of them (Xen. *Hell.* 1.2.1–10).

Not long after, Alcibiades brought up his own forces and joined Thrasyllus' unlucky troops at Lampsacus. But there were ill-feelings between the two forces: Alcibiades' men, not yet experiencing defeat, would have nothing to do with Thrasyllus' beaten men and made plain their reluctance to serve with them. Xenophon does not provide details, but it is plain enough to see what had happened. The courage of Thrasyllus' men was suspect and Alcibiades' men worried if they could trust them not to run the next time. In a society that put such a high premium on bravery and manliness in war, anything less was not simply failure to meet the standard but worse. In a fragment from Euripides' *Erechtheus* (c. 423–418?), lines such as 'sons who die in battle with others receive a tomb covered in glory' and 'those who die nobly live more than those who do not' clearly explain the scorn now directed at Thrasyllus' men.[12] Such a reaction among

Figure 10.1 The grave monument of Chairedemos and Lykeas, two hoplites killed in fighting during the Ionian War.[13]

Alcibiades' troops is not to be wondered at, and it might be noted that similar attitudes could be duplicated in other armies ancient as well as modern.

That Alcibiades recognized that there was a problem in his army which he then took steps to correct argues that he did possess some of the talents essential for an army commander. Over the course of the winter months, Alcibiades led his unhappy army against Pharnabazus and Abydus. In some successful fighting he was able to bring both groups together and forge them into a cohesive fighting unit (Xen. *Hell.* 1.2.14–18).

The fighting for the Hellespont and elsewhere in Greece raised to new levels the growing violence. At Cyzicus and in other fights in the eastern Aegean, the Athenians took a number of Syracusans, perhaps as many as 1000, prisoner. These were taken to Athens for 'special handling'. Upon the destruction of the Athenian expedition to Syracuse only five years before, the Syracusans had taken their Athenian prisoners, numbering in the thousands, and imprisoned them in quarries where during the course of cold winter months many perished. The few Athenian survivors had told of this and now, with Syracusans in their hands, the Athenians responded in kind, placing them in quarries in the Piraeus, subjecting them to the same cruelties. Whether or not the Athenians branded the Syracusans, as they had the Athenians taken in Syracuse, Xenophon does not state. But the Athenians and Samians had done so to each other in 440 and it perhaps happened again now.[14] Later some of the Syracusans were able to escape and make their way to the Spartans. This example of Athenian 'payback' reveals again the commonplace nature of the war's brutalities.[15]

But such treatment was not limited to foreigners. At about the same time that the Athenians took their Syracusan prisoners, they also captured on board one of the Syracusan ships one of their own. Alcibiades of Phegus, a cousin of Alcibiades the general, had fled Athens in 415, caught up in the controversy surrounding the mutilation of the Herms. How he ended up serving with the Syracusans is uncertain. As a fugitive he might well have turned to the Spartans for refuge as he shared the same social connections there as his more famous cousin. On becoming a renegade his options would have been few, which perhaps led him to join the other side. In these circumstances he may have even accompanied Gylippus and the Peloponnesian relief forces to Sicily which would explain his presence with the Syracusans now. In any case, the reviving fortunes of his namesake helped little. For a fugitive and outlaw, there were no protections and Thrasyllus, evidently the only or most influential general present, ordered him stoned to death on the spot.[16]

Ionian Glory?

Alcibiades' spectacular victory at Cyzicus and other advances elsewhere in Ionia were glorious achievements that more than compensated Thrasyllus' defeat at Ephesus. Yet the vicious payback meted out to the Syracusan prisoners in Athens and the execution of Alcibiades of Phegus reveal the sinking level of violence which participants experienced and saw had become the norm. Two dramas, the *Philoctetes* of Sophocles (c. 409) and the *Orestes* of Euripides (c. 408), appearing within a year of each other, reflect related dimensions of the suffering that was becoming more than commonplace.

Philoctetes was the hero essential to the conquest of Troy. On being wounded, his cries and stinking wound became so annoying that the other Greeks abandoned him on Lemnos, along with his magic bow, once Heracles'. As the Trojan War dragged on, those same Greeks learned that Troy would only fall with Philoctetes' help – that the bow was the key to victory. To secure this, Odysseus and young Neoptolemus, Achilles' son, traveled to Lemnos to get the bow (first), Philoctetes (second). One view argues that the drama is allegorical: that Philoctetes and the bow are really Alcibiades and his spear, that Troy is a stand-in for Sparta.[17] Another view suggests a more literal and historical reading, that Philoctetes represents Athenian and Greek wartime realities – the plight of the war wounded and the disabled.[18]

While there is a certain allure to the metaphorical interpretation, especially given Sophocles' political and military service, the drama has a much more human feel to it which argues that this is Sophocles' prime concern. As a tale of wartime trauma, the entire story revolves around pain and suffering. It could be objected that Philoctetes was not injured in battle, that he was only bitten by a snake. In fact this is no objection at all. Many men – past and present – are wounded or killed in non-combat type accidents and the serpent's bite is surely metaphorical. Moreover, the plight of the wounded in an era without pain killers must have been horrific. Imagine the injuries suffered by the crew of a rammed trireme, legs, arms, and hands crippled and shattered by splintered oars and smashed hulls. Texts from the Epidaurian miracle inscriptions describe men with spearheads or arrowheads buried in body parts for years.[19] In the warring towns of Greece, people lived close to one another.[20] The cries of the war-wounded, their hobbling about town, would have been commonplace sounds and sights, as the story of Epizelus told by Herodotus, Gorgias, and here Sophocles make clear. This is the reality behind the young Neoptolemus' question to Philoctetes (*Phil.* 752–3), 'what makes you cry out'?

There is also the wounding of the psyche. When told of the casualties at Troy, Philoctetes remarks that war never takes the bad except by chance, while the good always suffer this fate (*Phil.* 427–38). Such a remark placed in the experience of war finds parallels in Thucydides: his judgment that the Athenian hoplites killed in Ambracia with Demosthenes were the best to die in the war. Why them – why these 120 out of so many others? The same attitude may explain too his account of Cleon's cowardly death at Amphipolis.[21] The drama of Sophocles is rich in theme and content drawn from contemporary realities, and the damage inflicted by a sharp spear on body and soul must be seen as one of these.

A similar offering but on a broader canvas provides the inspiration for Euripides' *Orestes*, staged in spring 408. At first glance it appears to be a new story on an old theme – the murderous multi-generational family of Thyestes – but there is more here than simply the problems of Orestes and Electra after the killing of their mother Clytaemnestra. On closer inspection the similarity of this drama to Euripides' earlier works, *Hecuba, Andromache, Trojan Women*, and the issue of war again becomes clear. In *Orestes* brother and sister are condemned to die for the killing of their mother – the fact that they had no choice in this of no matter. As in the other war-plays, the idea of payback looms large. Orestes and Pylades decide that it is better to die on their feet than their knees, and that taking vengeance is no less good. This leads them first to plot the kidnapping and murder of Hermione, Helen and Menelaus' daughter, thus continuing a theme in Euripidean drama where the killing of women and children figures prominently.[22] Not satisfied with this, they then resolve to kill Helen herself, whose immorality and conduct had been the cause of so much more and greater suffering. Helen is again a symbol, not just of immorality but war itself (*Or.* 1133–5). While Apollo intervenes and thwarts the murderous acts planned by the two heroes, Euripides makes a statement here echoed elsewhere in his dramas: that 'war is a friend to lies', that victors' wreaths belong to those who lead their cities prudently and justly, who remove feuds and factions.[23] For more than twenty years Euripides had watched his city and all the Greeks slaughtering each other. In *Orestes* he advances a novel idea then as today, kill war, live in peace.

The Struggle for Byzantium

As crushing as the defeat at Cyzicus was, the Spartans still held Chalcedon and Byzantium, the latter as strategically a sited city as the world has ever known. From their stronghold at Decelea, Agis and other Spartans could see that their base had little impact on the Athenian markets, as ships sailed unmolested into and out of the Piraeus. The Spartans resolved to change this and to that effect ordered more forces into the Hellespont.[24] One contingent was placed in the hands of Clearchus, the son of Ramphias, and now headed north. Evidence makes it pretty clear that Clearchus' father was the same Ramphias who played a part in the pre-war negotiations and who later succeeded Brasidas in the north after his death in 421.[25]

The assignments and commands entrusted to Ramphias suggest that he was well connected to the Spartan leadership, particularly those friendly with the Eurypontid family of Archidamus. More importantly, these connections apparently followed into the next generation. Just as Archidamus had entrusted missions to Ramphias, now Agis did the same with Clearchus. This linkage may be confirmed in the assignment that would soon be handed to Lysander, the 'lover' of Agis' brother Agesilaus: command of Spartan forces in the Aegean. As Agis wanted a familiar in the southern Aegean, it stands to reason that he would push for the same in the northern region as well. That Clearchus was a Spartan of standing, well connected to its leadership, there should be little question.

Clearchus was also possessed by a passion for war, one that would be made legendary by another, the Athenian Xenophon, his comrade and biographer.[26] Now about forty years old, Clearchus had seen nearly two decades of non-stop war and, as so happens, had become *philopolemos*, a war-lover, someone hooked on the violence of war. In the fight for Cyzicus after Spartan naval forces had been defeated, Clearchus had given the Athenians a tough fight (Diod. 13.51.1–4). Now in command at Byzantium, he found himself isolated with no relief in sight as the Athenians moved against the remaining Spartan strongholds in the area.

After restoring Athenian morale, Alcibiades moved first against Chalcedon, forced to terms after Hippocrates, its commander and Mindarus' old deputy, fell in battle, and his troops were left leaderless. This victory enabled the Athenians to press Pharnabazus to accept a truce recognizing the return of Chalcedon to Athenian control and a reopening of negotiations with the Great King. Pending talks, the Athenians agreed not to make a move against the city. Pharnabazus then instructed a party of Athenian ambassadors to meet him in Cyzicus and there they were joined by ambassadors representing Sparta. With these under way, the Athenians turned their attention to Clearchus and Byzantium, determined to recover that strategic city.[27]

Clearchus repulsed every attack the Athenians threw at him, but they still pressed their siege. This led him to seek Persian aid, mostly money so that he could pay his troops and build ships to force the Athenians to lift their siege. To this end he left the defense to his subordinates and went off in search of Pharnabazus. But he had not been informed of the pending negotiations or that the satrap, from whom he sought funds, was no longer in the area. Clearchus then left his command, surely a poor decision on his part, especially so as the Athenians were not sitting by idly. Not content to remain bogged down in fruitless attacks, they resolved to end the siege by treachery and found willing conspirators among the Byzantine population.[28] These opened the gates to them. Clearchus' absence was decisive. His troops attempted to put up a fight, but on seeing the Athenians everywhere, surrendered (Xen. *Hell.* 1.3.14–22).[29] Byzantium was Athenian again.

What Should be Done About Alcibiades?[30]

In the spring 405, an Athenian audience watched Aristophanes' comedy *Frogs* and his commentary on the intellectual life of Athens, and heard an incarnate Dionysus ask, 'What should be done about Alcibiades?' By this date the one-time exile and condemned criminal, and savior of the city, had again gone into exile, not long after his grand homecoming and civic restoration. What had happened to bring about this sudden reversal?

By 407 Alcibiades had more than any other Athenian halted the slide into ruin that the Sicilian disaster had brought about: victories in the Hellespont and the islands had made him popular with the fleet and the people. As Athenian fleets commanded the seas as they had not for years, the Athenians conducted elections for the board of generals. Though officially in exile and not present, Alcibiades had friends at home. These included friends from the Socratic circle such as Critias, and these lobbied to bring him back. In the elections for 407/6, the Athenians elected Alcibiades and soon he received letters and pleas to return home.[31] Finally, at the festival of the Plynteria, Alcibiades sailed into the Piraeus with a squadron of ships. Ever fearful, but catching sight of relatives including his cousin Euryptolemus and friends like Critias among the waiting throng, he stepped off his ship to a hero's return (Xen. *Hell.* 1.4.7–19).

Within a short time he stood before the Council and assembly. Alcibiades denied any wrongdoing in the matters of the Herms and the Mysteries, claiming that he was innocent of all charges and had been unjustly treated. There was not a murmur of dissent. Most Athenians believed that only Alcibiades could reverse declining Athenian fortunes, and with so much at stake they were willing to take him at his word for the good of the city. Accordingly, he received not just the keys to the city, but appointment as senior *strategos* with authority over his nine colleagues.[32]

Soon Alcibiades demonstrated his leadership talents and his ability to inspire the Athenians with hope. It had been five years since the Mysteries at Eleusis had been celebrated as the Spartan garrison at Decelea was much too close for comfort. Alcibiades now organized the Athenians – the citizen population and every man able to bear arms – and as in the old days, they marched to Eleusis. The Spartans did nothing (Xen. *Hell.* 1.4.20).

The Athens that Alcibiades found was surely different from the one he left in the heady summer of 415 as the fleet sailed to Sicily. In the Kerameikos there would have been many more casualty lists and funeral monuments to memorialize the fallen, though Nicias, his unlucky rival and scapegoat of the Sicilian disaster, would have been conspicuously absent. Blamed for the disaster as much as for his surrender, Nicias' memory had been vilified as he was written out of the record.[33] On the acropolis, the *Nikai* on the balustrade of the temple of Athena Nike had only recently been finished. These graceful and beautiful figures of feminine Victory would have been matched by the graceful Ionic columns of the new home to Athena's olive tree, symbol of Athens' patron, the Erechtheum. With its graceful porch of the Caryatids, the heroic maidens, looking on to the Parthenon and the great statue of Athena Promachos, the Erechtheum was an impressive structure for all its eccentricity.[34] But Alcibiades probably had little time for sightseeing as the buoyant popular mood of the moment could give way as quickly again.

There were those who witnessed Alcibiades' return and believed it to be ill-omened. As he stepped ashore, other Athenians were conducting the rituals connected with the celebration of the Plynteria, the festival of the Washing of Athena. These required that the cult image of Athena herself be stripped of its robes and ornaments and then be covered up from sight. Then in procession the Athenians would walk out to the sea and there robes would be washed before returning. On this day the sacred precincts were kept shut and ropes marked them off limits. More importantly, no one did anything of importance on this day.[35] In short, the timing of Alcibiades' return could not have been worse. Yes, many Athenians were thrilled at his return and what that promised for Athens, who believed his protestations of innocence. But there were others who believed that he was responsible for the troubles of the past, both those he had brought on himself and Athens. This latter group believed that it was only a matter of time before Alcibiades would revert to form and bring Athens yet more grief (Xen. *Hell.* 1.4.12–17).

Figures 10.2 and 10.3 A *Nike* from the Temple of Athena Nike (left) and Callimachus' Aphrodite (right), both depicting the sensuous Rich Style in the later fifth century.[36]

Two Princes

As the Athenians readjusted to life with Alcibiades and were cautiously optimistic at their improved fortunes, important changes had also taken place in the Spartan camp. News of the fall of Byzantium had reached Pharnabazus and the party of ambassadors accompanying him in Gordium that winter (408/7). The following spring another party of Spartan ambassadors arrived, this returning from an audience with Darius, the Great

King. Their report must have sent chills down the backs of the Athenians: the King had declared for the Spartans, moreover he was sending his younger son Cyrus to Asia to guide Persian interests and ensure that his money was well spent. Cyrus produced a letter from his father empowering him, declaring him *caranus*, lord, over all.[37]

The arrival of Cyrus marked a decisive change in Persian policies. It coincided with another change no less significant, the arrival of Lysander to assume command of Spartan forces in the Aegean. Though Spartiate born, Lysander was a *mothax*. At birth, his family appears to have been impoverished so disqualifying him from the *agoge*. Despite his poverty, Lysander's father Aristocritus seems to have had good connections as he was able to place his son in the circle of the Eurypontid king Archidamus and his sons Agis and Agesilaus. These connections enabled Lysander to be admitted to the *agoge* where he not only received the traditional education but socialized with elite Spartans. Moreover, coming of age on the outbreak of the war and in the company of 'royal' brothers gave him opportunities to distinguish himself and redeem his origins.[38] That he had done just this by now there can be no doubt.

Lysander soon visited Cyrus in Sardis and with the Spartan ambassadors accompanying him, wasted no time in telling Cyrus of the many wrongs committed by Tissaphernes and urging him to take an active part in the war. Cyrus assured him that this was indeed his plan and soon the two men had worked out a new formula for the payment of the Spartan fleet, much to the dismay of the Athenians. Tissaphernes attempted to counsel Cyrus, advising him to follow his policy of helping both Athens and Sparta just enough, to ensure they remained weak thus susceptible to Persian strength. Cyrus rejected this advice, as also Athenian overtures to him, mediated by Tisssaphernes (Xen. *Hell.* 1.5.8–9).

The alliance of Cyrus and Lysander soon produced dividends. Lysander focused on rebuilding the battle-ravaged Spartan fleet around Ephesus and showed no signs of resuming the fighting. To the north there was much activity around Phocaea, now being blockaded by Thrasybulus, while nearby Clazomenae was threatened by some exiles. With his fleet at nearby Notium keeping watch on the Spartans, Alcibiades decided to exploit the lull. He took troops to the relief of Clazomenae and thought to confer with Thrasybulus too (Xen. *Hell.* 1.5.10–11, Diod. 13.71.1). Sometime in autumn 407 he departed, leaving command of his fleet in the hands of his pilot Antiochus, a loyal friend as well (Plut. *Alc.* 10.2). Before leaving, Alcibiades gave Antiochus strict orders not to engage Lysander.[39]

What happened next reveals not only the mysteries of war, but also the stresses to the Athenian war machine. That Alcibiades left Antiochus in command suggests a shortage of experienced commanders. On his return to Athens he had been granted an authority greater than that of the other generals and in the absence of experienced generals or trierarchs, he may have seen Antiochus, a friend and dependent, as an obedient subordinate.[40] No doubt an experienced pilot, Antiochus was still a pilot and perhaps believed that his abilities and talents had remained unappreciated.[41]

Desirous of glory and reputation, Antiochus may have decided to make a foray into the harbor at Ephesus and tease the seemingly docile Spartans. Sailing out from the Athenian anchorage at Notium with just one other ship, Antiochus passed within hailing distance and surely, sailors being sailors, a few risqué comments about mothers and cowards were exchanged. Lysander quickly ordered some ships into action. Attacked, other Athenian ships came to Antiochus' aid, but there was no plan of action, just one ship after the other engaging. Soon a full-scale battle, completely unrehearsed and unplanned, was underway as each side joined the fight. For the Athenians, the results were shocking. More than twenty ships were lost, though not many men, as the crews were able to beach their ships and escape. Antiochus was not so lucky: his ship was taken and he fell fighting, perhaps realizing his blunder. The blow to Athenian morale was staggering: an afternoon fight had wiped away all the recent successes.[42]

On receiving reports of this disaster, Alcibiades returned to Notium, quickly mobilized his fleet and then attempted to draw Lysander into another engagement. But Lysander declined the invitation forcing Alcibiades to move on to Samos, no doubt to regroup his forces which they surely required. But now Alcibiades compounded his problems. He picked a fight with the allied city of Cyme, probably as he needed money to pay his crews, surely a little grumpy after their recent defeat and to revive the flagging spirits of his men. The initial shock of being attacked quickly wore off, and the Cymaeans responded vigorously. Soon pressed hard, the Athenians abandoned their spoils and ran for their lives (Diod. 13.73.3–6).

Now twice defeated, Alcibiades came under fire at home. Thrasybulus of Kolluteus, probably one of the trierarchs in the fleet, sailed to Athens and attacked Alcibiades, claiming that blame for the disaster rested with Alcibiades alone. Antiochus, Thrasybulus claimed, was nothing more than a drinking companion appointed so that Alcibiades could cruise the Aegean looking for courtesans and a party.[43] The Cymaeans also sent a formal protest to Athens, denouncing Alcibiades for attacking them.

Attacks on him quickly multiplied: angry soldiers, enemies claiming that he was in league with the Spartans, the Persians – that he intended to become their lord and master. The Athenians were furious. Alcibiades recognized that with so many enemies now gathered together he could no nothing. Whether he simply sailed off into exile or suffered the humiliation of an official sacking along with the other generals is unclear.[44] Alcibiades and Athens were now history. Unpopular with everyone, the brilliant but erratic Alcibiades sailed off in a single trireme to a safe haven in the Chersonese. His earlier exile had taught him the need to anticipate reversal and in the region of the Chersonese he had carved out a mini-fiefdom with waiting allies and castles.[45] Alcibiades left Athens, never to return.

Alcibiades' departure and voluntary exile again threw Athens into chaos. Some Athenians seem to have given up hope for the city. Among these was Euripides who now left Athens for good. For some time he had decried the war's waste in his dramatic productions, but like critics in other times, his pronouncements had fallen on deaf ears. Now he accepted an invitation from Archelaus, the modernizing king in Macedonia, to attend as poet in residence at the new capital of Pella.[46] Here he joined other Greek intel-lectuals and artists, the poet Agathon and painter Zeuxis among them, who provided a hellenic accent to the Macedonian court. Macedonian kings since Alexander I had asserted their hellenic identity and Archelaus seems determined to make the point clearer. In the short time before his death (406/5) Euripides would write a drama, Archelaus, honoring his patron's ancestors and finish his final play Bacchae, a reflection perhaps on the overheated intellectualism of Athens.[47]

But there were other losses too. Critias, the one-time Socratic auditor, had promoted Alcibiades' recall home, and now he may have paid the price for his efforts. Enemies of Alcibiades went after his allies and friends too, including Critias. Exiled, Critias evidently found like-minded friends in Thessaly where he engaged in subversive political activities and planned how he might settle scores with his rivals at home.[48]

Notium was a debacle and what followed at Cyme only compounded Athenian problems. Not only were Athenian shortages and vulnerabilities at the command level revealed, but again Athenian arrogance toward the allies. There were only ten generals, and at least two of these and probably more, were in the Aegean, while a like number were back in Athens, where Agis brought out his full force and made a not very vigorous assault on the city walls (Diod. 13.72.3–73.2).

Alcibiades had succeeded in wrecking the fleet and upsetting Athens' few remaining allies. Money was in short supply. Much had to be done and done quickly, otherwise there was little hope of holding back the growing might of Sparta. Into the breach now stepped a number of officers and among these perhaps the most able was Conon. There was something lucky about Conon. As Demosthenes headed off to his appointment with destiny in Sicily, he had reinforced a small command of Conon's at Naupactus. Conon stayed and fought an inconclusive battle with the Corinthians, but this kept him out of harm's way in Sicily, alive to fight another day.[49] Now on Alcibiades' second downfall, Conon's luck held again: no connection to Alcibiades, eligible for election as general.[50] Elected to the new board of generals, Conon and several others arrived in Samos to take command of the fleet. What they found was a fleet in name only: more than 100 ships were present, but money to pay only seventy crews was in hand. What was worse, the morale of the crews was poor. To repair both, Conon led the fleet on a plundering expedition, this time into enemy country (Xen. *Hell.* 1.5.18–21).

Notes

1 Thuc. 8.96.1, 96.5. See also Lazenby 2004: 193.
2 Thuc. 8.107.1 notes the Athenians in Cyzicus after Cynossema, but Diod. 13.49.4, Xen. *Hell.* 1.1.13 show it shortly back in the hands of Pharnabazus and Mindarus. Kagan 1987: 225, 237–8 appears not to notice this.
3 Xen. *Hell.* 1.1.9–11 (arrest and escape), Plut. *Alc.* 28.1 (attacking Tissaphernes).
4 The chronology is uncertain here, but the fight to recover Cyzicus would have taken place sometime in late spring (perhaps early summer) 410 as Diod. 13.49.2 places the battle 'after winter'.
5 Xen.*Hell.* 1.1.16–22 and Diod. 13.49.5–51 (battle), 1.1.23 (dispatch); see also Lazenby 2004: 204–6.
6 Lazenby 2004: 206 suggests that the toll collected was in addition to the five percent tax imposed on all trade in the empire in 413 (Thuc. 7.28.3).
7 On the basis of 200 men per ship, and Xen. *Hell.* 1.5.4, the sum requested of Cyrus by the Spartan ambassadors in 407. While Cyrus demurred, he later agreed to a slight increase – an extra obol per day per sailor – at the request of Lysander (*Hell.* 1.5.6). The additional amount gave sailors a daily wage of four obols. Cyrus initially agreed to thirty minae per month for each ship (half the

sum the ambassadors had requested), but the extra that Lysander won meant that Cyrus now paid (approximately) another third.

8 Diod. 13. 52.2–53 (Endius' embassy), Thuc. 5.44.3 (Endius and the Peace of Nicias), 8.6.3 (Endius and Alcibiades). No mention is made of the Athenian garrison in Pylos, but removal of this would have been of prime concern to the Spartans, just as its continued operation was to the Athenians and their Messenian allies.

9 Diod. 13.65.1–2. See Parlama and Stampolidis 2000: 396–7, 399 for discussion of an Athenian cavalry casualty list from this fight, recently recovered in metro excavations.

10 Diod. 13.64.5–7; Anytus would prosecute Socrates some ten years later. Soph. *Aj.* 1135–6 (c. 440s) refers to corrupt votes among the judges (jurors or dicasts) who cheated Ajax out of Achilles' armor. Deceit such as this would have worried the Spartans in their dealings with the Athenians.

11 Xen. *Hell.* 1.1.27–31 records a regime change at Syracuse terminating Hermocrates' command of the Sicilian Greek contingent supporting the Spartans in the Aegean. Some of these men later received various civic rights from some of the Aegean Greek communities, such as the Selinuntines who received Ephesian citizenship after the Carthaginians destroyed Selinus.

12 Eur. *Erechtheus* 378–9, 390–1 (ed. Collard-Cropp).

13 Stewart 2008: 221 suggests that Chairedemos is a hoplite killed in 409, Lykeas a trierarch killed in 411 (referring to casualty lists). But both are depicted as hoplites and the identifications are not certain.

14 Plut. *Nic.* 29.2 (branding of Athenians), *Per.* 26.4 (branding of Athenians and Samians).

15 Xen. *Hell.* 1.1.18, 2.12 (Syracusan ships burned, crews captured, altogether some 300 men possibly), Thuc. 7.87.1–3 (Athenian and allied prisoners in the Syracusan quarries).

16 Xen. *Hell.* 1.2.13. Andoc. *Mys.* 65, with MacDowell 1962: 104. See also Thuc. 6.61.7 (death penalty for Alcibiades and those in flight with him); Harrison 1971: 31 (capital authority of Athenian generals), 169–70 (summary killing of outlaws).

17 Vickers 2008: 59–81.

18 Edwards 2000, and Tritle 2000: 195–6.

19 Texts in LiDonnici 1995. See also Salazar 2000: 16 and pp. 101–2.

20 Ratto 2006: 256–7 (with figures) makes clear the tight quarters in which people lived. Even today in Greece, in island villages such as Megalochori on Thira, houses are tightly packed and voices easily carry from house to house.

21 Thuc. 3.98.4, 5.10.9 (Cleon).

22 Eur. *Or.* 1346–53, and pp. 127–8 (on killing children).

23 Eur. *Bellerophon* 303; *Autolycus* 287 (ed. Collard-Cropp).

24 Thuc. 8.8, 39, 80 and Xen. *Hell.* 1.1.35–6 appear to refer to the same Spartan decision.
25 Thuc. 1.139.3, 5.12.1, 13.1, 14.1, with P-B 112. Probably sent to Athens as Archidamus' representative, Ramphias is likely to have shared the king's views regarding war, otherwise his service as ambassador makes little sense.
26 Xen. *Anab.* 2.6.6–15, with Tritle 2004.
27 Xen. *Hell.* 1.3.8–13 (Cyzicus conference), 1.3.13–22 (Athenians and Byzantium).
28 At least one of these Byzantine 'traitors', Anaxilaus, was apprehended by the Spartans after the war and put on trial for his actions. He defended himself on grounds that the women and children were starving, as Clearchus had given over all the food to the soldiers – the Spartans acquitted him (Xen. *Hell.* 1.3.19).
29 What Clearchus did after losing Byzantium is unknown. He next turns up serving under Callicratidas who appointed him deputy commander of the fleet just before the battle of Arginusae in 406. See pp. 207–9.
30 Ar. *Ran.* 1422–3.
31 Plut. *Alc.* 33.1, with Develin 1989: 165, 174 (noting that Alcibiades had commanded at Samos unofficially) and Ostwald 1986: 400–1.
32 Xen. *Hell.* 1.4.20. On appointing commanders with such authority see Thuc. 6.8.2 and the discussion in Gomme-Andrewes-Dover 4: 228.
33 But not history: see Paus. 1.29.9, with Gomme-Andrewes-Dover 4: 463–4.
34 Hurwit 1999: 200–9 and Pollitt 1972: 131–4, date the final touches to the Erechtheum to c. 421–405, so coinciding with Alcibiades' arrival. On the Nike see pp. 118–19.
35 Xen. *Hell.* 1.4.12; for other details see Parke 1977: 153–5, Parker 1996: 307.
36 On Callimachus see Stewart 1990: 1, 271, 2, 425–6.
37 Xen. *Hell.* 1.4.1–3, and Briant 2002: 593. The Athenian ambassadors accompanying Pharnabazus posed a diplomatic problem for the Persians who rightly feared their report on these changes. They were thus held for three years, released only after the war's end (*Hell.* 1.4.4–7).
38 Xen. *Xell.* 1.5.1, Plut. *Lys.* 2.1, with P-B 89–91 and Cartledge 1987: 28–9 noting that Lysander's brother Libys is not referred to as a *mothax*. This suggests that the family had become impoverished before Lysander's birth (possibly the result of the helot rising of the 460s–450s?).
39 On the chronology and the battle at Notium see *Hell. Oxy.* 4, with Bruce 1967: 35–9.
40 Xen. *Hell.* 1.4.20, and Kagan 1987: 314–15 (Alcibiades' authority). Develin 1989: 174–5 lists five generals for this year, so the possibility exists that other – inexperienced – generals might have been present.
41 On the role of pilots see Jordan 1972: 138–43, at 141, who suggests that Alcibiades' appointment of Antiochus to command of the fleet was irregular. But that was Alcibiades' way.

42 Xen. *Hell.* 1.5.11–14, Diod. 13.71, Plut. *Alc.* 35.6–7. See also Ellis 1989: 91–3 who suggests that Antiochus' attack was a battle plan executed poorly. Perhaps, but it is just as likely that it began as a sort of sailors' taunt that misfired.

43 Plut. *Alc.* 36.1–4. This Thrasybulus is not the general of the same name and veteran of the political controversies of 411 and of many battles. For details on Thrasybulus of Kolluteus see *PA* 7305 and *APF* 238–40.

44 Plut. *Alc.* 36.4 and Xen. *Hell.*1.5.16 suggest that new generals were now elected. This may be a false recollection on Xenophon's part. See Develin 1989: 174, 178.

45 Xen. *Hell.* 1.5.17, with Ellis 1989: 93–4.

46 Archelaus had succeeded his father Perdiccas c. 413 and in murky details, perhaps killing his father and other relatives in taking power. See Pl. *Gorg.* 471 a–c, with Borza 1990: 161–2.

47 Thuc. 2.100.2, with Beloch iii.2.55, Hornblower 1: 375–6 (Archelaus); Lefkowitz 1981: 88–104 (Euripides, life and career). On the *Bacchae* see (e.g.) Dodds 1960: xxxix–l.

48 On Critias see Guthrie 1971: 298–304, with sources.

49 Thuc. 7.31.4–5, 7.34 (Conon at Naupactus), Diod. 13.48.6 (Conon in Corcyra, 411/0), with Develin 1989: 153–5, 163.

50 On the election of new generals see Develin 1989: 174, 178–9.

11

'ATHENS IS TAKEN'

In the late spring or early summer of 406, Lysander's term as commander of Spartan forces in the Aegean ended. His successor Callicratidas arrived to take over the command, but feelings between the two were not cordial. At the change of command ceremonies, Lysander told his successor that he was passing on to him the title of master of the sea and conqueror in battle. Callicratidas' unfriendly reply was that if that were the case, Lysander should bring the fleet to Miletus and let the Athenians on Samos take a shot at him. Lysander ignored the taunt, saying only that others were now in command and they could do that. This unfriendly exchange reveals not only Spartan arrogance, but also the competition that drove Spartans like Lysander and Callicratidas. Both *mothakes*, they seemed determined to outperform their rival and so win greater prestige and authority for themselves and shine in the eyes of their mentors.[1]

Callicratidas soon found the going hard, as subordinate officers appointed by Lysander undermined his authority. In private sessions in the allied cities and with select groups of sailors and soldiers, these spoke of the folly of sending out inexperienced commanders to replace those who had demonstrated so much in action against the enemy. Callicratidas caught wind of this dissent and countered it, stating plainly that he would prefer to remain at home, but given the assignment he would carry it out to the best of his ability. He issued a challenge to his critics, asking them if he should remain in his command, or return home and report on the situation in the fleet?[2]

None dared answer the challenge, and Callicratidas decided to approach Cyrus on the matter of pay for the fleet. Lysander had done his work well sabotaging Callicratidas, as he had returned to Cyrus all the unused monies before his successor's arrival (Xen. *Hell.* 1.6.6–7). The practice of deceit was an old Spartan virtue, and Lysander was no stranger to its use. He once said that boys could be cheated with dice and men with oaths.[3] Now pinched hard by the lack of funds, Callicratidas called on Cyrus. The prince refused to see him and treated him little better than a court lackey, an attitude certain to offend any Spartan, especially one like Callicratidas who had labored for years against a stigma of inferiority. It is tempting to see in the clash between Lysander and Callicratidas a reflection of an internal debate in Sparta. Linked to King Agis and his brother Agesilaus, Lysander's goal was to make deals with the Persian 'other' and do what was necessary to achieve victory. In contrast others in Sparta, like the Agiad king Pleistonanx and the ephor Endius, advocated more pan-hellenic or anti-Persian interests, motivated either by personal clashes or genuine concerns.[4] Callicratidas seems to have belonged to the latter camp.

Callicratidas was furious at the slight, but it only convinced him that his beliefs about the Persians, or the 'foreigners' as he called them, were right: that they were even a greater threat than the Athenians they were fighting. In fact, he made it clear that he found it demeaning to ask the Persians for money and that once home, he would do all he could to bring about peace with Athens. Like Aristophanes in his play *Lysistrata* five years earlier, Callicratidas saw that a greater threat to all of them lay in the east and that the Greeks were now simply wearing each other out, making it easier for their old enemy to deprive them of their freedom.[5]

In sessions at Miletus and Chios, Callicratidas made his case vigorously and the allies responded generously with sufficient cash that he could now pay his sailors a bonus.[6] Inspired perhaps by this pan-hellenic rhetoric, Callicratidas' fleet and army took Methymna (on Lesbos) by storm. All the property that could be found was given over to the soldiery, while the Methymnaeans and the Athenian garrison were gathered into the marketplace. His allies urged him to sell all the prisoners as slaves. But Callicratidas refused to enslave fellow Greeks, at least until the next day when he gave in to the pressures and allowed the men of the Athenian garrison to be sold, along with any prisoner who had been a slave previously.[7]

After so many roadblocks, the victory at Methymna perhaps made Callicratidas overconfident. He now sent a message to Conon operating around Samos with a large squadron of seventy ships, telling him, euphemistically, that he intended to put an end to his fucking with the sea.[8] Immediately Callicratidas made for Conon and succeeded in blocking him up in Mytilene. But Conon's luck held again. Though he lost thirty ships, most of the crews escaped. He took the rest out of the water and drew them up under the city walls. Callicratidas pressed Conon even harder, bringing up land forces to place city and harbor under siege – and then money from Cyrus arrived (Xen. *Hell.* 1.6.16–18).

An Athenian Triumph

Trapped in Mytilene, Conon was in a difficult position and he knew it. With food in short supply for both his own forces and the city population, prospects were grim unless he could get word out of his plight. He did just that. Outfitting two fast ships with handpicked crews, a mid-day break succeeded in catching the Spartans napping. Heading in opposite directions, one for the Hellespont where word could be sent to Athens, the other into open sea, the race was on. The Athenians were lucky as it was the decoy that the Spartans caught, while that making its way to Athenian forces in the north safely made its journey. Word quickly reached Athens of Conon's plight (Xen. *Hell.* 1.6.19–22).

An emergency levy of every able-bodied man, free or slave, was made. Only months later (spring 405) Aristophanes staged *Frogs*, his comic masterpiece of literary criticism. At the play's beginning, the slave Xanthias ('Goldilocks'), loaded down with the god Dionysus' baggage, would complain that he had not volunteered for naval service and thereby earned his freedom.[9] Not only did slaves enlist, but so too did elite cavalrymen who volunteered for naval duty. A month's hard work succeeded in assembling a fleet of 110 ships which sailed to Samos where more than forty other ships joined them. Callicratidas learned that this relief force was approaching and made his own preparations for the looming showdown. Leaving behind fifty ships to keep Conon occupied, he quickly encountered the Athenian fleet at lunch at the Arginusae islands, opposite Mytilene (Xen. *Hell.* 1.6.24–5).

Outnumbered by the combined Athenian fleet, Callicratidas decided he must attack if he had any chance for success. Stormy weather delayed his surprise and so it was at first light that he sailed for the Athenians, hoping to catch them still asleep. His luck failed and he found the Athenians racing to meet him head on. His pilot, a Megarian named Hermon, told him it would be wise to retire as the Athenians had a numerical advantage. But a seer had predicted Callicratidas' death in the coming fight though his fleet would win. He now told Hermon that whatever happened, Sparta would live on, while for him flight would be dishonorable.[10] In a moment two great fleets collided. Callicratidas fought with all the courage of a man possessed, disabling several Athenian ships before becoming stuck in that of Pericles, son of the 'Olympian', after ramming it. Pericles' crew threw grappling irons onto Callicratidas' ship and a fierce fight, probably more like a brawl, followed between the crews of the entangled ships. Callicratidas fought to the bitter end, perhaps falling overboard not to be seen again (cf. Diod. 13.99.5 and Xen. *Hell.* 1.6.33).

Before the battle Callicratidas told his men that should he fall, command would pass to Clearchus, last seen losing Byzantium to the Athenians.[11] Whether Clearchus now gave an order to disengage is unknown, but on the death (or disappearance) of their commander the Peloponnesian ships began retreating. Though inexperienced the Athenian advantage in numbers overcame deficiencies in seamanship and gave the Athenians the victory. Some Spartan allies, particularly the Boeotian and Euboean ships on the left wing, continued the fight driven by their hate for Athens. But when Athenian numbers again proved too much, they too took to flight. Some of the Spartan and allied ships made for Chios, while the Athenians retired and reassembled in their anchorage in the Arginusae islands (Xen. *Hell.* 1.6.33).

The coastline around the battle site was strewn with corpses and wreckage. Drifting at sea were scores of battered and slowly sinking wrecks: triremes did not sink as much as they broke apart, and injured and exhausted men would have had a hard time hanging on.[12] The men on ten Spartan, more than sixty of their allies' ships, and twenty-five Athenian, were all in danger of joining their ships at the bottom. Roughly 5000 men were in danger aboard the damaged Athenian ships alone. Not all would have been Athenian, but given the community's *levée en masse* a high percentage would have been, which explains what the Athenian commanders now did. Orders were given to two experienced former generals now serving as trierarchs, Theramenes and Thrasybulus, to take a large squadron – some forty-seven warships – and aid the disabled ships and rescue survivors. The rest of the fleet, another seventy-five ships, raced off to Mytilene to relieve Conon and his trapped squadron (Xen. *Hell.* 1.6.34–5).

But the sea turned violent. Before Theramenes and Thrasybulus could act a fierce storm blew up, scattering the wrecked ships and only a few lucky survivors were found ashore. Many Athenians, and not a few of them elites, drowned and few bodies would have been recovered. Burial rituals, so important to the Greeks as any reader of Sophocles' *Antigone* will know, would have been impossible and this would only compound the grief and anger of loss. But the Athenian commanders, intent on relieving Conon, would have had no idea of the disaster behind them.

Meanwhile, a fast dispatch boat had reached Eteonicus, the Spartan officer holding Conon at bay in Mytilene. Receiving news of Callicratidas' defeat, Eteonicus told the boat to return to sea silently, but then return making lots of noise about a spectacular Spartan victory and the destruction of the Athenian fleet. Eteonicus then silently broke camp, ordering his ships to Chios, himself taking his ground forces back to Methymna. When Conon realized they were gone, he put to sea and met the relieving Athenian ships. The combined fleet now launched an attack against Chios but failed to achieve very much: several squadrons either returned to Samos or other locations while the bulk of the fleet returned to Athens where a storm of a different kind awaited the victorious generals (Xen. *Hell.* 1.6.35–8).

Xanthias – Would-be Sailor for Athens

How many slaves actually volunteered for the fleet that fought at Arginusae? One who missed the fight to his regret was Xanthias, Dionysus' slave, and while the character and the scene are comic, Aristophanes knew that both would get a laugh. This suggests that a number of slaves did take the Athenians at their word, served in the battle, and won their freedom and citizenship, most likely Plataean. Slaves had served in Athenian naval forces previously, what was unusual now were their number as well as the grant of freedom that came with their service.[13] While service for freedom tells much about the conditions of slavery and freedom in Athens, Xanthias' missed opportunity offers a glimpse into the sailor's life in the Peloponnesian War.

Life at sea on board a trireme, Athenian or Peloponnesian, was as hard as it was dangerous. Ships were largely propelled by manpower – men pulling on oars together – and this was not easy to learn, as Nicias reminded the Athenians from Sicily, a crew's efficiency and ability to pull together (literally) was brief.[14] A trireme was little more than a large racing scull with a ram mounted on the bow, and life aboard was full of labor: ships had to be brought up on land to dry out (and this was a problem for the Athenian fleet in Sicily where this was difficult and dangerous on account of Syracusan cavalry); cramped conditions made it difficult to eat, which also necessitated bringing ships in to land. Otherwise crews faced cold, dried food while pulling their oars at sea and while this could be done, it was difficult.[15] Life at sea was so hard that even the 'Old Oligarch', a conservative Athenian social critic, could admit that those who manned the ships, the poor and the needy, deserved holding political power in Athens ([Xen.] *Ath. Pol.* 1.2).

The trierarch's role in managing and keeping his ship fit was no less a challenge. Sailors deserted (why? See above.) or sometimes provided substitutes, this done by bribing trierarchs to look the other way, which lowered the overall effectiveness of the ship and the fleet of which it was a part (Thuc. 7.13.2). Mercenaries recruited to serve on board as marines frequently deserted when the fighting intensified, sometimes complaining that their servants had deserted, sometimes deserting to escape the dangers and hardships of service. The bitter fighting on board the entangled ships of Pericles and Callicratidas at Arginusae demonstrates clearly why men might choose desertion over service. But trierarchs sometimes caused their own problems too, not paying crews their full wages, even sailors who had fulfilled their terms of service. Aristophanes relates what would appear to be a common sailor's complaint – returning home to port and not being paid (*Eq.* 1366–7).

Life at sea and on land was full of danger and hard work, not to mention cold food and pay sometimes denied. In the end, maybe carrying Dionysus' bags was not such hard work after all.

An Athenian Tragedy

Triumph at Arginusae quickly became tragedy. In little time the Athenians deposed the generals who had just crushed a Spartan fleet, retaining on active service only Conon who had played no part in the battle. Erasinides, one of the Arginusae commanders, was brought up on charges of financial malfeasance and military misconduct by Archedemus, a popular politician – he was soon hauled off to prison. His former colleagues – Aristocrates, Diomedon, Lysias, Pericles, and Thrasyllus – soon found themselves defending their actions in the great battle, and after it, literally fighting for their lives as they too were charged with dereliction of duty.[16]

In highly charged proceedings, the generals reported on the course of the battle and especially the great storm that blew up afterwards that claimed so many Athenian lives. Another popular politician, Timocrates, proposed that the generals be handed over to the assembly for trial, a motion approved by the Council. The next day a meeting of the assembly heard many speakers attack the generals for their misconduct, with particular emphasis placed on their failure to save the crews of the damaged and sinking ships. On this none was more forceful or adamant than Theramenes – one of the trierarchs assigned this duty! Not only a former commander himself, Theramenes had participated in the political revolutions of the Four Hundred and Five Thousand and was no stranger to political intrigue or debate. His stature guaranteed him an attentive audience, while his oratory enabled him to obscure the fact that it was his failure that they were all debating. The generals attempted to rebut his accusations, but the length of the proceedings delayed a vote on the charges as darkness made it impossible to count votes. Accordingly, proceedings were held over.[17]

The delay would prove fatal. The celebrations of the Apaturia festival now intervened, a three-day affair conducted by the Athenian phratries or brotherhoods at which, among other events, family members gathered.[18] For the generals the timing could not have been worse. The bereaved would gather and family losses in the recent battle would be all too clear. But more damaging was the opportunity given to Theramenes and other angry and opportunistic Athenians to orchestrate public displays against the generals: men were bribed to attend the assembly in black with closely-shaved heads in mournful poses demanding justice. Then another politician, Callixenus, rose and proposed a sweeping – and unconstitutional – measure that the generals should be denied any further speeches in their defense and that they should be tried in bloc. The dramatics continued as a 'survivor' of the disaster rose and told the assembled crowd that before they died, men in the water around him screamed at him to tell the people how the generals had left them to die.

At this point, Euryptolemus, one of Alcibiades' relatives, rose and spoke in defense of the generals, arguing that the proposal brought by Callixenus was unconstitutional. While there were a number present who rallied behind him, more railed at him, demanding that the people should be able to do whatever they wanted. Another popular politician, Lyciscus, took up their cause and proposed that unless Euryptolemus withdrew his proposal, he and those supporting his measure would be judged by the same measure as the generals. Intimidated by the charge, and surely the crowd too, Euryptolemus backed down (Xen. *Hell.* 1.7.8–13).

Those Athenians trying to save the generals made one final effort. Several of the 'Presidents', the members of the Council's administrative committee or *prytaneis*, stated that they would not allow Callixenus' motion to go forward as it was clearly unconstitutional. But once more the anger and pain of the crowd spoke: Callixenus spoke out against the councilors, threatening them with the same charges as he had Euryptolemus and others, and the crowd yelled out its support. Once more level-headed Athenians were intimidated. The 'Presidents' retreated from their own motion and agreed to put Callixenus' to the vote. All, that is, but Socrates. The old soldier and friend of Alcibiades – and surely the young Pericles now on trial for his life – stood firm just as he had at Delium and Potidaea years before. Facing down the howling crowd, and surely angering many, Socrates plainly stated that he would not be party to a great wrong (Xen. *Hell.* 1.7.14–15). While not entirely certain, Socrates' action delayed proceedings until the next day. But then he would not be in a position to defend the generals further.[19]

After one last major effort in the generals' defense, another speech by Euryptolemus and another demand for separate trials, the issue was put to the vote. The outcome was never really in doubt. The Athenians rejected Euryptolemus' lawful proposal and adopted that illegally brought by Callixenus and now endorsed by an intimidated Council. The generals who had destroyed the Spartan fleet were condemned to death. Handed over to the jailers, the 'Eleven', the generals were marched to their deaths. On the way one of them, Diomedon, an experienced and distinguished commander, told the Athenians that they should make good on the generals' vow before the great battle: that on victory the generals would offer sacrifices to Zeus the Savior, Apollo, and the Holy Goddesses. While the irony of his officious and patriotic request did not go unnoticed, the executions were carried out as decreed (Diod. 13.102.2–3; Xen. *Hell.* 1.7.16–34).[20]

Disaster at Sea

Arginusae was an unlucky victory for the Athenians as its aftermath made clear. Not only had they killed the generals who won the battle, but in savoring the victory they may again have rejected Spartan peace overtures. Opposition to peace came most notably from Cleophon, a prominent popular leader, who on this occasion spoke boldly and drunkenly (perhaps) against any deal with the Spartans.[21] Some Athenians too were troubled by the freedom and citizenship granted to the fighting slaves of Arginusae, especially as so many free-born Athenian citizens had been exiled over the course of the war. Aristophanes voices this grievance in *Frogs* (ll. 33–4, 693–6) and the issue remained hot in 400 when Andocides defended himself against charges of impiety in his speech *On the Mysteries* (149). Battles not only took Athenian lives, but changed them in other ways too.

The executions required the election of new generals (probably in spring 405), and afterwards preparations began for a renewed offensive into the eastern Aegean. From their base in Samos the Athenian commanders, including Conon and some of the new generals, Cephisodotus, Menander, and Tydeus, raided Persian territories and those around Chios and Ephesus, all the while watching to see what response the Spartans would now make (Xen. *Hell.* 2.1.12, 16).

Arginusae may also have led the Spartans to reassess their old ways of doing things. A near revolt on Chios was just nipped in the bud by Eteonicus, the Spartan governor. This event, and allied demands that Lysander be reinstated as commander of Spartan and allied forces, reenergized the Spartan war effort. Lysander had been popular among the allies and he got on well with Cyrus, and while there were rules and regulations to be followed (i.e., the same man could not be admiral twice), they could be skirted. Spartan authorities returned Lysander to service, technically as the subordinate to a new commander, Aracus (in place of the fallen Callicratidas). But as far as anyone could see, it was Lysander who commanded Spartan Aegean forces (Xen. *Hell.* 2.1.1–7).

Lysander quickly began the rebuilding of the Spartan war effort. From his base at Ephesus, he began to assemble his forces: summoning Eteonicus and the Chian garrison (and fleet), Lysander begged and borrowed ships and crews wherever he could. Manipulative and scheming as ever, Lysander met with Cyrus. Again he pressed the prince for more money. While Cyrus went over the books, pointing out all the funds that he and his father had already invested in the Spartans, he still came up with more cash with which Lysander paid his crews. Cyrus also urged him to be careful in fighting the Athenians, to make sure that he held massive superiority before taking them on again – clearly Arginusae was on his mind (Xen. *Hell.* 2.1.10–15).

This new fleet needed a seasoning expedition and Lysander provided that with a punitive raid against Cedreiae, an Athenian ally in Caria, and then against shipping near Rhodes and the Ionian coast (Xen. *Hell.* 2.1.15–

16).[22] Lysander then moved north into the Hellespont which he had surely identified as the key to victory. Ostensibly aimed at the recovery of those cities lost to Alcibiades and the Athenians two years before, Lysander knew that moving there would draw the Athenian fleet to him, just like a moth to a flame.

Lampsacus, an Athenian ally mid-way up the Hellespont, fell to a Spartan attack by land and sea. The Athenians, trailing Lysander's fleet some twenty or thirty miles south, learned of this and immediately moved north, taking on new stores at Sestus, finally coming to Aegospotami, a landing opposite Lampsacus. Over the next four days the two fleets played a game of cat and mouse – a game that suited Lysander perfectly. He once said when the lion's skin was too small, it could be made bigger with the fox's (Plut. *Mor.* 229B). The Athenians were about to get a lesson in Spartan stealth.

Each morning the Athenian fleet, 180 ships strong, would sail across the narrow strait and assume battle stations opposite the Spartan anchorage. Lysander ordered his men to prepare their ships for battle but to await an Athenian attack. But there was no attack and at mid-day the Athenians retired for lunch. Lysander sent out a fast ship to watch and then report back on what the Athenians did on reaching their camp. What his scouts saw was encouraging: the Athenians pulled their ships up on the beach, prepared lunch, or went off in search of it as their supplies were fast running out. The Spartan fleet, however, remained on station as Lysander received this same report each day.

The danger lurking on the horizon was obvious to just about everyone perhaps but the Athenian commanders. This included the exiled Alcibiades whose Thracian perch a short distance away gave him a bird's eye view of the dangerous position taken up by the Athenian fleet. After watching for several days, Alcibiades visited the Athenian camp. He advised retiring to Sestus where there was food and a better anchorage which would enable them to attack wherever they desired. But the generals, especially Tydeus and Menander, rebuffed him harshly and told him to go away, that they were now in charge of things (Xen. *Hell.* 2.1.20–6).[23]

On the fourth day the scene replayed, but this time Lysander told his scout ship that upon following the Athenians back and observing the same routine as before, they should return as fast as possible and signal with a shield once they were halfway back. Keeping their routine, the Athenians scattered for lunch and the scout ship returned and flashed the ordered sign. Lysander sent his ships standing at battle station into the attack catching the Athenians completely off-guard. Only the still lucky Conon with eight other ships was able to get away before the Spartans were upon them all. In an hour, almost the entire Athenian force was captured, only a few men managing to get away on foot.[24] The last Athenian fleet was now in Spartan hands.

Lysander brought his prizes – both the ships and their crews – to Lampsacus and word was sent off to Sparta of the great victory. An assembly was convened and the allies were asked for recommendations in dealing with the prisoners, some 3000 of them Athenian (Plut. *Lys.* 13.1). Historically, from ancient Greece to Vietnam and Iraq, prisoners of war have always been in harm's way as previous acts of violence and killing demand payback. Moreover, keeping and looking after prisoners is a nuisance – they have to be fed, they have to be guarded, and they delay whatever plans a victorious commander wants to make. As Lysander now looked over the mass of Athenians in his hands and evaluated the situation, he may have seen a solution to his problem in his allies. Rage against the Athenians was palpable. To all the past crimes, the destruction of so many cities, the Athenians had recently added further horrors: a decree that all prisoners taken in sea fights should have their right hands cut off; the deliberate drowning of two ships' crews at the order of Philocles, one of the generals now in Lysander's hands.

The response of the allies was loud and clear – kill them. Only the general Adeimantus was spared, ostensibly for his opposition to the 'right hand' decree, though some thought he owed his survival to his betrayal of the fleet, bribed by Lysander (Xen. *Hell.* 2.1.32, Paus. 10.9.5). As for Philocles, Lysander asked him, 'What's a worthy punishment for acting like a criminal towards your fellow Greeks?'[25] Not intimidated, Philocles told Lysander not to play the part of the prosecutor where there was no judge, but rather that of the victor and do what would have been done to him had he lost. Then bathing and putting on his best clothes, he led his fellow Athenians to their deaths. How was such a mass execution carried out? A few rare scenes of the killing of prisoners from vase paintings suggests that the Athenians were bound and then were led off and executed, either drowned or killed by sword.[26] However carried out, the deliberate killing of so many unarmed men must be seen not only as a gruesome act itself, but also as an indicator of the level of violence the war had now reached.

The End

As Conon made his way to Cyprus where he entered the service of the Cypriote king Evagoras, the *Paralos*, a state trireme and another to escape Lysander's net, arrived in Athens with news of the disaster.[27] While Xenophon's account may be dramatically embellished, there should be little doubt that many must have realized the consequences as they also remembered what they themselves had also done to so many others.

The fleet destroyed at Aegospotami was Athens' last and except for its walls the city now lay defenseless. Moreover, a flood of refugees now began arriving. As Lysander consolidated his position in the Hellespont he forced the surrender of Byzantium and Chalcedon and their Athenian garrisons. The latter were not harmed and in fact were allowed to leave freely – as long as they went to Athens. Elsewhere as word of Aegospotami spread, the allies began deserting with only Samos holding firm, though here another slaughter of democratic enemies was carried out (Xen. *Hell.* 2.2.6). As Athens' empire crumbled, Athenians abroad would fly home for shelter and their arrival too would aggravate the food shortages and spread the panic. Lysander was surely right that the Athenians would have no choice but to agree to terms.

Within a short time the Spartans had Athens completely surrounded. Just north at Decelea sat Agis and his forces while to the south of the city, in the precinct of the Academy, the Agiad king Pausanias arrived with a second army. His arrival may have been fortuitous for the Athenians. On receiving Lysander's report of the Athenian fleet's destruction, Agis had discussed with Lysander Athens' total destruction.[28] Such policies were evidently not those of Pausanias and his father Pleistoanax, and whatever talk there might have been of wiping out the Athenians, Pausanias' arrival ended it. Not long after Lysander with his victorious fleet, some 200 ships, dropped anchor in the Piraeus and closed the harbor to all shipping. One story has it that Lysander now sent a dispatch to the ephors reporting 'Athens is taken', to which the ephors replied, '"Taken" is enough – [we know who the enemy is]'.[29]

It was now only a question of time. Soon the Athenians sued for peace, first approaching Agis who told them that he had no authority and they should go to Sparta. Before even reaching Sparta, the ephors, learning of the Athenian proposals – that they would join the Spartan alliance if they could keep their walls and the Piraeus – sent them home with the admonition to return with a better proposal.[30] On learning this, the Athenians were even more depressed and one, Archestratus, was thrown into prison when he proposed accepting Spartan terms – including the destruction of the Long Walls linking Athens to the Piraeus.

As the siege tightened and more and more Athenians succumbed to hunger, Theramenes, the same who had betrayed his commanders in the Arginusae affair, proposed to the assembly that he contact Lysander to learn why the Spartans insisted on the removal of the Long Walls. He was sent off and spent some four months waiting for an answer. Finally, Lysander released him, telling him to report to the Athenians that only the ephors possessed the authority to negotiate a settlement and that they should go to them. True desperation now prevailed in Athens. The assembly appointed a delegation of ten, including Theramenes, to negotiate a settlement, giving it full authority to do so.

At Sellasia in the Peloponnese, the ephors convened an assembly of their allies to hear the Athenian delegation, which stated that it possessed full authority to negotiate peace. A number of the allies, particularly the Corinthians and Thebans, urged the Spartans to destroy Athens and enslave its people, in effect to visit on the Athenians the same terror they had on the people of Greece. Erianthus of Thebes even proposed that not only should Athens be razed to the ground, but that its lands should be given over to sheep for grazing, in effect the same thing proposed by American diplomat Hans Morgenthau for Germany in 1944.[31] But the Spartans refused these extreme measures, arguing they would not deprive Greece of a city that had done such great things in the past (Xen. *Hell.* 2.1.19). In fact, the Spartans traditionally never pursued far a beaten enemy. They may have already recognized that allies like Corinth and Thebes might pose a threat too and that preserving Athens was in Sparta's best interests. The Spartans would have remembered Corinthian and Theban resistance to the Peace of Nicias and might have imagined future difficulties with them now.

Theramenes and his fellow ambassadors were obliged to accept a hard peace, but one that could have been much worse if men like Erianthus of Thebes had prevailed: the destruction of the Long Walls and those of the Piraeus, loss of all but twelve ships, recall of the exiles. The Spartans also required the Athenians to have the same friends and enemies and to follow the Spartans on whatever campaigns they required. In effect, if not technically, the Athenians were now members of the Peloponnesian League.[32] The ambassadors made their report before a hungry assembly. While some Athenians were for fighting on, most were relieved that they had been spared the fate of Melos and were willing to accept peace at the loss of the walls and a certain amount of autonomy. Soon afterwards Lysander sailed into the Piraeus with his fleet and a party of Athenian exiles (about March 404).[33] In a demonstration of his authority, he offered a gift to Athena on the acropolis. As he did so, perhaps work began dismantling the walls connecting Athens and the Piraeus, performed with great celebration and to the music of flute girls. Many thought that this day was the beginning of freedom for Greece.[34] For the Athenians one kind of war had been exchanged for another, though this horror still lay in the future. Brutal civil strife – *stasis* – would soon rip Athens apart and many Athenians would die before the ongoing violence finally yielded to peace.

Lysander and Post-War Sparta

Lysander had won the war for Sparta and made good on the claim to put an end to the 'tyrant city'. But Lysander's victory may have troubled more than a few, especially in Sparta. There was first the business of the public relations campaign that Lysander pushed. In Delphi a massive sculptural group, sometimes referred to as the 'Navarch's Monument', not only commemorated Lysander's victory but raised him to near divine stature (after 403). Created by the sculptor Polycleitus, his sons and students, the monument stood on a raised three meter base some eighteen meters long and nearly five deep. Some thirty to forty statues, mostly victorious commanders stood with Lysander's seer Agias and his helmsman Hermon, all around Lysander himself about to be crowned by Poseidon.[35] The association with Poseidon would have announced to viewers that Lysander was nearly a god himself.

If the imagery in Delphi was at all ambiguous, and it probably is not much, then what was done in Samos made it clear that Lysander had assumed greater than human standing. At Samos Lysander had restored the oligarchic party and in thanks and recognition of his achievements they had established a cult in his honor (September 404).[36] Complete with sacrifices, altar, and hymns, the Samians also changed the name of their principal festival, the Heraea, to the Lysandreia, revealing that Lysander now received divine worship and not simply heroic.[37]

Evidence of Lysander's heroics even penetrated the stubbornly conservative society of Sparta. At rural Amyklai two tripods were placed in commemoration of his victories while on the acropolis in Sparta itself, two victories or *nikai* standing on eagles were dedicated. Recognition of individual achievement by the living was unparalleled. No doubt Lysander imagined that he had accomplished more than any other man before, entitling him to this level of distinction.[38] Few even in Sparta might have dared challenge his claims.

Lysander's imposing heroics were matched only by the incredible wealth that now began to pour into Sparta. For any rural agrarian-based society, confronting piles of money and other forms of wealth must have been intoxicating as well as scary. Debate began among the Spartans themselves over what to do with all the loot. And there was lots of it: after Aegospotami, Lysander's forces had stormed Lampsacus, an Athenian ally. Lampsacus had provided Athens with an annual tribute of twelve talents a year, clear evidence of its prosperity. The soldiers were turned loose and stormed through the town, basically cleaning it out of food, wine, and everything else (Xen. *Hell.* 2.18–19).

A number of Spartans criticized Lysander for bringing such great wealth into Sparta and this resulted in the famous ban on coinage associated with the lawgiver Lycurgus.[39] But Lysander, with strong ties to the Eurypontid Agis and Agesilaus, had influential friends and these seem to have brokered a compromise: while private possession of coined money was prohibited, it could be used for the state. But temptations proved too great for some. Gylippus, the hero of Syracuse, had been charged with bringing to Sparta a vast quantity of monies taken from the Athenians. He apparently thought a small theft would go unnoticed but when the accounts did not tally he was caught red-handed, the missing money secreted away in the roof of his house. He fled into exile. More severe was the punishment of Thorax, one of Lysander's commanders, the same who had sacked Lampsacus. When he was caught in possession of silver, Spartan authorities ordered his execution.[40]

Notes

1 Xen. *Hell.* 1.6.2, Ael. *VH* 12.43 (*mothax* status of Callicratidas), with Cartledge 1987: 28.
2 Xen. *Hell.* 1.6.4–5.
3 Plut. *Mor.* 229b; see 229a–230a for other sayings attributed to Lysander.

4 See de Ste. Croix 1972: 144–7, especially at 147. The idea of 'party politics', however, must be restrained as there is a good deal of personality to these groupings and their conduct of 'policy'.

5 Xen. *Hell*. 1.6.7, Ar. *Lys*. 1128–36.

6 Xen. *Hell*. 1.6.12 (with Krentz 1989: 148) reads five drachmas per day per sailor. But this is surely a slip on Xenophon's part for five obols. See pp. 187–8 for discussion of pay rates.

7 Xen. *Hell*. 1.6.12–15. It is unclear, but the Athenian garrison may have been mostly non-Athenian, while former slaves serving as soldiers could probably be identified by owners' tattoos.

8 Xen. *Hell*. 1.6.15. Xenophon uses the verb *moicheuo* for Callicratidas' taunt, which LSJ delicately defines as 'commit adultery' or 'debauch a woman'. But the sexual innuendo and language is that of a brothel, hence the more vulgar translation of the passage here.

9 Ar. *Ran*. 33–4; see also Hellanicus *FGrHist* 323a F25.

10 Diod. 13.98.1 (prediction), Xen. *Hell*. 1.6.32 (Callicratidas' reply to Hermon). For the battle cf. Diod. 13.98.2–99 and Xen. *Hell*. 1.33–4. Hermon survived, later becoming Lysander's helmsman, immortalized in the victory monument at Delphi.

11 Diod. 13.98.1. Diodorus calls Clearchus 'a man proven in the deeds of war', a description matching the portrait of Clearchus in Xen. *Anab*. 2.6.2, arguing that they are the same man. For his later mercenary life see pp. 235–6.

12 On triremes and their fragility see Morrison and Coates 1986: 128.

13 Ar. *Ran*. 33–4, 693–4. Just what citizenship the slaves received is debated; see Hunt 1998: 87–95 for a summary of the arguments. Dover 1993: 279 notes that it is not clear if it was Athenian or Plataean, but of the grant of freedom there is no question.

14 Thuc. 7.14.1, with Gomme-Andrewes-Dover 4: 386–91; here Nicias reports on the situation in Sicily and in doing so relates much of life at sea. For full discussion see Jordan 1972 and Morrison and Coates 1986.

15 Thuc. 7.12.3 (ships on land), 7.13.2 (crews killed on land while looking for water, food). Thuc. 3.49.3 relates the extraordinary conditions of the trireme that saved the Mytilenians from death: the crews rowed constantly sleeping and rowing in shifts, eating as they did so. This would have been very hard work.

16 Xen. *Hell*. 1.7.2, names two other generals, Aristogenes and Protomachus, who also fought but did not return to Athens. Perhaps commanders of squadrons in Samos or elsewhere, their absence saved them the fate of their colleagues.

17 Xen. *Hell*. 1.7.3–7, with Krentz 1989: 158–61.

18 Sinclair 1988: 171 notes the interval caused by the festival that delayed the generals' trial.

19 Xen. *Hell*. 1.7.14–15, with Krentz 1989: 163–4 and references to Xen. *Mem*. 1.1.18, 4.4.2 and Pl. *Ap*. 32b, *Gorg*. 473e–474a.

20 In a footnote, Xen. *Hell.* 1.7.35 adds that the Athenians soon regretted what they had done and held Callixenus and several others responsible (so too Pl. *Ap.* 32b and Diod. 13.103.1). Most escaped prosecution. Callixenus returned to Athens after the war, but died of starvation, loathed by his fellow citizens.

21 [Arist.] *Ath. Pol.* 34.1, with Krentz 1989: 170; but *Ath. Pol.* is a later source and could be in error. See further Rhodes 1981: 424–5.

22 The fighting that follows leads to the Athenian defeat at Aegospotami, sometime in summer 405/4. See Diod. 13.104.1, [Arist.] *Ath. Pol.* 34.1, with Rhodes 1981: 426.

23 With this Alcibiades' role in the war ends and he disappears from Xenophon's account. His later murder at the hands of agents sent by the satrap Pharnabazus, in collusion with the Spartans, is told in Plut. *Alc.* Develin 1989: 180–1 lists the careless Athenian generals.

24 Plut. *Lys.* 11.11.

25 Xen. *Hell.* 2.1.30–2, with Plut. *Lys.* 13. Powell 2006: 290–3 links the killing of the Athenian prisoners to the later proposal to destroy Athens. While possible, what was discussed after Aegospotami falls more in the category of wartime vengeance rather than deliberate policy.

26 See the drawings in Krentz 2007: 181, 184. The mass execution is disputed, but the war's passions readily explain it; Krentz 1989: 179–80 cites several scholarly views.

27 Xen. *Hell.* 2.1.29 (Conon), 2.2.3 (the *Paralos* in Athens).

28 Reported by Paus. 3.8.6, a late source but generally well informed. See also Powell 2004: 290–1.

29 Plut. *Lys.* 14.6–7. Plutarch thinks the story is too pat for belief. Powell 2006: 290 questions his skepticism, linking the dispatch to a proposal by Lysander and Agis to destroy Athens, reported in Paus. 3.8.6.

30 Negotiations would take some time as the Spartans slowly surrounded Athens and isolated it. See below notes 33, 36 for references to chronology.

31 Plut. *Lys.* 15.3; Mearsheimer 2001: 151 (Morgenthau Plan).

32 Xen. *Hell.* 2.2.20, Diod. 13.107.4; see also de Ste. Croix 1972: 108, Kagan 1987: 410.

33 Xen. *Hell.* 2.2.23, Thuc. 5.26.3 (and Gomme-Andrewes-Dover 4: 12), with Krentz 1989: 188.

34 *IG* II^2 1388, l. 32, with Parker 1996: 222 (dedication); Xen. *Hell.* 2.2.23 (walls).

35 Paus. 10.9.4–5, who names twenty-nine of the allied commanders, noting also the four sculptors who created them. See also Stewart 2008: 228–9 and Cartledge 1987: 82–3.

36 Xen. *Hell.* 2.3.6–7, with Rhodes and Osborne 2003: 14–17 and Krentz 1989: 191 (date provided by a solar eclipse).

37 Plut. *Lys.* 18 (after Duris of Samos, *FGrHist* 76F26, 71), with Cartledge 1987: 83.

38 Stewart 2008: 228 and Cartledge 1987: 82–3. What Lysander did, or allowed to be done in his name, would go on to influence similar acts of (self) deification in the fourth century, most famously with Alexander the Great. See, e.g., Parker 1996: 263–4.
39 See Hodkinson 2000, Powell 2004: 297.
40 Plut. *Lys.* 16–17, with Powell 2006: 297–8.

12

'HERE'S TO THE NOBLE CRITIAS!'

For the Athenians, peace came at a high price. The war had taken the lives of perhaps a third of the population, maybe more.[1] Now with the walls coming down, oligarchic enemies of the democracy began asserting themselves. Quiet since the upheavals of 411, these now had in Lysander a powerful patron to whom they could and did turn for aid.

Not only had peace terms stipulated the destruction of the walls, but a new constitution and debate had become drawn out. Lysander now arrived and personally intervened on behalf of the oligarchs, telling the Athenians that they should select thirty men to take charge of affairs. This Theramenes challenged, telling Lysander that the peace provided for no such regime change and that having lost their freedom, he was now adding insult to injury. This was a brave thing to do, perhaps rare for Theramenes who had saved his own neck two years before, sacrificing six generals in the process.[2]

Theramenes not only confronted Lysander, but his Athenian allies now waiting to take power. Most notable of these was Critias, scion of an old aristocratic family, and one-time friend of Socrates.[3] Now home after several years in the wilderness, Critias was the Pol Pot of his day, embittered and vengeful, determined to cleanse Athens of its undesirable elements.[4] While the Pol Pot imagery may seem strained, Lysias specifically notes that the Thirty had a 'cleansing' agenda. His comments argue that Critias and other exiles had had time to contemplate the failure of the earlier oligarch coup. As their actions would later show, they would not settle for half measures or mercy on taking power.

Lysander threatened Theramenes with bodily harm if he did not stop his opposition. Sufficiently intimidated, Theramenes and other like-minded Athenians held their tongues. After discussion in the assembly, a measure proposed by Dracontides led to the election of thirty men who can only be described as enemies of the popular, democratic way of life.

Foremost among these were Critias and Theramenes, each representing in some ways extreme and moderate positions.[5] The Thirty then selected a 'rump parliament', 500 councilors from a pre-determined list (of 1000), as well as 300 enforcers (literally whip-bearers) and eleven jailors. To their own ranks they added another ten, including Critias' nephew Charmides, who were placed in charge of the Piraeus. The Thirty, as they came to be known, were empowered to purge the body of ancestral law and reform the constitution: in reality this amounted to authority to overthrow the democracy that the Athenians had followed for nearly 100 years.[6]

The Thirty

Once in power the Thirty began doing what they pleased and when asked about the reforms responded evasively. Their agenda became clear all too soon. While they announced their intention of restoring the 'ancestral constitution', it soon became clear that this amounted to regime change. Measures that had defined the democracy, laws of Solon, those of Ephialtes restricting the power of the old and aristocratic council the Areopagus, and the authority of the courts, were nullified.[7]

But soon the political maneuverings turned personal and violent. Athenians who had previously attacked aristocratic elites and/or oligarchs, or who had made a living as sycophants, informers who denounced lawbreakers or other wealthy public figures for real and imagined infractions, were rounded up and put on trial. Many of these were obnoxious persons and some Athenians may have thought they got what they deserved (Xen. *Hell.* 2.3.12). But as Dietrich Bonhoeffer would so poignantly relate two millennia later, once people began to disappear, fewer remained to stand up and fight back. Such a crisis now struck Athens.

Recognizing the need for support, the Thirty sent several of their number to Sparta to lobby Lysander for establishment of a garrison – a Spartan garrison – in Athens. Lysander willingly complied and soon Callibius and a force of soldiers arrived.[8] With this muscle the Thirty and their cronies now began arresting not just informers and other low-life types, but anyone they imagined might challenge their authority or resent losing their voice in politics. Fear of arrest and confiscation of property evidently prompted some Athenians to look for safe places to hide their valuables. In one instance Nicias and Euthynous, two cousins, agreed to a plan to hide a large sum of Nicias' money with Euthynous. Later when Euthynous kept some of it, Nicias brought a suit for its recovery.[9] The driving force behind these actions was Critias. His excesses led to a clash with Theramenes, who thought that such measures only created enemies. Moreover, Theramenes believed that to ensure their success they should broaden the citizen body their rule ostensibly represented and include more Athenians in the holding of power (Xen. *Hell.* 3.2.15–18).

Theramenes' 'moderate' opposition alarmed Critias and the more extreme oligarchs who feared his leadership potential. They now conceded to his proposal and agreed to expand it to 3000. Even with this Theramenes found fault, pointing out that this wider body threatened their own small clique at the same time. Such criticisms were perhaps unnerving and this led the Thirty to act against the entire population. Orders were given for the assembly of all citizens able to bear arms and staging areas were set up in different parts of the city. Once assembled, the Thirty, the Three Thousand and the Spartan garrison quickly moved in on the unsuspecting citizens who were disarmed, their weapons taken to the acropolis for storage. The city was now firmly in the hands of the Thirty. Those outside the oligarchic clique had no means to resist (Xen. *Hell.* 2.3.18–20).

Terror gripped Athens. Within a short time some 1500 Athenians were killed ([Arist.] *Ath. Pol.* 35.4), the toll climbing as the Thirty had to pay for the costs of maintaining the Spartan garrison. Two of the Thirty, Theognis and Peison, persuaded the others at a meeting that the metics, the wealthy resident aliens, of Athens were disaffected and posed a security risk. Moreover, as many of them were rich, the financial problems they faced could also be solved. It was agreed then to organize small groups of citizens for the arrest of ten metics, ostensibly for the public good but really as a revenue enhancement measure. To make it appear that public safety was the issue, two poorer metics were named among those designated for arrest (Xen. *Hell.* 2.3.21, with Lys. 12.6–7).

With brutal simplicity, the Thirty schemed to implicate as many Athenians as possible in their crimes. Critias and several others now told Socrates to join in the arrest of Leon of Salamis, a wealthy and prominent member of these elite aliens, that he was to be arrested and brought in for 'treatment'. Socrates had earlier stood up to the mob of Athenians demanding the deaths of the Arginusae generals. He acted so again. He simply ignored the order of his one-time friend and went home. Unfortunately for Leon, Critias found others less courageous, and possibly greedier, who were willing to carry out the death sentence.[10]

Leon's murder was a shocking crime, one that for more than two decades could be cited as an example of a notorious wrong, sometimes too as a crime that escaped punishment. Just a few years later (c. 400) Andocides, defending himself against charges of impiety, referred to it claiming that amnesties were sheltering its perpetrators from prosecution. Nearly twenty years later, Plato would refer to it again in dramatic terms and how it had affected his teacher Socrates, wrongly associated with the crimes of the Thirty.

Even more powerful and dramatic testimony comes from a survivor of the Thirty's terror, Lysias, an Athenian-born metic (c. 445) and latter day intellectual and speech-writer. Lysias' father Cephalas had come to Athens from Syracuse, ostensibly at Pericles' urging and had become a very successful businessman, a factory making shields among his profitable ventures. When the Thirty declared war on the metics, Lysias and his brother Polemarchus were placed on the proscribed list and both brothers were confronted by armed gangs and arrested. Lysias describes in detail his efforts to bribe his captors and only their greed exceeded their brutality. Placed under arrest, Lysias managed to escape only because he knew the layout of the house in which he was held. His brother was not so fortunate. Taken to prison, Polemarchus was condemned and sentenced to death, uncharged and without benefit of trial. Executed with hemlock, the Thirty surrendered his body to the family, but were forbidden to hold the usual funeral rituals in the home, instead being forced to rent a shed and clothes to dress the body.[11]

In recounting this story of terror and brutality, Lysias tells of his family's wealth: three homes, possession of more than 100 slaves, a factory with an inventory of 700 shields, a mass of gold and silver objects, plus other rich furnishings and luxurious clothes. He also details the brutality and corruption of the Thirty: their willingness to accept bribes to turn a blind eye; the earrings of Polemarchus' wife taken off her person (Lys. 12.8–9, 19). Why the Thirty targeted them and treated them as they did becomes abundantly clear in these details.

As with so many other revolutions, this one also devoured its own. Tension between Critias and Theramenes grew steadily and now Theramenes became another victim. At a meeting of the Council with the Thirty, Critias and several others set a trap. Young elite toughs, surely the enforcers or 'whip-bearers', were recruited for security. Once the stage was set, Critias denounced his one-time ally as an enemy of the cause. He ridiculed Theramenes for his duplicity, emphasizing his nickname, 'stage boot', so-called as these actors' shoes faced in opposite directions. Critias reminded his audience of Theramenes' ability to play both sides – both for and against the democracy and oligarchy – and how he had played such a pivotal role in the prosecutions of the Arginusae generals, condemning them for his failure. Such a man, he concluded, should be eliminated without mercy.

A persuasive speaker, Theramenes fired back: the generals convicted themselves, he claimed, in failing to save the men on the sinking ships; Critias' disarming of the democrats endangered them all, while arresting the metics only produced anger and resentment to their regime. Finally, Theramenes claimed that he had always held firm in his belief in a moderate constitution, as that briefly established in 411, and based upon the hoplite census. In short, he argued, Critias' methods were sure to encourage resistance and would be the undoing of them all (Xen. *Hell.* 2.3.23–50, [Arist.] *Ath. Pol.* 36).

At the conclusion of this speech, Critias could see the Council wavering and quickly introduced the young toughs assembled outside. Critias reminded the Council that while the Three Thousand were protected from arbitrary death sentences, the Thirty possessed greater authority and now had declared Theramenes' life forfeit. Theramenes grabbed hold of the Council's altar in a vain attempt to save himself. Religious scruple meant little to Critias. He summoned the Eleven, henchmen of the Thirty and led by a thug named Satyrus, who seized Theramenes and hauled him off to prison. With the armed youths standing over them and soldiers from the garrison outside, members of the Council could do nothing but watch. As he was led to the prison for immediate execution, Theramenes could be heard throughout the agora proclaiming his innocence. His protests continued even as he was handed the hemlock. Satyrus threatened him, and Theramenes replied, 'And I won't suffer if I stop?' Draining the cup, he saved a few dregs which he spat out as if playing a game of *kottabos* or 'wine throw', and said, 'Here's to the noble Critias!'[12]

An Athenian Civil War

Theramenes' killing removed the last brake on the Thirty who now consolidated their grip on Athens. Those not among the Three Thousand were forbidden entry into the city and many were driven into exile. Soon there were numerous refugees in Megara and Thebes – enemies not that long ago – which now provided sanctuary out of resentment to Sparta. At this moment, the ex-general Thrasybulus, a fervent democrat, and seventy others left Thebes and seized the frontier fortress of Phyle.[13]

On learning of this, the Thirty, joined by some volunteers from the Three Thousand, marched out thinking that it would be a relatively simple matter of eliminating these rebels. But the 'Men of Phyle', as they came to be called, easily repulsed a disorganized attack by the Thirty and then the weather turned cold and snowy. The Thirty decided to besiege the 'Men of Phyle', bringing up the Spartan garrison and a force of 'loyal' Athenian cavalry. This might have made sense had the rebel force remained small, but recruits continued to come in and before long Thrasybulus had gathered some 700 men. These were mostly 'working-class' types as well as foreigners and even slaves, but they were united in their resolve to restore the democracy. Under cover of night they advanced from their fortress home and took up a position only a half mile from their enemies. Watching quietly, they waited until dawn and just as the Spartans and the 'loyal' Athenians were rising and making breakfast, they attacked. The surprise was complete: some 120 men of the garrison were killed along with a number of the Athenians, some of whom were killed in bed. The rest fled leaving behind for the rebels their camp, weapons, and probably not a few horses.[14]

This defeat frightened the Thirty who may have begun to fear that their murderous ways were catching up with them. Accordingly, they shifted their base of operations to nearby Eleusis, smaller, more easily defended, and closer to Sparta. Here they carried out the same terror as in Athens, killing a large number of citizens. As the Thirty consolidated their hold on Eleusis, Thrasybulus made a move of his own. As more Athenians rallied to his cause, he advanced on the Piraeus, which now lay open thanks to the Spartan dismantling of the walls.[15] The Thirty hurried to intercept him but it was Thrasybulus who got there first. He seized the high ground, the hill of Munychia overlooking the port.[16]

Secure on the high ground, the Men of Phyle forced the Thirty to attack uphill and along a narrow roadway. They could only form up in ranks some fifty deep which blunted the force of their attack. This gave the advantage to Thrasybulus' outnumbered defenders, massed ten deep, but fighting under the cover of a large number of light-armed troops armed with missile weapons. A speech from Thrasybulus provided inspiration: the gods were on their side as witnessed by the weather that favored their cause and the high ground that they now defended. Encouraged, the Men of Phyle stood in place waiting for their rivals to strike first. This they did so that the guilt for taking the life of a fellow citizen might fall on the other side. On making this pronouncement, their seer then charged into the enemy and was promptly killed. Doubly inspired the Men of Phyle drove the forces of the Thirty downhill in fierce fighting. Critias, his nephew Charmides, as well as Hippomachus among the Thirty, were killed along with some seventy of their supporters. Losses for the Men of Phyle, unrecorded, were apparently light, which makes sense given the advantage of their position (Xen. *Hell.* 2.4.13–19).

This second defeat for the Thirty, this time in greater Athens and before a larger audience, doomed their revolution. Many Athenians were exhausted by the violence and moved toward reconciliation. The Men of Phyle did not strip naked and expose the bodies of their dead enemies, the usual practice, and under a truce allowed the relatives of the slain to take them home.[17] As this happened the two sides began talking and were then hushed by the fine voice of Cleocritus, the herald of the Eleusinian Mysteries. He passionately decried the killing of fellow citizens and admonished those loyal to the Thirty for giving in their murderous ways. His speech rallied those Athenians who wanted an end to the fighting.[18] At this moment the surviving members of the Thirty, already depressed by their defeats, could see that without Spartan help their cause was doomed. Moreover, support for them among the Three Thousand was weakening. In a meeting in the city, the Three Thousand voted to depose the Thirty and establish a new constitution. Ten were chosen to do this and negotiate a peace. But this new committee of Ten balked at this decision, instead appealing to the Spartans for money and aid. Civil war in Athens was not yet finished.[19]

Violence now escalated. Forces of the Ten and those of the Piraeus (formerly Men of Phyle) skirmished in the countryside as each side looked for food and material. Both sides committed murderous acts including the killing of prisoners. From their base in Eleusis remnants of the Thirty appealed to the Spartans for help, as did the Ten in Athens. In a move calculated perhaps to provoke a response, both groups claimed that the democrats were staging a revolt from the Spartan alliance (Xen. *Hell.* 2.4.28). This report troubled some in Sparta who saw their achievements in the recent war threatened, while others saw in it an opportunity.

Figure 12.1 The grave stele of Philoxenos and Philoumene: its simple nature reflects the economic hard times faced by the Athenians after years of war and civil strife.

Sparta between Power and Peace

In Sparta Lysander could see that his wartime accomplishments, as well as its settlement, were now threatened by the civil war in Athens. His Athenian allies did not have to wait long for an answer: quickly he sent them a large sum of money and began organizing a military response. Personally assuming command of a land force composed of Peloponnesians, Lysander delegated command of a naval taskforce to his brother Libys and the two closed in on the Athenian democrats in the Piraeus, squeezing them and restoring the confidence of the Athenian oligarchs (Xen. *Hell.* 2.4.28–9).

But this time the Spartans were not in agreement over how to handle affairs with the Athenians. Like his father Pleistoanax, the Agiad Pausanias saw in these events a means of weakening Lysander's power and influence in the Spartan state and institutions which he saw imperiled. Other motives perhaps motivated Pausanias, including a pan-hellenic view that envisioned a strong and united Athens and Sparta leading the rest of the Greeks.

In short Lysander may have become a liability: his incredible successes in the recent war had set him above everyone in Sparta, including the kings, the ephors, and the Spartan way of life. In particular his success may have weakened the support of his royal mentors Agis and Agesilaus. Neither apparently figured in these events and this may not have been accidental – the two royal houses had now combined as Lysander was simply too much of a threat to both.[20] With the support of three ephors (out of five), Pausanias decided that he too would go out on this expedition. The allies were called on to march with him and all responded except for the Corinthians and Boeotians. These declined, arguing that the Athenians were not violating the terms of the peace, little more than a convenient cover to their growing hostility to Spartan domination. Pausanias' decision could not be good news to Lysander who now had to face the opposing presence of a king and ephors in settling Athenian affairs.[21]

Spartan forces took up a position not far from the Piraeus and made a strong show of force. Several skirmishes were fought and most of these favored the Spartans, though on one occasion two senior officers, Chairon and Thibrachus, and the Olympic champion Lacrates, were killed (Xen. Hell. 2.4.33). Meanwhile Pausanias conducted a program of quiet diplomacy aimed at ending the fighting, bringing together the warring Athenian factions, and all as friends of Sparta. This he achieved with the result that both Athenian factions sent delegations to Sparta. On hearing these delegations the Spartan assembly resolved to send their own ambassadors to Pausanias, directing it to work with the king and make the best possible settlement possible for everyone.

In the end the extreme oligarchs – the Thirty and the Ten, or what of them remained, as well as their supporters – were allowed to retire to the stronghold they had established in Eleusis. This they would hold until 401/0 when the Athenians rallied to the local Eleusinians who rose in revolt. The Athenians marched out in full force: inviting the oligarchic generals to a meeting, they killed them and then brought about a peaceful reunion of Athens and Eleusis.[22] At last the Athenians had found peace, their civil war ended, ironically, thanks to Spartan intervention. Sometime later the Athenians decided to honor the Spartan intervention, building a *polyandrion*, a mass grave, in the public cemetery of the Kerameikos. In a tomb still visible today, they laid the thirteen Spartans killed restoring

Athenian freedom.[23] The argument has been made that this tomb reflects Spartan hostility to Athens, in effect a triumph over the Athenians. But this surely misjudges the background and moment.[24] By his intervention, Pausanias had supported the efforts of those Athenians like the Eleusinian herald Cleocritus who had appealed for an end to the fighting. A public burial for dead Spartans in the Kerameikos, hallowed ground for the Athenians, must be seen as an honor and as a monument to the return of democratic life in Athens.[25]

That the Athenians could now find a way to reconcile with the Spartans and bury their dead in the Athenian national cemetery, finds confirmation in the reconciliation that the Athenians made with each other. The factions that had fought each other so bitterly agreed to forget the troubles of the civil war: only the Thirty and their associates were excluded and even these could be restored by submitting to a scrutiny of their record.[26] Additionally, those men including slaves who had joined Thrasybulus and fought to restore the democracy were honored. Some received citizenship, while grants of equality (*isoteleia*) for taxation and military service went to others.[27] Later a decree by Theozotides enlarged upon these grants and made allowance for the care of the sons of those who had been killed in the fighting.[28] This was the first time that warring factions had agreed 'not to recall misfortunes of the past', and what the Athenians did is all the more remarkable when the communal suicide of Corcyra is recalled.

Further evidence of this effort to heal the wounds created by the Thirty and the civil war may be found in the last years of the life of Sophocles. As the events of a long war dragged on, Sophocles' sons challenged their father's mental competence and especially his handling of family finances. Brought into court, he recited choral songs from his current drama, *Oedipus at Colonus*. So moved were the jurors that the suit brought by his sons was thrown out (Plut. *Mor.* 785A-B).

While the story is probably just that, there are many issues in *Oedipus at Colonus* that with little doubt concern acceptance and reconciliation. This is seen clearly in Theseus' acceptance of Oedipus, the most reviled of men. When Oedipus wanders into a sacred precinct his polluted person terrifies the local Athenians who attempt to drive him out. Failing that they summon Theseus who merely accepts Oedipus for the man he is.[29] While written c. 406, *Oedipus at Colonus* was staged in 401 and on the heels of civil war and an amnesty. Its timing seems deliberate and perhaps was intended, as often said of Attic drama, to teach the Athenian about how to treat their fellow citizens.

Into the fourth century, intellectuals like Isocrates and Aristotle touted the reconciliation of 403, claiming that the lessons of the past had been learned, that citizens had since lived together as if they had never experienced such misfortunes.[30] This might be just so much wishful thinking. Several scholars have noted Athenian pretence to have forgotten the past, while in reality it was at best limited and in fact guided by a good deal of *Realpolitik*.[31] The attack on Socrates some four years later would appear to be only the most celebrated example of the exception to the rule that the misfortunes of the past would be allowed to fade from memory.

Plato made famous the prosecution of Socrates on charges of impiety and corrupting the youth brought by Anytus and Meletus in 399. The trial and speeches that Socrates gave in his defense are no less famous as also his connections to Alcibiades and members of the Thirty and their politics. All of this has been debated ever since the first attacks in the 390s which prompted numerous responses, Plato's only being the best known.[32]

While the politics of Socrates have been extensively discussed and analyzed, less attention has been paid to the soldierly dimensions of Socratic argument and thought. Xenophon, a soldier himself, created literary settings in which Socrates discussed with the younger Pericles and the disappointed Nicomachides various dimensions of military life: how did one learn the art of the general, how did one get elected general? As a serving soldier, and one who had extensive battle experience, Socrates was evidently fascinated by the nature of courage. How could some men look death in the face and stand and fight, while others ran in panic? This Socrates discussed in Plato's *Protagoras* and the *Gorgias* and reflects the very real world of the Peloponnesian War era.[33]

Lastly, the ethical model that Socrates advocated may also reflect his wartime experience. In the Greek world the customary action to any assault and act of wrongdoing, was to repay that in kind. In the *Crito* (*Cr.* 48d), Plato attributes to Socrates the idea that such a response was never right – that to return a wrong with wrong was always improper. Such an attitude reflects, I would argue, a lifetime in which Socrates had seen too much in the way of violence and force, particularly on the battlefield but elsewhere in life too. As Simone Weil comments, force 'petrifies the souls of those who undergo it and those who ply it', and Socrates, along with Gorgias and Euripides, was among the first to understand this.[34] Like others who have witnessed similar acts, Saints Francis of Assisi, Ignatius of Loyola are other examples that come to mind, Socrates embarked on a search for a new ethical value – a response to the violence of war.

The Man who would be Great King

Without the help of Cyrus, the younger son of Darius II, a Spartan victory over Athens might well have never happened. It was in spring 405 that Cyrus gave to Lysander another great sum of money and his thoughts on how to deal with the resurgent Athenian fleet.[35] While his advice might have struck the imperious Lysander as rather condescending, Cyrus' money, and what it symbolized, was crucial to the Spartan war effort.

After this conference, Cyrus returned home as Darius, sick and feeling the end near, wanted to see his younger son before dying (Xen. *Hell.* 2.1.15; *Anab.* 1.1.1–2). On Darius' death, sometime in 404, Cyrus' older brother Arsices (or Arses) took the throne as Artaxerxes II and before long palace intrigues and dislikes led to a break between the brothers. Behind this rupture probably was Tissaphernes, satrap of Sardis, whose stature and status in Aegean affairs Cyrus had displaced. Embittered perhaps, he now intrigued against the young prince. Artaxerxes apparently believed Tissaphernes' tales and only the intervention of Parysatis, their mother, secured Cyrus' release from jail and return to his command in the west.[36]

The danger and the disgrace from which Cyrus had escaped were not forgotten. Once beyond his brother's reach, Cyrus began to take measures to ensure that he would never again be so vulnerable. He cultivated relationships at the court where Parysatis, who favored him, did what she could to help. From his base in Sardis, he took care to look after the native peoples in his provinces, that they should not only regard him favorably but they should also be fit for military action.

Then, sometime early in 402/1, Cyrus began to exploit his network among the Greeks, directing his garrison commanders to recruit more soldiers, especially from that seemingly inexhaustible supply of mercenaries, the Peloponnese. The pretext for this measure was Tissaphernes, whom Cyrus claimed, planned to move against the Ionian cities, formerly his but now under Cyrus' control. Tissaphernes scented the plot and attempted to derail it. At court Parysatis helped veil events in the west, evidently persuading Artaxerxes that a 'private' war had erupted between Cyrus and Tissaphernes, which explained the military build-up going on in the west. For his part, Cyrus sent in the usual tribute further concealing his intentions. Artaxerxes then was doubly deceived and Cyrus' preparations for a war against his brother continued unimpeded.[37]

Cyrus assembled a number of native troops from among his provincial populations, but it was Greeks in whom he trusted. In his two years working with Lysander and the Spartan war effort in Ionia, Cyrus had met many soldiers and formed useful relationships with them. He now began making use of these. His first contact was the Spartan Clearchus who had served extensively in the Bosphorus, fighting the Athenians for control of Byzantium and at Arginusae. After the war Clearchus had persuaded Spartan authorities to send him against the Thracians on a punitive expedition. Recalled home on a change of policy, Clearchus refused orders and went rogue. Exiled, he took up the life of a mercenary soldier (c. 402/1?).[38]

Now a renegade soldier of fortune, Clearchus was just one of many men who had been displaced and/or alienated by wartime service. Cyrus now gave him a huge sum of money, 10,000 darics; Clearchus then recruited an army, hiring 1000 hoplites, 800 Thracian peltasts and 200 Cretan archers (Xen. *Anab*. 1.2.9). With this force he campaigned against the Thracians north of the Hellespont, earning even more money from grateful local towns, happy to see the 'barbarians' punished and a peace of sorts established (Xen. *Anab*. 1.1.9).

Cyrus' companionship and purse made him popular with other Greeks too and these he now contacted or assisted as occasion warranted. Aristippus of Thessaly, in a struggle with various rivals at home, asked Cyrus for enough money to recruit 2000 mercenaries for three months: Cyrus gave him money for 4000 for six months, stipulating that he not come to terms with his enemies without Cyrus' approval. Other commanders were asked for assistance in recruiting men for a prospective war against the Pisidians, ostensibly causing trouble in Cyrus' lands. Like the armies recruited by Clearchus and Aristippus, Meno (Thessaly), Proxenus (Boeotia), Sophaenetus (Stymphalia), and Socrates (Achaea) all assembled forces of mercenaries with Cyrus' money. Altogether these commanders found more than 13,000 Greeks looking for employment as well as opportunity and adventure.[39] Some, like Clearchus, were there simply because they liked to fight – who or where not mattering very much, if at all (Xen. *Anab*. 1.1.10–11).[40]

In spring 401 Cyrus was finally ready to move against his brother. The various Greek contingents assembled in Sardis where they made a great display of their military skills, frightening the natives who fled in panic, much to the soldiers' amusement (Xen. *Anab*. 1.2.18). This bit of soldierly and cynical humor reflects not only conventional notions of how the Greeks viewed non-Greeks, but also how soldiers regard non-soldiers. It is also an attitude that had evolved from the extensive wartime service these men had experienced which shaped their outlook on life in various other ways.

As Cyrus' army moved east, the soldiers gradually became aware that it was the Great King Artaxerxes himself whom they would be fighting. This produced some dissension within the ranks which Cyrus managed to ease with an increased rate of pay as well as the persuasive oratory – and a little intimidation from his leading commander, Clearchus. Armies on the march encounter many problems, some of them resulting from personal clashes of hard men not inclined to forgive easily. On one occasion soldiers of Clearchus got involved in a dispute with others, which Clearchus resolved but not fairly. Next day, men of the injured party belonging to Meno attacked Clearchus as he made his way through camp. Immediately Clearchus sounded the call to battle, and moved into battle formation planning to attack. Another officer, Proxenus, attempted to calm Clearchus but his words had little effect. Cyrus' intervention was helpful, but Xenophon, a witness to the affair, makes clear that what really happened was that Clearchus got a grip on himself and calmed down.[41]

Xenophon's emphatic portrait of Clearchus as a 'warlover' points to the enduring consequences of the battlefield experience (Xen. *Anab.* 2.6). No different are the actions taken by Clearchus' antagonists in this soldierly brawl. Clearchus, as many others in Cyrus' army, had fought through the recent war and had emerged changed from that experience with violence. Subsequent events make this clear. In September 401 Cyrus finally brought his brother Artaxerxes to battle on the plain of Cunaxa near Babylon. In the fight that followed Cyrus' Greek mercenaries did their job well, defeating the Persians and driving them from the field. But Cyrus had managed to get himself killed as he challenged his brother to single combat. With their employer dead, the Greek army was left surrounded by the enemy, and far from home. Within a short time they were also bereft of their own commanding officers, treacherously seized in a peace parley and viciously killed.

But the army did not dissolve. Its rank and file simply elected new officers and over the next nine months, simply fought their way home, reaching the Hellespont in summer 400. In the course of the march the Greeks committed various brutalities, the sort of thing that happens all too often in war. While fighting in the vicinity of the ancient Assyrian capital of Nimrud, they killed a number of Persians whom they then mutilated as a warning to the others (Xen. *Anab.* 3.4.5). Xenophon notes that this was done without cause. Among the men who did this were more than few who had spent too many years in battle witnessing and inflicting pain. In short they knew all too well the truth of Thucydides' dictum that war was a violent teacher – that what the inexperienced might see as despicable acts of violence could and did become 'normal'. The atrocities around old Nimrud had been anticipated many times in the Great Peloponnesian War – the horrors of Corcyra, the slaughter of the Athenians in Sicily, the despoiling of the dead in countless battles. Scenes of dramatic horror matched these too, as often depicted in the plays of Euripides with their multiple acts of violence on children and women or, again as but one example, the killing and mutilating of Achilles' son Neoptolemus by his Delphian enemies.[42]

Later, entering the mountains of Kurdistan, the Greeks were forced to fight as they marched. Assaulted on every side and losing men daily, they captured two natives to find another route, one that would take them around the enemy. Under interrogation the first prisoner would only say that there was no other path, at which he was killed. The second prisoner then became talkative and provided the desired information, adding that the first man had not cooperated in order to protect his family (Xen. *Anab.* 4.1.23–5). Both incidents give insight into the conduct of war by the Greeks, again many of whom had learned their trade in the violence of the Peloponnesian War.

In 399 the remnants of Cyrus' expeditionary force under the command of Xenophon joined Spartan forces in Ionia. Already the Spartans were conducting military operations against their former Persian allies – another war and old soldiers simply going on to the next fight.

Notes

1 See Akrigg 2007: 33, and discussion above pp. 48–50, 57.

2 For the debate over the generals of Arginusae, see above pp. 210–12.

3 On Critias see above p. 200. His political views and role during the crisis of the Four Hundred are ambiguous, but he now embraced that stance with a vengeance. His earlier association with Socrates also lies in the past, on which see Guthrie 1971: 300.

4 Lys. 12.5 tells of the Thirty's cleansing agenda. While Lysias' judgment might seem biased – the Thirty did later kill his brother – their actions do support his statement. Loraux 2002: 262 notes that Lysias struggled with the idea of forgetting, but this reflects his loss and the violence of the day.

5 See Krentz 1982: 49–56 for discussion, and the next note.
6 Xen. *Hell.* 2.3.2, Diod. 14.3.3–6, [Arist.] *Ath. Pol.* 34.3, 35.1. 'When' the Athenian democracy began is controversial and discussion is not possible here. The date suggested here begins with the lawgiver Clisthenes whom the Athenians themselves believed had started it, as alluded by Ar. *Eq.* 42, noting the age of Demos as 'sixtyish'. Staged in 424, this would yield a date of c. 490, not quite Clisthenes' time but close enough.
7 [Arist.] *Ath. Pol.* 35.2, with Rhodes 1981: 439–45. Opinion differed in Athens over the meaning of 'ancestral constitution' as now among modern scholars. For discussion see Fuks 1953, Finley 1971, Rhodes 1981: 376–7.
8 Xen. *Hell.* 2.3.13–14. The makeup of this force is unclear, but like that Brasidas took north in 425, it was probably composed of mercenaries and freed helots.
9 Isoc. *Against Euthynous*; see Whitehead 2004: 168–9.
10 Andoc. *Mys.* 94, Pl. *Ap.* 32c-d. Who was Leon of Salamis? MacDowell 1962: 133 and Gomme-Andrewes-Dover 5: 51 (on Thuc. 8.23.2) argue that he is the general of 412/1. Neither *PA* 9100 nor Develin 1989: 157 lists him as of 'Salamis'; the name is fairly common, and Xenophon (*Hell.* 2.3.21) makes clear that it was resident aliens who were now arrested.
11 Details in Lysias' speech against Eratosthenes, with Loraux 2002: 247–8, Todd 2007: 7.
12 Xen. *Hell.* 2.3.51–6. *Kottabos* concluded a drinking party at which participants spat the last of their wine at some target in a basin. For discussion see F.A. Wright and M. Vickers, 'games', *OCD*³ 624 and Becker 1866: 349–51, who notes that the dregs were spat, evidently not thrown from a cup.
13 Xen. *Hell.* 2.4.2–3. Snowfall about this time should place these events in late fall 404.
14 Xen. *Hell.* 2.4.5–7. Wolpert 2002: 26, 75 suggests that only a few Athenians joined Thrasybulus' 'rebel' force. Against it should be noted that his numbers increased tenfold, and that the arms of the citizens had been confiscated and locked away. In fact the determination of the Athenian democrats is remarkable.
15 A decree enacted by Thrasybulus himself in 401/400 honored those who had joined him in defeating the Thirty. See below and Rhodes and Osborne 2003: 20–6 for discussion.
16 Even today a casual walk in the Piraeus reveals the topography and makes clear the superior position that Thrasybulus now held.
17 Xen. *Hell.* 2.4.19.
18 Xen. *Hell.* 2.4.20, with Loraux 2002: 9–1039, 262, who stresses the conciliatory effect that Cleocritus now had on the Athenians.
19 Xen. *Hell.* 2.4.20–3, 28, and [Arist.] *Ath. Pol.* 38.1.
20 See Cartledge 1987: 94–6.

21 Xen. *Hell.* 2.4.29–30, Diod. 14.33.6, Plut. *Lys.* 21.4–7. See also de Ste. Croix 1972: 144–5 and Cartledge 1987: 283–4 for analysis of Spartan politics at this time.

22 Xen. *Hell.* 2.4.38, 43, with Cartledge 1987: 284.

23 See Camp 2001: 133, noting also that the tomb's dedication was in the Spartan Doric dialect, not the Athenian Ionic (*IG* II² 11678). Salazar 2000: 234 discusses the wounds that killed these Spartan soldiers (and see above pp. 101–2).

24 Low 2006: 98.

25 Todd 2007: 464 notes the importance of Pausanias' role in ending the civil war and also the reference in Lys. 6.38 (*Against Andocides*) to Spartan influence on the Athenian reconciliation.

26 Xen. *Hell.* 2.4.43, Andoc. *Mys.* 81, [Arist.] *Ath. Pol.* 39.6 (amnesty and oath). For discussion of the oath see Munn 2000: 279–80, Loraux 2002: 246–8, and Wolpert 2002: 30–59, though all seem to downplay the impact of nearly thirty years of war and suffering on the Athenians.

27 See Rhodes and Osborne 2003: 25–7 for discussion; the details are greatly disputed.

28 See Harding 1985: 13–15; as so many Athenians decrees this too was challenged, perhaps as financial resources were so reduced after the war.

29 Note Soph. *Oed. Col.* 226–34 (the fear and rejection of the Athenian chorus) and Theseus' acceptance (lines 560–8). Vickers 2008: 95–103 argues for a theme of reconciliation, though the parallels drawn to Alcibiades and Critias seem a bit strained.

30 Isoc. 18.46, [Arist.] *Ath. Pol.* 40.2,3, with Loraux 2002: 149–55.

31 Carawan 2004: 106. Cf. Loraux 2002: 145–69 who discusses the amnesty without comment on the trial of Socrates.

32 See Guthrie 1971: 59–65 (trial), 11 (attacks and defenses of Socrates), and most recently Wilson 2007.

33 See above p. 81 for Socrates with Pericles and Nicomachides. On Socrates and courage see Guthrie 1971: 132–3, 137 (citing *Protag.* 349e–350a, 360d, *Gorg.* 509d) and Miller 2000: 34–6, 281–2 who adds Socrates' discussion with Laches and Nicias from Plato's *Laches*.

34 Weil 2003: 61.

35 Xen. *Hell.* 2.1.13 places Cyrus in Media southwest of the Caspian Sea, where he was suppressing a rebellion among the Cadusians. Summoned, Lysander traveled to Cyrus, a journey that would have taken three months minimally. But as the Spartans were rebuilding their fleet (*Hell.* 2.1.10), Lysander would have had time to journey to Cyrus.

36 Xen. *Anab.* 1.1.2–4; cf. C.J. Tuplin, 'Tissaphernes', *OCD*³ 1531.

37 Xen. *Anab.* 1.1.6–8; cf. Briant 2002: 612–34.

38 See Xen. *Anab.* 2.6.1–4, with Lendle 1995: 133.

39 Additionally, the Greek contingent would have included numerous drovers, muleteers, and other support personnel; see Xen. *Anab.* 5.8.5 for an example. References (and figures) to these are infrequent, but for a military force in excess of 13,000 Greeks and even more native troops, they would have been substantial. See also Lee 2007: 255–75.

40 Xenophon of Athens later wrote an account of this expedition, the *Anabasis* or 'the march up country', at once an exciting adventure story filled with information regarding the Persian empire, its lands and peoples; what is revealed of the Greeks is no less valuable. See further, e.g., Tuplin 2004.

41 Xen. *Anab.* 1.5.11–17. See also Tritle 2004: 325–39 for fuller discussion.

42 Eur. *And.* 1153–5, dating to c. 430–424. See also above the horrors carried out in Corcyra (pp. 72–5), the treatment of the Athenian dead at Delium (p. 104), and the slaughter of the Athenians in Sicily (pp. 156–7).

Epilogue

LYSANDER'S TRIUMPH?

Why does the Peloponnesian War continue to attract attention and readers into the early twenty-first century? Within a few years Athens and Sparta were again at war, one later called the 'Corinthian War' (c. 395–387/6). But this time Corinth and Thebes joined with Athens in fighting their former ally and patron. 'Lucky' Conon, the survivor of Aegospotami, returned to Athens with a new fleet and a pile of money, courtesy of his eastern friends, Evagoras of Cyprus and the Great King himself, who no longer considered the Spartans his friends.

Lysander, the one-time power broker of Sparta and Greece, the man who would be king if only he could, had been cut down to size, a victim of his own arrogance. His old lover, Agesilaus, now king of Sparta, saw in him a threat and gradually shoved him aside. Less than ten years after defeating Athens, Lysander would die attacking Haliartus, an obscure Boeotian town, trying to recoup his lost power (395). Within thirty years of that, Sparta's power itself would be broken by the Thebans at Leuctra (371) – the victim of its own version of 'racial' politics and eugenics – the *homoioi* all but gone. Corinth was no longer of great political or military significance, and while Thebes, led by its brilliant soldiers Epaminondas and Pelopidas hung on a bit longer, after the former's death at Mantinea (362), it too faded away.

In Athens the amnesty held for the most part, though the revived democracy sacrificed Socrates to the memory of the Thirty. Probably not many Athenians really noticed or cared about that, except for one, Plato. But his voice was loud enough, and in a series of dramatic works Plato immortalized his teacher, creating a legend that continues to be read and studied today.

A little more than fifty years after its great defeat at Spartan hands only Athens still possessed substantial power or wealth, and the will to assert itself and resist a new challenge to its leadership – that made by Philip of Macedon. That challenge ended on the battlefield of Chaeronea (338/7) and a new power in the Greek world, Macedonia, presided over the Greeks. Despite that great effort, and a few minor ones, that followed, Athens afterwards lay at the foot of one royal or imperial power after the other, becoming little more than the college town of its day.

Lots of wars and lots of battles. Again then, why does the Peloponnesian War remain so important? The answer lies in part to the contribution of its great historian – Thucydides. In recording what happened in the Greek world at the latter half of the fifth century, he explored ideas and revealed realities that remain valid and pertinent today – the nature of great power politics, that war is a violent teacher, that it will pull you down to the level of your circumstances. No less important are the literary legacies of the great poets and minds of the Peloponnesian War era. From Euripides we learn of Heracles and the violent homecoming of a soldier, realities that we know in our own time, as also the effects of war on women. From Sophocles we hear the bitter and plaintive cries of Philoctetes, the wounded survivor of violence, while from Oedipus come cries of another kind as well as lessons on leadership and knowledge. While both poets reveal many other dimensions of Greek culture and society, they also ask eternal questions and issues that continue to attract interest. Additionally, all three wrote in the shadow of Homer who told the greatest tale of a city's destruction, which for them became reality. Confronted by the horrors of war and violence, all three responded with admonitions and reflections that remain valuable today as we watch and contemplate the use and abuse of power and the effects of war's violence.

The other part of the answer would seem to lie in the continuing image of Athens, witnessed even today by the millions of tourists who flock there to see its tattered remains of greatness. Athens is the story of a democratic society, even one flawed in modern eyes by its slavery and other abuses, with its startling developments and innovations in art, literature, and philosophy. These would influence and encourage the activities and accomplishments of future generations, first in the Greek world, then the Greco-Roman world of the Roman Empire, and eventually the modern world. That reality says something about the nature and value of history and the connections between past and present.

Appendix A

A NOTE ON SOURCES

Without the account of Thucydides, a history of the Peloponnesian War would be very different. Informed, connected politically and socially to many of the war's Athenian participants, he was known, or became known, to others, both Athenians and other Greeks. As participant and observer, Thucydides saw the war to its conclusion with the surrender of Athens in 404, possibly returning home after some twenty years in exile. A grand revision to his account may have then begun, as his text breaks off suddenly with the events of 411/10 and his death, coming perhaps within a few years of his homecoming, seems the likeliest explanation.[1] Often regarded as a model of accuracy and truth (though readers should look at the introduction he gives Cleon at 3.36.6), Thucydides' relentless focus on matters of state, war and the pursuit of power, and politics both domestic and interstate was an incredible achievement.[2] But many Greeks might well have seen his work as idiosyncratic and remote from their own understanding of past and present, which explains the absence of later historians like him. Rediscovered by Thomas Hobbes in the seventeenth century, Thucydides has not wanted for attention since.

Slightly less critical is Xenophon, Thucydides' continuator and another Athenian. No less connected than Thucydides, Xenophon knew people like Agesilaus and Clearchus, Socrates, and maybe even Thucydides. A contemporary (though a younger one) to the events, he probably began to write later in his life, perhaps in the 370s. Readers will note quickly that Xenophon is a different kind of writer. His style is more conversational and generally congenial and this seems best explained by an approach to the past conceived as personal memoir.[3] Xenophon's interests remain focused on military and political events, and his analytical powers are considerably less than those of Thucydides (though for this many readers might be grateful).[4] While true that his *Hellenika* or 'Greek things' suffer in comparison with Thucydides' history, it is also true that without them the record of how the war ended would be much poorer. No less important is Xenophon's great adventure story, the *Anabasis* or the 'March up country'. Though not a part of the Peloponnesian War proper, the event itself – Cyrus' effort to take the throne from his brother Artaxerxes, with the help of 13,000 Greek mercenaries, all veterans (or mostly so) of the recent war – reveals the impact of the war in social-economic terms. It also suggests that the reality of an 'end' to the war in 404 was imperceptible to many of its participants, certainly these soldiers who merely fought in a new theater of war.[5]

Additional contemporary sources include the epigraphic testimony, or inscriptions. As a democracy, the Athenians recorded the many public decisions of the assembly and Council on stone, as well as the collections of tribute from the allies. These were displayed in the agora and on the acropolis and provide historians with information complementing the literary accounts of Thucydides and Xenophon. On the other hand, the epigraphic evidence seldom survives intact and reconstructing the chronology of decrees as well as the full text of a particular decree is far from simple.[6] For example, scholars have assigned dates for a number of decrees relating Athenian imperial administration – the Weights and Measures Decree, the Clinias or Tribute Delivery Decree – to dates ranging from the 440s, the 420s, or simply before 414. The debate here has focused on the use of the three bar sigma which many scholars have argued ended after 445. At stake is the dating of these aggressive acts of the Athenian state, whether they should be assigned to the statesman Pericles or the demagogue Cleon and those who succeeded him. Recent studies of inscriptions using such sophisticated technology as laser have argued that this might not be the case – that the three bar sigma indeed may be found after 445. On the other hand, it has also been shown that old and new letter forms may be found on the same inscription, so in a sense the debate proves little. Consensus then remains elusive. In the end, however, the debate appears to have little impact on the picture of aggressive Athenian imperialism in the years preceding the outbreak of the war.[7]

A wide range of evidence also contemporary to the Peloponnesian War survives in the works of later generations of scholars, some of it of late Roman imperial date. This includes the historical accounts of the Sicilian Greek author Diodorus (hence called 'Siculus') who wrote a 'Library' or *Bibliotheke* in the first century. For the period of the Peloponnesian War, he followed the historian Ephorus (*fl.* fourth century) who sometimes provided information unrecorded by Thucydides or Xenophon. As a western Greek, Diodorus knew the historiography coming out of Greek Sicily, especially the work of Timaeus of Tauromenium. Not always discriminating or critical in what he wrote, and influenced by the philosophical ideas of his own era, Diodorus' account remains of some value.[8]

The same might be said of Plutarch of Chaeronea, the great essayist of the Trajanic Age of Rome. From his home in central Greece but close enough to consult sources of all kinds in Athens, Plutarch wrote his famous *Lives* of noble Greeks and Romans, and his *Moralia*, or 'Moral Essays' of which the *Sayings of the Spartans* is but one.[9] Of the former, those of *Pericles, Nicias, Alcibiades,* and *Lysander* provide accounts or biographies, in reality 'lives', of four important personalities of the Peloponnesian War.[10] It is important to stress that Plutarch did not write history, but lives and what interested him in these were the moral dimensions of his subjects. The focus and object of his accounts then are not those of the modern era. But these freely composed and conversational accounts were derived from a wide variety of sources, many of which were contemporary, that Plutarch found in Athens and elsewhere. From his extensive research and reading he reassembled all this material into a literary whole, and again without these the modern researcher would have much less to study.

The sources that Plutarch found ranged from prose accounts including those of Thucydides and Ion of Chios, to plays of the comic poets, e.g., Aristophanes, Cratinus, Eupolis, the Atthidographers or local historians of Athens such as Philochorus, and philosophers of diverse views including Plato. It is clear that he had been in Athens and knew the city and its sites and monuments well. Plutarch's *Life of Pericles* provides some idea of how he integrated the above-named sources into a creative interpretation of his own design. This work is so well done that a close reading will make clear the difficulty of detecting the principal source of any 'life' he wrote. Such detective work will also make clear that at times either he did not understand what his source was telling, or on occasion, he chose to bend what he found to his own views based on his philosophy as well as the spirit of his time.[11]

Plutarch's accounts of Pericles and Nicias, for example, will refer to and cite lines from the poets contemporary to these Athenian statesmen and generals of the Peloponnesian War. The *Pericles* includes references to

Cratinus' plays *The Tutor*, *Nemesis*, and *Thracian Women*, as well as Eupolis' *The Demes*; the *Nicias* refers to Eupolis' *Maricas*, Aristophanes' *Knights* and *Birds*, as well the poet Telecleides. Tragic poets also find mention: Euripides' *Iphigenia at Aulis* and *Erechtheus* in the *Nicias*; Ion of Chios in the *Pericles*.

How are these poets, both comic and tragic, to be interpreted in relation to the events and persons of the Peloponnesian War? Generations ago, and dating back to the nineteenth-century foundational work of German philologists such as Ulrich von Wilamowitz-Moellendorff, the idea that either Attic comedy or tragedy could be usefully interpreted as contemporary evidence would have been met with howls of protest. Just as Wilamowitz dismissed Nietzsche's *The Birth of Tragedy* as 'future philology' (1872–3), he argued against the idea that any of the plays of Sophocles had a connection to contemporary life.[12]

As Jasper Griffin's thoughtful essay on Sophocles shows, this interpretation has largely passed away.[13] On the other hand, expecting every piece of drama to be full of contemporary references whether to events or people probably does go too far in the other direction. Michael Vickers rightly suggests that the Athenians no more went to the theater to learn about Oedipus and his family than we read *Animal Farm* today to learn about life in the country.[14] But his determination to see Pericles or Alcibiades seemingly on every page of Aristophanes or Sophocles is a bit of a stretch.[15] The tragedies of both Euripides and Sophocles should not be imagined as simply stories of heroes and gods and some remote past. Instead, as Victor Ehrenberg noted, their poetical visions at once reflect the voice of the artist, the voice of the contemporary critic, and the voice of the eternal witness.[16] What this means for the historical-minded is that they are filled with reflections on current thoughts and issues, as well as allusions to contemporary persons and events.

Attic comedy should not be viewed any differently. As Keith Sidwell argues, the great comic poets of the Peloponnesian War era – Cratinus, Aristophanes, and Eupolis – were not simply writing funny stories of their politicians and generals, or just taking pot shots of various kinds at their fellow Athenians. While they were doing this, they were also engaged in sometimes bitter dramatic or theatrical battle as they competed for the honor of winning the title of voice of the people. But this also led them to enter the battle over domestic issues and concerns, as well as politics and war and peace. And all of this was couched in allusive and sometimes vulgar language.[17]

Notes

1 The commentaries of Gomme, Gomme-Andrewes-Dover, and Hornblower are fundamental (references cited in Abbreviations). Useful translations (listed in Bibliography) include those of Lattimore and Warner, and the Loeb edition (English with Greek text facing) of C.F. Smith. Also recommended is Woodruff 1993, a translation of such critical passages as the Mytilenian Debate and Melian Dialogue.

2 Ehrenberg 1954: 14–15. A complete Thucydidean bibliography would be immense, but among important works see Connor 1984, Hornblower 1987 and 1996–2008 (listed in Abbreviations), Woodhead 1970, and the collection of essays in Rengakos and Tsakmakis 2006.

3 See further Cartledge 1987: 61–5.

4 Commentary in Krentz 1989, with accessible translation in Warner; see also the collection of essays on Xenophon in Tuplin 2004 (not limited to the *Hellenika* and *Anabasis*).

5 Commentary in Lendle 1995, with accessible translation in Warner (see also Tuplin 2004).

6 Fornara 1977 provides a useful collection of inscriptions in translation.

7 Fornara 97, 98 (for the inscriptions), Mattingly 1996 (arguing for the three bar sigma after 445), Rhodes 2006: 52–4 (arguing and showing the coexistence of old and new letter forms).

8 K.S. Sacks, 'Diodorus (3)', OCD^3 472–3, with translation in Loeb edition of Oldfather.

9 A Plutarchan bibliography would be an extensive undertaking, but useful works include Duff 1999, Pelling 2002, and Stadter 1965.

10 English commentaries for *Nicias* (Holden 1887) and *Pericles* (Stadter 1989); Italian for *Alcibiades* (Raffaelli and Prandi); translations only for *Lysander* (Loeb and Budé).

11 See de Romilly 1988.

12 Wilamowitz's famous attack appeared in 1872–3 and ignited a storm of controversy; see Gründer 1969: 27–55, 113–35. See Vickers 2008: 1, n.1 citing other criticisms of Wilamowitz *et al.*

13 Griffin 1999.

14 Vickers 2008: 16.

15 See the criticism of Vickers 1997 in Dover 2004: 243–5; the same might be said of Vickers 2008.

16 Ehrenberg 1954: 7–8.

17 Sidwell 2009. See also Rhodes 2004: 223–38 and Ehrenberg 1962 (still useful for its collection of material).

Appendix B

WHO'S WHO IN THE PELOPONNESIAN WAR[1]

Agis II (c. 450–400), P-B 11–13. Agis succeeded his father Archidamus II as Eurypontid king of Sparta in 427. Not much is known of him until 418 when he leads Spartan and Peloponnesian forces to victory at the battle of Mantinea, what Thucydides called the greatest set battle fought in many years. The garrison he established in Athenian territory (413) at Decelea clearly influenced the war's outcome.

Alcibiades (c. 451/50–404/3), *PA* 600, *APF* 9–22. Alcibiades belonged to the influential Alcmeonid family of Athens through his mother. He gained prominence with the treaty he negotiated with Argos, bitter enemy of Sparta (419). He later promoted the ambitious plan to invade Sicily. Though he sailed as co-commander of the expedition, he was recalled to Athens to stand trial for his alleged role in several religious controversies. Fearing condemnation, he defected to Sparta where he revealed details of the Athenian campaign. In exile, Alcibiades attempted to win Persian support for Athens, or so he claimed. He won over the sailors of the Athenian fleet enabling him to return to Athens where he was reinstated (408/7). Elected general and given wide authority, his efforts in Asia failed and he again abandoned the Athenian cause. After the war he was murdered, probably at Spartan instigation.

Alcidas P-B 18. A Spartan commander in the Archidamian War, Alcidas distinguished himself by his harsh methods, especially in the Aegean. This conduct clashed with the Spartan image of fighting to liberate the Greeks from Athenian tyranny as Thucydides notes.

Archelaus (c. 413–399), [7] *RE* 2 (1895): 446–8. Successor to Perdiccas II in Macedonia, Archelaus continued Macedonian involvement in the war on the Athenian side, supplying Athens with timber and other resources. Archelaus established a new capital at Pella and in a sense 'modernized' Macedonia. A philhellene, he invited artists and intellectuals to his court (e.g., Zeuxis, Euripides).

Archidamus II (c. 489–427/6), P-B 32–3. Spartan king (Eurypontid house) for more that forty years (ca. 470–427), Archidamus gained prominence by his skillful handling of affairs after the earthquake which ignited a major helot rising (c. 464–456). Before the outbreak of the Peloponnesian War, Archidamus failed to dampen Spartan enthusiasm for war.

Aristeus [3] *RE* 2 (1895): 898. Corinthian military leader and statesman, Aristeus engaged the Athenians around Potidaea and gave them a good fight. While ambassador en route to Persia he was intercepted and turned over to the Athenians by the Thracian warlord Sitalces. He was killed in Athens without trial.

Aristophanes (c. 460/50–386), *PA* 2090. The greatest writer of Attic old comedy, Aristophanes wrote over forty plays (eleven survive) that are themselves a rich source of information regarding virtually every aspect of life in classical Athens, as well as events in the Peloponnesian War. A keen satirist, his critical eye missed nothing – he attacked and satirized politicians and generals, poets and intellectuals with equal enthusiasm and zeal, just as he did the common citizen.

Aspasia (c. 465–?), *APF* 458–9. Born in Miletus, the daughter of a prosperous businessman, Aspasia perhaps practiced the world's oldest profession, what in classical Greece were called *hetairai*. She became Pericles' companion c. 445 and he divorced his wife to live with her. Their relationship provided rich material for humor and political attack. Aspasia gave birth to Pericles' son, also named Pericles, later made legitimate by a special vote, as Pericles' own law barred his son from citizenship. After Pericles' death in the plague (c. 429), Aspasia soon became the companion of Lysicles, another politician, proof perhaps of her 'profession'.

Brasidas (c. 455–422), P-B 36–7. Energetic and innovative, Brasidas won a number of successes in the Archidamian War. In 424 he entered northern Greece and with a small force disrupted Athenian fortunes. He captured the strategic city of Amphipolis and prompted the revolts of others in the region. In 422 he ambushed an Athenian army led by Cleon outside Amphipolis. Mortally wounded, Brasidas lived long enough to learn of his soldiers' victory.

Callicratidas (d. 406), P-B 70–1. Spartan commander who succeeded Lysander in the Aegean, Callicratidas attempted to implement a new program of decreased reliance on Persian money and more enlightened conduct with the Aegean Greeks. He engaged the Athenian fleet at Arginusae and died fighting.

Clearchus (c. 451–400), P-B 73–4. During the Ionian War, Clearchus led Spartan forces into the northern Aegean. After the war he refused to follow the orders of Spartan home authorities and went rogue, taking up the life of a mercenary general. He joined the mercenary army of Cyrus (401), bringing to the prince a private army of some 2000 men. Clearchus won a battle, but the prince's death created a crisis. Invited to a peace parley with Tissaphernes, Clearchus was seized and later executed.

Cleon (c. 462–422), *PA* 8674, *APF* 318–20. The best-known political figure in Athens after the death of Pericles, Cleon came to prominence in the debate over Mylitene (427), notoriously proposing that the men of that city be executed; his proposal failed. In operations against the Spartans at Pylos, Cleon became a major figure (425). In a stunning success, Cleon captured and brought to Athens 292 Spartan prisoners; on their account the Spartans stopped their annual invasions of Attica. In 422 he led an expedition to turn back Brasidas. In a battle before the walls of Amphipolis, Cleon proved an unworthy opponent: his army was defeated, he was killed.

Conon (c. 444–389), *PA* 8707, *APF* 506–9. Perhaps the luckiest of Athenian commanders in the war, Conon drew an assignment to Corcyra that kept him out of Sicily and certain death, while at Aegospotami he escaped Lysander's trap. After some ten years in Cypriot service, Conon returned to Athens in 393 with a fleet and money that guaranteed his restoration into the good graces of the Athenians. He later died in Cyprus commanding Athenian forces.

Cratinus (c. 520–423), *PA* 8755. A noted Athenian writer of comedy and critic of Pericles (he dubbed him the 'Olympian'). Little of his work survives other than in fragments, but he rivaled Aristophanes in popularity.

Critias (c. 460–403), *PA* 8792, *APF* 326–8. The Athenian oligarch, 'student' of Socrates, and one of the 'Thirty Tyrants', Critias led the oligarchy that subjected Athens to a reign of terror after the surrender of Athens in 404. Critias vigorously fought the democratic rising of Thrasybulus and died fighting in the Piraeus.

Cyrus (c. 423–401), [7] *RE* suppl. v. 4 (1924): 1166–77. The younger son of the Persian king Darius II and Parysatis, Cyrus was ambitious and favored by his mother. Placed in general command of Asia by his father (408), Cyrus supported the Spartans against the Athenians. Upon the accession of his older brother, Arsicas, who took the regal name Artaxerxes (II), Cyrus began plotting against his brother. He organized an army including 13,000 Greek mercenaries and invaded his homeland. While his

Greeks won the battle (at Cunaxa), Cyrus himself was killed as he attacked Artaxerxes.

Demosthenes (c. 457–413), *PA* 3585, *APF* 112–13. An innovative Athenian general, Demosthenes first gained a reputation in western Greece where he won several spectacular victories, in one instance knocking Ambracia out of the war with devastating loss (Thuc. 3.105–13). He won greater fame the next year with his stunning victory over the Spartan force on Sphacteria. Demosthenes led a relief force to Sicily (413) to assist Nicias in the attack on Syracuse. After failures on land and at sea, Demosthenes finally persuaded Nicias to retreat, but too late. Both were taken prisoner, the Syracusans later executing them.

Endius P-B 50. The son of Alcibiades; Endius' family enjoyed connections with the family of the Athenian Alcibiades and through these represented Spartan interests in Athens. He signed the Peace of Nicias for Sparta and unsuccessfully offered peace terms to the Athenians in 410 upon their recovery of Cyzicus.

Eupolis (c. 450–400?), *PA* 5936. The noted rival of Aristophanes, Eupolis' politics may have had a conservative flavor. This probably resulted in his exile from Athens following the suppression of the oligarchic movements, ending his literary career. Pausanias' description of his grave in Sicyon argues that he did not die in a naval battle during the war as is sometimes thought. Little of his work survives other than in fragments, but he rivaled Aristophanes in popularity.

Euripides (c. 485/4–406/5), *PA* 5953. The youngest of the three great writers of tragic drama, Euripides wrote ninety-two plays of which nineteen survive in a career stretching from 455–406. As the the target of Aristophanic comedy in the *Frogs* (405), Aristophanes leaves Euripides in Hades bringing Aeschylus back to Athens. This may suggest what Aristophanes thought of him. Popular opinion in Athens seems to have associated Euripides with the intellectual theories and views of the sophists. Toward 408 and perhaps repelled by the war and political turmoil in Athens, Euripides retreated to Macedonia at the invitation of its king, Archelaus.

Gorgias (c. 485–380), [8] *RE* 7 (1912): 1598–619. The noted sophist and rhetorician, Gorgias was from Leontini in Sicily. His arrival in Athens c. 427 on an embassy seeking aid against Syracusan aggression was a cause célèbre, as his oratorical displays were a marvel to behold. During the war Gorgias traveled widely in Greece, giving lectures and demonstration speeches, including the *Encomium of Helen* which absolves Helen of blame in starting the Trojan War.

Gylippus (c. 450–?), P-B 38–9. A Spartan officer sent with modest reinforcements from Corinth to aid Syracuse in 415. His presence restored morale and bolstered Syracusan efforts. On the final Athenian defeat, Gylippus attempted to save the lives of the Athenian generals Nicias and Demosthenes, but failed. He returned to the Aegean where he joined Lysander's staff; after the war, he brought back to Sparta Persian-supplied gold and loot seized from the Athenians at Aegospotami. He embezzled a large sum, was detected, and fled into exile.

Hermocrates [1] *RE* 8 (1912): 883–7. A prominent leader in Syracuse, Hermocrates persuaded the Sicilians, Greek and non-Greek, at the Congress of Gela (424) to force the Athenians to leave Sicily. On the arrival of the Athenian expedition in 415, Hermocrates played a key role in rallying the Syracusans, initially overwhelmed by the prospect of fighting the Athenians, and led them to victory. After the Athenian defeat Hermocrates led a Syracusan squadron into the Aegean to support the Spartan war effort.

Laches (d. 418), *PA* 9019. An Athenian general who commanded forces in Sicily, Laches died in the battle of Mantinea. Later Plato would make him famous as a participant in his dialogues as a companion and associate of Socrates.

Lamachus (d. 414), *PA* 8981. A soldier's soldier, Lamachus joined Nicias and Alcibiades in command of the Sicilian expedition. He argued unsuccessfully for an immediate attack on a still unprepared Syracuse; as a result the Athenians became bogged down in positional warfare attempting to starve Syracuse into surrender. In a minor skirmish, he was killed and the Athenian effort stalled.

Lysander (c. 440–395), P-B 89–91. The Spartan commander whose leadership defeated Athens in spring 404, Lysander rose from poverty to become king-maker. Appointed to a naval command in the Aegean (408/7), he won the support of the Persian prince Cyrus and with his funding created a navy that could challenge the Athenians. In 405 he destroyed the Athenian fleet at Aegospotami and then blockaded Athens, forcing the city's surrender. Lysander empowered in Athens a group of murderous oligarchs later known as the Thirty Tyrants, the precedent for which was the decarchies (boards of ten) that he had created in the Aegean the previous four years. Later Spartan authorities abandoned the decarchies, but Lysander's influence remained, as seen in the election of Agesilaus to the kingship (400).

Lysimache *PA* 9470, *APF* 170–1. Priestess of Athena Polias for some sixty-four years, Lysimache belonged to the aristocratic family of the

Eteoboutadae. As priestess of the cult of Athena Polias (centered on the acropolis where an ancient wood state represented the goddess), Lysimache enjoyed social as well as religious prominence in the city. The cult over which she presided was the most important in the city and her position was the most significant that an Athenian woman could occupy. Her stature possibly gave Aristophanes the initial inspiration for his drama *Lysistrata* (411).

Mindarus (d. 410), *P-B* 94. A Spartan commander in the Hellespont and Aegean; Alcibiades surprised him at Cyzicus where the Athenians inflicted a crushing defeat, Mindarus losing his fleet and life.

Nauclides. Among the elites of Plataea, Nauclides wanted political power. He negotiated with the Thebans, eager to make Plataea part of a Theban-dominated 'Greater Boeotia'. Thus was launched the Theban sneak attack on Plataea; Nauclides may be the man who started the Peloponnesian War.[2]

Nicias (c. 470–413), *PA* 10808, *APF* 403–7. Nicias rose to political prominence after the death of Pericles. A moderate, he apparently opposed the aggressive form of imperialism advocated by Pericles and Cleon. On Cleon's death (422), Nicias asserted his moderate views and persuaded the Greeks to accept the peace named for him, the Peace of Nicias (421). He found a greater challenge in Alcibiades who promoted the ambitious scheme to invade Sicily, something he opposed. As sole commander after the flight of Alcibiades and death of Lamachus, Nicias continued the struggle against Syracuse despite his declining health. Despite the arrival of Demosthenes' relief force, setbacks continued. Finally Nicias and Demosthenes attempted to disengage but could not. Hounded by the Syracusans, Nicias surrendered the remnants of his army to save them from slaughter. The Syracusans later killed him.

Paches (d. 427/6?), *PA* 11746. The Athenian general who reduced rebellious Mytilene and Lesbos in 427. Prosecuted either for negligence or some private crimes, Paches dramatically took his own life in court.

Pausanias (c. 460–380?), *P-B* 103–4. The Spartan king whose father Pleistoanax (Agiad royal house) seems to have been pro-Athenian, clinching the Peace of Nicias for the Spartans in 421, Pausanias succeeded his father and played a key role in the restoration of the Athenian democracy. Leading a force into Attica as the democrats battled the Thirty Tyrants, Pausanias intervened on the democratic side. Opposition to the influence of Lysander explains his action in no small way. In the fighting and negotiations that followed, the Thirty were overthrown, and the Athenian democracy was restored.

Perdiccas II (c. 450–413), [2] *RE* 19 (1937): 590–602. The Macedonian king had long supported the Athenians, but their settlement at Amphipolis in 436 changed that. Perdiccas supported the rebellion of Potidaea and other northern Greeks against Athens; he invited Brasidas north in 425. This alliance was directed at his Lyncestian rival Arrabaeus. Brasidas, however, was more intent on driving the Athenians out of the northern Aegean. By 423 the two had broken and Perdiccas, in true Macedonian fashion perhaps, called in his former enemies the Athenians to help him now get rid of Brasidas. This led to the battle at Amphipolis and the deaths of Brasidas and Cleon. Perdiccas focused on two goals: limit outside intervention and build up the power of his own house.

Pericles (c. 495–429), *PA* 11811, *APF* 455–60. From the most notable circle of Athenians, Pericles' mother Agariste was related to Clisthenes the 'founder' of Athenian democracy, and his father Xanthippus was a Persian War hero. In the twenty years before the Peloponnesian War, Pericles emerged as the leader of the pre-war Athenian democracy. Elected *strategos* frequently, he held extensive authority prompting Thucydides (2.65.10) to comment that while a democracy in theory, Athens was in reality ruled by one man – Pericles (and Plato [*Gorg.* 515e] thought he made the Athenians lazy, cowardly, and avaricious). He took interest in and facilitated the rebuilding of Athens after the war with Persia ended (perhaps with the so-called Peace of Callias, c. 449).

In the crisis leading up to the outbreak of the Peloponnesian War (432/1), Pericles refused to negotiate with the Spartans, forcing them to seek arbitration as prescribed by the terms of the Thirty Years Truce (446/5). He persuaded the Athenians to rebuff Spartan overtures and seek shelter behind the city walls, trusting in the fleet and the accumulated wealth of Athens. Soon afterwards he died along with many others in the plague that swept Athens (429).

Phidias *PA* 14149. Athenian sculptor, Phidias was one of the great artists of the classical Greek world. He was regarded as the most accomplished of Greek sculptors and his students were influential into the following generations. Among his earliest works was the colossal bronze statue of Athena Promachus, or 'Champion' (literally the one who fights in front). Association with Pericles made Phidias. A member of Pericles' circle, he played a major part in the rebuilding of Athens in the 440s and 430s, possibly holding major responsibility for the new temple of Athena, the Parthenon.

Phormio *PA* 14958. An Athenian general of the older generation, Phormio took Athenian naval forces into the Corinthian Gulf where he won some spectacular victories over larger Peloponnesian fleets. He was famous for his rough soldier's life, caricatured in Eupolis' play *Taxiarchs*.

Plato (c.429–346), *PA* 11855, *APF* 322–35. Plato belonged to one of the ancient families of Athens. In the fifth century this family was well placed politically and enjoyed elite status; its ranks included later radical oligarchs, most notably Critias and Charmides. Born at the start of the war, Plato would have been old enough to listen to Socrates debate ideas with the great Sophists of the day, men like Gorgias and Protagoras. Later when he began to write philosophy these individuals and arguments would provide dramatic background and title to his famous dialogues.

Socrates (c. 469–399), *PA* 13101. Perhaps the most famous Greek of the classical age, Socrates was the son of Sophroniscus, a stone mason or sculptor, and Phaenarete, famous for her skills as a midwife. His father's occupation argues for a moderate though not elite economic status, and this is seen further in Socrates' own wartime service. As a hoplite he fought in numerous campaigns of the Archidamian War; he later served on the Council of Five Hundred, defending the generals placed on trial for their supposed dereliction of duty in failing to rescue shipwrecked sailors after the battle of Arginusae (406).

It was probably during the 420s that Socrates' life as a philosopher and noted intellectual in Athens matured. Plato and Xenophon identify his 'circle' of students: Critias and Charmides, as well as Alcibiades; these relationships would later be turned against him when he was placed on trial for 'corrupting the youth' of Athens (399). While it is clear that he could have slipped away into exile, Socrates chose to abide by the laws of his city and accept its judgment. His death gave birth to the 'Socratic Legend' which influenced later philosophy and literature.

Sophocles (c. 496–406) *PA* 12834. Arguably the greatest of Athenian playwrights, Sophocles' literary career began in c. 468 when he competed with Aeschylus and ended in 401 when his namesake grandson posthumously staged his last play, *Oedipus at Colonus*. Sophocles was prolific, writing more than 120 plays, and victorious more often than any other playwright, winning first prize twenty times. He also played an active role in affairs of state, holding a number of responsible political positions, e.g., general c. 438, *hellenotamias* (443/2), and *proboulos*, the executive committee established after the Sicilian disaster (413).

Theramenes (d. 404), *PA* 7234, *APF* 227-8. Theramenes played an important role in the right-wing coup in Athens that brought the Four Hundred to power (411). Theramenes broke with the hardcore oligarchs and migrated to support of the Five Thousand, and then joined in with the restoration of democracy. Theramenes brought Spartan terms of 'peace' to Athens after the Aegospotami disaster and he ranked among the Thirty Tyrants who ruled Athens once peace came. He broke ranks with Critias and the more radical members of the Thirty and this cost him his life. Theramenes was perhaps not as radical an oligarch as some, but he was also a manipulator: in 406 after the battle of Arginusae, the generals assigned him the task of rescuing the shipwrecked sailors. While a storm did make this impossible, it also seems clear that he dodged responsibility and supported the proposals that cost the generals their lives.

Thrasybulus of Steiria (c. 440–388), *PA* 7310, *APF* 240-1. An Athenian democrat, Thrasybulus was with the fleet at Samos when the Four Hundred seized power. His support of Alcibiades allowed for the return of democracy and the rest of the war he fought in the Aegean. Banished by the Thirty Tyrants, he seized the fortress at Phyle (late autumn 404) and began a rebellion that the Thirty could not suppress. From Phyle he seized the Piraeus and again the Thirty could not dislodge him: in street fighting Critias and others were killed, opening the door to Spartan intervention and the restoration of democracy.

Thrasyllus (d. 406), *PA* 7333. A staunch democrat, Thrasyllus led the fleet against the oligarchic conspiracy of the 400. He later commanded Athenian forces in the eastern Aegean. In 406 he was one of the generals who won the battle of Arginusae. On returning to Athens, he was prosecuted along with five of his colleagues for dereliction of duty – allowing many Athenians to die at sea after the battle – and was executed.

Thucydides (c. 460–395?), *PA* 7267, *APF* 230-7. The historian of the Peloponnesian War, Thucydides was related to the influential family of Cimon: that his family possessed substantial wealth seems clear in his travels during his life of exile. Thucydides served as general at least in the year 424; his failure to save Amphipolis from Brasidas led to exile, possibly made legal by a decree proposed by Cleon. That Thucydides did not like Cleon is plain in the introduction given Cleon in the *History*: the most violent man in Athens (3.36.6), and the apparent satisfaction in describing his cowardly death at Amphipolis (5.10.9). During the war Thucydides traveled the Greek world, talking to those who participated and then wrote down what he learned.

Tissaphernes *RE* supp. v. 7 (1940): 1579–99. The Persian satrap of Sardis after 413, Tissaphernes belonged to an elite Persian family. Upon arriving in Asia Minor, he had responsibility over the entire region. His orders were to cooperate with Sparta, but the arrival first of Alcibiades and then Cyrus stymied his efforts. Cyrus' successes perhaps made Tissaphernes jealous leading him to denounce the prince to his brother Artaxerxes even before the war ended. When the royal brothers broke irrevocably and Cyrus attempted to seize the throne (401), Tissaphernes won royal favor by supporting the king. When the Spartan and Persian friendship later broke down, Tissaphernes attempted a dangerous game of deceit that cost him royal favor and his life.

Women of Plataea. The Plataean–Athenian garrison at Plataea included 110 women who cooked for the defenders. Sometimes thought to be slaves (see Thuc. 3.78.3, 3.68.2, with Gomme 2: 212), a number might have been free who remained with their men. Women seldom figure in the sources for the war (see Hornblower 1: 241–2) and their heroics seem worthy of mention.

Xenophon (c. 430–360), *PA* 11307. Xenophon belonged to an elite Athenian family. As a young man he associated with Socrates, a connection that perhaps influenced his political beliefs. His elite status qualified him for service in the cavalry, which played a controversial role in the events in Athens after the Peloponnesian War, supporting the Thirty Tyrants against the democracy. Xenophon probably fought in this civil war and afterwards, in spite of the proclaimed amnesty, left Athens. He served in the famously unsuccessful expedition of Cyrus against his brother Artaxerxes. On Cyrus' death Xenophon played a key role in the heroic march of the stranded Greek mercenary army, events which he later recorded as the *Anabasis*, the 'March up country'.

Notes

1 Individuals listed here are identified as cited in *APF* and/or *PA* (for Athenians) and P-B (for Spartans); other Greeks and Persians are identified as listed in *RE* (with bracketed numbers) or may be found by consulting the index. For the most part, references in this Who's Who are omitted.

2 Not listed in *RE*.

Appendix C

A PELOPONNESIAN WAR GLOSSARY[1]

Attica. The region surrounding and including the city of Athens in central Greece. Boeotia and its dominant city Thebes lies to the northwest, the large island of Euboea with its many *poleis*, or city-states (on which see below), lies to the northeast.

Choregos/choregia. Productions of Athenian dramas, whether comedy or tragedy, were expensive and required costumes and training. A wealthy Athenian – the *choregos* – assumed responsibilities and the costs of training and equipping the chorus that danced and sang in these festive productions. Such financial burdens were collectively known as liturgies or *litourgia.*

Cleruch(s). These were Athenian citizens who received grants of land outside of Athens, as a form of social welfare – those receiving land sometimes came from the lowest social-economic group (called *thetes*). The cleruchs held their land in return for military service and provided the Athenians with an additional military force. Such settlements symbolized Athenian imperialism and power.

Delian League. The alliance created by Athens after the Persian Wars when Sparta yielded leadership of the Greeks to Athens (478/7). Apollo's island home of Delos became the center for the alliance and was the site of the league treasury, until 454 when it was moved to Athens. Originally the larger allied states contributed ships and crews to military operations (e.g., Samos, Lesbos, Chios) while the smaller paid tribute (*phoros*), monetary payments, assessed and collected by Athens. Those whom the Athenians once recognized as allies came to be regarded, as Aristophanes makes plain in his plays, as 'subjects' as the alliance became the Athenian empire.

Democracy. 'People-power', the political system best known from the Athenian experience dates c. 500–280 (i.e., other communities, Argos and Chios were regarded also as democratic but evidence for these is slim). Principal institutions were the assembly (*ekklesia*) of free citizens (men, born of citizen parents after c. 451/0), the Council of Five Hundred (*boule*) that prepared business for the assembly and administered the city on a daily basis, and the law courts. It has been estimated that approximately 700 Athenians held public offices in the mature Athenian democracy.

Helot(s). The serf-like inhabitants of Sparta, the helots may be distinguished as 'Messenian' or newly conquered helots (c. 650) who remembered they had once been free, and 'Laconian', helots conquered earlier and perhaps more wedded to the society and culture of the elite Spartiates or 'equals' (*homoioi*). Helots considerably outnumbered their Spartan masters (7:1 being a frequently cited ratio, though the evidence for this figure is contested). The great number of helots was a constant worry to the Spartan elite who feared that they might rebel at any moment. Helots were different from slaves as usually defined in that they lived in their own communities and enjoyed family life, which slaves did not. During the Peloponnesian War, the Spartans recruited soldiers from the helots who were later emancipated and called *neodamodeis*, or 'new men' (literally 'new of the people').

A related category were the *mothakes* (sing. *mothax*) or *mothones* (sing. *mothon*), who were sometimes the children of mixed parentage (i.e., Spartiate and helot) who became the 'pets' or 'foster brothers' of young Spartiates; others were the children of impoverished Spartans (e.g., Lysander) and regarded as 'Inferiors'. Both, however, might be reared in the Spartan educational structure, the *agoge*, and so could recoup lost status and/or wealth. They largely identified with the elite Spartiates.

Hoplite. The core of the armies that fought the Peloponnesian War were citizen militias composed of heavy infantry or hoplites. Hoplite derives from the Greek *hopla* referring to the equipment that soldiers carried and wore into battle: the large shield, about three feet across, carried for personal protection (on the left arm), along with a spear (about eight feet) and a short slashing sword (roughly twenty-four inches in length). For personal protection soldiers wore a bronze helmet of various styles (remarkably light) that afforded some protection. Some soldiers also wore greaves (bronze shin guards) and a breastplate, though these items appear to have become unpopular, perhaps because they slowed men down (see above Figures 3.3, 5.2, 5.3, 10.1, 12.1 for illustrations; also

Ratto 2006: 78–9, 182). Increasingly during the fifth century and especially through the Peloponnesian War, hoplites fought alongside lighter armed troops called peltasts who carried even lighter equipment but more weapons, and other specialty troops such as slingers and archers (see Ratto 2006: 80). The Athenian general Demosthenes was one commander who achieved some fame (e.g., at Pylos) in combining these different types of troops (though his luck ran out in Sicily, 413).

Metics. Sometimes called resident aliens, the metics were a commercially prominent and affluent group in Athens and other Greek cities. In Athens they bore many obligations – financial and military service – yet possessed no political voice, reflecting the ambivalence of their citizen neighbors.[2]

Oligarchy. Meaning 'rule by the few', oligarchy at the time of the Peloponnesian War was an ancient and still practiced political form among the Greeks. Its opposite is democracy, or 'people-power'.

Peloponnese/Peloponnesos. The southern-most part of Greece (below the Isthmos), dominated by Sparta which drew its strength from the Eurotas river valley in the south central area and the Pamisos river valley in Messenia. To the northeast lay Sparta's longtime rival Argos.

Peloponnesian League. This was the alliance led by Sparta, founded in the later part of the sixth century. The name is a modern convenience. In antiquity the alliance was the 'Lacedaemonians (Spartans) and their allies', the latter being not at all Peloponnesian. The term 'league' is again a modern idea. The 'allies' were only allied to Sparta and in times of peace could be found fighting each other. It was only to Sparta that the allies swore oaths of allegiance, and in return Sparta pledged to aid any ally attacked by a third party. In a league assembly it was 'one state, one vote' and the Spartans could ignore an inconvenient allied vote. Sparta always held the command and prescribed the numbers of men each ally was to contribute to a campaign. The Spartans moved to transform the League into an empire after the victory over Athens in 404. In the fourth century, as Spartan power declined so too did the League which dissolved in 366 upon the suggestion of Corinth, always the most powerful of the 'allies'.

Persian empire. The Greeks knew the Persians and their empire well, especially the Greek cities in Ionia (Aegean coast of Turkey today) which bordered the Persian empire. After the conquests of Cyrus the Great (546) and until the fifth-century Persian War victories (479/8 and later), the Ionian or eastern Greeks had been at the mercy of the Persians.

Forced into retreat by the Athenian-led Delian League (c. 450 and the Peace of Callias), a Persian revival in Ionia began as the Peloponnesian War distracted Athens and provided the Spartans with a devil's bargain: money to defeat Athens at the cost of surrendering the Ionian Greeks to Persia.

Polis. Usually translated 'city-state', the concept is a modern convenience. What the term refers to is a self-governing community (in which the idea of 'government' is somewhat anachronistic[3]) that controls the surrounding area, e.g., Athens over Attica, and which is free from external authority. A community that was not autonomous (= self-governing), in Greek eyes, was not free. Control over the surrounding rural area allowed a town or city to flourish as the rural population supplied the food that the townspeople would consume, while the townspeople would produce goods and services for those in the country.

Spartan kings. Unusually the Spartans had two lines of kings – the Agiads and Eurypontids – who ruled jointly. The two houses were frequently at odds and both acted under close scrutiny of the Spartans themselves. During the Peloponnesian War the Agiads were Pleistoanx and Pausanias (father and son, descended from Pausanias, the victor of Plataea), the Eurypontids Archidamus II and Agis II (also father and son).[4] The chief role of Spartan kings was the command of military forces.

Strategos. The Greek word for general is *strategos* (cf. strategy). The Athenians elected ten generals (pl., *strategoi*) every year by popular vote, unlike the usual selection of officials by lot. These men commanded Athenian military forces both on land and at sea, though military ability was not a prerequisite for election. Athenian generals possessed political authority and privilege as well (they could call a meeting of the Council for example), and could, as the example of Pericles shows, occupy a dominating position of leadership within the democracy.

Trireme. The basic warship of the classical age, the trireme was a long fighting ship rowed by 170 oarsmen. An additional group (about thirty) of marines and other sailors rounded out the ordinary complement of a trireme and some of these, especially the helmsman (*kubernetes*), were specialists in their own right and highly sought after. The principal weapon was a large bronze ram mounted on the trireme's bow and the object was to steer this into another warship, disable and/or sink it. A ship that was rammed usually did not sink immediately – wood construction usually kept a damaged ship afloat for some time before it finally sank. In other situations, ships would become entangled in which cases there would be hand-to-hand fighting until one side literally cleared the decks of the other. Triremes were costly. In democratic Athens, the trierarchy (*trierarchia*) ranked among the costliest of the liturgies for well-to-do citizens. Service as a trierarch demonstrated one's civic pride and advertised one's wealth by paying for a ship's maintenance and the crew's wages.

Notes

1 References are mostly omitted here; see related entries in the index.
2 D. Whitehead, 'metics', *OCD*[3] 969.
3 See Sealey 1993: 5, 271–2, and Whitley 2001: 336.
4 See Cartledge 1987: 101 for a full listing of the Spartan kings.

BIBLIOGRAPHY

(Not listed here are entries in *OCD*[3] and *RE*, citations of which may be found in the Abbreviations)

I. Classical Studies

Akrigg, B. 2007. The nature and implications of Athens' changed social structure and economy. In R. Osborne, ed., *Debating the Athenian Cultural Revolution* (pp. 27–43). Cambridge.

Allan, W., ed. 2008. *Euripides. Helen.* Cambridge.

Arrowsmith, W., ed. and trans. 1956. *Euripides II. The Cyclops and Heracles.* Chicago.

Arrowsmith, W., ed. and trans. 1958. *Euripides III. Hecuba.* Chicago.

Badian, E. 1966. Alexander the Great and the Greeks of Asia. In E. Badian, ed., *Ancient Society and Institutions, Studies Presented to Victor Ehrenberg on his 75th Birthday* (pp. 37–69). Oxford.

Badian, E. 1993. *From Plataea to Potidaea. Studies in the History and Historiography of the Pentecontaetia.* Baltimore.

Bagnall, N. 2004. *The Peloponnesian War. Athens, Sparta, and the Struggle for Greece.* New York.

Barlow, S.A., ed. 1996. *Euripides Heracles.* Warminster.

Baynham, E.J. 2009. Power, passion, and patrons. Alexander, Charles Le Brun, and Oliver Stone. In W. Heckel & L.A. Tritle, eds., *Alexander the Great: A New History* (pp. 294–312). Oxford.

Becker, W.A. 1866. *Charicles or Illustrations of the Private Life of the Ancient Greeks.* Ed. by F. Metcalfe. London.

Bond, G.W., ed. 1981. *Euripides Heracles.* Oxford.

Borza, E. 1990. *In the Shadow of Olympus. The Emergence of Macedon.* Princeton.

Bosworth, A.B. 1992. *Autonomia*: the use and abuse of political terminology. *Studi italiani di filologia classica*, **10**: 122–52.

Bosworth, A.B. 1993. The humanitarian aspect of the Melian Dialogue. *Journal of Hellenic Studies*, **113**: 30–44.

Bradeen, D.W. 1960. The popularity of the Athenian empire. *Historia*, **9**: 257–69.

Briant, P. 2002. *From Cyrus to Alexander. A History of the Persian Empire*. Trans. by P.J. Daniels. Winona Lake.

Broneer, O. 1938. Excavations on the north slope of the Acropolis, 1937. *Hesperia*, **7**: 228–43.

Bruce, I.A.F. 1967. *An Historical Commentary on the 'Hellenica Oxyrhynchia'*. Cambridge.

Burckhardt, J. 1998. *The Greeks and Greek Civilization*. Trans. by S. Stern. Ed. with Introduction by O. Murray. New York.

Burckhardt, L.A. 1996. *Bürger und Soldaten. Aspekte der politischen und miliarischen Rolle athenischer Bürger im Kriegwesens des 4.Jahrhunderts v. Chr. Historia Einzelschriften* 101. Stuttgart.

Busolt, G. & Swoboda, H. 1920–26. *Griechische Staatskunde*. 2 vols. Munich.

Calhoun, G.H. 1913. *Athenian Clubs in Politics and Litigation*. Austin.

Camp, J.M. 2001. *The Archaeology of Athens*. New Haven.

Carawan, E. 2004. Andocides' defence and MacDowell's solution. In D.L. Cairns & R.A. Knox, eds., *Law, Rhetoric, and Comedy in Classical Athens. Essays in Honour of Douglas M. MacDowell* (pp. 103–12). Swansea.

Cartledge, P. 1987. *Agesilaos and the Crisis of Sparta*. Baltimore.

Cawkwell, G. 1997. *Thucydides and the Peloponnesian War*. London.

Christ, M. 2001. Conscription of hoplites in classical Athens. *Classical Quarterly*, **51**: 398–422.

Clark, M. 1999. Thucydides in Olympia. In R. Mellor & L.A. Tritle, eds., *Text and Tradition. Studies in Greek History and Historiography in Honor of Mortimer Chambers* (pp. 115–34). Claremont.

Cohen, E.E. 1992. *Athenian Economy and Society. A Banking Perspective*. Princeton.

Collard, C. & Cropp, M., eds. and trans. 2008. *Euripides. VII. Fragments, Aegeus-Meleager*. Cambridge.

Connor, W.R. 1984. *Thucydides*. Princeton.

Develin, R. 1989. *Athenian Officials, 684–321 B.C.* Cambridge.

Dodds, E.R., ed. 1960. *Euripides Bacchae*, 2nd edn. Oxford.

Dover, K.J. 1972. *Aristophanic Comedy*. Berkeley and Los Angeles.

Dover, K.J., ed. 1993. *Aristophanes Frogs*. Oxford.

Dover, K.J. 2004. The limits of allegory and allusion in Aristophanes. In In D.L. Cairns & R.A. Knox, eds., *Law, Rhetoric, and Comedy in Classical Athens. Essays in Honour of Douglas M. MacDowell* (pp. 239–29). Swansea.

Ducat, J. 2006. The Spartan 'tremblers'. In S. Hodkinson & A. Powell, eds., *Sparta & War* (pp. 1–55). Swansea.

Duff, T. E. 1999. *Plutarch's Lives. Exploring Virtue and Vice*. Oxford.

Eckstein, A. 2003. Thucydides, the outbreak of the Peloponnesian War, and the foundation of international systems theory. *Bulletin of the Institute of Historical Research*, **24**: 757–74.

Eddy, S.K. 1970. On the peace of Callias. *Classical Philology*, **65**: 8–14.

Eddy, S.K. 1973. The cold war between Athens and Persia, ca. 448–412 B.C. *Classical Philology*, **68**: 241–58.

Eddy, S.K. 1973a. Review, D. Kagan, *The Outbreak of the Peloponnesian War* (Ithaca, 1969). *Classical Philology*, **68**: 308–10.

Edwards, M.J. 2000. Philoctetes in historical context. In D.A. Gerber, ed., *Disabled Veterans in History* (pp. 55–69). Ann Arbor.

Edwards, M.J. 2004. Antiphon the revolutionary. In D.L. Cairns & R.A. Knox, eds., *Law, Rhetoric, and Comedy in Classical Athens. Essays in Honour of Douglas M. MacDowell* (pp. 75–86). Swansea.

Ehrenberg, V. 1954. *Sophocles and Pericles*. Oxford.

Ehrenberg, V. 1962. *The People of Aristophanes*. New York.

Ellis, W. 1989. *Alcibiades*. London.

Finley, M.I. 1971. *The Ancestral Constitution*. Cambridge.

Finley, M.I. 1982. *Economy and Society in Ancient Greece*. Ed. with introduction by B.D. Shaw & R.P. Saller. New York.

Flower, M.A. & Marincola, J., eds. 2002. *Herodotus, the Histories. Book IX*. Cambridge.

Fränkel, H. 1973. *Early Greek Poetry and Philosophy*. Trans. by M. Hadas & J. Willis. New York.

Frost, F. 1980. *Plutarch's Themistocles. A Historical Commentary*. Princeton.

Fuks, A. 1953. *The Ancestral Constitution*. London.

Goldhill, S. 1986. *Reading Greek Tragedy*. Cambridge.

Goldhill, S. 1990. The Great Dionysia and civic ideology. In J.J. Winkler & F.I. Zeitlin, eds., *Nothing to do with Dionysos? Athenian Drama in its Social Context* (pp. 97–129). Princeton.

Goldhill, S. 1997. Modern critical approaches to Greek tragedy. In P.E. Easterling, ed., *The Cambridge Companion to Greek Tragedy* (pp. 324–47). Cambridge.

Goldhill, S. 2000. Civic ideology and the problem of difference: the politics of Aeschylean tragedy, once again. *Journal of Hellenic Studies*, **120**: 34–56.

Green, P. 1970. *Armada from Athens*. New York.

Green, P. 1999. War and morality in fifth-century Athens: the case of Euripides' *Trojan Women. Ancient History Bulletin*, **13**: 97–110.

Griffin, J. 1999. Sophocles and the democratic city. In J. Griffin, ed., *Sophocles Revisited. Essays Presented to Sir Hugh Lloyd-Jones* (pp. 73–94). Oxford.

Griffith, M., ed. 1999. *Sophocles: Antigone*. Cambridge.

Gründer, K., ed. 1969. *Der Streit um Nietzsches 'Geburt der Tragödie'*. Hildesheim.

Guthrie, W.K.C. 1971. *Socrates*. Cambridge.

Guthrie, W.K.C. 1971a. *The Sophists*. Cambridge.

Habicht, C. 1985. *Pausanias' Guide to Ancient Greece*. Berkeley and Los Angeles.

Hale, J.R. 2009. *Lords of the Sea. The Epic Story of the Athenian Navy and the Birth of Democracy*. New York.

Hammond, N.G.L. & Griffith, G.T. 1979. *A History of Macedonia*. Vol. II. *550-336 B.C.* Oxford.

Hansen, M.H. 1988. Three studies in Athenian demography. *Historisk-filosofiske Meddelelser*, **56**: 3–28.

Hanson, V.D. 1999. Hoplite obliteration: the case of the town of Thespiae. In J. Carman & A. Harding, eds., *Ancient Warfare* (pp. 203–17). Stroud.

Hanson, V.D. 2005. *A War Like No Other. How the Athenians and the Spartans fought the Peloponnesian War*. New York.

Harding, P., ed. 1985. *Translated Documents of Greece & Rome*. Vol. **2**. From the End of the Peloponnesian War to the Battle of Ipsus. Cambridge.

Harrison, A.R.W. 1971. *The Law of Athens. Procedure*. Oxford.

Harvey, D. 2004. The clandestine massacre of the Helots. In T.J. Figueira, ed., *Spartan Society* (pp. 199–217). Swansea.

Havelock, E.A. 1972. War as a way of life in classical culture. In E. Gareau, ed., *Classical Values and the Modern World* (pp. 19–78). Ottawa.

Henderson, B.W. 1927. *The Great War between Athens and Sparta*. London.

Henderson, J., ed. 1987. *Lysistrata*. Oxford.

Hodkinson, S. 2000. *Property and Wealth in Classical Sparta*. Swansea.

Hodkinson, S. 2006. Was classical Sparta a military society?' In S. Hodkinson & A. Powell, eds., *Sparta & War* (pp. 111–62). Swansea.

Hodkinson, S. & Powell A., eds. 1999. *Sparta. New Perspectives*. Swansea.

Holden, H.A., ed. 1887. *Plutarch's Life of Nicias*. Cambridge.

Hornblower, S. 1987. *Thucydides*. Baltimore.

How, W.W. & Wells, J. 1912. *A Commentary on Herodotus*. 2 vols. New York.

Hunt, P. 1998. *Slaves, Warfare, and Ideology in the Greek Historians*. Cambridge.

Hurwit, J.M. 1999. *The Athenian Acropolis. History, Mythology, and Archaeology from the Neolithic Era to the Present*. Cambridge.

Hussey, E. 1985. Thucydidean history and Democritean theory. In P. Cartledge & F. Harvey, eds., *Crux: Essays in Greek History Presented to G.E.M. de Ste. Croix* (pp. 118–38). London.

Hutchinson, G. 2006. *Attrition. Aspects of Command in the Peloponnesian War*. Stroud.

Huxley, G.L. 1970. *Early Sparta*. New York.

Jehne, M. 1994. *Koine Eirene. Untersuchungen zu den Befriedungs- und Stabilisierungsbemühungen in der griechischen Poliswelt des 4. Jahrhunderts v. Chr.* *Hermes Einzelschriften* 63. Stuttgart.

Jenkins, I. 2006. *Greek Architecture and its Sculpture*. London.

Jordan, B. 1972. *The Athenian Navy in the Classical Period*. Berkeley and Los Angeles.

Kagan, D. 1969. *The Outbreak of the Peloponnesian War*. Ithaca.

Kagan, D. 1974. *The Archidamian War*. Ithaca.

Kagan, D. 1981. *The Peace of Nicias and the Sicilian Expedition*. Ithaca.

Kagan, D. 1987. *The Fall of the Athenian Empire*. Ithaca.

Kagan, D. 2003. *The Peloponnesian War*. New York.

Kallet, L. 2001. *Money and the Corrosion of Power in Thucydides*. Berkeley and Los Angeles.

Kassel, R., & C. Austin, eds. 1984. *Poetae Comici Graeci*. 7 vols. Berlin.

Kerferd, G.B. 1981. *The Sophistic Movement*. Cambridge.

Konstan, D. 2007. War and reconciliation in Greek literature. In K.A. Raaflaub, ed., *War and Peace in the Ancient World* (pp. 191–205). Oxford.

Krentz, P. 1982. *The Thirty at Athens*. Ithaca.

Krentz, P., ed. 1989. *Xenophon Hellenika I-II.3.10*. Warminster.

Krentz, P. 2007. The Oath of Marathon, not Plataia'? *Hesperia*, **76**: 731–42.

Krentz, P. 2007a. War. In P. Sabin *et al.*, eds. *The Cambridge History of Greek and Roman Warfare. Vol. 1: Greece, the Hellenistic World and the Rise of Rome* (pp. 147–85). Cambridge.

Lattimore, S., ed. and trans. 1998. *Thucydides. The Peloponnesian War*. Indianapolis.

Lattimore, S. 2006. From Classical to Hellenistic art. In K.H. Kinzl, ed., *A Companion to the Classical Greek World* (pp. 456–79). Oxford.

Lazenby, J.F. 1985. *The Spartan Army*. Warminster.

Lazenby, J.F. 2004. *The Peloponnesian War. A Military Study*. London.

Lebow, R.N. 2003. *The Tragic Vision of Politics, Ethics, Interests and Orders*. Cambridge.

Lee, J.W.I. 2007. *A Greek Army on the March. Soldiers and Survival in Xenophon's Anabasis*. Cambridge.

Lefkowitz, M.R. 1981. *The Lives of the Greek Poets*. London.

Lendle, O. 1995. *Kommentar zu Xenophon's Anabasis (Bücher 1–7)*. Darmstadt.

Lendon, J.E. 2005. *Soldiers and Ghosts. A History of Battle in Classical Antiquity*. New Haven.

Lesky, A. 1966. *A History of Greek Literature*. Trans. by J. Willis and C. de Heer. London.

Lewis, D.M. 1977. *Sparta and Persia*. Leiden.

Lewis, D.M. 1997. *Selected Papers in Greek and Near Eastern History*. Ed. by P.J. Rhodes. Cambridge.

Lewis, R.G. 1988. An alternative date for Sophocles' *Antigone*. *Greek, Roman and Byzantine Studies*, **29**: 35–50.

LiDonnici, L.R. 1995. *The Epidaurian Miracle Inscriptions*. Atlanta.

Littman, R.J. 2006. The plague of Athens: current analytic techniques. *Amphora*, **5**: 10–12.

Lloyd-Jones, H., ed. and trans. 1996. *Sophocles. III. Fragments*. Cambridge.

Loomis, W.T. 1992. *The Spartan War Fund: IG V 1, 1 and a New Fragment. Historia Einzelschriften* 74. Stuttgart.

Loraux, N. 1986. *The Invention of Athens. The Funeral Oration in the Classical City*. Trans. by A. Sheridan. Cambridge.

Loraux, N. 2002. *The Divided City. On Memory and Forgetting in Ancient Athens*. Trans. by C. Pache with J. Fort. New York.

Low, P. 2003. Remembering war in fifth-century Greece: ideologies, societies, and commemoration beyond democratic Athens. *World Archaeology*, **35**: 98–111.

Low, P. 2006. Commemorating the Spartan war-dead. In S. Hodkinson & A. Powell, eds., *Sparta & War* (pp. 85–109). Swansea.

Low, P. 2007. *Interstate Relations in Classical Greece. Morality and Power*. Cambridge.

Ma, J. 2008. Chaironeia 338: topographies of commemoration. *Journal of Hellenic Studies*, **128**: 72–91.

MacDowell, D.M., ed. 1962. *Andokides. On the Mysteries*. Oxford.

MacDowell, D.M. 1995. *Aristophanes and Athens: An Introduction to the Plays*. Oxford.

McAusland, I., & P. Walcot, eds. 1998. *Homer*. New York.

McNeill, W.H. 1995. *Keeping Together in Time. Dance and Drill in Human History*. Cambridge.

Mattingly, H.B. 1996. *The Athenian Empire Restored. Epigraphic and Historical Studies*. Ann Arbor.

Meier, C. 1993. *The Political Art of Greek Tragedy*. Trans. by A. Webber. Baltimore.

Meiggs, R. 1972. *The Athenian Empire*. Oxford.

Michelini, A.N. 1987. *Euripides and the Tragic Tradition*. Madison.

Michell, H. 1952. *Sparta*. Cambridge.

Mitchell-Boyask, R. 2008. *Plague and the Athenian Imagination. Drama, History, and the Cult of Asclepius*. Cambridge.

Morris, I. 2009. The greater Athenian state. In I. Morris & W. Scheidel (eds.), *The Dynamics of Ancient Empires. State Power from Assyria to Byzantium* (pp. 99–177). Oxford.

Morrison, J.S. & Coates, J.F. 1986. *The Athenian Trireme: The History and Reconstruction of an Ancient Greece Warship*. Cambridge.

Morwood, J., ed. and trans., 2000. *Euripides: Hecuba, The Trojan Women, Andromache*. Intro by E. Hall. Oxford.

Munn, M. 2000. *The School of History. Athens in the Age of Socrates*. Berkeley and Los Angeles.

Nims, J.F. ed. and trans. 1958. *Euripides III. Andromache*. Chicago.

Oakley, J.H. 2004. *Picturing Death in Classical Athens. The Evidence of the White Lekythoi*. Cambridge.

Ober, J. 1996. *The Athenian Revolution. Essays on Ancient Greek Democracy and Political Theory*. Princeton.

Osborne, R. 1998. *Archaic and Classical Greek Art*. New York.

Ostwald, M. 1986. *From Popular Sovereignty to the Sovereignty of Law. Law, Society, and Politics in Fifth-Century Athens*. Berkeley and Los Angeles.

Papadopoulou, T. 2005. *Heracles and Euripidean Tragedy*. Cambridge.

Paradiso, A. 2004. The logic of terror: Thucydides, Spartan duplicity and an improbable massacre. In T.J. Figueira, ed., *Spartan Society* (pp. 179–98). Swansea.

Parke, H.W. 1977. *Festivals of the Athenians*. Ithaca.

Parker, R. 1996. *Athenian Religion: A History*. Oxford.

Parlama, L., & N.C. Stampolidis, eds. 2001. *Athens: the City Beneath the City*. Athens.

Pelling, C., ed. 1997. *Greek Tragedy and the Historian*. Oxford.

Pelling, C. 2002. *Plutarch and History*. Swansea.

Podlecki, A.J. 1998. *Perikles and His Circle*. London.

Pollitt, J.J. 1972. *Art and Experience in Classical Greece*. Cambridge.

Powell, A. 2006. Why did Sparta not destroy Athens in 404, or in 403 BC? In S. Hodkinson & A. Powell, eds., *Sparta & War* (pp. 287–303). Swansea.

Quinn, T.J. 1981. *Athens and Samos, Lesbos, and Chios, 478–404 B.C.* Manchester.

Raaflaub, K.A. 1985. *Die Entdeckung der Freiheit. Zur historischen Semantik und Gesellschaftsgeschichte eines politischen Grundbegriffes der Griechen*. Munich.

Raaflaub, K.A. 1994. Democracy, power, and imperialism in fifth-century Athens. In J.P. Euben *et al.*, eds., *Athenian Political Thought and the Reconstruction of American Democracy* (pp. 103–46). Ithaca.

Raaflaub, K.A. 1998. The transformation of Athens in the fifth century. In D. Boedeker, & K.A. Raaflaub, eds., *Democracy, Empire, and the Arts in Fifth-Century Athens* (pp. 15–41). Cambridge.

Raaflaub, K.A. 2001. Father of all – destroyer of all: war in late fifth-century Athenian discourse and ideology. In B. Strauss, & D. McCann, eds., *War and Democracy: A Comparative Study of the Korean War and the Peloponnesian War* (pp. 307–56). New York.

Raaflaub, K.A. 2001a. Political thought, civic responsibility, and the Greek polis. In J.P. Arnason, & P. Murphy, eds., *Agon, Logos, Polis. The Greek Achievement and its Aftermath* (pp. 72–117). Stuttgart.

Raaflaub, K.A. 2002. Herodot und Thukydides: Persischer Imperialismus im Lichte der athenischen Sizilienpolitik. In N. Ehrhardt & L.-M. Günther, eds. 2002. *Widerstand-Anpassung-Integration. Die griechische Staatenwelt und Rom. Festschrift für Jürgen Deininger* (pp. 11–40). Stuttgart.

Raaflaub, K.A. 2004. *The Discovery of Freedom in Ancient Greece*. Chicago [translation, with additional material of *Die Entdeckung der Freiheit*, 1985].

Raaflaub, K.A., & N. Rosenstein, eds. 1999. *War and Society in the Ancient and Medieval Worlds. Asia, the Mediterranean, Europe, and Mesoamerica*. Cambridge.

Raffaelli, L.M., trans. 1993. *Plutarco Alcibiade*. Intro. by L. Prandi. Milan.

Ratto, S. 2006. *Greece. Dictionaries of Civilization*. Trans. by R.M.G. Frongia. Berkeley and Los Angeles.

Rawlings, L. 2007. *The Ancient Greeks at War*. Manchester.

Rengakos, A., & Tsakmakis, A., eds. 2006. *Brill's Companion to Thucydides*. Leiden.

Rhodes, P.J. 1972. *The Athenian Boule*. Oxford.

Rhodes, P.J. 1981. *A Commentary on the Aristotelian Athenaion Politeia*. Oxford.

Rhodes, P.J. 1984. *What Alcibiades Did or What Happened to Him*. Durham.

Rhodes, P.J. 1987. Thucydides on the causes of the Peloponnesian war. *Hermes*, **115**: 154–65.

Rhodes, P.J. 2004. Aristophanes and the Athenian assembly. In D.L. Cairns & R.A. Knox, eds., *Law, Rhetoric, and Comedy in Classical Athens. Essays in Honour of Douglas M. MacDowell* (pp. 223–37). Swansea.

Rhodes, P.J. 2006. The literary sources. In K.H. Kinzl, ed., *A Companion to the Classical Greek World* (pp. 26–44). Oxford.

Rhodes, P.J., & Osborne, R., eds. 2003. *Greek Historical Inscriptions, 404–323 BC*. Oxford.

Roisman, J. 1993. *The General Demosthenes and His Use of Military Surprise. Historia Einzelschriften 78*. Stuttgart.

de Romilly, J. 1988. Plutarch and Thucydides or the free use of quotations. *Phoenix*, **42**: 22–34.

de Romilly, J. 1992. *The Great Sophists in Periclean Athens*. Oxford.

Rosen, W. 2007. *Justinian's Flea. Plague, Empire, and the Birth of Europe*. London.

Rubincam, C. 1991. Casualty figures in the battle descriptions of Thucydides. *Transactions and Proceedings of the American Philological Association*, **121**: 181–98.

Rutherford, R. 2005. *Classical Literature. A Concise History*. Oxford.

Ryder, T.T.B. 1965. *Koine Eirene. General Peace and Local Independence in Ancient Greece*. Oxford.

Sabin, P. 2000. The Roman face of battle. *Journal of Roman Studies*, **90**: 1–17.

Sabin, P., H. van Wees, & M. Whitby, eds. 2007. *The Cambridge History of Greek and Roman Warfare*. Vol. **1**: Greece, the Hellenistic World and the Rise of Rome. Cambridge.

de Ste. Croix, G.E.M. 1972. *The Origins of the Peloponnesian War*. Ithaca.

Salazar, C. 2000. *The Treatment of War Wounds in Graeco-Roman Antiquity*. Leiden.

Samons, L.J. II. 1996. The 'Kallias Decrees' (*IG* i^3 52) and the inventories of Athena's treasure in the Parthenon. *Classical Quarterly*, N.S. **46**: 91–102.

Samons, L.J. II., ed. 2007. *The Cambridge Companion to the Age of Pericles*. Cambridge.

Scheidel, W. 2003. Helot numbers: a simplified model. In N. Luraghi & S. Alcock, eds., *Helots and their Masters in Laconia and Messenia: Histories, Ideologies, Structures* (pp. 240–7). Cambridge.

Sealey, R. 1976. *A History of the Greek City-States*. Berkeley and Los Angeles.

Sealey, R. 1993. *Demosthenes and His Time*. New York.

Sekunda, N. 2000. *Greek Hoplite, 480-323 BC*. Oxford.

Shay, J. 1995. The birth of tragedy – out of the needs of democracy. *Didaskalia: Ancient Theater Today* [on-line journal], **2**, 2.

Shear, J.L. 2007. Cultural change, space, and the politics of commemoration. In R. Osborne, ed., *Debating the Athenian Cultural Revolution* (pp. 91–115). Cambridge.

Shipley, D.R. 1997. *Plutarch's Life of Agesilaos. Response to Sources in the Presentation of Character*. Oxford.

Sidwell, K. 2009. *Aristophanes the Democrat. The Politics of Satirical Comedy during the Peloponnesian War*. Cambridge.

Sinclair, R.K. 1988. *Democracy and Participation in Classical Athens*. Cambridge.

Smith, C.F., ed. and trans. 1920–35. *Thucydides. The Peloponnesian War*. 4 vols. Cambridge.

Solmsen, F. 1975. *Intellectual Experiments of the Greek Enlightenment*. Princeton.

Sommerstein, A.H., ed. and trans. 1980. *Aristophanes, Acharnians*. Warminster.

Sommerstein, A.H., ed. and trans. 1985. *Aristophanes, Peace*. Warminster.

Sommerstein, A.H. 2004. Comedy and the unspeakable. In D.L. Cairns & R.A. Knox, eds., *Law, Rhetoric, and Comedy in Classical Athens. Essays in Honour of Douglas M. MacDowell* (pp. 205–22). Swansea.

Sprague, R.K., ed. 1972. *The Older Sophists. A Complete Translation by several hands of the Fragments in Die Fragmente der Vorsokratiker edited by Diels-Kranz with a New Edition of Antiphon and of Euthydemus*. Indianapolis.

Stadter, P. 1965. *Plutarch's Historical Methods*. Cambridge.

Stadter, P. 1989. *A Commentary on Plutarch's Pericles*. Chapel Hill.

Stewart, A.F. 1990. *Greek Sculpture. An Exploration*. 2 vols. New Haven.

Stewart, A.F. 2008. *Classical Greece and the Birth of Western Art*. Cambridge.

Storey, I. C. 2003. *Eupolis. Poet of Old Comedy*. Oxford.

Sutton, D.F. 1990. Aristophanes and the transition to middle comedy. *Liverpool Classical Monthly* **15**: 81–95.

Taplin, O. 1998. The shield of Achilles within the *Iliad*. In I. McAusland & P. Walcot, eds., *Homer* (pp. 96–115). New York.

Taylor, M.C. 2002. Implicating the *Demos*: a reading of Thucydides on the rise of the Four Hundred. *Journal of Hellenic Studies*, **122**: 91–108.

Todd, S.C. 2004. Revisiting the Herms and the Mysteries. In D.L. Cairns & R.A. Knox, eds., *Law, Rhetoric, and Comedy in Classical Athens. Essays in Honour of Douglas M. MacDowell* (pp. 87–102). Swansea.

Todd, S.C. 2007. *A Commentary on Lysias, Speeches 1–11.* New York.

Tritle, L.A. 1988. *Phocion the Good.* London.

Tritle, L.A. 1997. Hector's body: mutilation of the dead in Ancient Greece and Vietnam. *The Ancient History Bulletin,* **11**: 123–36.

Tritle, L.A. 2000. *From Melos to My Lai. War and Survival.* London.

Tritle, L.A. 2002. The frontiers of ancient history: Thucydides, survival and the writing of history. In S.M. Burstein, & C. Thomas, eds. 2002. *Current Issues and the Study of Ancient History* (pp. 69–79). Publications of the Association of Ancient Historians, 7. Claremont.

Tritle, L. 2003. Alexander and the killing of Cleitus the Black. In W. Heckel & L.A. Tritle (eds.), *Crossroads of History. The Age of Alexander.* (pp. 127–46). Claremont.

Tritle, L.A. 2004. Xenophon's Portrait of Clearchus: a study in post-traumatic stress disorder. In C. Tuplin, ed., *Xenophon and His World. Historia Einzelschriften* 172 (pp. 325–39). Stuttgart.

Tritle, L.A. 2007. 'Laughing for Joy': war and peace among the Greeks. In K.A. Raaflaub, ed., *War and Peace in the Ancient World* (pp. 172–90). Oxford.

Tuplin, C. 1979. Thucydides 1.42.2 and the Megarian Decree. *Classical Quarterly,* N.S. **29**: 301–7.

Tuplin, C. 1982. Fathers and sons: *Ecclesiazusae* 644–45. *Greek, Roman and Byzantine Studies,* **23**: 325–30.

van Wees, H., ed. 2000. *War and Violence in Ancient Greece.* Swansea.

van Wees, H. 2004. *Greek Warfare. Myths and Realities.* London.

Vickers, M. 1997. *Pericles' On Stage. Political Comedy in Aristophanes.* Austin.

Vickers, M. 2008. *Sophocles and Alcibiades. Athenian Politics in Ancient Greek Literature.* London.

Warner, R., trans. 1949/1972. Intro. and Notes by G. Cawkwell. *Xenophon. The Persian Expedition.* London.

Warner, R., ed. and trans. 1954. *Thucydides. The Peloponnesian War.* New York.

Weil, S. 2003. *Simone Weil's the Iliad, or the Poem of Force: a Critical Edition.* Ed. and Trans. by J.P. Holoka. New York.

West, S. 1999. Sophocles *Antigone* and Herodotus Book Three. In J. Griffin, ed., *Sophocles Revisited. Essays Presented to Sir Hugh Lloyd-Jones* (pp. 109–36). Oxford.

Westlake, H.D. 1969. *Essays on the Greek Historians and Greek History.* Manchester.

Westlake, H.D. 1975. Paches. *Phoenix,* **29**: 107–16.

Wheeler, E.L., ed. 2007. *The Armies of Classical Greece.* Aldershot.

Whitehead, D. 2004. Isokrates for hire: some preliminaries to a commentary on Isokrates 16–21. In D.L. Cairns & R.A. Knox, eds., *Law, Rhetoric, and Comedy in Classical Athens. Essays in Honour of Douglas M. MacDowell* (pp. 151–86). Swansea.

Whitley, J. 2001. *The Archaeology of Ancient Greece*. Cambridge.

Whitley, J. *et al.* 2007. Archaeology in Greece 2006–2007. In *Archaeological Reports for 2006–2007*. Athens.

Wilson, E. 2007. *The Death of Socrates. Hero, Villain, Chatterbox, Saint*. Cambridge.

Wilson, J. 1982. The customary meaning of words changed – or were they? A note on Thucydides 3.82.4. *Classical Quarterly*, N.S. **32**: 18–20.

Winkler, J.J. 1990. The ephebes' song: tragoidia and Polis'. In J.J. Winkler & F.I. Zeitlin, eds., *Nothing to do with Dionysos? Athenian Drama in its Social Context* (pp. 20–62). Princeton.

Wolpert, A. 2002. *Remembering Defeat. Civil War and Civic Memory in Ancient Athens*. Baltimore.

Woodhead, A.G. 1970. *Thucydides on the Nature of Power*. Cambridge.

Woodhouse, W.J. 1933. *King Agis of Sparta and His Campaign in Arkadia in 418 B.C.* Oxford.

Woodruff, P., ed. and trans. 1993. *Thucydides. On Justice Power and Human Nature*. Indianapolis.

Wycherley, R.E. 1978. *The Stones of Athens*. Princeton.

II. Modern History (including Psychology and Trauma Studies)

Audring, G., Hoffmann, C., & von Ungern-Sternberg, J., eds. 1990. *Eduard Meyer Victor Ehrenberg. Ein Briefwechsel, 1914–1930*. Stuttgart.

Collingwood, R.G. 1946. *The Idea of History*. Oxford.

Doyle, M.W. 1997. *Ways of War and Peace. Realism, Liberalism, and Socialism*. New York.

Duncan, R., & Klooster, D.J., eds. 2002. *Phantoms of a Blood-Stained Period. The Complete Civil War Writings of Ambrose Bierce*. Amherst.

Eksteins, M. 1989. *Rites of Spring. The Great War and the Birth of the Modern Age*. Boston.

Filkins, D. 2008. *The Forgotten War*. New York.

Fussell, P. 1975. *The Great War and Modern Memory*. New York.

Gibbs, P. 1920. *Realities of War*. London.

Herman, J., 1992. *Trauma and Recovery. The Aftermath of Violence – from Domestic Abuse to Political Terror*. New York.

Herr, M. 1978. *Dispatches*. New York.

Keegan, J. 1976. *The Face of Battle. A Study of Agincourt, Waterloo, and the Somme*. Harmondsworth.

Keeley, L.H. 1996. *War Before Civilization*. New York.

Kolata, G. 1999. *Flu. The Story of the Great Influenza Pandemic of 1918 and the Search for the Virus that Caused it*. New York.

Langer, W. 1958. The next assignment. *American Historical Review*, **63**: 283–304.

Mearsheimer, J. 2001. *The Tragedy of Great Power Politics*. New York.

Miller, W.I. 2000. *The Mystery of Courage*. Cambridge.

O'Brien, T. 1990. *The Things They Carried*. New York.

Sapolsky, R. 1994. *Why Zebras Don't Get Ulcers*. New York.

Sapolsky, R. 1997. *The Trouble with Testosterone and Other Essays on the Biology of the Human Predicament*. New York.

Scarry, E. 1985. *The Body in Pain. The Making and Unmaking of the World*. New York.

Shay, J. 1994. *Achilles in Vietnam. Combat Trauma and the Undoing of Character*. New York.

Shay, J. 2004. *Odysseus in America. Combat Trauma and the Trials of Homecoming*. New York.

Shephard, B. 2000. *A War of Nerves. Soldiers and Psychiatrists 1914–1994*. Cambridge.

Wills, G. 1992. *Lincoln at Gettysburg. The Words That Remade America*. New York.

Wills, G. 2002. *A Necessary Evil. A History of American Distrust in Government*. New York.

Winter, J. 1995. *Sites of Memory, Sites of Mourning. The Great War in European Cultural History*. Cambridge.

INDEX

Principal entries are noted in **BOLD**; references to communities, peoples, and states should be understood to refer as well to their inhabitants. References to literary works will be found listed by author. Readers may also wish to consult the entries in the Who's Who and Glossary, which are not (for the most part) listed here. DP indicates a literary figure (*dramatis persona*).

CPSIA information can be obtained
at www.ICGtesting.com
Printed in the USA
LVOW04s1917061215

465598LV00018B/89/P

9 781405 122511